Safety Symbols

These symbols appear in laboratory activities. They warn of possible dangers in the laboratory and remind you to work carefully.

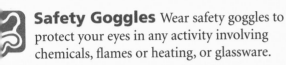 **Safety Goggles** Wear safety goggles to protect your eyes in any activity involving chemicals, flames or heating, or glassware.

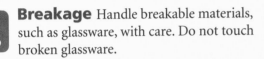 **Lab Apron** Wear a laboratory apron to protect your skin and clothing from damage.

Breakage Handle breakable materials, such as glassware, with care. Do not touch broken glassware.

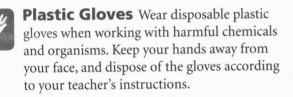 **Heat-Resistant Gloves** Use an oven mitt or other hand protection when handling hot materials such as hot plates or hot glassware.

Plastic Gloves Wear disposable plastic gloves when working with harmful chemicals and organisms. Keep your hands away from your face, and dispose of the gloves according to your teacher's instructions.

Heating Use a clamp or tongs to pick up hot glassware. Do not touch hot objects with your bare hands.

Flames Before you work with flames, tie back loose hair and clothing. Follow instructions from your teacher about lighting and extinguishing flames.

No Flames When using flammable materials, make sure there are no flames, sparks, or other exposed heat sources present.

Corrosive Chemical Avoid getting acid or other corrosive chemicals on your skin or clothing or in your eyes. Do not inhale the vapors. Wash your hands after the activity.

Poison Do not let any poisonous chemical come into contact with your skin, and do not inhale its vapors. Wash your hands when you are finished with the activity.

 Fumes Work in a ventilated area when harmful vapors may be involved. Avoid inhaling vapors directly. Only test an odor when directed to do so by your teacher, and use a wafting motion to direct the vapor toward your nose.

 Sharp Object Scissors, scalpels, knives, needles, pins, and tacks can cut your skin. Always direct a sharp edge or point away from yourself and others.

 Animal Safety Treat live or preserved animals or animal parts with care to avoid harming the animals or yourself. Wash your hands when you are finished with the activity.

 Plant Safety Handle plants only as directed by your teacher. If you are allergic to certain plants, tell your teacher; do not do an activity involving those plants. Avoid touching harmful plants such as poison ivy. Wash your hands when you are finished with the activity.

 Electric Shock To avoid electric shock, never use electrical equipment around water, or when the equipment is wet or your hands are wet. Be sure cords are untangled and cannot trip anyone. Unplug equipment not in use.

 Physical Safety When an experiment involves physical activity, avoid injuring yourself or others. Alert your teacher if there is any reason you should not participate.

 Disposal Dispose of chemicals and other laboratory materials safely. Follow the instructions from your teacher.

 Hand Washing Wash your hands thoroughly when finished with the activity. Use soap and warm water. Rinse well.

 General Safety Awareness When this symbol appears, follow the instructions provided. When you are asked to develop your own procedure in a lab, have your teacher approve your plan before you go further.

PRENTICE HALL

FORENSIC SCIENCE

CLARENCE COCROFT

PEARSON

Boston, Massachusetts • Chandler, Arizona • Glenview, Illinois • Shoreview, Minnesota • Upper Saddle River, New Jersey

PRENTICE HALL
Forensic Science

Resources

- **Student Edition**
- **Teacher's Guide**
- **Student Handbook**
- **Student Handbook, Annotated Teacher's Edition**
- **Chapter and Unit Tests**
- **Forensic Science Videos**
- **Materials Kits**

Acknowledgments appear on page 163, which constitutes an extension of this copyright page.

13-digit ISBN 978-0-13-362746-6
10-digit ISBN 0-13-362746-2

2 3 4 5 6 7 8 9 10   12 11 10 09 08

Author

Clarence A. Cocroft II

Clarence Cocroft brings practical experience in both forensics and science education to Prentice Hall *Forensic Science*. After earning an M.S. in Microbiology and Chemistry from the University of Memphis, Clarence worked as a biochemist in forensic laboratories. His area of expertise was DNA electrophoresis. Then, Clarence decided to pursue his interest in science education. While teaching high school biology, Clarence developed and taught forensic science seminars for teachers. At the urging of the teachers, he began to speak to middle grades and high school students about careers in forensic science and biotechnology. As a member of the National Youth Leadership Forum on Medicine (NYLF), Clarence developed workshops for college students. He continues to act as a mentor for students who want to do research in forensic science and biotechnology. Clarence Cocroft is also a licensed private investigator.

Contributing Writers

Susan Eldert
Middle School Science Teacher
The Fessenden School
West Newton, Massachusetts

Chuck McMillan
Science Consultant
Port Huron, Michigan

Barbara Brooks Simons
Science Writer
Boston, Massachusetts

Content Reviewers

David C. Coleman
Public Defender
Contra Costa County
Martinez, California

Charles Curtis
Assistant Director
Oklahoma State Bureau of Investigation
Oklahoma City, Oklahoma

Phyllis Goldfarb
Professor of Law and Associate Dean
    for Clinical Affairs
George Washington University
    Law School
Washington, D.C.

Walter F. Rowe
Professor of Forensic Sciences
George Washington University
Washington, D.C.

Roberta Sue Salem
Forensic Chemical Science Coordinator
Washburn University
Topeka, Kansas

Norman L. Starks
Detective Sergeant
Clarksdale Police Department
Clarksdale, Mississippi

James L. Streeter
Forensic Evidence Examiner
North East Forensics, LLC
Groton, Connecticut

David G. Tate
Director Clinical & Forensic Sciences
Purdue University
West Lafayette, Indiana

Safety Reviewer

Ruth Hathaway, Ph.D.
Hathaway Consulting
Cape Girardeau, Missouri

Teacher Reviewers

Mark A. Atkinson
Federal Way Public Academy
Federal Way, Washington

Colleen Campos
Cherry Creek Schools
Aurora, Colorado

Luz M. Castillo
Hawthorne Math and Science Academy
Hawthorne, California

Suzanne Foxworth
Watauga Middle School
Watauga, Texas

Veronica Gaier
Piqua Junior High School
Piqua, Ohio

Carol McMillan
Larson Middle School
Troy, Michigan

John Lawrence Parsons
Blake Middle School
Medfield, Massachusetts

John Brent Warford
Turkey Foot Middle School
Edgewood, Kentucky

Richard Wilkerson
Pitt County Schools
Greenville, North Carolina

Contents

Forensic Science

First segment

Second segment

Reference Section

Discovery EDUCATION™

Go Online
SCi LINKS™ NSTA

Activities

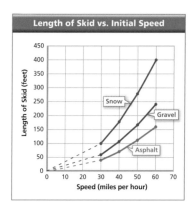
Distribution of Blood Types in the U.S. Population			
Type	Frequency of Blood Type	Can Receive Blood From	Can Donate Blood to
O+	37%	45%	84%
O–	7%	7%	100%
A+	35%	85%	37%
A–	6%	13%	44%
B+	9%	56%	12%
B–	2%	9%	15%
AB+	3%	100%	3%
AB–	1%	16%	4%

Length of Skid vs. Initial Speed

Length of Skid (feet) / Speed (miles per hour)

Snow
Gravel
Asphalt

Focus on the
BIG Idea
Scientific Inquiry

What inquiry skills do crime scene teams use as they develop an explanation for a crime?

Each chapter begins with a **Focus on the Big Idea** question that links the lessons in the chapter.

Built-In Reading Support

Every lesson is organized with *before*, *during*, and *after* reading support that provides a clear and consistent structure for learning about forensic science.

Before You Read

Key Concept questions identify the important concepts in the upcoming lesson.

Key Terms preview the vocabulary for each lesson.

Target Reading Skills provide practice in using the reading skills that you will need to learn science successfully.

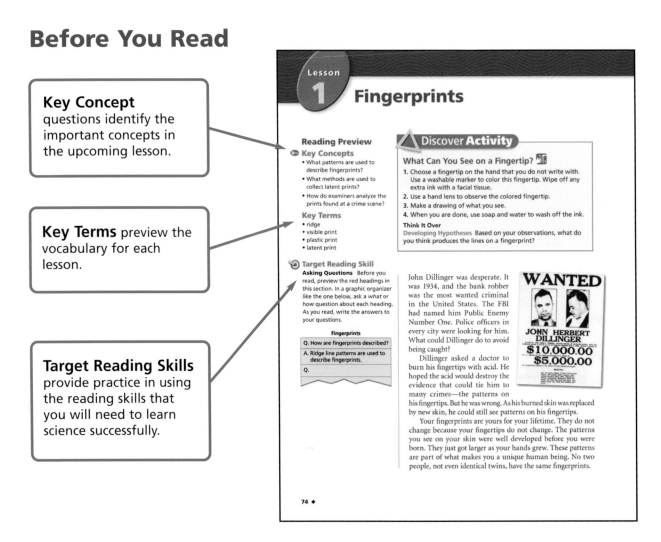

Lesson 1

Fingerprints

Reading Preview

Key Concepts
- What patterns are used to describe fingerprints?
- What methods are used to collect latent prints?
- How do examiners analyze the prints found at a crime scene?

Key Terms
- ridge
- visible print
- plastic print
- latent print

Target Reading Skill

Asking Questions Before you read, preview the red headings in this section. In a graphic organizer like the one below, ask a *what* or *how* question about each heading. As you read, write the answers to your questions.

Fingerprints

Fingerprints
Q. How are fingerprints described?
A. Ridge line patterns are used to describe fingerprints.
Q.

Discover Activity

What Can You See on a Fingertip?

1. Choose a fingertip on the hand that you do not write with. Use a washable marker to color this fingertip. Wipe off any extra ink with a facial tissue.
2. Use a hand lens to observe the colored fingertip.
3. Make a drawing of what you see.
4. When you are done, use soap and water to wash off the ink.

Think It Over
Developing Hypotheses Based on your observations, what do you think produces the lines on a fingerprint?

John Dillinger was desperate. It was 1934, and the bank robber was the most wanted criminal in the United States. The FBI had named him Public Enemy Number One. Police officers in every city were looking for him. What could Dillinger do to avoid being caught?

Dillinger asked a doctor to burn his fingertips with acid. He hoped the acid would destroy the evidence that could tie him to many crimes—the patterns on his fingertips. But he was wrong. As his burned skin was replaced by new skin, he could still see patterns on his fingertips.

Your fingerprints are yours for your lifetime. They do not change because your fingertips do not change. The patterns you see on your skin were well developed before you were born. They just got larger as your hands grew. These patterns are part of what makes you a unique human being. No two people, not even identical twins, have the same fingerprints.

WANTED
JOHN HERBERT DILLINGER
$10,000.00
$5,000.00

74 ◆

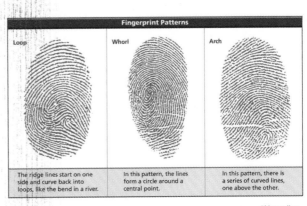

Fingerprint Patterns

Loop	Whorl	Arch
The ridge lines start on one side and curve back into loops, like the bend in a river.	In this pattern, the lines form a circle around a central point.	In this pattern, there is a series of curved lines, one above the other.

Describing Fingerprints

For thousands of years, people have known that fingerprints could be used to identify a person. In ancient China, for example, people could sign a legal paper with a thumbprint. Over time, signatures replaced fingerprints as a form of identification. But not in a crime lab.

When you take a close look at your fingertips, you can see a series of raised lines, or **ridges**. These ridges make it easier for your fingers and thumb to grasp and hold on to objects. The ridges also make the lines that you see on your fingerprints. **There are three typical patterns of ridge lines—loops, whorls, and arches.** Figure 1 compares these patterns.

Print examiners look for more than the overall pattern of a print. They look for the details that make the print unique. There may, for example, be places where a ridge ends. Or there may be places where a single ridge splits into two ridges, like a fork in a road. A fingerprint may have as many as 150 specific details.

 What are ridges?

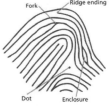

FIGURE 1
Fingerprint Patterns
Of the three patterns, loops are the most common and arches are the least common. Only about five percent of people have prints with arches.
Observing Look at the drawing with some details labeled. On a fingerprint, what is a fork? What is an enclosure?

As You Read

Key Concepts in boldface sentences allow you to focus on the important ideas of the lesson.

Protecting the Investigators

It's not only evidence that must be protected at a crime scene. People who work at the scene can be at risk. They may have to handle blood that is infected. They may find explosives or drugs. What crime scene investigators do to protect themselves is similar to what you do during a lab at school. **Crime scene investigators protect themselves by following established safety rules and procedures.** Here are a few examples.

▶ Poisons, viruses, and bacteria can enter a person's body through the skin, nose, or mouth. So a CSI does not eat, drink, chew gum, or put on makeup at a crime scene.

▶ At some crime scenes, a CSI adds a mask, goggles, and an extra pair of gloves. If a piece of protective clothing is torn, it must be replaced.

▶ A CSI handles knives, razor blades, broken glass, and other sharp objects with care.

▶ Sometimes a CSI must work in a building that has been damaged where there is a danger of injury from falling objects. The CSI needs to wear a helmet and sturdy shoes.

Some situations call for people with extra training. For example, disarming an explosive device is a task for a bomb squad. They, in turn, may use a hazardous duty robot like the one shown in Figure 25.

FIGURE 25
Hazardous Duty Robot
At a bank, the bomb squad finds a device that they suspect will explode. They use a robot to place the device into a bucket.

Lesson 4 Assessment

Target Reading Skill Outlining Use the information in your outline about collecting evidence to help answer Question 2.

Reviewing Key Concepts

1. a. Reviewing Why is it important to search a crime scene in an organized way?
   b. Applying Concepts What factors influence the choice of a search pattern?
   c. Comparing and Contrasting How do a line search and a grid search differ?
2. a. Summarizing What are four things a CSI needs to do to keep evidence useful?
   b. Inferring A CSI is using a hand lens and tweezers. What does this tell you about the evidence the CSI is trying to collect?

3. a. Listing What are three hazards that investigators may face at a crime scene?
   b. Making Generalizations How do crime scene investigators protect themselves at a crime scene?
   c. Drawing Conclusions Why should a CSI replace torn clothing quickly?

Math Practice

4. Area Twenty people use a strip pattern to search a field. Each strip is 2 meters wide and 80 meters long. What is the area of the field in square meters? *Hint:* It might help to draw a diagram of the field.

After You Read

The Lesson Assessment tests your understanding of the Key Concepts. Each set of questions focuses on one of the Key Concepts.

If you can't answer these items, go back and review the lesson.

Hands-On Investigations

Like a forensic scientist, you can develop your own scientific questions and perform labs and activities to find answers. Follow the steps below when doing a lab.

1 Read the whole lab.

2 Write a purpose. What is the purpose of this activity?

3 Write a hypothesis. What is a possible explanation? Hypotheses lead to predictions that can be tested.

4 Follow each step in the procedure.

5 Record your data.

Skills Lab

Measuring Writing

Problem
What measurements can you use to describe a writing sample?

Skills Focus
measuring, calculating, designing experiments

Materials
- ruled paper
- metric ruler
- protractor
- tracing paper

Procedure
1. Write the following words on a sheet of ruled paper: Forensic scientists analyze evidence. They do not convict or clear suspects.
2. Draw a line through each letter in the sample as shown in the photo. The line should have the same slant as the letter.
3. Select a line. Use a protractor to measure the angle the line makes with the ruled line on the paper. Measure the angle for two other lines. Enter your data in a table like the one below.
4. Place tracing paper over your sample. Draw vertical lines between each letter. Select a pair of lines. Use a metric ruler to measure the distance between the lines (the spacing) in millimeters. Repeat the measurement for two other pairs of lines. Record your data.

Analyze and Conclude
1. **Designing Experiments** Why do you think you were asked to make three separate measurements for slant and spacing?
2. **Calculating** Calculate the mean, or average, slant and spacing. Enter the results in your table and record them on your sample.
3. **Designing Experiments** Select another feature of the writing sample that you could measure. Describe the method you would use to measure this feature.
4. **Interpreting Data** Make a class display of the samples. What is the range of data for average slant? For average spacing?
5. **Drawing Conclusions** How could measurements be used to identify a writing sample?

Communicating
Pick two samples to compare. Write a paragraph explaining how an analyst could tell that the samples were written by different people.

Data Table				
Feature	Trial 1	Trial 2	Trial 3	Average
Slant (degrees)				
Spacing (mm)				

100 ◆

6 Analyze your results. Answering the questions will help you draw conclusions.

7 Communicate your results in a written report or oral presentation. Your report should include:
- ◆ a purpose
- ◆ a hypothesis
- ◆ the steps of the procedure
- ◆ a record of your results
- ◆ a conclusion

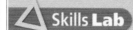

Lab Report

Purpose: To determine whether measurements can be used to describe a writing sample.

Hypothesis:

Visuals in *Forensic Science*

Your *Forensic Science* textbook is rich with images that teach and support the Key Concepts. Captions describe image content and relate it to the lesson content. Skills questions prompt you to analyze the image further or apply its content to new situations.

FIGURE 16
Handwriting Samples
These samples show how writing styles can vary among people. *Comparing and Contrasting In what ways are the two writing samples similar? In what ways are they different?*

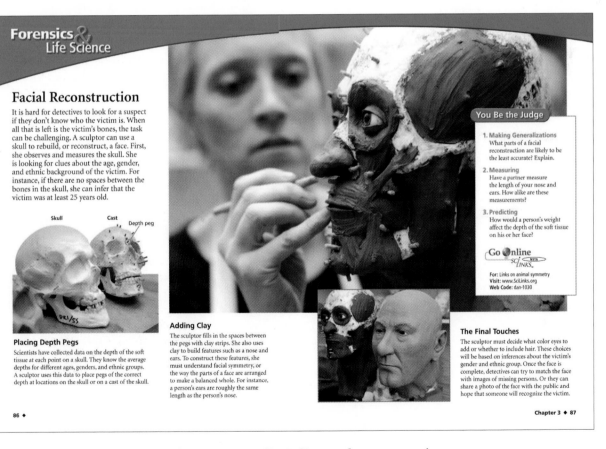

Forensics & Life Science

Facial Reconstruction

It is hard for detectives to look for a suspect if they don't know who the victim is. When all that is left is the victim's bones, the task can be challenging. A sculptor can use a skull to rebuild, or reconstruct, a face. First, she observes and measures the skull. She is looking for clues about the age, gender, and ethnic background of the victim. For instance, if there are no spaces between the bones in the skull, she can infer that the victim was at least 25 years old.

Skull   Cast   Depth peg

Placing Depth Pegs
Scientists have collected data on the depth of the soft tissue at each point on a skull. They know the average depths for different ages, genders, and ethnic groups. A sculptor uses this data to place pegs of the correct depth at locations on the skull or on a cast of the skull.

Adding Clay
The sculptor fills in the spaces between the pegs with clay strips. She also uses clay to build features such as a nose and ears. To construct these features, she must understand facial symmetry, or the way the parts of a face are arranged to make a balanced whole. For instance, a person's ears are roughly the same length as the person's nose.

The Final Touches
The sculptor must decide what color eyes to add or whether to include hair. These choices will be based on inferences about the victim's gender and ethnic group. Once the face is complete, detectives can try to match the face with images of missing persons. Or they can share a photo of the face with the public and hope that someone will recognize the victim.

You Be the Judge

1. **Making Generalizations**
   What parts of a facial reconstruction are likely to be the least accurate? Explain.

2. **Measuring**
   Have a partner measure the length of your nose and ears. How alike are these measurements?

3. **Predicting**
   How would a person's weight affect the depth of the soft tissue on his or her face?

Go Online
SciLINKS

For: Links on animal symmetry
Visit: www.SciLinks.org
Web Code: dan-1030

Each chapter includes an interdisciplinary feature such as the one above. These features are designed to spark your imagination and help you see how forensic science relates to other sciences and to real-world situations.

If you look closely at this crime scene, you will see several clues. At the beginning of each chapter in this book, there is an activity related to the crime. If you do all the activities, you will be able to solve the crime.

PAINTING STOLEN!

MYSTERIOUS, USA Police were called to a Main Street mansion early this morning. A woman reported hearing an alarm and seeing a car speed out of the driveway. When police entered the house, they noticed that a painting was missing. Police are in the process of

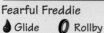 Brand of Pen
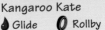 Brand of Tire
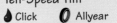 Blood Type

Investigators have identified 36 suspects in the Missing Masterpiece mystery. They know each suspect's brand of pen, brand of tires, and blood type. You will use the data as you solve the crime.

Fearful Freddie
Glide Rollby A

One-Eyed Ayla
Glide Trend A

Mustache Max
Glide Allyear A

Kangaroo Kate
Glide Rollby B

Three-Point Paul
Glide Trend B

Lazy Larry
Glide Allyear B

Pool-Hall Patti
Click Rollby A

Ornery Olivia
Click Trend A

Two-Tone Trish
Click Allyear A

Virtual Val
Click Rollby B

Zany Zoë
Click Trend B

Ten-Speed Tim
Click Allyear B

Nine-Ring Nellie
Penz Rollby A

Crafty Carl
Penz Trend A

Flat-Top Freddy
Penz Allyear A

Frankie Four-Eyes
Penz Rollby B

Spooky Stephanie
💧 Penz 🅾 Trend 💧 B

Chilly Cindi
💧 Penz 🅾 Allyear 💧 B

Gentle Giovanni
💧 Glide 🅾 Rollby 💧 AB

Seven-Foot Sal
💧 Glide 🅾 Trend 💧 AB

Toothless Tony
💧 Glide 🅾 Allyear 💧 AB

Uptight Ursula
💧 Glide 🅾 Rollby 💧 O

Jittery Jim
💧 Glide 🅾 Trend 💧 O

Ava the Astronaut
💧 Glide 🅾 Allyear 💧 O

Artistic Al
💧 Click 🅾 Rollby 💧 AB

Baby-Faced Betty
💧 Click 🅾 Trend 💧 AB

Eagle-Eye Earl
💧 Click 🅾 Allyear 💧 AB

Quincy the Quarterback
💧 Click 🅾 Rollby 💧 O

Dizzy Diane
💧 Click 🅾 Trend 💧 O

Sixth-Sense Sandy
💧 Click 🅾 Allyear 💧 O

Young Yasmin
💧 Penz 🅾 Rollby 💧 AB

Hairy Harry
💧 Penz 🅾 Trend 💧 AB

Pedro the Pest
💧 Penz 🅾 Allyear 💧 AB

Nervous Nancy
💧 Penz 🅾 Rollby 💧 O

Wily Winona
💧 Penz 🅾 Trend 💧 O

Regal Ranida
💧 Penz 🅾 Allyear 💧 O

Chapter 1

Crime Scene Investigation

Focus on the BIG Idea
Scientific Inquiry

What inquiry skills do crime scene teams use as they develop an explanation for a crime?

Chapter Preview

① Using Science to Solve Crimes

② Securing and Recording a Crime Scene

③ Types of Evidence

④ Collecting Physical Evidence

A CSI must wear protective gear when ▶ working on a case of anthrax poisoning.

▲ Chapter **Project**

Investigating a Crime Scene

A valuable painting has been stolen from a home. There are 36 possible suspects. Before you can begin to solve this crime, you need to investigate the scene of the crime.

Your Goal To protect and record the crime scene, and identify evidence

To successfully complete this project, you must

- make notes about what you observe at the crime scene
- decide how to secure the crime scene
- make a sketch of the crime scene
- interview an eyewitness
- identify useful physical evidence

Plan It! Brainstorm with your team ways that you can accomplish each task. Then decide who will be responsible for which tasks. Make sure to record all of your descriptions, notes, and sketches in your Student Handbook.

Using Science to Solve Crimes

Reading Preview

Key Concepts
- What skills do people who investigate crimes use?
- How does working as a team help solve crimes?
- How do the methods used to solve crimes today compare with those used in the past?

Key Terms
- burglary
- forensic science
- observing
- evidence
- inferring
- predicting
- hypothesis
- crime scene investigator
- medical examiner
- autopsy
- density

Target Reading Skill
Building Vocabulary After you read this lesson, use what you have learned to write a definition of each Key Term in your own words. Define a term by telling its most important feature or function.

Discover **Activity**

What Do You Know About Solving Crimes?

Which of these statements about solving crimes do you think are true and which do you think are false?

1. Every crime that is reported to the police gets solved.
2. It takes just a few hours to solve most crimes.
3. Crime scene investigators work only on murder cases.
4. One task of crime scene investigators is to track down and arrest suspects.

Think It Over

Making Judgments Where do you think most people get their information about how crimes are solved? Do you think this source gives people true or false ideas about how crimes are investigated? Give an example to support your answer.

Exclusive:

SCHOOL BUS VANISHES!

"All My Homework Was On That Bus" says distraught student athlete.

Shocking bus disappearance leaves few clues.

"I only left it for a minute to get some snacks."
-driver

A 9-1-1 call comes in to a police station. Someone broke into a ground-floor apartment. A valuable stamp collection that was kept in a locked desk drawer is missing. Breaking into a building to steal an object is a **burglary.**

The first officers to arrive see a broken window. Inside, there are shoe prints on the carpet. One officer says, "Those shoe prints come from two different shoes. There was more than one burglar." Then she looks at the desk. "Here are marks left by a tool. They must have pried open the drawer."

The other officer sniffs the air. "That smells like a perfume my wife wears," he says. "One of the burglars may be a woman." In the bedroom he finds a parrot who keeps saying, "Hurry up, Pat!" Could one burglar be named Pat?

This investigation shows science in action. From the time that investigators arrive at a crime scene, they use skills that scientists use. They observe details. They interpret what they see. They ask questions. They draw conclusions about what happened.

Science at a Crime Scene

The use of scientific knowledge and methods to answer legal questions is called **forensic science.** People sometimes call this field just "forensics." However, the complete term helps stress the connection between science and law.

Some members of an investigative team are scientists. Some are not. But all of them approach the situation with the same questions: What happened? When did it happen? Who could have done it? To find out, each investigator must think like a scientist. **The investigative team uses inquiry skills to help solve crimes. These skills include observing, inferring, predicting, and developing a hypothesis.**

"Hurry up, Pat!"

Observing What were the officers at the burglary scene doing when they saw shoe prints, smelled perfume, and listened to a parrot? They were observing the crime scene. **Observing** is using one or more of your senses to gather information. People who investigate crime scenes rely on their senses of sight, smell, and hearing. They rarely use taste or touch.

Observing is a skill used to find evidence. In the legal system, **evidence** is something that can be presented in court to make a point during a trial. The evidence can be a statement from a witness. Evidence can also be an item collected at a crime scene or the results of tests done on that item. The place where an item is found can also be evidence. All the observations made at a crime scene can be used as clues to help solve a crime. But not every clue can be used as evidence, as shown in Figure 1.

 Which senses do people who investigate crimes use most often?

FIGURE 1
Clues vs. Evidence
Shoe prints on a carpet and words spoken by a parrot can both be clues. But only the shoe prints could be used as evidence in a trial.

Skills **Activity**

Observing
Your teacher will give you a list of five items to find in your classroom. When you find an item, record its location on the list. After you finish the task, answer these questions: Were some items harder to find than others? If so, what made these items harder to find?

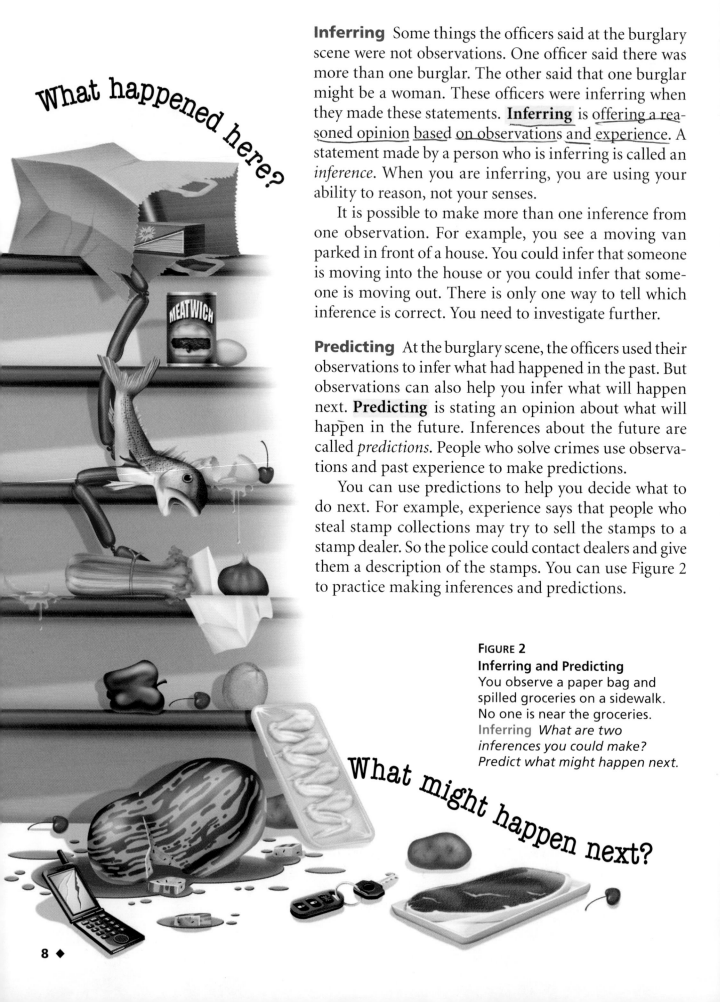

What happened here?

Inferring Some things the officers said at the burglary scene were not observations. One officer said there was more than one burglar. The other said that one burglar might be a woman. These officers were inferring when they made these statements. **Inferring** is offering a reasoned opinion based on observations and experience. A statement made by a person who is inferring is called an *inference*. When you are inferring, you are using your ability to reason, not your senses.

It is possible to make more than one inference from one observation. For example, you see a moving van parked in front of a house. You could infer that someone is moving into the house or you could infer that someone is moving out. There is only one way to tell which inference is correct. You need to investigate further.

Predicting At the burglary scene, the officers used their observations to infer what had happened in the past. But observations can also help you infer what will happen next. **Predicting** is stating an opinion about what will happen in the future. Inferences about the future are called *predictions*. People who solve crimes use observations and past experience to make predictions.

You can use predictions to help you decide what to do next. For example, experience says that people who steal stamp collections may try to sell the stamps to a stamp dealer. So the police could contact dealers and give them a description of the stamps. You can use Figure 2 to practice making inferences and predictions.

FIGURE 2
Inferring and Predicting
You observe a paper bag and spilled groceries on a sidewalk. No one is near the groceries.
Inferring *What are two inferences you could make? Predict what might happen next.*

What might happen next?

Inquiry Skills	Description	Forensic Science Examples
Interpreting Data	Analyzing data to look for patterns or trends	Deciding if a suspect's fingerprints match those at a crime scene; mapping locations of similar crimes
Classifying	Grouping together objects that are alike in some way	Typing blood; distinguishing cat hair from human hair
Making Models	Using a drawing, diagram, or a 3-D structure to represent a complex object or process	Making sketches or 3-D models of a crime scene; making a computer simulation of a crime
Communicating	Sharing ideas and information with other people	Taking notes at a crime scene; interviewing witnesses
Measuring	Making quantitative observations about the properties of an object or of a set of objects	Measuring the length of skid marks; using body temperature to determine time of death
Posing Questions	Asking questions that can be answered by gathering evidence	Which automobile models have this type of paint? Is the person who lost this contact lens nearsighted or farsighted?

Developing a Hypothesis Sometimes what happened at a crime scene is obvious from the beginning. Sometimes the people who solve crimes must dig deeper to find an explanation. Scientists call a possible explanation for a set of observations a **hypothesis.**

There may be more than one reasonable hypothesis for a given set of facts. Think again about the case of the stolen stamps. Here are three possible hypotheses.

▶ One of the burglars knew about the collection and where it was stored.

▶ The burglars didn't know that the owner had a valuable stamp collection. They chose the apartment at random.

▶ The owner hid the stamps and staged the burglary to collect the insurance money.

The third hypothesis seems least likely. The first and second hypotheses fit the known facts. As of now, there is not enough evidence to support one hypothesis and reject the other.

Other Inquiry Skills Figure 3 lists some other inquiry skills that can be used to solve crimes. You will learn more about these skills in later lessons. In Lesson 2, for example, you will see why it is important to communicate and to make measurements at a crime scene.

FIGURE 3
Other Inquiry Skills
An investigator uses many inquiry skills to solve a crime.
Interpreting Data *Which skill is used to interview a witness?*

Discovery EDUCATION™

Forensic Science Video
Clues From a Murder

Reading Checkpoint | What do people who solve crimes base their predictions on?

FIGURE 4
Roles at a Crime Scene
These North Carolina emergency medical technicians are trying to save a life. They may treat victims at a crime scene. They may also treat an injured suspect.

Teamwork at a Crime Scene

In some mystery novels, one person does all the work. He or she finds the body, interprets the clues, and solves the mystery. With real-world mysteries, it usually takes a team of people working together to solve the mystery.

Each member of an investigative team brings specific skills and knowledge to the team. Each has an assigned role. Some team members work at the crime scene. Others get involved later, after the evidence is collected. Figure 4 shows one task that might take place at a crime scene.

First on the Scene The person who answers a 9-1-1 call has an important task. He or she must decide who should respond to the call. Uniformed police officers almost always respond first. Fire and ambulance crews may also be sent.

This group's first responsibility is to save lives. They rescue people who are trapped inside burning buildings. They pull people from wrecked cars. They provide emergency medical treatment as they rush seriously injured people to a hospital.

Crime Scene Investigators What happens next? It depends on what the first people on the scene find when they respond. If a crime has taken place, someone needs to record and collect the evidence. For some crimes, a uniformed officer may do this task. At major crime scenes, crime scene investigators do this task. A **crime scene investigator (CSI)** is trained to record, collect, and test evidence from a crime scene. In later lessons, you will learn much more about this process.

A detective may come to view the scene before the evidence is collected. Detectives are experienced police officers whose only job is to solve crimes. They usually must pass a test before they can become a detective.

Medical Examiners When there is a sudden or suspicious death, a medical doctor will come to observe the body. These doctors are called **medical examiners.** By law, they need to confirm that the person is dead. They also do a few simple tests at the crime scene. For example, they may measure air and body temperature to help estimate the time of death.

If there is evidence of "foul play," the doctor will later do an autopsy. An **autopsy** (AW tahp see) is a detailed exam of a dead body. It includes cutting the body open to look inside.

Police use a different type of examiner when a victim has been dead for years. They use people who know how to find clues in bones, like the bones in Figure 5.

Discovery EDUCATION™

Forensic Science Video

The Mysterious Ice Man

 **Reading Checkpoint** What does the person who answers a 9-1-1 call have to decide?

FIGURE 5
Forensic Anthropologists
Forensic anthropologists are experts on human bones. They use the bones they collect to figure out who a victim was and how he or she died.
Making Judgments *Why might an anthropologist use a soft brush to uncover bones?*

FIGURE 6
Telling Gold From Silver

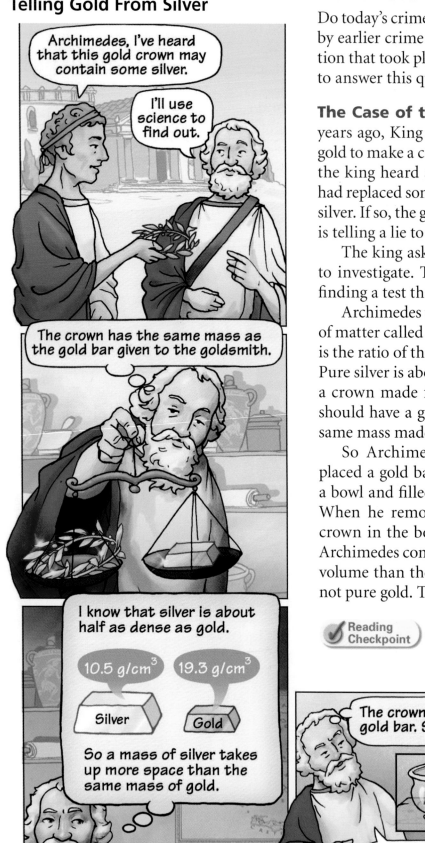

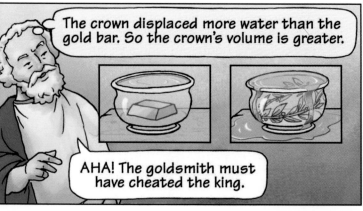

Forensic Science Methods

Do today's crime solvers use the same methods used by earlier crime solvers? This story of an investigation that took place long ago is a good place to start to answer this question.

The Case of the Golden Crown About 2,300 years ago, King Hiero II gave a goldsmith enough gold to make a crown like the one in Figure 6. Later, the king heard a troubling rumor. The goldsmith had replaced some of the gold with an equal mass of silver. If so, the goldsmith was guilty of fraud, which is telling a lie to obtain money or other property.

The king asked the Greek scientist Archimedes to investigate. The challenge for Archimedes was finding a test that would not damage the crown.

Archimedes used what he knew about a property of matter called density to solve the crime. **Density** is the ratio of the mass of a substance to its volume. Pure silver is about half as dense as pure gold. Thus a crown made from a mixture of silver and gold should have a greater volume than a crown of the same mass made from pure gold.

So Archimedes designed an experiment. He placed a gold bar of equal mass to the crown into a bowl and filled the bowl with water to the brim. When he removed the gold bar and placed the crown in the bowl, water flowed out of the bowl. Archimedes concluded that the crown had a greater volume than the bar of gold. Thus, the crown was not pure gold. The goldsmith was guilty of fraud!

Reading Checkpoint Which property of matter did Archimedes use to solve a crime?

The Case of the Fake Painting What if forensic scientists today were faced with the problem Archimedes faced? They would still have to design an experiment. But they would have some advantages. **Scientists still design tests to solve crimes. But now they have better technology for doing the tests.**

Consider a fraud that could happen in the art world. The value of a painting depends on the identity of the painter. Some artists' paintings sell for millions of dollars. With this much money at stake, a talented crook might make a fake that looked like a painting by a well-known artist. The crook would copy the style of the artist and forge the artist's signature. On the surface, the fake would look real.

What could an art dealer do to detect a fake? The dealer could ask a forensic scientist to run some tests on the painting without damaging it. One way is to use the equipment shown in Figure 7 to analyze the paint the artist used. The equipment bombards a painting with X-rays. In response, elements in the paint give off energy. Each element gives off distinctive wavelengths of energy that can be used to identify the element.

The chemical makeup of paints has changed over time. Some elements that were used long ago are not used now. So analyzing paint can help a scientist tell if a painting is a fake.

FIGURE 7
Using Paint to Detect Fake Art
This equipment bombards a painting with X-rays. It also measures the energy that is given off by elements in the paint.
Applying Concepts *Why doesn't the scientist take a sample of paint from the painting to test?*

Lesson 1 Assessment

Target Reading Skill Building Vocabulary Use your definitions to help you answer the questions below.

Reviewing Key Concepts

1. a. Listing Name four skills that people use in investigating a crime.
   b. Comparing and Contrasting How are inferences different from predictions?
2. a. Identifying What is the role of a crime scene investigator?
   b. Sequencing Which task happens first at a crime scene: a CSI collects evidence or a victim receives medical treatment? Give a reason for your answer.
   c. Applying Concepts At a crime scene, which tasks require an understanding of human biology? Explain your choices.

3. a. Reviewing What objects did Archimedes use to test the density of the gold crown? How can a modern investigator identify the elements in paint?
   b. Summarizing What advantage does a modern crime investigator have over earlier crime solvers like Archimedes?
   c. Developing Hypotheses What is the hypothesis that Archimedes was testing?

In the Community

9-1-1 People don't call 9-1-1 just to report a crime. They may call to report a fire or a heart attack. Young children can save lives if they know about 9-1-1. Design a poster that teaches young children when to call 9-1-1.

Skills Lab

Who Stole Dave's MP3 Player?

Problem

What hypothesis can you develop about who stole your friend's MP3 player based on your review of the evidence?

Skills Focus

observing, inferring, developing hypotheses

Procedure

At noon, your friend Dave goes to his locker and discovers that it is open. His MP3 player and his favorite pen are missing. So is a brown paper bag containing a sandwich and a large pretzel. Dave asks you to help him find the thief and the MP3 player before the end of the school day. To catch the thief, you need to interpret the data shown on these pages.

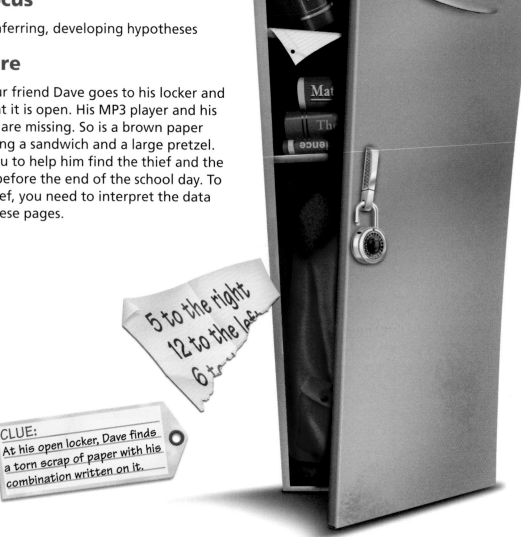

5 to the right
12 to the left
6 to...

CLUE:
At his open locker, Dave finds a torn scrap of paper with his combination written on it.

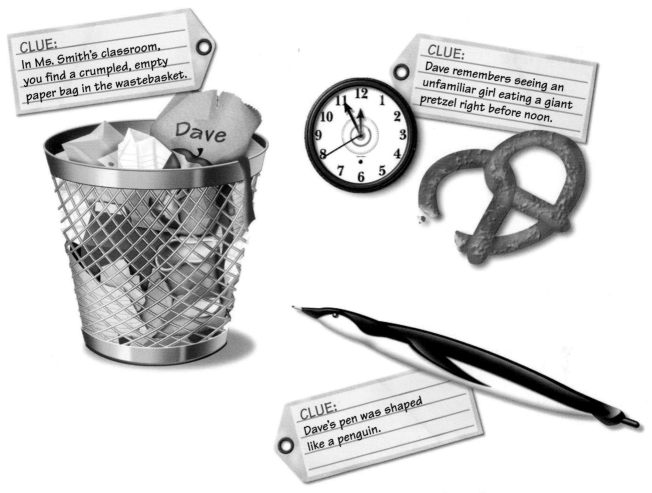

CLUE:
In Ms. Smith's classroom, you find a crumpled, empty paper bag in the wastebasket.

Dave

CLUE:
Dave remembers seeing an unfamiliar girl eating a giant pretzel right before noon.

CLUE:
Dave's pen was shaped like a penguin.

Analyze and Conclude

1. **Observing** List two observations you can make from the illustrations on these pages.

2. **Inferring** Based on where the brown paper bag was found, what can you infer about the thief?

3. **Inferring** Think about the scrap of paper. What are two possible inferences you could make about the thief from this evidence?

4. **Inferring** Why does Dave think the thief might be a girl?

5. **Interpreting Data** How would you use the fact that Dave's favorite pen is missing to help you catch the thief?

6. **Developing Hypotheses** Use your inferences to write a hypothesis about who stole Dave's MP3 player.

Communicating

You have narrowed down the list of possible suspects to one or two students. You want the principal to search their lockers and backpacks for the MP3 player. Write a one-paragraph summary of the evidence and your inferences that will persuade the principal to take action.

Securing and Recording a Crime Scene

Reading Preview

Key Concepts
- How do police secure a crime scene?
- What methods do investigators use to record a crime scene?

Key Terms
- sketch
- scale
- communicating

Target Reading Skill
Sequencing As you read, make a flowchart that shows the steps for securing and recording a crime scene. Place each step in a separate box in your flowchart.

Secure and Record Scene

Establish boundaries.

How Many Footsteps?
1. Observe three classmates walking from the doorway of your classroom to their desks. Count and record the number of steps each classmate takes.
2. Add up the total number of steps and divide by three to get an average number of steps from the doorway to a desk.
3. Also, record the number of students in your class.

Think It Over

Calculating You are investigating a crime scene in a room the size of your classroom. Estimate how many total footsteps your classmates would make if each person walked through the crime scene once. Then think of two ways you could reduce the total number of footsteps.

The fictional detective Sherlock Holmes understood forensic science. In one story, Holmes is examining the scene of a murder. He looks at the trampled grass at the scene and gets angry. "Oh, how simple it would all have been had I been here before they came like a herd of buffalo and wallowed all over it," he exclaims. "Here is where the party with the lodge-keeper came, and they have covered all tracks for six or eight feet round the body."

Modern crime scene investigators would understand how Holmes felt. They often face the same problem. Too many people at a crime scene are like a "herd of buffalo." They trample on evidence. They walk over footprints or fragile traces of evidence. They may leave fingerprints. They interfere with the important first steps in investigating a crime.

Sherlock Holmes in a scene from "The Boscombe Valley Mystery," written by Sir Arthur Conan Doyle in 1891

Securing a Crime Scene

In many TV shows, crime scenes are busy places. They are filled with detectives and officers in blue uniforms. Curious neighbors gather around. But a crime scene is no place for a crowd.

Sometimes people must rush into a crime scene to save a life or keep a suspect from escaping. These acts are necessary even if they disturb the scene and damage evidence. Afterward, the police must secure the site to prevent more damage. **Two ways to make a crime scene secure are to establish clear boundaries and limit entry to the crime scene.**

Establish Boundaries Figure 8 shows the most common way to protect a crime scene. The police are using bright yellow "crime scene" tape to mark the boundaries of the scene. Police may also use ropes, orange traffic cones, or parked police cars to seal off the area. It helps if there are natural boundaries at the scene, such as fences, gates, and doors.

If the crime scene is indoors, police place a seal on windows and doors. Those actions warn people who are not part of the crime scene team to stay out. Officers may be posted at the scene to make sure that no one ignores the warning.

Police commonly tape off an area larger than the crime scene itself. This keeps reporters and other people away from the crime scene. It also provides a place to park official vehicles, talk with witnesses, and meet with other team members.

Control Entry People who walk through a crime scene can leave objects, such as hairs, behind by accident. These objects can cause confusion later when the team collects and tests evidence. So police may map out a single path for people to use as they come and go. They also keep a record, or log, of all visitors.

 Reading Checkpoint | Why do police tape off an area larger than the actual crime scene?

FIGURE 8
Sealing a Crime Scene
These police are using yellow tape to seal off a crime scene.

Long Range These photographs provide an overview, or "big picture," of a crime scene.

Medium Range These photographs focus on locations where there are pieces of evidence.

FIGURE 9
Types of Photographs

These photographs are views of the Bethesda Fountain in Central Park in New York City.

Observing *How can you tell that these photographs were not taken at a crime scene?*

Recording a Crime Scene

At last, the crime scene is secure. The chief investigator can do a "walk-through" of the area with other team members. The team needs to look at the "big picture" before they make a detailed record of the crime scene. It is important to have a record of the scene before any evidence is removed. **Investigators can use photographs, videos, sketches, and notes to make a record of a crime scene.**

Photographs Investigators take photographs to make a visual record of the crime scene. The team will refer to the photographs as they investigate the crime. They may notice a detail that didn't seem important at the start. Or they may check to see if their memories of the crime scene are accurate.

Photographs can also record evidence that is likely to be destroyed. When snow melts, footprints in the snow disappear. Rain may start to fall, washing away traces of evidence. Some crime scenes, such as a busy street, cannot easily be sealed off for long periods. In cases like those, photographs can show what conditions were like when the investigators arrived at the scene.

Showing what the crime scene looked like is also important during a trial. Trials often take place years after a crime happens. Photographs are used to show the crime scene as it looked at the time of the crime. With photographs, people in the courtroom can see where the evidence being presented was found at the crime scene.

Point of View These photographs show what a witness might see from this location. The photos can support or oppose the statement of a witness.

Close-ups These photographs focus on the details of evidence. Close-ups are taken from the side and from above.

Photographs are classified as long range, medium range, point of view, and close-ups. In some close-ups, a ruler is placed next to the object. The photographer can use the photo with the ruler to make a print of the object at its actual size. Figure 9 shows an example of each type of photograph.

The type of camera used at the crime scene is important. With a digital camera, photographers can see right away if they got the right image. Also, the photos can be quickly stored in a computer. They don't need to be sent to a photo lab. On the other hand, it is easy to alter the images with a computer. That makes digital photos less reliable as evidence than photos taken with film.

Videos A photographer may also make a video of a crime scene. He often follows a path from the outside of the scene to the center. This is the path an investigator takes when she first walks through the scene. The photographer does not want team members to be seen in the video. Nor does he want to record their remarks as part of the permanent record. So he usually turns the sound off.

Videos don't show details as clearly as still photographs do. But videos can provide a dramatic "you are there" experience. They give people a sense of being at the original crime scene. A video can also be used to introduce new members of the team to the case.

Skills Activity

Observing
Look at the photographs in Figure 9. They are examples of the four types of photos that might be taken at crime scenes. Use details from the photos to compare long-range, medium-range, and point-of-view photos.

Reading Checkpoint What types of photographs does a photographer take at a crime scene?

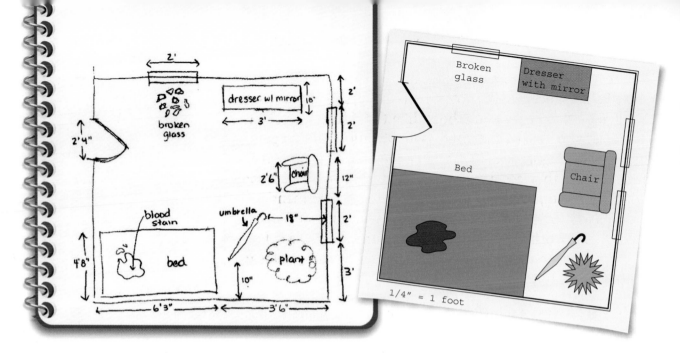

Figure 10
Sketch vs. Scale Drawing
A CSI made the measurements recorded on the sketch at a crime scene. An artist used the measurements and a computer program to make a scale drawing of the room.

Skills **Activity**

Calculating

You are investigating a bank robbery that is similar to one that took place in Spain. The detective in Spain asks for a sketch of the bank vault at your crime scene. Before you send the sketch, you need to convert the measurements from feet to meters—a unit of length used in Spain. The vault is 12 feet wide, 16 feet long, and 11 feet high.

Hint: 1 meter = 3.28 feet

Sketches The next task is making sketches of the crime scene. A **sketch** is a rough drawing that is done quickly and without much detail. Like photographs, sketches are visual records of a crime scene. But a sketch doesn't include everything a viewer could observe at the scene. Investigators decide which objects to include in a sketch and which to ignore.

The sketch in Figure 10 includes measurements. It shows the length of the walls, the width of the doorway, and the width of each window. There are also measurements for the bed and other items in the room. Measurements are used to mark the locations of objects, such as an umbrella. All the measurements must be accurate. If not, investigators won't be able to use the sketch to make models of the crime scene that can be shown in court.

Scale Drawings An artist can use the sketches from a crime scene to make two-dimensional drawings, or models, of the scene. The drawings will be larger or smaller than the area they represent, but they will be drawn to **scale.** The scale is the ratio of the model to the actual size of the object. For example, suppose the scale is 1 inch equals 1 foot. Then a 3-inch line on the drawing will represent 3 feet at the crime scene.

Today, most artists use **c**omputer-**a**ided **d**rafting (CAD) software to make scale drawings. Most CAD programs include drawings of rooms or street intersections. Operators use data from the crime scene sketches to complete the drawings. Programs may include symbols for cars, furniture, and even splashes of blood. A CAD program lets the artist zoom in on areas of the crime scene. Or the artist can make a large version of the drawing for use in court.

Written Notes The record of a crime scene also includes notes. Police officers make notes when they respond to a 9-1-1 call. They often carry a notebook like the one in Figure 11. They use it to record the time, date, location, and type of emergency. They also record what they observed and what they did. Did they see a car speeding away from the scene? Did they force open a door to gain entry to an apartment?

Handwritten notes must be easy to read and well organized. A police officer wants to respond quickly when a detective asks a question. Officers will also refer to their notes if they are called to testify in a trial.

Dictated Notes An investigator often carries a small voice recorder. He uses the recorder to make notes as he does tasks at the crime scene, such as taking photographs. Later, he can listen to the tape and type up the notes.

Dictating notes is faster than writing notes. It also allows others to listen as the notes are being recorded. For example, an investigator describes what she sees during a walk-through of a crime scene. She is recording her first impressions. She is also communicating with other team members. When people share their ideas with other people, they are **communicating.** The ideas may be written or spoken. So team members need to be good readers, writers, speakers, and listeners.

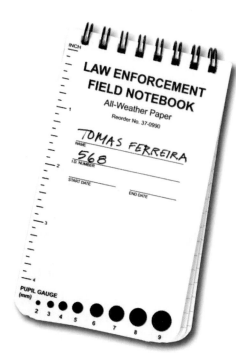

FIGURE 11
Taking Notes
This notebook is small enough to fit in a pocket. It has a waterproof cover that keeps the notes dry.

Lesson 2 Assessment

Target Reading Skill Sequencing Use your flowchart of actions at a crime scene to help you answer the questions below.

Reviewing Key Concepts

1. a. **Describing** How do police establish boundaries at an outdoor crime scene?
   b. **Explaining** Why do police establish one path to exit and enter a crime scene?
   c. **Making Judgments** Which type of crime scene do you think would be easier to control—an outdoor or an indoor crime scene? Give a reason for your choice.
2. a. **Identifying** List four methods that are used to make a record of a crime scene.
   b. **Classifying** What type of photo taken at a crime scene is likely to include a ruler? Why is the ruler in the photo?

c. **Problem Solving** A CSI is getting ready to testify in court. The CSI needs to know the distance from the front door to the back door at the crime scene. Where should the CSI look for this data?

At-Home **Activity**

Measuring a Room Work with your family to make a sketch of a room in your home. Measure the length and width of the room. Mark the location of doors and windows. Include large items such as a table, a couch, a bed, or a refrigerator. Use measurements to show the location of objects in the room.

Forensics & Earth Science

Mapping Crime

In the past, police would use pins to mark the locations of crimes on large wall maps. They often used different colored pins to represent different types of crimes. Now police can use crime-mapping software to display and analyze crime data. With computer maps, police have more control. They can choose a geographic area, a time period, a type of crime, and how they want to display the data.

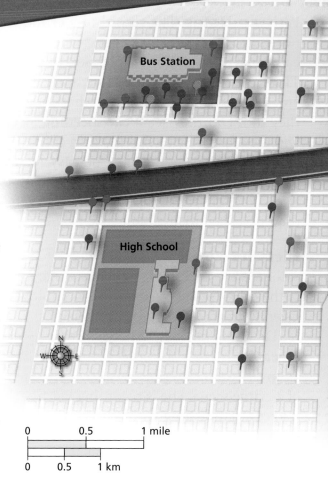

Coding Crime Data

When police enter data about crimes into a database, they assign codes to locations where crimes occur so they can plot these locations on maps. The codes are often based on latitude and longitude. Latitude is the distance north or south of the equator. Longitude is the distance east or west of the prime meridian.

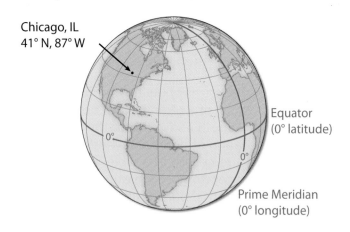

Chicago, IL
41° N, 87° W

Equator
(0° latitude)

0°

0°

Prime Meridian
(0° longitude)

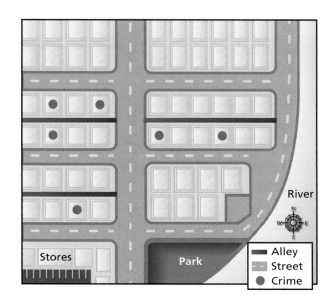

Solving Crimes

One person has stolen items from six homes in the same neighborhood. When the police plot the crime sites on a map, they notice a pattern that can help them predict future targets. All six homes back onto alleys.

Key
- Auto theft
- Burglary
- Murder
- Vandalism

Park

Highway

Mall

Identifying Hot Spots

Police can use crime maps to identify areas in a community that have a higher than average crime rate. These areas are called "hot spots." A police department may assign more police to work in hot spots. They may also change the type of patrols in an area.

Police on bicycles may be used to patrol a downtown area, a park, or a college campus.

You Be the Judge

1. Reading Maps
Look at the map showing four types of crimes. Pick two areas you think are hot spots and explain why.

2. Graphing
Make a bar graph for each hot spot you chose. Plot the number of crimes for each type of crime. How are the graphs alike? How are they different?

3. Problem Solving
Write a plan that the police could use to reduce crime in one hot spot.

Go Online
SciLINKS NSTA

For: Links on longitude
Visit: www.SciLinks.org
Web Code: dan-1010

Types of Evidence

Reading Preview

🔑 Key Concepts
- What are the benefits and drawbacks of direct evidence?
- What methods are used to help witnesses identify suspects?
- Why is physical evidence key to solving crimes?

Key Terms
- eyewitness
- direct evidence
- modus operandi
- surveillance camera
- physical evidence

🎯 Target Reading Skill

Posing Questions Before you read, preview the red headings in this section. In a graphic organizer like the one below, ask a *what* or *how* question about each heading. As you read, write the answers to your questions.

Question	Answer
What is direct evidence?	Direct evidence is observed by an eyewitness.

Discover **Activity**

Who Was That Person?
Your teacher will organize an event for you to observe.

1. Take a few minutes to record what you observed in your notebook. Include details that you think would help identify the person.

2. After about 10 minutes, the person will return to the classroom. Take a few minutes to observe the person again and revise your description.

Think It Over

Observing How accurate was your first description? Why was it difficult to write a detailed description?

People are in a convenience store picking out snacks. Two people are leaning on the counter talking to the store clerk. They're both wearing jeans and sweatshirts. Suddenly one of them says, "We have a gun. Give us all your cash. Then no one will get hurt!" The customers gasp and shrink back.

The clerk's hands shake as he empties the cash register and hands over the cash. The robber laughs and hands one of the dollar bills back to him. "Here. Buy yourself some chips."

After the robbers pull their hoods over their faces and leave, the clerk calls the police. Then everyone starts talking at once. "Did you see the gun?" "Were they both men?" "One was kind of short. Maybe it was a girl." "She had awfully big feet for a girl!"

When the police arrive, they will find the people who witnessed the crime. They will also find the dollar bill the robber gave to the clerk. The people and the bill provide two different types of evidence—direct evidence and physical evidence.

Direct Evidence

After the robbery, the convenience store clerk is excited. He calls his mother to tell her what happened. Now both of them know what happened. But only one has firsthand knowledge of the event—the clerk. He is an eyewitness.

Eyewitnesses An **eyewitness** is a person who directly observes an event. The clerk and customers at the convenience store are eyewitnesses. When the police arrive, they will ask each person to say what he or she saw or heard. These firsthand observations by eyewitnesses are **direct evidence.** This evidence can be used in court to prove a fact. For example, the clerk could testify to the fact that he saw two robbers.

Identifying witnesses is one of the first things officers do at a crime scene. They collect names, addresses, and phone numbers. The officers may also search the surrounding area to see if anyone else saw or heard what happened. **Some witnesses give accurate descriptions of what they saw or heard. But what a witness says is not always accurate.**

Problems With Direct Evidence The descriptions that eyewitnesses give at a crime scene may not match. One witness says the person drove a gray car. The other says the car was red. One witness says the person was wearing boots. Another can identify the brand of boot. One recalls things the person said. The other does not. Why are their observations different?

People's physical abilities, experiences, and emotions can affect their observations. A red car may look gray to a person who is colorblind, like the young man in Figure 12. Someone who works in a shoe store may recognize a boot brand. Or a witness may be too scared or angry to notice anything!

Another problem is that witnesses may be asked to recall events weeks or months after they happen. This can be difficult. If you were asked to say what you did on a given day last month, do you think you could remember?

 **How is direct evidence used?**

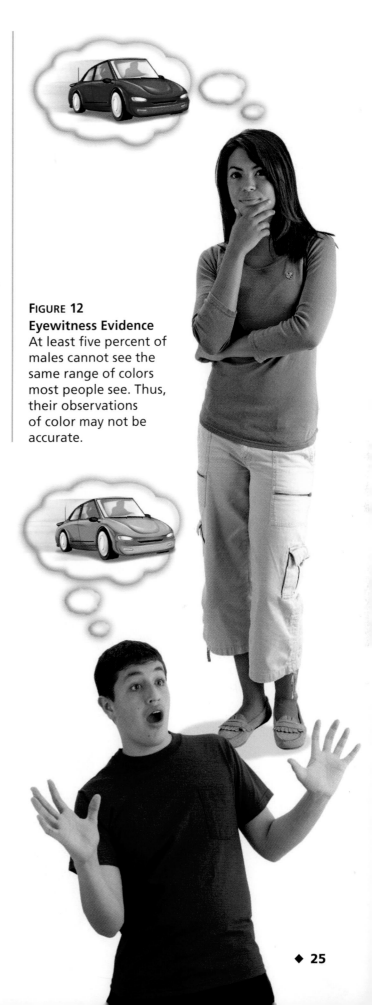

FIGURE 12
Eyewitness Evidence
At least five percent of males cannot see the same range of colors most people see. Thus, their observations of color may not be accurate.

Using Lineups and Mug Shots

Police have ways to help witnesses supply evidence that is useful. **Police may ask a witness to view a lineup or look at mug shots to help identify suspects.**

The Lineup You may have seen a lineup on TV or in a movie. If so, you know that the witness looks at the lineup through a one-way mirror so the suspect can't see the witness. The witness is looking for the person he or she saw at the crime scene. A person in the lineup may be asked to step forward so the witness can get a better view. Or each one may be asked to repeat words the witness recalls hearing at the crime scene.

When is the lineup useful? First, investigators need a likely suspect. Then they must design a lineup that is fair. All the individuals in the lineup must be similar in appearance. The lineup in Figure 13 isn't good. A good lineup would not include a person who is clearly older than the others.

The results of a lineup may be misleading. Most witnesses assume that the person who committed the crime is in the lineup. Even if they are told that it is fine not to make a choice, they may feel pressured to identify *someone*. They may point out a person who only vaguely resembles the one they saw at the crime scene. If everyone looks similar, it is harder for a witness to pick out a suspect at random.

FIGURE 13
A Mock Lineup
This is an example of a poorly designed lineup. If this group were used in an actual lineup, the suspect could claim that the process was not fair.
Interpreting Photographs *Give three reasons why all of these people should not appear in the same lineup.*

Mug Shots If the suspect has a criminal record, police can show witnesses mug shots, like the one in Figure 14. Mug shots are the photos taken when a person is arrested. The photographer takes a front and side view. The same rules apply to mug shots that apply to lineups. For the process to be fair, a witness must view photos of similar-looking people.

Police can use mug shots even when there is no specific suspect. They may ask a witness to browse through books filled with mug shots. This isn't an ideal situation. Police in large cities have so many photos on file that it is not practical for witnesses to look at them all. Besides, when people spend hours looking at photos, they may begin to lose interest or they may pick out the wrong person by mistake.

The police can speed up the process by narrowing the task. They can show photos of criminals with a **modus operandi,** or MO, that fits the crime. This Latin term means "mode of operation." A person's MO describes the way he or she approaches a task. For a criminal, this could mean working alone, picking a lock to gain entry to a building, or targeting older people.

 **What is a mug shot?**

FIGURE 14
Mug Shot
This 1975 photo is of Patricia Hearst. It was taken when she was arrested for her part in a bank robbery. Patty claimed she was forced to take part in the robbery by a group who kidnapped her in 1974.

Picturing a Criminal

Mug shots won't help if the person who committed a crime has never been arrested. What other tools do investigators have? **Investigators can use sketches made by forensic artists to identify criminals. They can also use surveillance videos and facial recognition software.**

Making Sketches In 1995, a bomb destroyed a federal building in Oklahoma City. The blast killed 168 people. The FBI needed the public's help. A forensic artist talked with people at the agency where the truck that delivered the bomb was rented. She used what they told her to make the sketch in Figure 15. This sketch helped the FBI identify the bomber.

Until 1959, sketch artists drew their sketches by hand. In 1959, many artists began to use a kit that contained a library of facial features. The artist would choose features such as "wide-set eyes," "thin eyebrows," or "pointed nose." The witness might say, "No, the cheekbones were broader." They would go back and forth, working together to build a reliable portrait like the one in Figure 16.

Today, artists can use a software version of the kit to draw their sketches. With a computer, the process of building up a portrait is faster. Plus, the library of facial features is larger.

Some artists still think the choices are too limited. They prefer to sit with a witness and a sketchpad. These sketches take longer to draw, but they include more details and can account for unusual features.

FIGURE 15
Sketch Made by Hand
A forensic artist interviewed witnesses. Then she drew this sketch of Timothy McVeigh.
Comparing and Contrasting
Compare the sketch to the photo of Timothy McVeigh. Would you change any feature to make the sketch more realistic? Explain.

 Reading Checkpoint **What tool used by forensic artists was invented in 1959?**

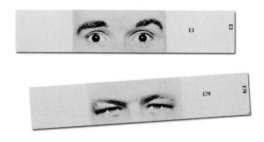

FIGURE 16
Sketch Made With Kit
An artist made this sketch by selecting facial features from a kit.

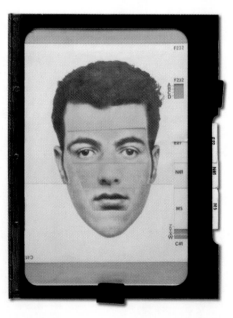

Surveillance Cameras When you're in a public place, there may be a camera watching. The cameras in banks, stores, and other public places are **surveillance cameras** (sur VAY luns). *Surveillance* comes from a French word meaning "to watch over." Sometimes you know that these cameras are watching. There's a sign saying "CCTV in use." CCTV stands for closed circuit TV.

If a crime takes place within view of a surveillance camera, the camera records the action. In theory, this evidence should be very useful. Unfortunately, the images on these videos are often gray and blurry. It is hard to match the images with an actual suspect's face.

Facial Recognition Software Investigators may need to show that a suspect was at a specific place at a given time. The place could be a cash machine, a gas station, or a store. A camera at the location may have captured a video image of the suspect. If so, the video has a date and time stamp. What can be done to convince a viewer that the image on the video is really the suspect?

There is computer software that can match a video image to an image in a database of mug shots. The software works by measuring distances between facial features. It measures these distances on the face in the video image. Then it searches for mug shots with similar measurements. The software can search up to 60 million images a minute. If the software makes a match, a person checks to make sure the match is accurate.

FIGURE **17**
Surveillance Videos
In a large store, there may be many surveillance cameras. One person can sit in a room and watch what is happening at locations throughout the store.

Forensic Science Video
Interviewing Witnesses

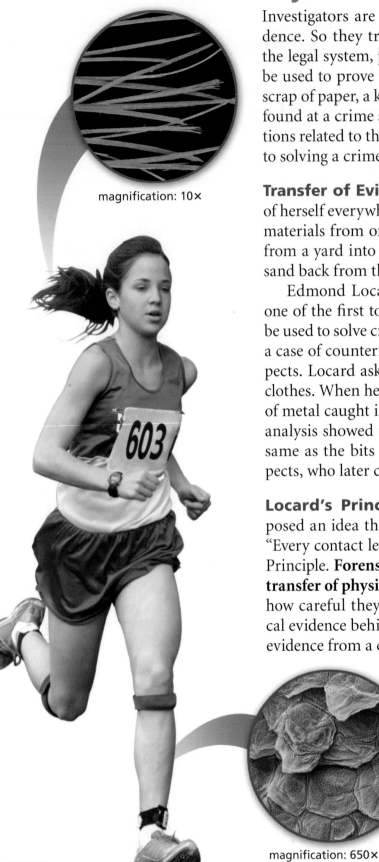

magnification: 10×

Physical Evidence

Investigators are aware of the problems with direct evidence. So they try to rely more on physical evidence. In the legal system, **physical evidence** is any object that can be used to prove that a fact is true. The object could be a scrap of paper, a knife, or a hair. Some physical evidence is found at a crime scene. Some may be found at other locations related to the crime. Physical evidence can be the key to solving a crime.

Transfer of Evidence The girl in Figure 18 leaves a bit of herself everywhere she goes. You do, too. You also move materials from one place to another. You may track mud from a yard into a kitchen on your shoes. You may carry sand back from the beach in your bathing suit.

Edmond Locard (1877–1966), a French scientist, was one of the first to see how the transfer of materials could be used to solve crimes. One time Locard was investigating a case of counterfeit, or fake, coins. There were three suspects. Locard asked the police to bring him the suspects' clothes. When he examined the clothes, he found tiny bits of metal caught in the seams and other creases. Chemical analysis showed that the metal of the fake coins was the same as the bits in the clothing. Police arrested the suspects, who later confessed.

Locard's Principle Based on his work, Locard proposed an idea that is central to forensic science. He said, "Every contact leaves a trace." This idea is called Locard's Principle. **Forensic scientists know that there is always a transfer of physical evidence at a crime scene.** No matter how careful they are, criminals always leave some physical evidence behind. Plus, they always carry away physical evidence from a crime scene.

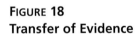

Figure 18
Transfer of Evidence
People leave physical evidence wherever they go. This girl will shed about 100 hairs a day and about 50,000 flakes of skin every minute. *Predicting What materials might she pick up while running cross country?*

magnification: 650×

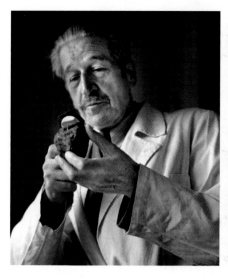

FIGURE 19
Role of Technology
Edmond Locard's tools were much simpler than those used by modern forensic scientists. *Making Judgments Do you think it is easier for modern scientists to solve crimes than it was for Locard? Why or why not?*

Locard's Influence Locard had studied both medicine and law. In 1910, he set up his own police laboratory in Lyons, France. He worked in a cramped attic room and had only a few simple instruments, like the one in Figure 19. But he soon became famous for his research into forensic science. His work inspired police in other countries to set up laboratories. In the United States, the FBI set up its first lab in 1932. Today, the FBI lab is one of the largest forensic labs in the world.

Lesson 3 Assessment

Target Reading Skill Posing Questions Use your graphic organizer and the answers you wrote to help you answer the questions below.

Reviewing Key Concepts

1. a. Defining What is direct evidence?
   b. Making Generalizations When is direct evidence useful? Why is direct evidence not always reliable?
   c. Predicting An off-duty detective sees a person trying to steal a car. Would you expect the detective to provide accurate direct evidence? Why or why not?
2. a. Reviewing What methods do police use to help witnesses identify a likely suspect?
   b. Relating Cause and Effect Why might an eyewitness identify the wrong person?
   c. Problem Solving When investigators don't have a likely suspect, what are two ways a witness can help identify a suspect?

3. a. Defining What is physical evidence? List three examples.
   b. Describing What did Locard say happens to physical evidence at a crime scene?
   c. Applying Concepts Show how Locard used his principle to solve the case of the fake coins.

Writing in Science

Descriptive Paragraph You want an artist to make a sketch of a family member or friend. The problem is you do not have a recent photo of the person. Using your memory, write a "word picture" of the person. Provide details that will help the artist make a lifelike portrait.

Collecting Physical Evidence

Reading Preview

Key Concepts
- What should investigators do before they begin to search a crime scene?
- How do investigators make sure that evidence found at a crime scene can be used in court?
- What can investigators do to keep safe at a crime scene?

Key Terms
- contamination
- chain of custody

Target Reading Skill
Outlining As you read, make an outline about collecting physical evidence. Use the red headings for the main ideas and the blue headings for supporting ideas.

Collecting Physical Evidence
I. Organizing a Search
A. Consider the Crime Scene
B. Pick a Search Pattern
II. Keeping Evidence Useful

Discover Activity

How Would You Collect This Evidence?
Your teacher has placed evidence at different locations in your classroom. Each location has a number. Do Step 1 as you move around the classroom. Then return to your seat and do Step 2.

1. Observe and identify each piece of evidence. Record this information in your notebook. Do not touch or remove any of the evidence.

2. For each piece of evidence, describe how you could collect the evidence if you were a CSI.

Think It Over

Drawing Conclusions What equipment do you think a CSI should bring to a crime scene to collect evidence?

It is your first day working as a CSI at an actual crime scene. You want to show your boss that you know how to do your job. You have a kit full of equipment for gathering evidence. You pull on gloves to make sure that any fingerprints found at the scene won't be yours! You look around and wonder where to start.

The way that a CSI searches for evidence can have a big effect on a case. If searchers don't find evidence early on, it may never be found. So how a team organizes a search is important.

FIGURE 20
Searching in a Line
When people form a line and search as a group, they are less likely to miss a small object.

Organizing a Search

Each search is a little different. But one rule applies to all crime scenes. The crime scene team must search in an organized way. If not, they are likely to miss some important pieces of evidence. **The team needs to consider the crime scene and pick a search pattern before they begin a search.**

Consider the Crime Scene Some crimes occur in a small space—a store or an apartment. Others, such as an explosion, scatter evidence over a huge area. For crimes that take place outdoors, weather is an issue. Because weather can destroy evidence, these crimes scenes may have to be searched quickly. If the crime scene is a car, a CSI is likely to do a quick initial search at the scene. Then the CSI will have the car towed to a garage for a more detailed search.

Pick a Search Pattern Search patterns are designed to cover every inch of a crime scene. A team picks a search pattern based on the size of the crime scene and the size of the objects they are looking for. The investigators in Figure 20, for example, are creeping along the ground in a line, shoulder-to-shoulder. They are using a strip, or line, pattern. This pattern can be used to look for a small object in a large area.

Figure 21 shows other search patterns. A grid pattern is like a strip pattern, except that every area is searched twice. Searchers cross the scene in one direction. Then they cross it again at right angles. Searchers may also divide a crime scene into zones. The zones are labeled so that searchers can record where evidence is found.

Reading Checkpoint When might a CSI need to do a quick search?

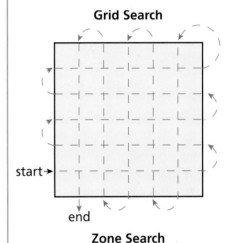

FIGURE 21
Grid and Zone Searches
These drawings compare two typical types of search patterns. *Predicting Which pattern are investigators likely to use to search a house? Explain.*

Search and Rescue Events

Rangers who work for the National Park Service may need to rescue visitors who are lost, ill, or injured. So the rangers need to understand search patterns. The graph shows data about some search and rescue events that took place in national parks in one year.

1. **Reading Graphs** For which activity were there 187 events?

2. **Calculating** How many people were injured or became ill while boating or swimming?

3. **Estimating** What is the ratio of swimming events to swimming injuries or illnesses?

4. **Interpreting Data** There are about six times as many hiking events as climbing events. Yet you could argue that hiking is a safer activity than climbing. What data could you use to support this argument?

5. **Developing Hypotheses** If hiking is generally safer than climbing, how can you explain the difference in number of events?

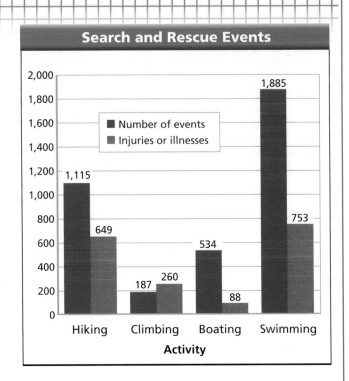

Search and Rescue Events

- ■ Number of events
- ■ Injuries or illnesses

Hiking: 1,115 — 649
Climbing: 187 — 260
Boating: 534 — 88
Swimming: 1,885 — 753

Activity

Go Online

SciLINKS NSTA

For: Links on careers in science
Visit: www.SciLinks.org
Web Code: dan-1014

Keeping Evidence Useful

Investigators don't just collect evidence to solve a crime. They want to be able to use the evidence later in a trial. What if a judge says key pieces of evidence can't be used in a trial? The case may have to be dropped for lack of evidence and a guilty person may go free. There are steps investigators can take to keep this from happening. **Crime scene investigators must prevent contamination at the crime scene. They also must have the right equipment, package the evidence correctly, and keep a chain of custody.**

Preventing Contamination The adding of unwanted material to an object is called **contamination.** A CSI wears clothing that is designed to prevent contamination of a crime scene. A head cover, for example, keeps the CSI from adding hairs to the scene. Booties protect shoes so that soil caught in shoe treads won't be left at the scene. Gloves allow a CSI to pick up an object without transferring dead cells, sweat, or oil from his skin to the object.

Having the Right Equipment What evidence do investigators look for? For most crimes, they look for fingerprints. For a burglary, they may look for tool marks where burglars forced open a door or window. For a hit-and-run, they look for evidence they can use to identify the vehicle. This could be glass from a broken headlight or marks made by tire treads. With violent crimes, they look for evidence that may have been transferred to the victim from the attacker.

Investigators need to be prepared for any situation. They start with an equipment kit like the one in Figure 22. The kits have tools for collecting different kinds of evidence. If a CSI needs to cut out a piece of carpet that is stained with blood, for example, she can reach for a box cutter or scalpel. Here are some other examples of how some tools are used.

▶ A brush, powder, and tape are used to collect fingerprints.

▶ A hand lens is used to get a closer view of a small object.

▶ Tweezers and forceps are used to pick up small objects.

▶ Swabs are used to collect evidence from a victim.

▶ A small vacuum cleaner with an attached filter and screen can be used to sweep a rug or a car's interior.

▶ A screwdriver can be used to remove a doorknob or even a door so it can be sent to the crime lab.

Reading Checkpoint What can a CSI use to pick up small objects?

FIGURE 22
Equipment Kit
Some items in an equipment kit are standard, such as fingerprint powders. But other items will vary depending on the kit.
Applying Concepts *Most kits include an evidence ruler. When might a CSI use this item?*

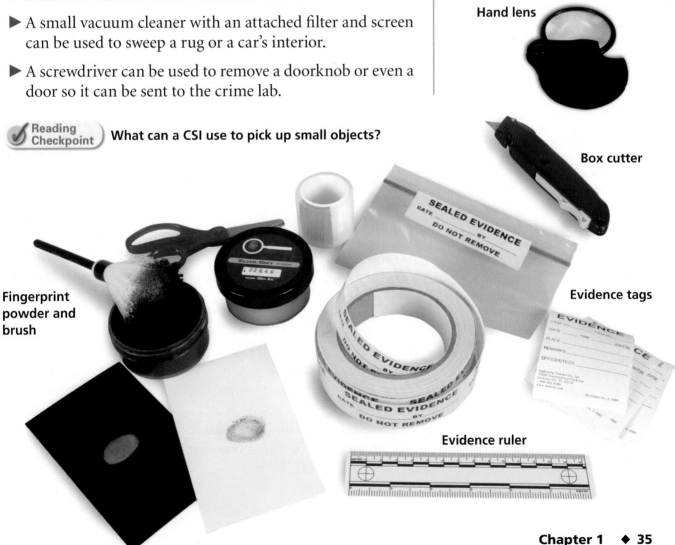

Tweezers

Scalpel

Hand lens

Box cutter

Fingerprint powder and brush

Evidence tags

Evidence ruler

Packaging Evidence Correctly Evidence kits have containers a CSI can use to package evidence. These may include paper bags, envelopes, and plastic bottles. In general, each piece of evidence is packaged separately. The CSI has to choose the right container for each item. For example, a bloody shirt would first be allowed to dry. Then it is packed in a paper bag. Figure 23 explains how to pack five other pieces of evidence.

The CSI must make sure evidence isn't lost as it moves from a crime scene to a storage area or crime lab. Containers must be sealed so the contents cannot leak or spill out. Some evidence is fragile, or easily damaged. A drinking glass, for example, can break if it is dropped. So investigators may use plastic wrap with bubbles, cardboard, or cotton cloth to protect fragile items.

Some police departments have vans that are called mobile crime scene labs. These vans are expensive, but they do help to keep the evidence safe. They carry refrigerators and other equipment for packaging and storing physical evidence. The word *lab* in mobile crime scene lab is a bit misleading. Most vans do not carry equipment for testing evidence.

FIGURE 23
These instructions for packing evidence come from a handbook written by the FBI.
Interpreting Data *Which items should not be packed in a plastic container?*

Evidence Packing Instructions

Sample	Instructions
A drop of blood on a windowsill	Use a cotton swab. Leave part of the swab unstained as a control. Air-dry the swab and pack in clean paper or an envelope with sealed corners. Do not use a plastic container.
Cigarette butts from a sidewalk	Pick up with a gloved hand or forceps. Air-dry and pack in clean paper or an envelope with sealed corners. Do not use a plastic container.
Hair from a pillow	Pick up with forceps. Package in clean paper or an envelope with sealed corners. Do not use a plastic container.
Bits of glass from a broken window	Package in a leakproof container such as a plastic film canister or pill bottle. Do not use a paper or glass container.
Soil caught in the sole of a shoe	Do not remove the soil from the shoe. Air-dry the shoe. Then put the shoe in a paper bag.

FIGURE 24
Chain of Custody

Evidence could be in a lab, in a storage room, or in a courtroom. The people who handle the evidence at each location need to maintain a chain of custody.

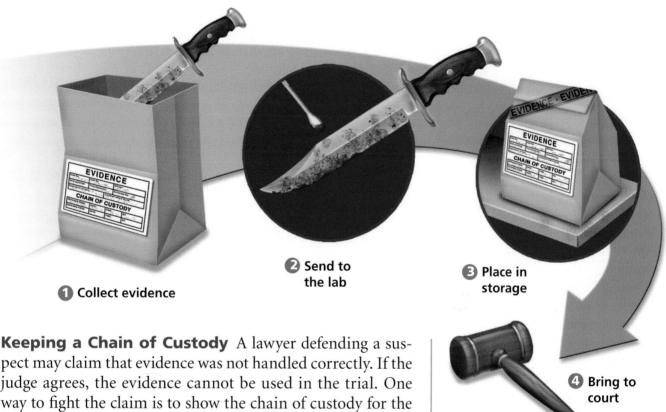

① Collect evidence

② Send to the lab

③ Place in storage

④ Bring to court

Keeping a Chain of Custody A lawyer defending a suspect may claim that evidence was not handled correctly. If the judge agrees, the evidence cannot be used in the trial. One way to fight the claim is to show the chain of custody for the evidence. A **chain of custody** is a written record of who had control of a piece of evidence from the time it was collected. The record contains names, dates, and places. There must be no gaps in the record, that is, no times when the evidence is not secured.

An accurate chain of custody helps show that an item being presented in court is the item that was found at the crime scene. When a CSI packages an item, she labels the outside of the container with the date and adds her name or initials. She makes sure the evidence is secure until it is handed off to someone else.

The log shows everyone who had contact with the evidence. For example, an investigator may check out a piece of evidence from storage, observe the evidence, and return it. The evidence may be sent to a lab for testing. If so, the log will show when it was sent, who tested it, what he did, and when it was sent back. Figure 24 illustrates one possible chain of custody.

 **Reading Checkpoint** When does a chain of custody begin?

Protecting the Investigators

It's not only evidence that must be protected at a crime scene. People who work at the scene can be at risk. They may have to handle blood that is infected. They may find explosives or drugs. What crime scene investigators do to protect themselves is similar to what you do during a lab at school. **Crime scene investigators protect themselves by following established safety rules and procedures.** Here are a few examples.

▶ Poisons, viruses, and bacteria can enter a person's body through the skin, nose, or mouth. So a CSI does not eat, drink, chew gum, or put on makeup at a crime scene.

▶ At some crime scenes, a CSI adds a mask, goggles, and an extra pair of gloves. If a piece of protective clothing is torn, it must be replaced.

▶ A CSI handles knives, razor blades, broken glass, and other sharp objects with care.

▶ Sometimes a CSI must work in a building that has been damaged where there is a danger of injury from falling objects. The CSI needs to wear a helmet and sturdy shoes.

Some situations call for people with extra training. For example, disarming an explosive device is a task for a bomb squad. They, in turn, may use a hazardous duty robot like the one shown in Figure 25.

FIGURE 25
Hazardous Duty Robot
At a bank, the bomb squad finds a device that they suspect will explode. They use a robot to place the device into a bucket.

Lesson 4 Assessment

Target Reading Skill Outlining Use the information in your outline about collecting evidence to help answer Question 2.

Reviewing Key Concepts

1. a. **Reviewing** Why is it important to search a crime scene in an organized way?
   b. **Applying Concepts** What factors influence the choice of a search pattern?
   c. **Comparing and Contrasting** How do a line search and a grid search differ?

2. a. **Summarizing** What are four things a CSI needs to do to keep evidence useful?
   b. **Inferring** A CSI is using a hand lens and tweezers. What does this tell you about the evidence the CSI is trying to collect?

3. a. **Listing** What are three hazards that investigators may face at a crime scene?
   b. **Making Generalizations** How do crime scene investigators protect themselves at a crime scene?
   c. **Drawing Conclusions** Why should a CSI replace torn clothing quickly?

Math Practice

4. **Area** Twenty people use a strip pattern to search a field. Each strip is 2 meters wide and 80 meters long. What is the area of the field in square meters? *Hint:* It might help to draw a diagram of the field.

The BIG Idea The team at a crime scene observes, infers, and communicates. They also measure, pose questions, and develop hypotheses.

1 Using Science to Solve Crimes

Key Concepts

- The investigative team uses inquiry skills to help solve crimes. These skills include observing, inferring, predicting, and developing a hypothesis.
- Each member of an investigative team brings specific skills and knowledge to the team. Each has an assigned role.
- Scientists still design tests to solve crimes. But now they have better technology for doing the tests.

Key Terms

- burglary
- observing
- inferring
- hypothesis
- medical examiner
- autopsy
- forensic science
- evidence
- predicting
- crime scene investigator (CSI)
- density

2 Securing and Recording a Crime Scene

Key Concepts

- Two ways to make a crime scene secure are to establish clear boundaries and limit entry to the crime scene.
- Investigators can use photographs, videos, sketches, and notes to make a record of a crime scene.

Key Terms

- sketch
- scale
- communicating

3 Types of Evidence

Key Concepts

- Some witnesses give accurate descriptions of what they saw or heard. But sometimes what a witness says is not accurate.
- Police may ask a witness to view a lineup or look at mug shots to help identify suspects.
- Investigators can use sketches made by forensic artists to identify criminals. They can also use surveillance videos and facial recognition software.
- Forensic scientists know that there is always a transfer of physical evidence at a crime scene.

Key Term

- eyewitness
- modus operandi
- physical evidence
- direct evidence
- surveillance camera

4 Collecting Physical Evidence

Key Concepts

- The team needs to consider the crime scene and pick a search pattern before they begin a search.
- Crime scene investigators must prevent contamination at the crime scene. They also must have the right equipment, package the evidence correctly, and keep a chain of custody.
- Crime scene investigators protect themselves by following established safety rules and procedures.

Key Terms

- contamination
- chain of custody

Review and Assessment

Organizing Information

Concept Mapping Copy the concept map about evidence onto a separate sheet of paper. Then complete the map by adding the correct missing words or phrases. (For more on Concept Mapping, see the Skills Handbook.)

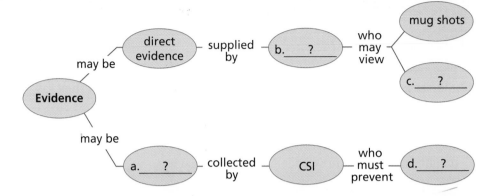

Reviewing Key Terms

Choose the letter of the best answer.

1. Using your senses to gather evidence at a crime scene is called
   a. sensing.   b. observing.
   c. hearing.   d. touching.

2. Giving an opinion about an event based on observations and experience is called
   a. observing.
   b. classifying.
   c. inferring.
   d. communicating.

3. In science, a possible explanation for a set of observations is called
   a. direct evidence.
   b. a prediction.
   c. an inference.
   d. a hypothesis.

4. To record measurements at a crime scene, investigators make a
   a. sketch.
   b. CAD drawing.
   c. surveillance video.
   d. scale drawing.

5. The chain of custody is
   a. the log of visitors to a crime scene.
   b. a record of who had control of evidence.
   c. a list of eyewitnesses to a crime.
   d. a way to secure a crime scene.

If the statement is true, write _true_. If it is false, change the underlined word or words to make the statement true.

6. Stating an opinion about what will happen in the future is called <u>classifying</u>. F predicting

7. In the legal system, <u>evidence</u> is something that can be presented in court to make a point during a trial. F

8. An <u>autopsy</u> is a detailed examination of a dead body. T

9. The evidence given by eyewitnesses at a crime scene is called <u>physical evidence</u>. F directed

10. A CSI wears protective clothing in order to prevent <u>loss</u> of evidence at a crime scene. F protect from clues

Writing in Science

Analogy Crime scene investigators are not the only ones who worry about contamination. People who buy medicines have the same concern. They need to be sure that these products are safe to use. One way to check for safety is to look at the packaging. Write a paragraph describing what buyers can look for to check that medicines are safe to use. Compare how medicines are packaged to how evidence is packaged at a crime scene.

Checking Concepts

11. What two tasks should team members do first at a crime scene? ~~S Sc~~

12. Why do investigators make a record of a crime scene?

13. What is the difference between direct evidence and physical evidence?

14. When do police use a lineup and mug shots to help witnesses identify a suspect?

15. In your own words, explain Locard's ideas about the transfer of physical evidence.

16. Give two reasons why investigators wear protective clothing at a crime scene.

Thinking Critically

17. **Relating Cause and Effect** What could happen if police don't secure a crime scene? *People could walk around in it and leave traces to confuse police.*

18. **Comparing and Contrasting** How are a sketch and a scale drawing similar? How are they different?

19. **Predicting** Investigators are organizing a search inside a mall. What kind of search pattern are they likely to use, and why? *Grid search*

Math Practice

After a crime, a CSI needs to search a tennis court. Use the sketch to answer Questions 20 and 21. The green area is the playing surface.

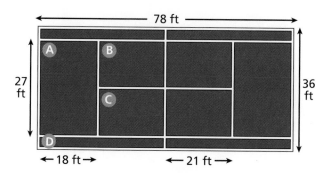

20. **Area** What is the area of the playing surface in square yards?

21. **Area** What is the area of zone A in square yards? What is the area of zone D?

Applying Skills

Use the photo to answer Questions 22–26.

Hit from back, No airbag, hit house

22. **Observing** List at least three observations that a police officer might make at the scene.

23. **Inferring** Use these observations to make three inferences about what happened.

24. **Posing Questions** What are three questions you would ask an eyewitness? *Was the hit intentional? Was there another car involved? If so, what did it look like?*

25. **Problem Solving** How would you secure the scene? *caution tape or orange cones,*

26. **Applying Concepts** What kind of search grid would you use? *line search,*

Chapter **Project**

Performance Assessment Work with your team to present a brief summary of your experience investigating a crime scene. Which step was easiest to do? Which step was the most challenging? What problems, if any, did you have working as a team?

Prints and Trace Evidence

Focus on the BIG Idea

Properties of Matter

How do investigators identify and compare materials they find at a crime scene?

Chapter Preview

▶ Print examiner comparing prints from a suspect's shoes to a print from a crime

△ Chapter **Project**

Analyzing Print and Trace Evidence

Investigators found a ransom note and tire tracks at the Missing Masterpiece crime scene. Later, the detectives were allowed to collect pens from the suspects and make prints of the tires on the suspects' cars.

Your Goal To use evidence to narrow the list of suspects

To successfully complete this part of the unit project, you must

● compare prints of tire tread sections with a database of tire brand photographs
● use paper chromatography to analyze ink from three pens and compare the results to the test done on ink from the ransom note
● follow the safety guidelines in Appendix A

Plan It! Read the instructions for doing the tire tread comparison and the chromatography test. Discuss the instructions with your team and decide how to accomplish each task. If you are not sure about any of the procedures, make a list of questions for your teacher. Get answers to your questions before you proceed.

Prints

Reading Preview

Key Concepts
- What kinds of prints do investigators look for at crime scenes?
- How are prints preserved, and how is print evidence used?
- Why do investigators need search warrants?

Key Terms
- print
- imprint
- impression
- skid mark
- cast
- search warrant

Target Reading Skill

Previewing Visuals When you preview, you look ahead. Look at Figure 7. Write two questions you have about the figure in a graphic organizer like the one below. As you read, answer your questions.

Impressions and Casts

Q. What is an impression?
A.
Q.

Discover **Activity**

What's the Difference?

Look carefully at the two photographs. Use what you observe to answer these questions.

1. What type of object made the marks shown in the photographs?
2. Was each mark made by the same object? Why or why not?
3. What do you think is the key difference between the marks?

Think It Over

Forming Operational Definitions The mark in photo B is an impression. The mark in photo A is not. Based on these examples, how would you define an *impression*?

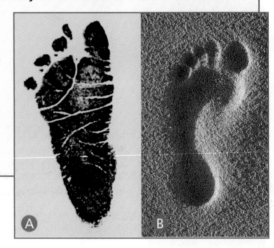

The "Shadow Wolves" are a Native American unit of the U.S. Customs Service. The unit hunts smugglers who bring drugs into Arizona from Mexico. The officers often use footprints as clues. They know, for example, that a person carrying a heavy load leaves deep footprints. They can tell where a smuggler stopped to rest and where he turned around to look back.

Most detectives are less likely to use footprints to track a person. But they do use footprints and other marks to show that a person, a car, or a tool was present at a crime scene.

Marks left when an object is pressed against the surface of another object are **prints.** In forensic science, flat prints with only two dimensions are called **imprints.** Prints that have three dimensions—length, width, and depth—are called impressions. An **impression** is the pattern left when an object is pressed into a surface. An object can make an impression when a surface is soft or the object is pressed hard enough against the surface. Your teeth, for example, make an impression when you bite into an apple.

Types of Prints

Some prints found at crime scenes are extremely useful. **Investigators look for imprints and impressions made by objects that leave a distinctive pattern.** Some patterns are so distinctive that they can be used to identify a suspect. This is true for fingerprints, which you will study in Chapter 3. Prints left by other objects can be used to narrow a list of possible suspects. These objects include shoes, tires, tools, and gloves.

Shoe Prints There are many ways one shoe can differ from another. One shoe might be white and the other red. One shoe might be made of leather and the other made of cloth. These differences are important when you buy shoes, but are not important when a CSI finds a shoe print at a crime scene. The features that interest investigators most are shoe size—both length and width—and the pattern on the sole of a shoe. These are features that can be detected in an imprint or impression.

Figure 1 shows a pair of shoes with a distinctive pattern on the soles. But shoe stores may have sold thousands of pairs of shoes with this same pattern. Other than size, would there be any way to tell one pair from the others?

The soles on the boots in Figure 2 are worn down. But they are not all worn down in exactly the same way. The way a person walks affects how a sole wears down. Look at the bottom of a shoe you've worn for a while. Is it worn down more on one edge than on the other? Can you see places where the sole has been cut or scratched? Sometimes print examiners can use such differences to connect a particular shoe to a print.

 **Reading Checkpoint** What are two things you can tell about a shoe from a shoe print?

FIGURE 1 Shoe Soles
The pattern on these shoe soles is distinctive, but it is not unique. Many pairs of shoes with the same pattern may have been sold.

FIGURE 2 Worn Soles
As people walk, they wear down the soles of their shoes.
Comparing and Contrasting *How could you tell prints made by these cowboy boots apart?*

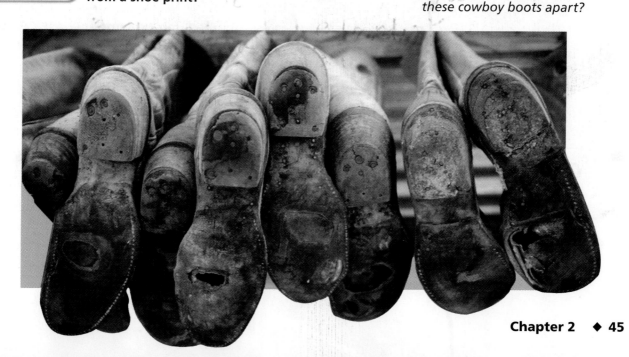

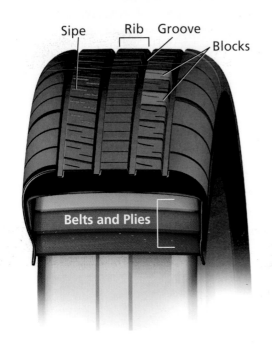

FIGURE 3
Tire Treads
Tire treads have a distinctive pattern of ribs and grooves.

Sipe   Rib   Groove

Blocks

Belts and Plies

Tire Treads The part of a tire that touches the road is called the tread. It can leave an impression in soft earth, sand, or snow. Figure 3 shows how a tread is made up of alternating ribs and grooves. Wide ribs help the tire grip the road on a dry day. Wide, deep grooves help the tire grip the road on a wet day. The pattern of ribs and grooves is distinctive for each brand and model of tire.

Tires gradually wear down from the constant contact with hard road surfaces. Just as with shoe soles, tire treads do not wear down evenly. There may also be marks on a tire tread, such as a cut or a missing chunk of rubber. A print examiner may be able to use these marks and wear patterns to connect a specific tire to an impression.

Skid Marks Sometimes a driver has to make a sudden, unplanned stop. The driver may be trying to avoid hitting a person, an animal, or another vehicle. When the driver presses hard on the brake pedal, the wheels on the car may lock, so that the wheels can no longer turn.

When the wheels lock, rubber from the tires can make a skid mark like the ones in Figure 4. A **skid mark** is the mark left when a vehicle with locked wheels slides along a road surface. A tire may also leave a skid mark when a driver takes a sharp turn at high speed. Investigators can use skid marks to figure out a car's direction and speed.

FIGURE 4
Skid Marks
A fire engine rolled over after turning a corner.
Relating Cause and Effect *What do you think caused the fire engine to roll over?*

Tool Marks A burglar could use one of the tools shown below. If the burglar presses the tool against the window frame, the tool leaves a mark. Each type of tool leaves a different mark. A forensic scientist can often infer what tool was used just by looking at the mark.

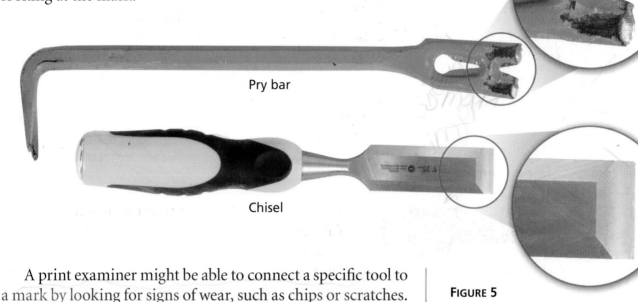

Pry bar

Chisel

A print examiner might be able to connect a specific tool to a mark by looking for signs of wear, such as chips or scratches. These flaws appear on the working edge, or blade, of the tool. Flaws on a tool are like nicks on a shoe sole or tire tread. Tool marks are generally less useful as evidence than are shoe prints. Here are three reasons why.

▶ New tools from the same factory are likely to leave the same mark unless the tools have been sharpened.

▶ If a tool used in a crime remains in use, nicks and scratches may be added to the blade. So investigators need to find the tool quickly in order to compare it to a tool mark.

▶ Criminals may steal or borrow a tool. Or they may use a tool they find at the crime scene. Thus, tool marks may lead investigators to a tool's owner—but not necessarily to the person who did the crime.

Gloves Criminals may wear gloves to keep from leaving fingerprints at a crime scene. But gloves can leave prints, too. Suppose a person wearing a pair of gloves leaves an imprint on a dusty mirror. Print examiners match the pattern on the print to the pattern on a specific brand of gloves. If a pair of those gloves are found in a suspect's house, the print can be used as evidence.

 **Reading Checkpoint** **Where would a print examiner look for flaws on a tool?**

FIGURE 5
Tools
These tools leave different marks on a hard surface.
Inferring How would marks left by a chisel differ from those left by a pry bar?

Skills **Activity**

Drawing Conclusions

1. Examine the tool marks your teacher has displayed. The marks are labeled "A," "B," and so on.

2. Then examine the tools. Don't put a tool into a tool mark to find a match.

3. In your notebook, record which tool you think made each mark, and why.

Estimating Speed From Skid Marks

Investigators measure the length of skid marks. Then they use the data to estimate the speed of a vehicle when the driver applied the brakes. The graph has data for skid marks on three surfaces.

1. **Interpreting Graphs** If a car's speed on asphalt is 40 miles per hour, about how far will it skid?

2. **Estimating** A car skids 125 feet on gravel. About how fast was the car traveling?

3. **Comparing and Contrasting** Based on the data, which surface is most slippery? Which is least slippery?

4. **Drawing Conclusions** How does the speed of a vehicle affect the length of a skid?

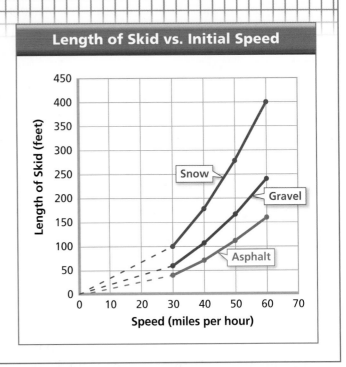

Length of Skid vs. Initial Speed

Preserving Prints

Some prints are easy to destroy. A neighbor rushing into a house to help a victim may walk over a shoe print. Rain can wash muddy prints from a sidewalk. So what can investigators do to make sure they don't lose the evidence from prints? **Investigators can preserve prints by taking photographs, making casts, or removing objects from a crime scene.** They can also "lift" some types of prints, as you will learn in Chapter 3.

Taking Photographs It can be a challenge to take good photos of impressions. Photographers need to capture every possible detail of the impressions. If not, the people who look at the photos later won't be able to see those details.

Figure 6 shows how to photograph an impression. The camera is attached to a stand directly above the impression. A ruler is placed next to the impression to show scale.

A photographer would need a series of photos to record a trail of shoe prints in a muddy yard. The photographer would first take long-range and medium-range photos. Then he would place a number beside each impression. Finally, he would take close-ups of each impression. A photographer would use the same approach for long tire tracks or skid marks.

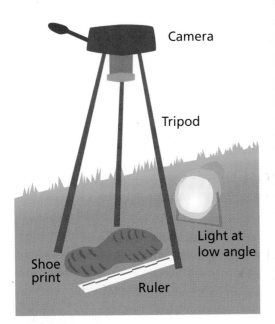

FIGURE 6
Photographing Impressions
A light held close to the ground creates shadows that highlight details in the impression. For each shot, the photographer moves the light to a new spot.

What shoe made this impression?

Liquid is poured into the impression. After the liquid sets, the cast is removed.

Investigators search for a shoe to compare to the cast.

Shoe

Making Casts Investigators can also make a cast of an impression. A **cast** is an object made by filling a mold with a liquid that takes the shape of the mold as it changes to a solid. Because an impression can be filled with a liquid, it can act as a mold. Figure 7 shows an impression, a cast, and the shoe that made the impression.

Casts of impressions are usually made from "dental stone." If you wear braces, a dentist may have used dental stone to make a cast from an impression of your teeth. When dental stone is mixed with the right amount of water, it forms a liquid with a thickness similar to pancake batter.

Removing Objects Investigators prefer to send some prints back to the lab for analysis. Suppose someone used a tool to force open a door. At the crime scene, a CSI could take photos as a record of the evidence. Then she could carefully remove and pack up all or part of the door.

If it is not practical to remove an object with a tool mark, a CSI makes a cast of the tool mark. To preserve tool marks, the CSI uses a casting material that can be spread, poured, or sprayed onto the tool mark.

Investigators may find a tool at the crime scene that they think made a tool mark. Even so, they should not try to fit the tool into the mark. Touching the tool to the mark could alter the mark and destroy its value as evidence. The tool mark and the tool need to be packaged separately and sent to the lab.

FIGURE 7
Impressions and Casts
A cast of an impression should have the same pattern as the object that made the impression. Interpreting Photographs *Would it be easier to compare a shoe to an impression or a shoe to a cast, and why?*

Reading Checkpoint Why can an impression act as a mold?

Comparing Prints

What do forensic scientists do with the photos, casts, and tool marks that are sent to a crime lab? **Forensic scientists use computer databases to identify and compare prints. They also compare prints found at a crime scene to objects that belong to a suspect.**

Searching a Database A print examiner wants to know what shoe made a print found at a crime scene. Luckily, there are databases that the examiner can use to identify the shoe. Most databases are organized sets of computer records. They are designed to make it easy to search for records.

The examiner starts by adding a record and a scanned image of the shoe print to a database of crime scene prints. Then she can search for similar records in the database. The computer displays any likely matches on the screen. She could also look for a match in two other databases. One has data about makes and models of shoes from companies that manufacture shoes. The other has records of shoe prints from suspects.

To compare tire prints, examiners use data supplied by companies that make tires. The data may be part of an online database. Or it may be in a reference book or on a CD-ROM.

Comparing Prints to Objects If the crime lab has a suspect's shoes, a technician can make a print of the shoe sole. Then he can compare the print to a print from the crime scene. If the lab has a suspect's car, someone can compare a tire from the car to a cast of a tire impression, as shown in Figure 8.

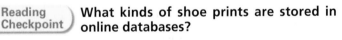

Reading Checkpoint What kinds of shoe prints are stored in online databases?

FIGURE 8
Comparing a Tire to a Cast
This print examiner is comparing a tire from a suspect's car to a cast of an impression from a crime scene.
Interpreting Photographs *What is the examiner measuring?*

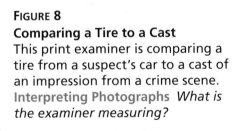

Search Warrants

How does a crime lab get a suspect's shoe to compare it to a print? Maybe a police officer caught the suspect at the crime scene. More likely, investigators searched the suspect's home. Before doing the search, they had to get a search warrant. A **search warrant** is a written court order that allows police to search for specific objects at a given place and time. The warrant allows police to seize property as evidence. But they can only take items listed on the warrant.

Why do police need a search warrant? **A search warrant protects a suspect's rights and ensures that a search is legal.** The U.S. Constitution states that a person must be protected from "unreasonable searches and seizures." So, to obtain a search warrant, police have to show that their planned search is reasonable. They must explain why they expect to find evidence of a crime during the search.

Why is it important to make a legal search? Suppose police find a key for a locker at a YMCA when they arrest a suspect. They use the key to open the locker and find a gun that was used in a crime. If the police don't have a search warrant for the locker, the gun may be thrown out as evidence in court.

FIGURE 9 Seizing Evidence
An officer can remove objects from a crime scene if the objects were listed on a search warrant.

Lesson 1 Assessment

Target Reading Skill Previewing Visuals Refer to your graphic organizer about Figure 7 to help you answer Question 2.

Reviewing Key Concepts

1. a. **Summarizing** How are prints made by shoes, tires, tools, and gloves useful to investigators?
   b. **Explaining** Explain why it can be difficult to connect a tool to a suspect.
   c. **Making Judgments** An examiner has a print made by a new shoe and a print made by a shoe that was worn only for a few months. Which print do you think will be more helpful, and why?

2. a. **Identifying** What is the preferred method for collecting tool marks?
   b. **Comparing and Contrasting** How are taking photographs and making casts similar? How are they different?

   c. **Making Generalizations** How do databases make it easier to identify shoe prints or tire tracks?

3. a. **Listing** What are two reasons why police officers need a search warrant before they enter a suspect's home?
   b. **Applying Concepts** Is it reasonable for police officers to search every house on a street to look for a tool used in a burglary? Explain your answer.

Writing in Science

Wanted Poster Design a wanted poster for a pair of your shoes. Assume that you don't have a photo of the shoes to use on the poster. Write a description of the shoes. Include details that could help someone recognize your specific pair of shoes.

Analyzing Shoe Prints

Problem

How can you match an unknown shoe print to a specific shoe in a shoe print database?

Skills Focus

observing, measuring, calculating, classifying

Materials

- washable black ink
- felt pad
- plastic tray
- large sheet of plain white paper
- newspaper
- metric ruler
- transparency grid
- dry erase marker
- database of shoe prints

Procedure

Part 1: Making Shoe Prints

1. Spread newspaper over the area where you will be making prints.

2. Place the felt pad in the plastic tray. Spray or pour washable black ink evenly over the surface of the felt pad.

3. Step carefully into the plastic tray with your right foot. While your shoe is in contact with the felt pad, gently rock your foot back and forth a few times. This motion will distribute the ink evenly over the sole of your shoe.

4. Step from the tray directly onto the white paper. Don't rock your foot back and forth or turn it in any way.

5. Lift your foot straight up from the white paper and walk to the sink. Be sure to walk only on the newspaper.

6. Remove your shoe. Use the materials at the sink to clean the ink off the shoe.

Data Table		
Feature	Observation or Measurement	
Length of print		
Width of print		
Shoe size		
Marks on shoe sole	Grid Box	Description

Part 2: Analyzing a Shoe Print

7. Once the print is completely dry, use a metric ruler to measure the total length and width of the print. Record the measurements in your data table.

8. Use the shoe size conversion chart to determine the approximate size of your shoe. Record the shoe size in your data table.

9. Place a transparency grid over the print. Line up the top of the grid with the top of the print. Center the grid, left to right, over the print. Then use the marker to draw an outline of the print on the grid.

10. Carefully examine the print under the grid. Identify any marks in the shoe sole, such as nicks and cuts. Draw these marks on the grid. Also note any places where the sole is worn down. Then record your observations in your data table. Be sure to include the location of each mark (A1, C12, and so on).

Part 3: Matching a Shoe Print

11. Your teacher will assemble all the prints into a database. Use the database to find a match for a print your teacher will give you.

Analyze and Conclude

1. **Designing Experiments** Look at the database of prints. Are there prints that are smeared? Are some prints incomplete because ink was not spread evenly on the sole? Suggest two ways to change the procedure in Part 1 to reduce these problems.

2. **Calculating** What would the shoe size be for a man's shoe with a length of 27.6 cm? What would the size be for a woman's shoe?

3. **Interpreting Data** When a grid is used to collect data about a print, the data can be entered into an online database of prints. Explain why it would be important to line up the print and the grid in the same way for every print.

4. **Classifying** Describe the steps you followed to match the print your teacher gave you with a print in the database.

5. **Drawing Conclusions** Assume a CSI was able to match a shoe print from a crime scene to a shoe belonging to a suspect. Using only the shoe print evidence, what conclusion could the CSI reach?

Communicating

Write a paragraph comparing the steps you used to analyze a shoe print to the steps a print examiner might use in a crime lab.

Shoe Size Conversion Chart															
Men	3½	4	4½	5	5½	6	6½	7	7½	8	8½	9	10½	11½	12½	14
Women	5	5½	6	6½	7	7½	8	8½	9	9½	10	10½	12	13	14	15½
Length (cm)	22.8	23.1	23.5	23.8	24.1	24.5	24.8	25.1	25.4	25.7	26	26.7	27.3	27.9	28.6	29.2

Trace Evidence

Reading Preview

🔑 Key Concepts
- How does a CSI collect trace evidence?
- What are five major types of trace evidence?
- How do crime labs use technology to test trace evidence?

Key Terms
- trace evidence
- classifying
- concentration
- chromatography
- microscope

🎯 Target Reading Skill

Using Prior Knowledge Before you read, write one thing you know about hair, paint, glass, and soil in a graphic organizer. As you read, fill in four things you learned that you didn't know before.

What You Know
1. Hair varies in color and length.
2.

What You Learned
1.
2.

🔺 Discover **Activity**

What Clues Does Sand Contain?

Use a hand lens to examine the sand provided by your teacher. Record your answers in your notebook.

1. What color are most of the particles of sand? What other colors can you see?
2. What size are most of the particles? Are they closer in size to grains of table salt, to seeds in a banana, or to poppy seeds?
3. List one property other than color and size you could use to describe the sand.

Think It Over

Developing Hypotheses A CSI finds sand at a crime scene. How could she begin to determine where the sand came from?

Jada wakes up from a nap because she hears a dog barking. When she looks out her window, Jada can see her neighbor Eva get into her van and drive away. She thinks, "As long as I'm up, I'll check on my new puppy." But her puppy is missing! When she can't find the puppy, she calls the police. She tells them what she saw and how much her puppy is worth.

When Eva returns home, the police ask her about the dog. She says, "I didn't take the dog." Then she offers, "Feel free to search my van." The van appears spotless inside and out. It looks as if it was just cleaned. Yet a CSI still finds a few hairs in the van. The hairs might be from the missing puppy. The hairs are an example of trace evidence.

The word *trace* can mean "a tiny amount." It can also mean "a sign of a person that remains after the person has left." So it makes sense that tiny amounts of physical evidence that are transferred at a crime scene are called **trace evidence.**

Collecting Trace Evidence

Investigators must find trace evidence before they can collect it. Given the size of the evidence, this isn't always an easy task. But trained investigators know what to do. **To collect trace evidence, investigators need to know where to look. They also must have the right tools.**

Knowing Where to Look Consider the stolen puppy. What did investigators observe at the crime scene? A glass pane in Jada's back door was broken. A CSI looked for fibers from Eva's clothing on the door. There was soil on the floor where a flowerpot had been knocked over near the puppy's bed.

After getting a search warrant for Eva's house, a CSI looked for the clothing Jada said Eva was wearing. He expected to find bits of glass and soil in the soles of Eva's shoes and dog hairs on Eva's sweater. Even if Eva had brushed the sweater, some hairs could still remain.

Using the Right Tools Evidence kits usually have a hand lens and tweezers. With these tools, a CSI can find and pick up larger pieces of trace evidence, such as the hair in Figure 10. He might also use tape to collect a hair. Objects that are likely to contain trace evidence, such as a sweater, are folded, packed separately, and sent to the lab.

A CSI might use a vacuum cleaner to collect dust. Like the vacuum cleaners people use at home, it draws bits of material onto a filter. But the filters in a forensic vacuum cleaner are designed to be changed frequently. That way the CSI can keep track of where each bit of evidence was found.

> ✓ **Reading Checkpoint** What does the CSI need before he can search Eva's house?

FIGURE 10
Collecting Trace Evidence
Tweezers can be used to collect trace evidence such as hairs.
Applying Concepts What might a CSI use instead of a tweezers to collect hairs?

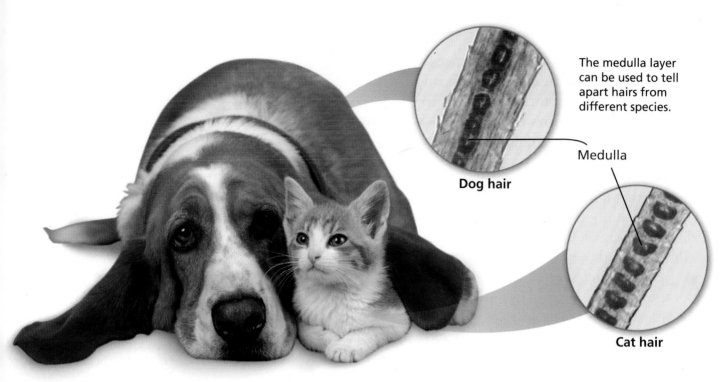

The medulla layer can be used to tell apart hairs from different species.

Dog hair

Medulla

Cat hair

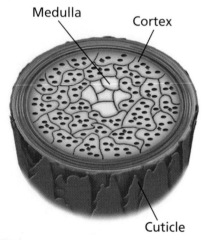

Medulla

Cortex

Cuticle

FIGURE 11
The Structure of Hair
Overlapping scales in the cuticle form an outer protective layer. The pigments that give hair its color are found in the cortex. A thick hair often has a visible inner layer called a medulla.
Comparing and Contrasting *What shape are the cells in the medulla of dog hair and cat hair?*

Types of Trace Evidence

Grouping objects together that are alike in some way is called **classifying.** Forensic scientists use this skill to organize the trace evidence they collect. All the samples in a group share certain properties. **Five major groups, or types, of trace evidence are hair, fibers, paint, glass, and soil.**

Hair Sometimes a victim will struggle with his attacker. During the struggle, hairs from the attacker may end up on the victim. If detectives can collect hairs from a suspect, those hairs can be compared to the hairs found on the victim.

The examiner will look at a hair found on the victim under a microscope. She will note its color, length, and diameter. She can tell if the hair was dyed. With the right microscope, she will see the layers that are described in Figure 11. The central layer, the medulla, may be wide or thin. It may be full of cells separated by pockets of air. Or it may not be visible at all!

Then the examiner looks at a hair from the suspect under a microscope. She may see clear differences between this hair and the one found on the victim. For example, one hair may be thicker than the other. Hairs can be used to narrow the list of suspects. But they can't be used to positively identify a suspect because many people have hair with a similar structure.

Many crime labs use visual exams of hair to decide if it is worth doing other tests on the hair. These tests might result in a positive identification, but they are very expensive. You will learn about these tests when you study DNA in Chapter 3.

Fibers Your clothes, the sheets you sleep on, and the towels you dry yourself with all contain fibers. These are long, slender strands that can be woven or knitted together. Figure 12 shows examples of natural fibers and synthetic fibers.

▶ **Natural Fibers** These fibers come from animals and plants. Wool, for example, comes from sheep, and cotton comes from a plant grown in warm climates. Wool and cotton are common fibers. Fibers that are less common, such as silk and cashmere, can be more useful in solving a crime.

▶ **Synthetic Fibers** Today, many fabrics contain synthetic fibers. These fibers do not come from animals or plants. Chemists develop these fibers in a lab. Examples are nylon and polyester.

Fibers that a suspect *carries from* a crime scene may not be useful unless the suspect is found right away. After all, clothes can be washed, dry-cleaned, or even thrown away. Fibers that a suspect *brings to* a crime scene can be more useful. If these fibers come from an object in a suspect's home, such as a rug, they may help solve the case.

Suppose an examiner is able to match a fiber found at a crime scene to a fiber found at a suspect's house. Can this match be used to positively identify a suspect? No, but the match can help to make a case against the suspect. Even then, the team will need evidence other than fibers to use in court.

FIGURE 12
The Structure of Fibers
Wool has scales that are typical of animal hair. Cotton fibers are like flat ribbons. Every now and then the "ribbon" twists. Synthetic fibers, such as polyester, have a uniform shape because of the way they are manufactured.

✓ Reading Checkpoint **What is the main difference between natural fibers and synthetic fibers?**

Wool fibers

Polyester fibers

Cotton fibers

FIGURE 13
Paint, Glass, and Soil Evidence

A car involved in a hit-and-run is likely to contain different types of trace evidence. **Applying Concepts** *How could paint, glass, and soil evidence be used to connect this car to a crime scene?*

This soil contains daisy, cherry, and hornbeam pollen.

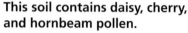

Skills **Activity**

Making Models

Changing the composition of a mixture can affect the mixture's properties.

1. Pick two colors. Decide how many "dabs" of each color you want to use.
2. Transfer the chosen number of dabs from each master container to your container. Do not contaminate the swabs.
3. Use a clean swab to mix the dabs together.
4. After the paint dries, add a label describing its composition. Add your sample to the class display.

Paint A driver speeding along a road hits a man on a bicycle. Instead of stopping to help, the driver speeds off. Police call this type of case a hit-and-run. If investigators find paint at the crime scene, they may be able to identify the make and model of car.

Paint is a mixture, meaning that its composition can vary. For example, the red paint used on one make and model is not likely to match the red paint used on another make and model. Even the red paint used at two factories making the same model can vary. These differences may not be visible to the human eye. But they will show up in the lab.

There is a database for paint samples called the Paint Data Query, or PDQ. The FBI and the Royal Canadian Mounted Police worked together to develop the database. It contains test results for hundreds of thousands of automotive paint samples. Any crime lab can use the database for free. But the lab must send 60 new samples to the PDQ each year. The samples can come from junkyards, body shops, or automakers.

Paint is applied to a car in very thin layers. Even a new car can have four or five layers of paint. If a car has been repaired or repainted, there will be additional layers. These extra layers of paint can make it easier to match a sample from a crime scene to a sample from a suspect's car.

 **Reading Checkpoint** **What does the Paint Data Query contain?**

58 ◆

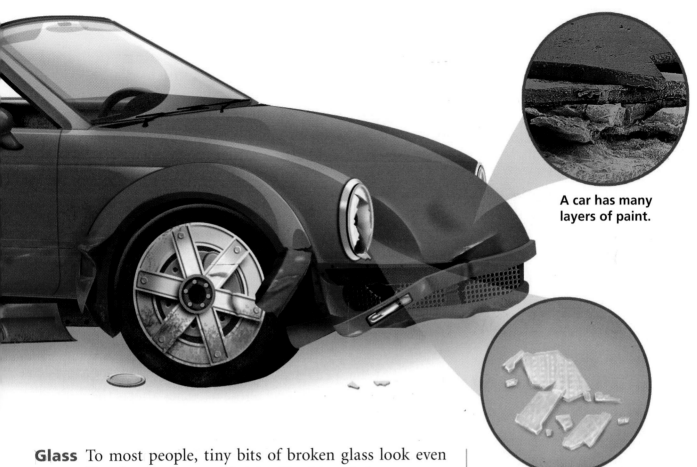

A car has many layers of paint.

Glass from the crime scene may fit the broken headlight.

Glass To most people, tiny bits of broken glass look even more alike than paint samples do. But bits of glass are not all the same. Glass is made from a mixture of sand and other materials. Forensic scientists can use differences in the composition of glass to compare samples of glass.

A scientist can measure the concentration of elements in a sample of glass. **Concentration** is the amount of a substance in a given mass or volume of a mixture. The scientist tests for elements that are present in very small amounts.

If the type of glass is common, scientists won't be able to use its composition to solve a crime. But they still may be able to use the shape of the glass. For example, bits of broken glass may fit cracks in a broken headlight.

Soil Like paint and glass, soil is a mixture. So the composition of soil can vary, and so can its properties. These properties can be used to match a sample to a specific location. A forensic scientist might, for example, be able to show that soil on the wheels of a car came from a crime scene.

The scientist often begins by looking at the color of the samples. Next, he might look at the size and types of particles in the soil. Seeds or pollen from flowering plants can be very useful. If, for example, the scientist finds seeds from a plant that doesn't grow in the local area, investigators know to search in areas where the plant does grow.

Go Online

SCiLINKS NSTA

For: Links on soil types
Visit: www.SciLinks.org
Web Code: dan-1022

Using Chromatography

There are tests a forensic scientist can use to positively identify a substance. But there is a catch. The tests provide the best results when the substance being tested is pure. In other words, the substance should not be mixed with other substances. **Trace evidence is often a mixture. So a forensic scientist needs a way to separate mixtures.**

Suppose you mix table salt with water. If you heat the mixture, the water changes to a gas, but the salt does not. You are able to separate table salt from water because these substances have different properties. Every method a scientist uses to separate mixtures takes advantage of such differences.

Chromatography (kroh muh TAHG ruh fee) is one way to separate mixtures based on their properties. You may have seen this simple example. A spot of food coloring is placed on paper. The food coloring spreads out as water moves along the paper. This happens because some particles in the dye move faster than others. The size of the particles affects their speed. So does their ability to dissolve in water.

The chromatography methods used in a crime lab are not simple. But the concept is the same. Particles in a mixture move through the equipment at different speeds. In a crime lab, a gas that does not react easily is often used to carry the sample being tested. The sample may be a gas, a liquid, or even a solid. Figure 14 explains how gas chromatography can be used to test a paint chip.

FIGURE 14
Gas Chromatography
Chromatography is used to separate substances in a mixture. Particles of different substances will move through the equipment at different speeds.
Interpreting Diagrams *Why is the paint chip heated?*

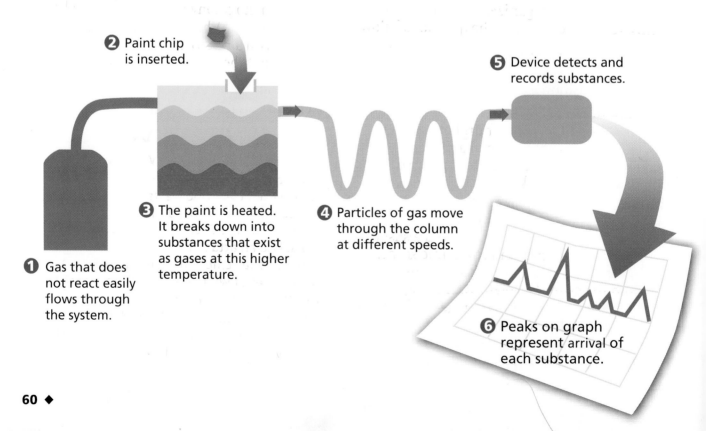

❷ Paint chip is inserted.

❺ Device detects and records substances.

❸ The paint is heated. It breaks down into substances that exist as gases at this higher temperature.

❹ Particles of gas move through the column at different speeds.

❶ Gas that does not react easily flows through the system.

❻ Peaks on graph represent arrival of each substance.

Using Microscopes

A hundred years ago, when Edmond Locard worked in his lab in France, he had very few tools. But he did have a microscope. A **microscope** is an instrument that makes very small objects look larger. The microscope is still an important tool for forensic science. **With a microscope, scientists can see details of evidence that are not visible to the unaided eye.** Those details help scientists identify and compare trace evidence.

Crime labs often have a comparison microscope like the one in Figure 15. It has two microscopes joined together. Looking through the eyepiece, a scientist can see two images side by side. The scientist can adjust the images to see if marks on one sample line up with marks on the other.

To magnify tiny traces many hundreds of times, scientists use a scanning electron microscope (SEM). An SEM does not use light to produce an image. It uses a stream of electrons— the tiny negatively charged particles found in atoms. An SEM was used to make the image of pollen in Figure 13.

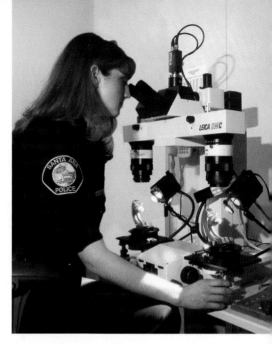

FIGURE 15
Comparison Microscope
This microscope is ideal for comparing a sample from a crime scene to a sample from a suspect.

 **Reading Checkpoint** **What does the SEM use to produce images?**

Lesson 2 Assessment

Target Reading Skill Using Prior Knowledge Use your graphic organizer about trace evidence to help you answer the questions below.

Reviewing Key Concepts

1. a. **Defining** What is trace evidence?
   b. **Describing** Give two examples of how a CSI might collect trace evidence.
   c. **Applying Concepts** A burglar breaks a window and forces open a door to steal a computer. What kinds of trace evidence would a CSI look for at the crime scene?

2. a. **Identifying** Give two examples of natural fibers and two of synthetic fibers.
   b. **Making Judgments** A hair from a suspect matches a hair found at a crime scene. Does this match prove that the suspect did the crime? Explain your answer.
   c. **Making Generalizations** In general, which evidence is more useful—evidence that is brought to a crime scene or evidence that is carried from a crime scene? Why?

3. a. **Making Generalizations** Why is chromatography used in a crime lab?
   b. **Explaining** What can forensic scientists see with a microscope that they can't see without the microscope?

 At-Home Activity

Collecting Trace Evidence Work with family members to collect trace evidence from a car. First remove large items from the floor and seats. Put an unused filter bag into a vacuum cleaner. Then vacuum the floor and seats. Use an attachment that can reach into narrow spots. Empty the filter bag onto a clean sheet of white paper. Put on gloves to sort through the contents. Use a hand lens to identify the materials. Record the results in your notebook. How might a CSI use the trace evidence you found?

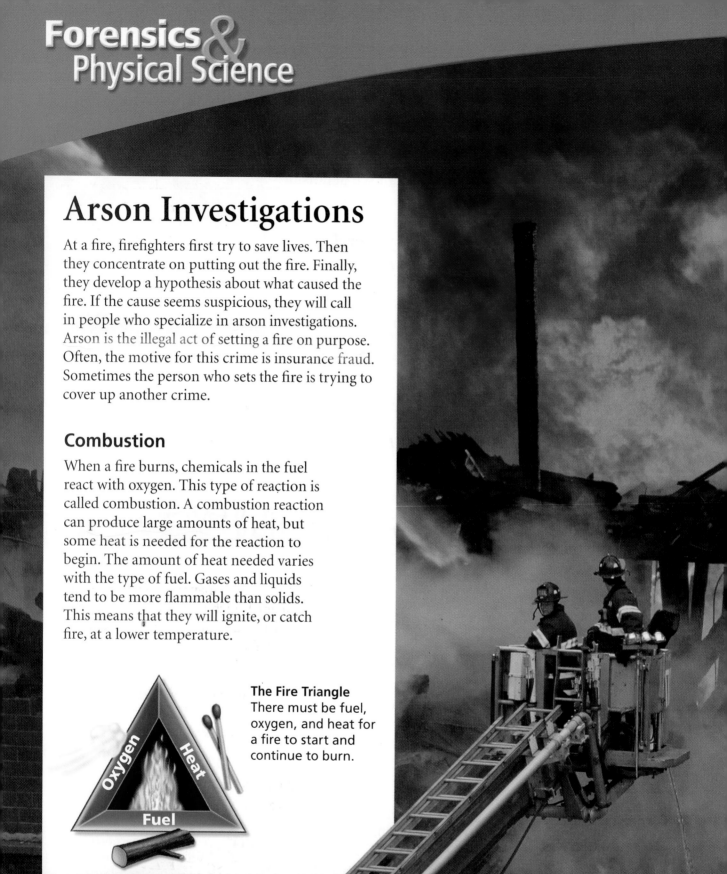

Arson Investigations

At a fire, firefighters first try to save lives. Then they concentrate on putting out the fire. Finally, they develop a hypothesis about what caused the fire. If the cause seems suspicious, they will call in people who specialize in arson investigations. Arson is the illegal act of setting a fire on purpose. Often, the motive for this crime is insurance fraud. Sometimes the person who sets the fire is trying to cover up another crime.

Combustion

When a fire burns, chemicals in the fuel react with oxygen. This type of reaction is called combustion. A combustion reaction can produce large amounts of heat, but some heat is needed for the reaction to begin. The amount of heat needed varies with the type of fuel. Gases and liquids tend to be more flammable than solids. This means that they will ignite, or catch fire, at a lower temperature.

The Fire Triangle
There must be fuel, oxygen, and heat for a fire to start and continue to burn.

Oxygen Heat Fuel

DISCOVERY EDUCATION™

Forensic Science Video

Arson-Sniffing Dogs

Dogs can be trained to sniff out an accelerant at the scene of a suspicious fire.

Accelerants

Liquids, such as gasoline or paint thinner, are often used to get a fire started quickly. These liquids are accelerants (ak SEL ur unts). They are easy to detect because they have distinct odors. Traces of the liquids can be found on objects at a fire. A scientist can use gas chromatography to identify the accelerant.

An object that has absorbed traces of an accelerant is sealed in an airtight jar or can. This keeps the liquid from evaporating.

You Be the Judge

1. **Applying Concepts**
   Firefighters may smother a fire with foam. Which part of the fire triangle are the firefighters trying to reduce? Explain.

2. **Classifying**
   People who cook over charcoal often pour lighter fluid on the charcoal. How would you classify lighter fluid?

3. **Making Judgments**
   What effect might incidents of arson have on an entire community?

Go Online

SciLINKS™ NSTA

For: Links on fire triangle
Visit: www.SciLinks.org
Web Code: dan-1020

Identifying Firearms

Reading Preview

🔑 Key Concepts
- What kinds of evidence can investigators collect when a weapon is fired?
- How is the evidence from firearms analyzed?

Key Terms
- cartridge
- rifling
- gunshot residue

🎯 Target Reading Skill

Relating Cause and Effect As you read, identify three effects of firing a gun. Choose effects that can be used as evidence. Write the information in a graphic organizer like the one below.

Effects

Cause

| Gun fired | → | Impressions on cartridge cases |

⚠️ Discover **Activity**

Where Does the Powder Go?

Your teacher will ask for volunteers to do this demonstration. Record your observations in your notebook.

1. Use a plastic spoon and a funnel to transfer a spoonful of cornstarch into a small balloon. Have your partner hold the neck of the balloon open.
2. Blow up the balloon and tie off the end.
3. Hold the balloon at arm's length while your partner uses a pin to burst the balloon. Observe what happens to the powder. CAUTION: Take care not to slip on the cornstarch.

Think It Over

Making Models Make a drawing in your notebook showing the location of the balloon, the path of the powder, and where the powder ended up. Refer to this drawing when you read about trace evidence from firearms.

If you watch the winter Olympics, you may see athletes on skis carrying a rifle. The athletes are taking part in an event called a biathlon (by ATH lahn). As the athletes race cross country on skis, they must stop at times to shoot at targets. To win the race, an athlete must ski fast and be accurate with a rifle.

The sport started in Northern Europe. In countries such as Norway, people used skis when they hunted for food. Soldiers also skied with weapons to protect their country's borders.

Not every use of a rifle is as innocent as in a biathlon. Many crimes in the United States involve the use of rifles and handguns. Forensic scientists have the task of identifying the firearms used in those crimes.

Russian Olga Zajceva takes aim during a biathlon 7.5 km sprint competition.

Evidence From Firearms

Crime scene investigators may find a gun or a person with a gun at the scene of a shooting. But this doesn't happen in most cases. So what else can investigators do? **Investigators look for the evidence that is left behind when a weapon is fired.**

How Firearms Work Firearms are designed to shoot an object at high speed toward a target. In a pistol like the one in Figure 16, the object is a bullet. A bullet is shaped like a cylinder with a pointed tip. Bullets are typically made from lead. Each bullet is packed in a metal case, or **cartridge.** The cartridge also contains gunpowder and a primer.

Pulling a trigger makes the firing pin strike the cartridge. This pressure causes the primer to ignite, which in turn ignites the gunpowder. The hot gases produced by the reaction push the bullet through the barrel of the gun at high speed.

Evidence From Cartridge Cases A CSI can learn many things by just observing empty cartridge cases. The size of the cases can help narrow down the list of possible firearms. When cases are found, they are typically near the spot where a weapon was fired. From the number of cases, the CSI can infer how many bullets were fired.

Firing a gun leaves impressions on a cartridge case. The firing pin leaves a small, distinctive dent. Marks are also stamped on the case when it is pressed against the inside of the firing chamber and when it is ejected from the gun.

FIGURE 16
Inside a Handgun
Firing a gun leaves impressions on bullets and cartridge cases.
Interpreting Diagrams *What happens to the empty cartridge case after the gunpowder ignites?*

Firing chamber

Firing pin

Muzzle

Barrel

Rifling

Ejector mechanism

Hammer

Trigger

Safety

Bullet

Gunpowder

Cartridge

Primer

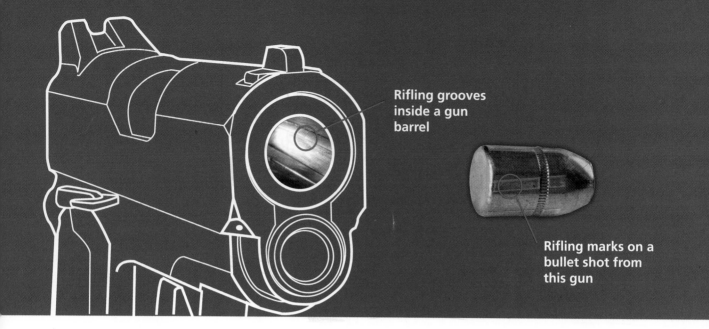

Rifling grooves
inside a gun
barrel

Rifling marks on a
bullet shot from
this gun

FIGURE 17 Rifling
The grooves inside a gun barrel
make marks on a bullet as it
passes through the barrel.

Skills **Activity**

Making Models

1. Cut a 5-cm piece from a plastic straw. Use a push pin to make four holes in the straw.

2. Roll a grape-size piece of clay into a tube that is narrow enough to fit in the straw, but wide enough to fill the straw.

3. Insert the clay into the straw. Use a cotton swab to gently force the clay through the straw.

4. Look for marks on the surface of the clay. Where do you think these marks came from?

5. Explain how this activity models what happens to a bullet when a gun is fired.

Evidence From Bullets First investigators must find the bullets. X-rays are used to locate bullets in shooting victims. If the victim is alive, the bullets may be removed during an operation. If the victim is dead, the medical examiner will retrieve the bullets during an autopsy.

A bullet may miss the victim. A CSI can search for that bullet at the crime scene and use its location to trace a path back to the spot where the gun was fired.

A CSI can also use marks on a bullet as evidence. **Firing a gun leaves impressions on a bullet.** Inside a gun barrel, there are spiral grooves called **rifling.** The grooves cause a bullet to spin as it passes through the barrel. Rifling leaves marks on a bullet that match the size, spacing, and angle of the grooves, as shown in Figure 17. The marks help narrow down the list of possible weapons. A gun barrel also has tiny nicks and bumps. These flaws leave a unique pattern of scratches on the bullet.

Evidence From Gunpowder Impressions are not the only physical evidence produced when a gun is fired. **Firing a gun leaves trace evidence on the person who fires the gun.** Often, some of the gunpowder and primer in a cartridge does not burn. This material is called **gunshot residue.** As the residue sprays out of the barrel and trigger hole, some lands on the hands, face, and clothes of the person who fires the gun. If the gun is close to the victim, some residue lands on the victim.

A CSI can use a swab or tape to collect gunshot residue from a person's hands. The residue is fairly easy to wash or wipe off. So a CSI will also look for traces on a suspect's clothes.

 Reading Checkpoint   **What causes a bullet to spin inside a gun barrel?**

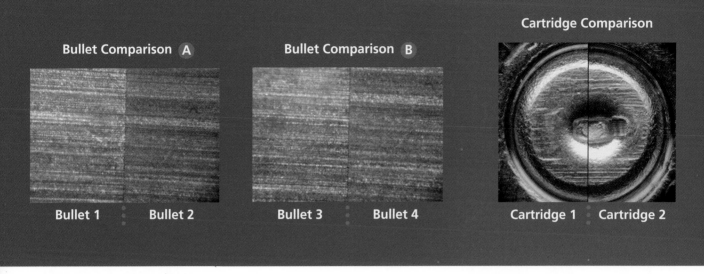

Bullet Comparison Ⓐ

Bullet 1　Bullet 2

Bullet Comparison Ⓑ

Bullet 3　Bullet 4

Cartridge Comparison

Cartridge 1　Cartridge 2

Analyzing Firearms Evidence

A firearms analyst wants to identify the weapon used in a crime and the person who used the weapon. **Microscopes and chemical tests are used to check for gunshot residue. Microscopes and databases are used to compare impressions from firearms.**

Testing for Gunshot Residue Some particles in gunshot residue have a distinctive shape. When the particles are magnified with a scanning electron microscope, the shape is easy to see. A CSI uses tape to collect residue that will be magnified.

Gunshot residue contains traces of the chemical elements lead, barium, and antimony. There are chemical tests that can identify these elements. A CSI uses swabs to collect residue that will be tested chemically.

Testing a Firearm To figure out if a gun was used in a crime, an analyst needs a bullet to compare with one from the crime scene. So she uses the gun to fire a bullet. The bullet is fired into water or a gel so it is not damaged.

The analyst compares the rifling on the test bullet with a bullet from the crime scene. If the rifling matches, she has the right type of gun. But does she have the actual gun that was used? To find out, she must take a closer look at the bullets.

Using a comparison microscope, an analyst can see if two bullets have the same pattern of scratches. If they do, the analyst has proof that a bullet from the crime scene was fired from the gun being tested. The microscope is also used to compare marks on cartridge cases, as shown in Figure 18. Those marks can also help to match a specific gun to a crime.

FIGURE 18
Comparing Impressions
When the images of two bullets or cartridge cases are lined up, an analyst can compare the marks made by a barrel or firing pin.
Drawing Conclusions *Which pair of bullets was fired from the same gun? Explain your answer.*

Discovery
EDUCATION™
Forensic Science Video
Firearms Evidence

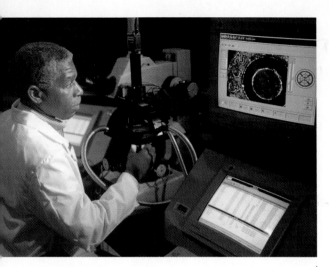

FIGURE 19
Using a Firearms Database
This analyst is checking an image of a cartridge case that was found during a computer search.

Using Computer Databases What happens if the analyst doesn't have a gun to test? There is another way to use the evidence from the crime scene. A criminal may have used the gun before. If so, images of evidence from the previous crime may be stored in an online database. A technician can search the database to match firearms evidence from one crime to evidence from other crimes.

The FBI keeps a national database of firearms evidence. It has more than 900,000 images from crime scenes and test firings. A technician starts a search by scanning an image of a bullet or cartridge case. Then the software searches for a match. If a likely match is found, he uses a microscope to check the match. If he accepts the match, the system has a "hit." A hit is a link between two unrelated crimes.

Using a database saves time. A computer can do a search in minutes that might take an analyst months. When crime labs in different states use the same database, each lab has more data to compare with its data. So it is less likely that a criminal can avoid capture by simply moving from one place to another.

 **Reading Checkpoint** | **What kinds of images are stored in a firearms database?**

Lesson ❸ Assessment

Target Reading Skill Relating Cause and Effect Use the information in your graphic organizer about the effects of firing a gun to help you answer Question 1.

Reviewing Key Concepts

1. a. Describing How does trace evidence end up on the person who fires a gun?
   b. Comparing and Contrasting Firing a gun leaves two types of marks on a bullet. How are these marks similar? How are they different?
   c. Making Generalizations Why does a CSI record the location of bullets and cartridge cases at a crime scene?
2. a. Describing What are two tests that can be done to check for the presence of gunshot residue?

   b. Sequencing What steps does a firearms analyst use to figure out if a firearm was used in a crime?
   c. Making Generalizations What are two advantages of using a firearms database to match firearms evidence?

In the **Community**

Reducing Crime Some communities use "gun buy-back" programs to reduce crime. Interview a police officer to find out if your police department has such a program. If not, ask the officer to describe programs the police do use to reduce crime. Write a paragraph summarizing your research.

The BIG Idea — Scientists do tests to separate and identify materials. They also compare one sample to another.

① Prints

🔑 Key Concepts

- Investigators look for imprints and impressions made by objects that leave a distinctive pattern.
- Investigators can preserve prints by taking photographs, making casts, or removing objects from a crime scene.
- Forensic scientists use computer databases to identify and compare prints. They also compare prints found at a crime scene to objects that belong to a suspect.
- A search warrant protects a suspect's rights and ensures that a search is legal.

Key Terms

print
imprint
impression
skid mark
cast
search warrant

② Trace Evidence

🔑 Key Concepts

- To collect trace evidence, investigators need to know where to look. They also must have the right tools.
- Five major groups, or types, of trace evidence are hair, fibers, paint, glass, and soil.
- Trace evidence is often a mixture. So a forensic scientist needs a way to separate mixtures.
- With a microscope, scientists can see details of evidence that are not visible to the unaided eye.

Key Terms

trace evidence
classifying
concentration
chromatography
microscope

③ Identifying Firearms

🔑 Key Concepts

- Investigators look for the evidence that is left behind when a weapon is fired.
- Firing a gun leaves impressions on a cartridge case and on a bullet. Firing a gun leaves trace evidence on the person who fires the gun.
- Microscopes and chemical tests are used to check for gunshot residue. Microscopes and databases are used to compare impressions from firearms.

Key Term

cartridge
rifling
gunshot residue

Review and Assessment

Organizing Information

Concept Copy the concept map about prints onto a separate sheet of paper. Then complete the map by adding the correct missing words or phrases. (For more on Concept Mapping, see the Skills Handbook.)

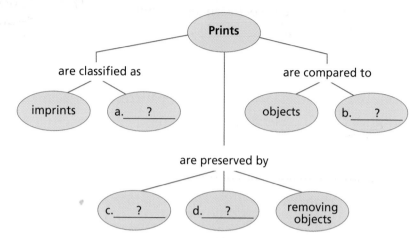

Reviewing Key Terms

Choose the letter of the best answer.

1. The pattern left when something is pressed into a soft surface is called
   a. a cast.
   b. an impression.
   c. a skid mark.
   d. an imprint.

2. A search warrant allows police to
   a. search every place a suspect has been seen.
   b. stop and search suspects on the street.
   c. search for specific objects at a given place.
   d. collect any object at a given place.

3. Grouping items together that share certain characteristics is called
   a. matching.   b. comparing.
   c. contrasting.   **d.** classifying.

4. A CSI can use tweezers or a vacuum cleaner to collect
   a. trace evidence.
   b. direct evidence.
   c. gunshot residue.
   d. impressions.

5. When a person fires a gun, rifling in the gun barrel leaves impressions on
   a. a cartridge case.
   b. the person's hand.
   c. a bullet.
   d. the target.

If the statement is true, write *true*. If it is false, change the underlined word or words to make the statement true.

6. If a driver takes a turn at high speed, the tires may leave <u>tool marks</u> on the road. F

7. Hair and fibers are two kinds of <u>trace evidence</u>. T

8. <u>Concentration</u> is the amount of a substance in a given mass or volume of a mixture. True

9. Scientists use <u>chromatography</u> to see details that are not visible to the unaided eye. F

10. The case that holds a bullet and gunpowder is called the <u>gun barrel</u>. F

Writing in Science

How-To Instructions You are a trained CSI. You are asked to teach a new CSI about collecting evidence from a muddy shoe print on a kitchen floor. Write a list of instructions for recording and collecting both the imprint and the trace evidence.

Checking Concepts

11. What is the difference between an imprint and an impression?

12. What types of information can investigators get from a shoe print?

13. Why is it a mistake to touch a tool mark with the tool that may have made it?

14. What do investigators do to record and preserve the evidence from prints?

15. What are five major types of trace evidence?

16. Why is a comparison microscope helpful in matching samples of evidence?

17. What kinds of evidence are left when a gun is fired?

Thinking Critically

18. **Comparing and Contrasting** Suppose you were comparing prints made by these soles. What features could help you tell them apart?

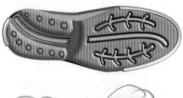

19. **Inferring** A car runs off a road and strikes a tree. Witnesses say that the car was traveling at high speed. The police don't find any skid marks on the road. What might the police infer from this observation?

20. **Applying Concepts** Visual exams of hair samples cannot identify a specific person. So why would a scientist do the exam?

21. **Drawing Conclusions** A bullet test fired from a gun matches a bullet from a crime scene. The gun is owned by Mr. Green. Can you conclude that the gun was used in the crime? Can you conclude that Mr. Green fired the gun? Explain.

Applying Skills

This table describes evidence collected from a hit-and-run crime scene. Use the table to answer Questions 22–26.

Type of Evidence	How to Preserve	Item Needed for Comparison
Skid marks	Take series of photographs. Measure length.	Tires from suspect's car
Impression of tire tread	Take photos and make cast. Pack some soil in plastic container.	Tires and wheels from suspect's car
Glass particles	Pack in plastic container.	Headlight from suspect's car
Paint chips	Pack in plastic vial or film canister.	Chip showing all layers of paint collected from undamaged area

22. **Interpreting Data** Which type of evidence will remain at the crime scene?

23. **Predicting** What might a CSI expect to find on the tires and wheels of a suspect's car?

24. **Relating Cause and Effect** What could an investigator learn by measuring the length of the skid marks?

25. **Classifying** What are two things scientists can do once they have a suspect's headlight?

26. **Problem Solving** Why would scientists want a chip from an undamaged area of the suspect's car? *Hint:* Recall Locard's principle.

Chapter **Project**

Performance Assessment Work with your team to prepare a report on your investigation of the art theft. Present the results of the tests you did on the ink and tire prints. Then use these results to explain how you were able to narrow the list of possible suspects.

Chapter 3
Identifying an Individual

Focus on the
BIG Idea
Variation

What are some traits scientists can use to identify an individual?

① **Fingerprints**

② **Evidence From Blood**

③ **DNA Evidence**

④ **Handwriting and Voice Identification**

A forensic scientist tests blood ▶
collected from a pair of jeans.

▲ Chapter **Project**

Identifying the Thief

In the last chapter, you used evidence collected from the Missing Masterpiece crime scene and from suspects to narrow your list of suspects. Now you will use evidence from blood to identify the thief.

Your Goal To identify the thief

To successfully complete this part of the unit project, you must

- analyze a sample of blood from the crime scene to determine its blood type
- determine if any of the remaining suspects have the same blood type as the blood found at the crime scene
- follow the safety guidelines in Appendix A

Plan It! Read through the instructions for testing blood. Discuss the instructions with your team. If you are not sure about any of the procedures, make a list of questions for your teacher. Get answers to your questions before you proceed. Be sure to record your data in your Student Handbook.

Reading Preview

🔑 Key Concepts
- What patterns are used to describe fingerprints?
- What methods are used to collect latent prints?
- How do examiners analyze the prints found at a crime scene?

Key Terms
- ridge
- visible print
- plastic print
- latent print

🎯 Target Reading Skill

Asking Questions Before you read, preview the red headings in this section. In a graphic organizer like the one below, ask a *what* or *how* question about each heading. As you read, write the answers to your questions.

Fingerprints
Q. How are fingerprints described?
A. Ridge line patterns are used to describe fingerprints.
Q.

▲ Discover **Activity**

What Can You See on a Fingertip? 🖐

1. Choose a fingertip on the hand that you do not write with. Use a washable marker to color this fingertip. Wipe off any extra ink with a facial tissue.
2. Use a hand lens to observe the colored fingertip.
3. Make a drawing of what you see.
4. When you are done, use soap and water to wash off the ink.

Think It Over
Developing Hypotheses Based on your observations, what do you think produces the lines on a fingerprint?

John Dillinger was desperate. It was 1934, and the bank robber was the most wanted criminal in the United States. The FBI had named him Public Enemy Number One. Police officers in every city were looking for him. What could Dillinger do to avoid being caught?

Dillinger asked a doctor to burn his fingertips with acid. He hoped the acid would destroy the evidence that could tie him to many crimes—the patterns on his fingertips. But he was wrong. As his burned skin was replaced by new skin, he could still see patterns on his fingertips.

Your fingerprints are yours for your lifetime. They do not change because your fingertips do not change. The patterns you see on your skin were well developed before you were born. They just got larger as your hands grew. These patterns are part of what makes you a unique human being. No two people, not even identical twins, have the same fingerprints.

WANTED

JOHN HERBERT DILLINGER

On June 23, 1934, HOMER S. CUMMINGS, Attorney General of the United States, under the authority vested in him by an Act of Congress approved June 6, 1934, offered a reward of

$10,000.00
for the capture of John Herbert Dillinger or a reward of

$5,000.00
for information leading to the arrest of John Herbert Dillinger.

DESCRIPTION

Age, 32 years; Height, 5 feet 7-1/2 inches; Weight, 153 pounds; Build, medium; Hair, medium chestnut; Eyes, grey; Complexion, medium; Occupation, machinist; Marks and scars, 1/2 inch scar back left hand, scar middle upper lip, brown mole between eyebrows.

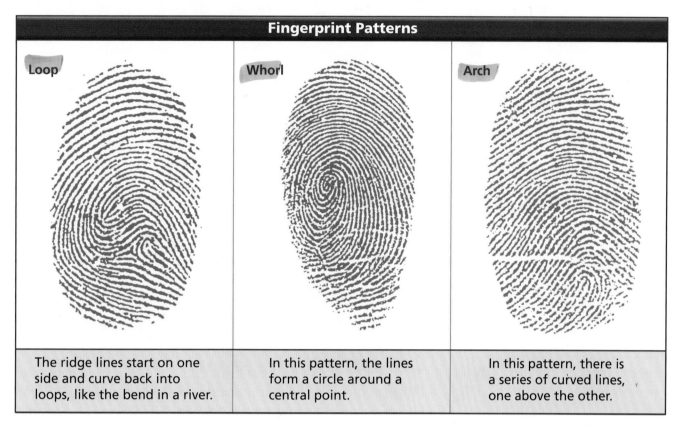

Fingerprint Patterns

Loop	Whorl	Arch
The ridge lines start on one side and curve back into loops, like the bend in a river.	In this pattern, the lines form a circle around a central point.	In this pattern, there is a series of curved lines, one above the other.

Describing Fingerprints

For thousands of years, people have known that fingerprints could be used to identify a person. In ancient China, for example, people could sign a legal paper with a thumbprint. Over time, signatures replaced fingerprints as a form of identification. But not in a crime lab.

When you take a close look at your fingertips, you can see a series of raised lines, or **ridges.** These ridges make it easier for your fingers and thumb to grasp and hold on to objects. The ridges also make the lines that you see on your fingerprints. **There are three typical patterns of ridge lines—loops, whorls, and arches.** Figure 1 compares these patterns.

Print examiners look for more than the overall pattern of a print. They look for the details that make the print unique. There may, for example, be places where a ridge ends. Or there may be places where a single ridge splits into two ridges, like a fork in a road. A fingerprint may have as many as 150 specific details.

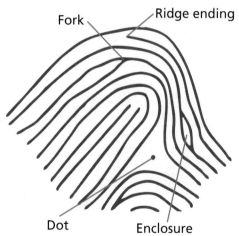

Fork
Ridge ending
Dot
Enclosure

FIGURE 1
Fingerprint Patterns
Of the three patterns, loops are the most common and arches are the least common. Only about five percent of people have prints with arches.
Observing *Look at the drawing with some details labeled. On a fingerprint, what is a fork? What is an enclosure?*

 **Reading Checkpoint** What are ridges?

Dusting with a fine powder works well on glass, tile, or painted wood.

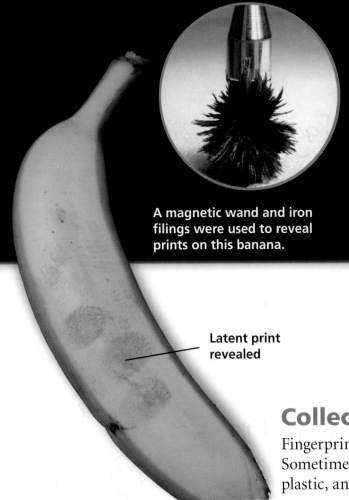

A magnetic wand and iron filings were used to reveal prints on this banana.

Latent print revealed

FIGURE 2
Revealing Latent Prints

There are several ways to reveal latent prints. A CSI often begins by dusting with a fine powder or with iron filings. He may also use chemicals or lighting.

Problem Solving Would you use a light or a dark powder to dust for latent prints on a glass surface? Explain your answer.

Collecting Fingerprints

Fingerprints left at a crime scene are rarely complete or clear. Sometimes they cannot even be seen. A CSI may find visible, plastic, and latent prints at a crime scene.

► If you touch a colored material and press your finger on a surface, you will leave a **visible print**, a print that can be seen. Blood, paint, and ink leave visible prints.

► If you touch a soft material, such as wax or dust, you will leave an impression, or **plastic print.** Plastic means "able to be shaped." A CSI can take photographs or make casts of plastic prints.

► When you transfer sweat or oil from the ridges on your fingers to the surface of an object, you leave a **latent print** (LAY tent). The word *latent* means "hidden."

Methods that are used to reveal and improve latent prints include dusting, chemical reactions, and lighting. Some methods can be used at the crime scene. Others must be done at the crime lab.

Dusting Figure 2 shows a CSI trying to reveal latent prints. He uses a soft brush to dust a surface with a fine powder. The powder clings to the ridge patterns left by oil and sweat. A CSI chooses a color that allows the print to stand out. On a dark surface, a CSI might use a gray powder.

It isn't practical to dust every surface at a crime scene. So the CSI dusts only surfaces that a suspect may have touched.

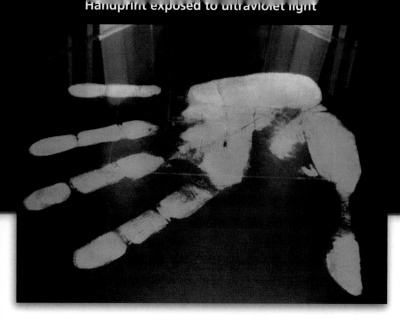

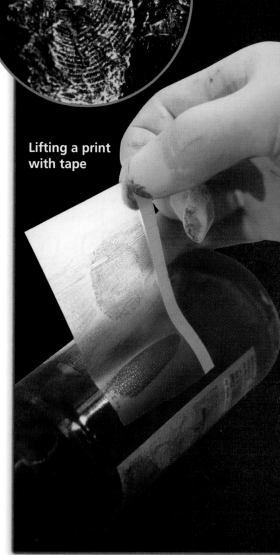

Lifting a print with tape

Chemical Reactions

Chemical Reactions Most dusting powders don't work on paper or cardboard. These materials have tiny holes, or pores, that can absorb sweat and oil. The term used to describe such surfaces is *porous* (PAWR us).

For an object with a porous surface, a CSI might use a chemical that reacts with the chemicals in sweat. The CSI sprays the chemical on the object. When the object is warmed, the latent prints become visible.

In a lab, scientists can use the vapor produced when a liquid or solid is heated to reveal latent prints. This method is called fuming. Vapor from a type of glue can reveal prints on metal, plastic bags, and leather objects, such as wallets.

Lighting When you hold a drinking glass up to the light, you may see fingerprints on the glass. A forensic photographer can use a beam of white light to make prints stand out. Some dusting powders produce prints that glow when they are exposed to ultraviolet (UV) light. Prints produced by fuming with glue may be dyed so that they glow, too. That approach was used for the print on aluminum foil shown in Figure 2.

Lifting Prints Once a print is visible, a CSI uses transparent tape to "lift," or remove, the print from a surface. It is placed on a card with a contrasting color, such as a white card for black powder. The tape must be sticky enough to lift the print but not so sticky that it can't be peeled off the surface.

 **Reading Checkpoint** What is a porous surface?

FIGURE 3
Scanning Fingerprints
A camera in this scanner takes a picture of a fingertip that is pressed against the glass. The image is stored and viewed on a computer.

Identifying Fingerprints

A crime scene is likely to contain many more prints than those of the person who did the crime. **Fingerprint examiners first try to eliminate some prints. Then they try to match the remaining prints with those of a suspect or with prints in a database.**

Eliminating Prints Remember the stamp collection that was stolen from the desk drawer? Fingerprints that were found on the drawer might belong to the owner of the stamps. Police would collect prints from the owner to compare them to the prints on the drawer. If there is a match, an examiner can eliminate those prints as evidence.

After a theft at a museum, police would take prints from the staff and security guards. These workers might have touched a doorknob or a picture frame while doing their jobs. At some crime scenes, police may collect prints from witnesses or the people who were first to respond to the scene.

Taking Prints From a Person For years, police used an ink pad to take fingerprints. Each finger was inked and rolled onto the correct place on a fingerprint card. Now some police departments use a scanner like the one in Figure 3.

Analyzing Prints When an examiner compares two prints, she does three levels of review. She looks at the ridge patterns. Do the prints have loops, whorls, or arches? Then she looks for details such as places where a ridge ends or splits. Finally, she looks for small variations, such as a difference in the width of ridge lines. Try these steps with the prints in Figure 4.

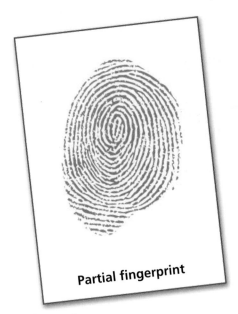

Partial fingerprint

FIGURE 4
Comparing Prints
An examiner uses fine details and small variations to compare prints.
Identifying *Which print is the best match for the partial print, and why?*

Fingerprint A

Fingerprint B

Computer Identification Systems Identifying fingerprints takes a great deal of skill, experience, and time. Computers can now help to sort and match prints. These systems are **automated fingerprint identification systems** (AFIS). The computer does the sorting. It compares prints from a suspect with prints stored in a database. Then it makes up a list of the most likely matches. The computer has done its part. Now it is time for the print examiner to review the prints. She will decide whether any of the prints is a good match for the suspect's prints.

With an automated system, local police and sheriffs have much more data. Suppose police have prints from a crime scene but no suspect. They can search for a suspect in state and federal databases. The FBI, for example, has the largest collection of fingerprints in the world. The FBI's system can make up to 85,000 searches in a day.

Using AFIS also saves time. Police in Los Angeles were looking for man who had killed at least 13 people. They found his print in a stolen car. At the time, the city of Los Angeles had 1.7 million fingerprints on file. If a person had searched through all the prints by hand, it might have taken 67 years. But AFIS took only three minutes to match the print.

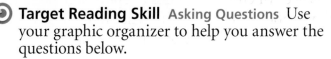

Lesson 1 Assessment

Target Reading Skill Asking Questions Use your graphic organizer to help you answer the questions below.

Reviewing Key Concepts

1. a. **Naming** What are three typical patterns of ridge lines?
   b. **Classifying** The lines on a fingerprint circle around a central point. What is the pattern of this print?
   c. **Making Generalizations** Why are fingerprints very useful as evidence?

2. a. **Defining** What is a latent print and how does it form?
   b. **Describing** What are three methods that a CSI can use to reveal latent prints?
   c. **Predicting** What method might be used to reveal latent prints on a drinking glass? On a doorknob? On a paper envelope?

3. a. **Explaining** Why do police officers collect fingerprints at a crime scene from people who are not suspects?
   b. **Sequencing** List the three steps an examiner follows to compare prints.
   c. **Making Generalizations** How can a computer make it easier to find a match for a print?

At-Home **Activity**

Family Fingerprints Use carbon from a soft pencil or an ink pad and index cards to make one fingerprint of each family member. Choose either the thumb or index finger of one hand. Explain the typical patterns of prints to your family. Then work together to classify the prints.

Evidence From Blood

Reading Preview

Key Concepts
- What can investigators do to detect blood?
- How is blood classified?
- What can investigators learn from patterns of blood at a crime scene?

Key Terms
- hemoglobin
- luminol
- antibody

Target Reading Skill
Comparing and Contrasting As you read, complete a graphic organizer like the one below for Type A, Type B, Type AB, and Type O blood.

Blood Type	Marker	Clumps With
Type A	A	Anti-A
Type B		

Discover Activity

What Can Blood Drops Reveal?

1. Place a large piece of white paper on a hard surface, such as a floor or desk.
2. Hold a dropper bottle of fake blood about 20 cm above the paper. Squeeze one drop of blood onto the paper.
3. Move the bottle to a height of 100 cm. Squeeze one drop of blood onto a different part of the paper.
4. Write a description of each drop in your notebook. How do the drops differ?

Think It Over
Predicting Jabar cuts himself while slicing a tomato. He leaves a trail of blood on the floor as he goes to get a bandage. What would the drops look like, and why?

In a room of a farmhouse in Pennsylvania, a detective sweeps a bright light across a wood floor. In the dark room, the light sharpens the contrast between wood and blood that had soaked into the floor. The detective sees the outline of a small-boned man on the floor.

This detective is not collecting evidence from a crime scene. He is studying Civil War history. In July 1863, the house was a hospital. The man whose blood is on the floor was wounded at the Battle of Gettysburg. Given the large amount of blood, the detective suspects that surgeons operated in this room.

Two Confederate soldiers

Even if there are only trace amounts of blood at a scene, the blood can be detected. This is true even when a person tries to clean away the blood or when the blood is old.

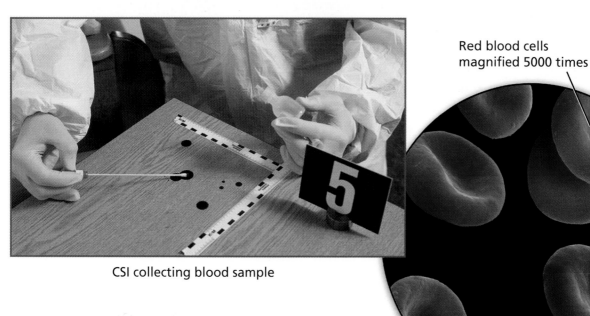
CSI collecting blood sample

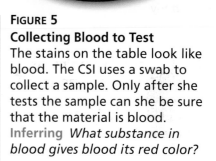
Red blood cells
magnified 5000 times

Searching for Blood

Blood is a water-based mixture, with cells suspended in the water. Figure 5 shows an enlarged view of one type of cell found in blood—red blood cells. These cells consist mainly of **hemoglobin** (HEE muh gloh bin), the molecule that carries oxygen to cells in the body. **Some chemicals produce light or change color in the presence of hemoglobin. The chemicals can be used to detect or test for blood at a crime scene.**

Finding Blood A CSI can use UV light to find blood at a crime scene. If this method fails, he can spray a chemical called luminol on surfaces where he suspects there is blood. **Luminol** emits a blue glow when it comes in contact with blood. The glow lasts about 30 seconds, which is long enough to photograph the evidence.

Luminol can be used to search large areas quickly. It can also detect the small traces of blood left behind when someone tries to clean up a crime scene. Luminol does have one drawback: Blood is not the only material that can cause luminol to glow. So a positive test with luminol may be a false alarm.

Testing Blood Stains that look like blood may not be blood. A CSI can run an initial test on a stain at the crime scene. She can use a moist cotton swab to take a sample of the stain. Then she rubs the swab against a strip that contains chemicals that change color in the presence of blood.

Some materials, such as horseradish, can produce the same results. But these materials are not found at most crime scenes. So a positive test is usually a reliable first test for blood. Another test must be done at the lab to confirm the results.

FIGURE 5
Collecting Blood to Test
The stains on the table look like blood. The CSI uses a swab to collect a sample. Only after she tests the sample can she be sure that the material is blood.
Inferring What substance in blood gives blood its red color?

 **Reading Checkpoint** **What does hemoglobin do in the body?**

FIGURE 6
Typing Blood
When Anti-A antibodies are mixed with blood that has A molecules, the blood clumps.
Interpreting Data *Which types of blood will clump when Anti-B antibodies are mixed with the blood?*

Blood Type	Blood Sample	Antibodies	
		Anti-A	**Anti-B**
A			
B			
AB			
O			

Blue and yellow tints were used to highlight the clumps.

Classifying Blood

At the lab, scientists can test to see if blood is human. They may also do some quick, inexpensive tests to narrow the list of possible suspects. To understand how these tests work, you need to know more about blood.

ABO Blood Groups In the early 1900s, doctors were looking for a way to save patients who had lost large amounts of blood. They tried to transfer blood from a healthy donor to the patient. Most of the time, the transfer didn't work. One doctor, Karl Landsteiner, was able to figure out what happened.

He discovered that human blood can be classified into four major groups, or blood types. These types are A, B, AB, and O. The groups are named after marker molecules found on the surface of red blood cells. Some people have only A molecules. Some have only B molecules. People with type AB blood have both A and B molecules. People with type O blood have neither A nor B molecules.

Antibodies Marker molecules act as tags. They say, "These cells are part of your body." Or they say, "These cells are not part of your body." **Antibodies** are molecules that bind to marker molecules. Each antibody will bind to one specific molecule. **Scientists can use antibodies to classify blood.** Figure 6 shows what happens when Anti-A and Anti-B antibodies are mixed with different blood types.

Skills **Activity**

Interpreting Data
Tests were done on four blood samples. Use these results to decide the possible blood type or types of each sample.

1. Blood clumps with Anti-A.

2. Blood does not clump with Anti-B.

3. Blood does not clump with Anti-A, but does with Anti-B.

4. Blood does not clump with Anti-A or Anti-B.

Using Blood Types as Evidence Blood types are not like fingerprints. They cannot be used to identify a suspect. But they can point investigators in the right direction.

For example, police find a bloodstain on a suspect's shirt. "I cut myself while shaving," the suspect explains. But he has Type A blood, and the blood on the shirt is Type O. The police will wonder why the suspect lied to them. If the victim's blood is also Type O, the police will be even more suspicious.

Data on blood types can reduce the number of suspects. For example, a thief with Type A blood cuts herself while taking jewelry from a display case. Drops of her blood are found on the case. This evidence points directly to the thief. So suspects with blood types other than Type A can be eliminated.

There are about 250 possible marker molecules for red blood cells. If scientists had a large blood sample and enough time, they might be able to use blood types to identify a suspect. But scientists now have a better option. They can do some quick, initial tests on blood. Then they can use the blood to do DNA tests, which you will read about in Lesson 3.

For: Links on blood type
Visit: www.SciLinks.org
Web Code: dan-1032

 **Reading Checkpoint** What problem was Karl Landsteiner trying to solve when he discovered the major blood types?

Math / Analyzing Data

Blood Type Distribution

Some blood cells have a marker molecule called the Rh factor. People who have this marker are Rh positive (Rh+). The rest are Rh negative (Rh−). The table shows the frequency of certain blood types in the United States. The data is based on A, B, and Rh markers only. Use the data to answer these questions.

1. **Interpreting Data** Which blood type is the most common? Which is the least common?

2. **Calculating** What percentage of people do not have the Rh factor?

3. **Inferring** Why are people with O− blood called "universal donors"?

4. **Predicting** A person is Rh negative. How does this fact affect her ability to receive donated blood?

Distribution of Blood Types in the U.S. Population			
Type	Frequency of Blood Type	Can Receive Blood From	Can Donate Blood to
O+	37%	45%	84%
O−	7%	7%	100%
A+	35%	85%	37%
A−	6%	13%	44%
B+	9%	56%	12%
B−	2%	9%	15%
AB+	3%	100%	3%
AB−	1%	16%	4%

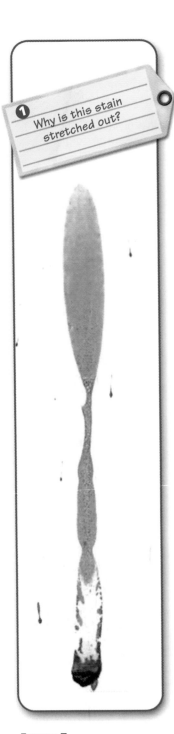

FIGURE 7
Analyzing Bloodstains
The shape and size of bloodstains can provide important clues.
Applying Concepts *After you read about bloodstain patterns, answer the questions in Figure 7.*

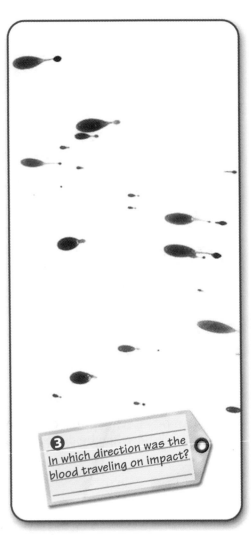

Bloodstain Patterns

Investigators may find drops, splashes, or pools of blood at a crime scene. Each stain tells a story. Did blood drip from a cut? Did blood spurt from an artery? Did a victim leave smears of blood while crawling across a floor? **Investigators analyze patterns of bloodstains to figure out what happened at a crime scene.** The number and location of bloodstains is important. So is the shape of the bloodstains.

Distance and Angle of Impact Blood that falls a short distance usually leaves a round stain on a hard surface. If the surface is soft or porous, there is likely to be some spatter and the stain will have ragged edges.

A round stain also means that the blood hit the surface at a 90-degree angle. In other words, the source of the blood was perpendicular to the surface. Figure 7 shows what happens when blood hits a surface at an angle less than 90 degrees. The stain is stretched out and loses its round shape.

Size of Drops Blood that is sent flying through the air by a blow will break into smaller drops when it hits a surface. Investigators can estimate the force of the blow by the size of the drops. Generally, as the force increases, the size of the drops decreases.

Direction of Travel An analyst can also use the shape of bloodstains to figure out the location of an attack. He knows that the tip of a stain always points in the direction that the blood had been moving. If there are multiple stains on a surface, he can draw a line through the long axis of each stain. Then, he can follow the lines back to the point where they meet. This is the spot where the blood was released.

Analysts used to do all this work by hand. But now there are computer programs that can analyze the pattern of blood spatter. These programs can accurately plot the path that blood traveled from its source.

Absence of Stains There may be a space in the middle of a blood spatter pattern where there is no blood. This absence of blood can be an important clue. Investigators will suspect that there was an object in that location at the time of the attack. If investigators find the object, they are likely to find the rest of the blood pattern.

DISCOVERY EDUCATION™
Forensic Science Video
Clues From Bloodstains

Lesson 2 Assessment

Target Reading Skill Comparing and Contrasting Use the data in your graphic organizer to help you answer Question 2.

Reviewing Key Concepts

1. a. Explaining How does hemoglobin make it possible to detect traces of blood?
   b. Applying Concepts What are two advantages of using luminol to detect blood? What is one drawback?
2. a. Naming What two molecules can be used to determine a blood type?
   b. Comparing and Contrasting How are Type A and Type AB blood alike? How are they different?
   c. Drawing Conclusions Blood found at a crime scene and a suspect's blood are both Type B. Can this evidence be used to identify the suspect? Why or why not?

3. a. Reviewing What properties can an investigator use to analyze bloodstains?
   b. Inferring A CSI finds a round drop of blood on a floor. What might the CSI infer about the source of the blood?
   c. Relating Cause and Effect What could cause an empty space in the middle of blood spatter?

In the Community

Blood Donors The American Red Cross keeps a supply of donated blood for emergencies. Interview a Red Cross representative to find out about blood donation in your community. Ask questions such as these: What blood types do they need most? Are there times during the year when the blood supply is low? Who can be a blood donor?

Facial Reconstruction

It is hard for detectives to look for a suspect if they don't know who the victim is. When all that is left is the victim's bones, the task can be challenging. A sculptor can use a skull to rebuild, or reconstruct, a face. First, she observes and measures the skull. She is looking for clues about the age, gender, and ethnic background of the victim. For instance, if there are no spaces between the bones in the skull, she can infer that the victim was at least 25 years old.

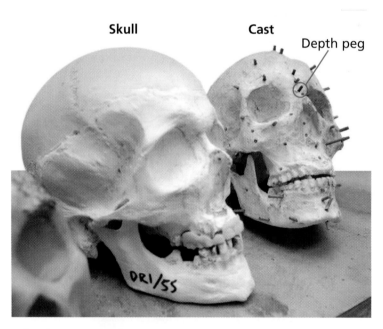

Skull   Cast   Depth peg

DRI/55

Placing Depth Pegs

Scientists have collected data on the depth of the soft tissue at each point on a skull. They know the average depths for different ages, genders, and ethnic groups. A sculptor uses these data to place pegs of the correct depth at locations on the skull or on a cast of the skull.

Adding Clay

The sculptor fills in the spaces between the pegs with clay strips. She also uses clay to build features such as a nose and ears. To construct these features, she must understand facial symmetry, or the way the parts of a face are arranged to make a balanced whole. For instance, a person's ears are roughly the same length as the person's nose.

You Be the Judge

1. **Making Generalizations**
   What parts of a facial reconstruction are likely to be the least accurate? Explain.

2. **Measuring**
   Have a partner measure the length of your nose and ears. How alike are these measurements?

3. **Predicting**
   How would a person's weight affect the depth of the soft tissue on his or her face?

Go Online
SCi LINKS NSTA

For: Links on animal symmetry
Visit: www.SciLinks.org
Web Code: dan-1030

The Final Touches

The sculptor must decide what color eyes to add or whether to include hair. These choices will be based on inferences about the victim's gender and ethnic group. Once the face is complete, detectives can try to match the face with images of missing persons. Or they can share a photo of the face with the public and hope that someone will recognize the victim.

DNA Evidence

Reading Preview

🔑 Key Concepts

- Why is DNA a valuable tool for forensic scientists?
- What is the process for making a DNA profile?
- Why are DNA profiles accepted as evidence, and how are they used?

Key Terms

- DNA
- protein
- gene
- DNA profile
- replication
- probability
- cold case
- endangered species

🎯 Target Reading Skill

Sequencing As you read, make a flowchart that shows the steps for making a DNA profile. Place each step in a separate box in your flowchart.

Making a DNA Profile

Collect DNA evidence.

↓

〜〜〜〜〜〜〜〜

⚠ Discover **Activity**

How Long Can You Make a Match?

1. Your teacher will give you a cup of snap cubes. Select any three cubes and connect them in a 3-cube string. How many students have matching 3-cube strings?
2. Select three more cubes and connect them to the existing string, making a 6-cube string. How many students have matching 6-cube strings?
3. Select three more cubes and connect them to the existing string, making a 9-cube string. How many students have matching 9-cube strings?

Think It Over

Interpreting Data How does the number of cubes in a string affect the number of matching strings?

One fall evening, a deer rancher in Pennsylvania discovered that his prize buck, Goliath, was missing. The stolen buck was worth about $100,000. Someone had cut a hole in the fence. From the drag marks near the fence, the rancher inferred that the thief had drugged the deer before taking it away.

Four years later, the rancher got a tip that Goliath was on a ranch about 50 miles away. When the rancher saw the deer, he was sure it was Goliath. But he needed some way to prove that he was right.

Scientists were able to use DNA to confirm the identity of the deer. DNA tests are expensive. But they are an excellent way to identify individuals, even an individual deer. Why is DNA so useful? The answer lies in the structure of DNA.

DNA Molecules

Do you have curly hair? Brown eyes? These characteristics are traits that are carried from parents to offspring by **DNA,** or deoxyribonucleic acid (dee ahk see ry boh noo KLEE ik). DNA controls the production of proteins in the human body. **Proteins** are molecules that your body uses to build tissues and organs. Proteins also control the chemical reactions that take place in cells.

DNA is found in the nucleus, or control center, of body cells. This nuclear DNA is a combination of the DNA you inherit from each of your parents. It is the same in every body cell—hair, skin, muscle, and so on.

Structure of DNA Figure 8 shows the structure of a DNA molecule. Two long strands of DNA are coiled around one another. Weak chemical bonds between pairs of nitrogen bases connect the strands. The letters A, T, G, and C are used to represent these pairs of bases, or base pairs. **Except for identical twins, no two people have nuclear DNA with the exact same sequence of base pairs.**

Genes DNA strands are divided into sections. A **gene** is a section of DNA that contains information your cells need to make a protein. The order of the bases in a gene is a code that determines which protein is produced. Humans have about 24,000 genes with a total of three billion base pairs.

 **Reading Checkpoint** What do proteins control?

Nitrogen bases

Guanine   Adenine

Thymine   Cytosine

T
A

Base pair   C

G   G

V
C

A
U
T

Deoxyribose (a sugar)

Phosphate group

Adenine

Cytosine

Guanine

Thymine

Drawing Conclusions

Some DNA profiles are like a bar code. Your teacher will give you a partial bar code and a sheet of paper with complete bar codes. Compare your partial bar code to the bar codes on the sheet to find a match. Then explain why it is a match.

FIGURE 9
Collecting and Isolating DNA
The hole in the swab box allows air to circulate and dry the blood. At the lab, the DNA is isolated.
Applying Concepts What are two reasons why a CSI wears gloves while collecting blood evidence?

Making a DNA Profile

You might expect that a strand of DNA is filled with genes. But this isn't true. Some sections of DNA are non-coding; that is, they do not contain instructions for making a protein. In non-coding DNA, a sequence of bases can be repeated many times. The number of times a sequence repeats is an inherited trait.

The number of repeats for a sequence can vary. Scientists use this variation to make DNA profiles. A **DNA profile** is a distinctive pattern of DNA fragments. The pattern is used to match a biological sample to an individual. **To make a profile, scientists must collect, isolate, multiply, and sort DNA.**

Collecting DNA A CSI may find a suspect's blood or skin under a victim's fingernails. There could be saliva on a pillow or a licked stamp. A discarded facial tissue might contain a suspect's sweat or blood. All of these materials contain DNA.

Investigators may use a swab to take cells from the inside of a suspect's cheek. They can also find DNA on a toothbrush or a comb. A CSI must be careful to avoid contamination when collecting samples for DNA analysis. Tools, such as the swab box in Figure 9, can help.

Isolating DNA DNA must be removed from a biological sample before it can be tested. Suppose a scientist has a sample of blood. She uses a microfuge like the one in Figure 9 to spin the blood at high speed. As the blood spins, the cells separate from the liquid. Then she adds chemicals to release the DNA from the white blood cells. Finally, she adds alcohol, and a sticky blob of DNA settles out of the mixture.

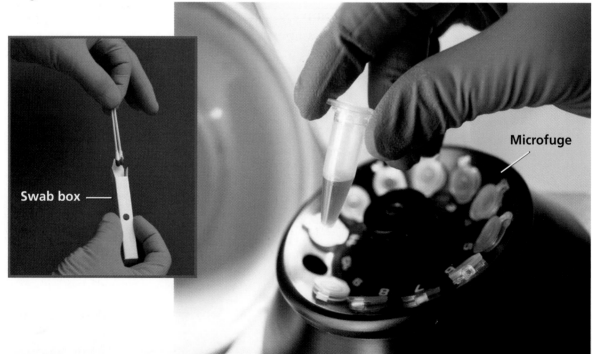

Swab box

Microfuge

Multiplying DNA To understand what happens next, you need to know how a DNA molecule makes a copy of itself. This process is called **replication.** The bonds between the base pairs break. The strands begin to separate and unwind, like a zipper unzipping. Nitrogen bases in the nucleus bond to the bases on the single strands. The bases are added according to the rule that A always bonds with T and C always bonds with G. As the bases are added, the original molecule and the copy rewind, as shown below.

FIGURE 10
DNA Replication
The nuclear DNA in a cell must be copied before the cell can divide into two cells. Scientists use this process to multiply DNA samples.

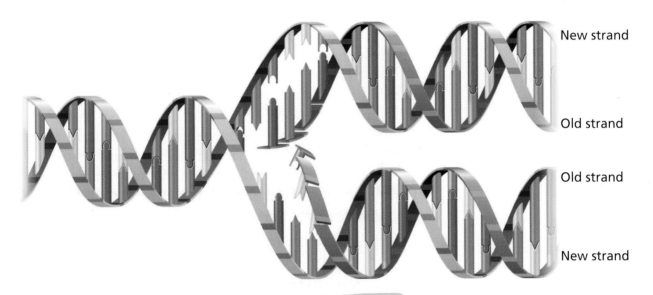

New strand

Old strand

Old strand

New strand

Trace evidence often does not contain enough DNA to make a profile. A forensic scientist can use DNA replication to increase the amount of DNA. The scientist starts with the DNA that was isolated. He doesn't copy all the DNA. He copies only 13 segments of non-coding DNA.

Each time the segments are copied, the amount of DNA doubles. The process can be repeated again and again. In just an hour, a scientist can repeat the process about 30 times. If he does, he will have about a million times as much DNA as he had at the start.

FIGURE 11
DNA Profile
The bands on this gel represent different DNA fragments. The DNA is stained so the bands are visible on the profile.

Sorting DNA The result of the DNA "multiplication" is a mass of DNA fragments. These fragments need to be sorted to produce a visual profile. In one method, an electric field pulls the fragments through a thick gel. The fragments travel at different speeds depending on their length. The shorter fragments move more quickly than the longer fragments. The process produces a pattern of bands like the one in Figure 11.

 **What is replication?**

Figure 12
DNA Variations
In one non-coding segment of DNA, the sequence A-A-T-G can repeat from 5 to 11 times.
Interpreting Diagrams *How many times does the sequence repeat in the first segment?How many times does it repeat in the second segment?*

Probability

Some people refer to a DNA profile as a DNA "fingerprint." But most forensic scientists do not. They don't like to imply that a profile is unique the way a fingerprint is. It is possible that two people could have the same profile. It just isn't probable.

Probability is a measure of the chance that an event will happen. When you toss a coin, it can land heads up or tails up. The probability of either event is 1 in 2 or 50 percent. Suppose you select any two people in the world. Scientists can calculate the probability of their having the same number of repeats in a given DNA segment.

Here is an example. The DNA segment known as TH01 contains the base sequence A-A-T-G. There are 7 variations of TH01 with from 5 to 11 repeats. Figure 12 shows the one with 6 repeats and the one with 8 repeats. A person could inherit both variations. She could inherit the one with 6 repeats from her mother and the one with 8 repeats from her father. About 3.6 percent of people in the world have this combination.

Scientists often test at least 13 different segments. **As the number of segments tested increases, the probability of two people having the same DNA profile decreases.** What is the probability when 13 segments are tested? It is less than 1 in 500 trillion (500,000,000,000,000). With odds like this, courts are likely to accept DNA evidence.

Reading Checkpoint   **What is the repeating base sequence in TH01?**

First segment

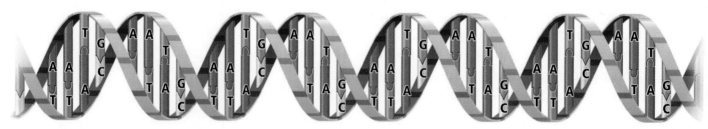
Second segment

Uses of DNA Profiles

DNA is rarely the only evidence in a case. But it is often the most persuasive evidence. **DNA profiles are used to connect a suspect to a crime. They also help solve cold cases, free the innocent, identify human remains, and protect endangered species.**

Connecting a Suspect to a Crime Newer methods for making DNA profiles are faster than earlier methods. But they are still expensive. So DNA profiles are used most often to solve very serious crimes. If police have a suspect, the lab can compare a profile of the suspect's DNA to one prepared with evidence from the crime scene. Figure 13 shows one way profiles are compared.

Police can also search for a suspect in a DNA database. Every state has a DNA database. These databases store profiles of offenders who were convicted of certain violent crimes. The profiles are stored as a series of numbers. So finding a match is a fairly quick process, if a match exists.

The FBI keeps a national database called CODIS. That stands for Combined DNA Index System. It has data from the 50 states, the armed forces, and the FBI. CODIS gives every crime lab access to more data. CODIS includes profiles of known offenders and missing persons. It also has data from forensic evidence.

Solving Cold Cases Not every case gets solved. The police may not have enough evidence or any good leads. If a case isn't solved within a year, the case may be filed away. Old, unsolved cases are known as **cold cases.** Many police departments have set up special units to look into cold cases.

Some crimes happened before DNA testing existed. Suppose police have biological evidence from a cold case. They could send the evidence to a lab and ask for a DNA profile. Adding the profile to a database could help solve the crime.

In Ohio, for instance, a man was sent to prison for a robbery. His DNA profile went into a database. It matched the profile of DNA found at the scene of an unsolved murder.

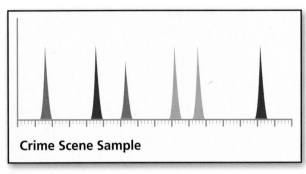

Crime Scene Sample

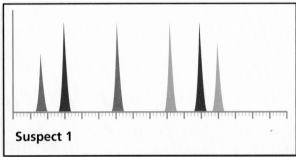

Suspect 1

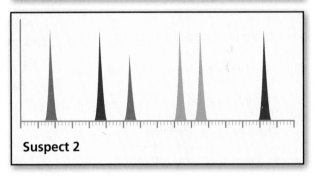

Suspect 2

FIGURE 13
Comparing DNA Profiles
With one method for making DNA profiles, the result is a graph. Each peak on the graph represents a different DNA segment.
Interpreting Graphs *Look at the DNA profiles. Based on the profiles, was one of the suspects at the crime scene? Explain.*

Freeing the Innocent Many people who are in prison claim that they are innocent. Most are guilty of the crime for which they are being punished. Some, however, are innocent.

In 1992, some lawyers in New York City set up a free legal service. Its goal was to defend prisoners whose claims of innocence could be proven by DNA testing. The idea spread. Law students, journalism students, and lawyers who defend poor clients set up similar services in other states.

Sometimes a DNA test shows that a prisoner's claims of innocence are false. But many times, the evidence has helped free innocent people. In 1997, for instance, Ryan Matthews was accused of shooting a man during a robbery. He was found guilty and sentenced to death. In 2004, Matthews was released from prison. The key was DNA found on the inside of a ski mask left at the crime scene. The DNA profile matched the DNA profile of another man.

Identifying Human Remains Most DNA tests use nuclear DNA. But sometimes it is not possible to get DNA from the nucleus. Some cells don't have a nucleus. Also, nuclear DNA can be damaged when a body decays or is burned.

To identify human remains, scientists can turn to DNA that is found outside the nucleus. This DNA, which is found in all cells, comes only from a person's mother. It is more abundant than nuclear DNA and is less likely to decay. This method was used to identify the bones of Tsar Nicholas II. Figure 14 shows the tsar, his wife, and their children. They were all murdered in 1918 during the Russian Revolution.

✓ **Reading Checkpoint** How did DNA testing free Ryan Matthews?

FIGURE 14
Tsar Nicholas II and His Family
After the family was murdered, their bodies were thrown into a pit and covered with acid. Their bones were dug up in 1991.
Applying Concepts Why did scientists have to use DNA from outside the nucleus to identify the bones?

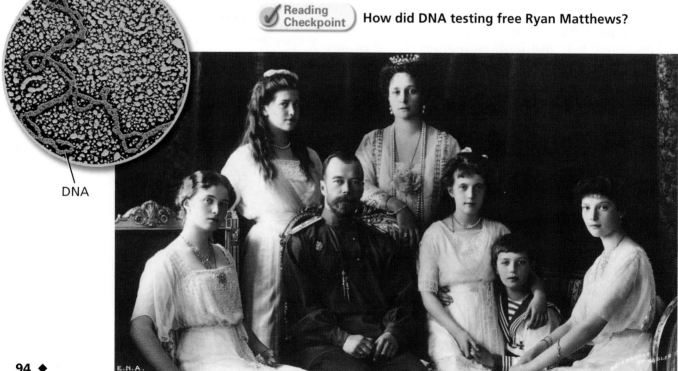

DNA

Protecting Endangered Species DNA is not just used to identify human beings. It can be used to identify other species. Some species have been classified as endangered. An **endangered species** is a species whose numbers are so small that the species may disappear from the world.

Some people work hard to protect endangered species. But other people try to use them to make a profit. They may sell protected animals to restaurants. Or they sell specific parts of an animal's body—an elephant's tusk or the skin from a tiger like the one in Figure 15. Some people will buy rare animals, especially birds, to keep as pets.

How can DNA tests help? In Florida, scientists were able to show that the "tuna" on some restaurant menus was really sailfish. Sailfish is protected by federal law. Tests also showed that whale meat being sold in Japan came from species that were protected by international law.

FIGURE 15
Endangered Tigers
Bengal tigers are an endangered species. If a person tried to sell the skin of this tiger, a DNA test could prove that the person had committed a crime.

Lesson 3 Assessment

Target Reading Skill Sequencing Use your flowchart to help you answer Question 2.

Reviewing Key Concepts

1. a. **Describing** What is the general structure of a DNA molecule?
   b. **Summarizing** How is the information your cells need stored in a DNA molecule?
   c. **Applying Concepts** Do a child and a parent have the same nuclear DNA? Explain your answer.

2. a. **Describing** What feature of non-coding DNA do scientists use to make a DNA profile?
   b. **Sequencing** List the four general steps scientists follow to obtain a DNA profile.
   c. **Relating Cause and Effect** What property determines which DNA fragments travel most quickly through a thick gel?

3. a. **Explaining** Why do scientists use 13 DNA segments instead of just one segment to make a DNA profile?
   b. **Summarizing** How do forensic scientists use DNA profiles?
   c. **Problem Solving** Scientists have a DNA profile for a suspect. What are two ways they can use the profile to connect the suspect to a crime?

Math Practice

4. **Probability** There are 7 variations of DNA segment TH01. A person inherits one from each parent. Figure out how many possible combinations there are of two variations. Then show why the probability of having any one combination is about 3.6 percent.

Handwriting and Voice Identification

🔈 Reading Preview

Key Concepts
- What clues are used to compare writing samples?
- What methods do scientists use to compare voice samples?

Key Terms
- voiceprint

🔄 Target Reading Skill

Identifying Main Ideas Make a graphic organizer like the one below about handwriting. As you read, add three supporting details that help explain the main idea.

Main Idea

Handwriting experts look at the style of the handwriting and the content.

Discovery EDUCATION™

Forensic Science Video

Voice Stress Analysis

⚠️ Discover **Activity**

Can Handwriting Identify a Person?

Your teacher will give you a sheet of paper on which several people have signed their names.

1. Pick a vowel that appears in many of the signatures. Is the shape of the vowel the same in all the signatures? If not, describe any differences you observe.
2. Does the size of the letters vary within a signature? Does it vary between signatures?
3. List one other characteristic that you think could be used to compare signatures.

Think It Over

Inferring Do you think it is possible to use handwriting to identify a suspect? Why or why not?

Charles Lindbergh was the first person to fly a plane solo across the Atlantic Ocean in 1927. This deed made him rich and famous, but it also made him a target. On March 1, 1932, Bruno Hauptmann climbed a ladder to the second floor of Lindbergh's house. Then Bruno grabbed Lindbergh's 20-month-old son and left a ransom note asking for $50,000.

When Lindbergh paid the ransom on April 2, he didn't know that his son was dead. The added weight of the child may have caused the ladder to break as Bruno climbed down. Although the child probably died on March 1, his hidden body wasn't discovered until May 12.

The evidence at Bruno's trial included 45 writing samples. There were 15 ransom notes. There were 9 auto registration forms that Bruno had filled out. There were also samples that Bruno agreed to write as he was questioned by the police. Experts were able to use the samples to explain why it was likely that Bruno had written the ransom notes. People's handwriting styles are distinctive.

Handwriting Identification

A robber hands a bank teller a note. A thief forges the signature on a stolen check. When detectives have this type of evidence, they call on a handwriting expert. **Handwriting experts look at the style of the handwriting and for content clues.**

Handwriting Features When you look at someone's writing, you probably notice whether it's hard or easy to read. But that's not what handwriting experts look for. They start with the general style. Some people print each letter separately. Some people join the letters together within a word.

An expert looks at the shape, the slant, and the size of letters. He notices whether the lines are thin or thick. He looks for personal touches. For instance, does the writer circle the dot over an "i"? Figure 16 compares two writing samples.

Comparing Writing Samples Experts need samples of a suspect's writing to compare with their written evidence. Few people today write letters by hand. They use a computer to send e-mail or to type a report for school. But handwritten samples still exist. People hand write grocery lists, entries on a calendar, or a note on a birthday card. They sign legal documents, such as checks. A person's signature appears on the front of a driver's license and the back of a credit card.

Ideally, experts want a writing sample with some of the same words as in the evidence sample. This makes it easier to compare the samples. If it isn't possible to compare words, then the experts will look at individual letters.

FIGURE 16
Handwriting Samples
These samples show how writing styles can vary among people. *Comparing and Contrasting In what ways are the two writing samples similar? In what ways are they different?*

My handwriting looks like this

FIGURE 17
Sketch of Ted Kaczynski
In 1987 in Salt Lake City, Utah, a bomb exploded outside a computer store. A woman was able to describe the man who left the package. Content clues in an article Ted wrote helped identify him as the bomber.

Skills Activity

Observing
Your teacher will play a recording of several voices. As you listen, try to identify each voice. Were you able to identify all the voices? If not, why not?

Content Clues Handwriting experts also look for clues in the content of a writing sample. The clues could include word choice, spelling, and punctuation. Experts can also apply this type of analysis to text messages. With text messages, the trick is to look for letters that a writer tends to leave out.

Content clues helped catch the man shown in Figure 17. In 1978, he began mailing pipe bombs to people. His bombs killed 3 people and injured 23 others. In 1995, the bomber offered to stop. In return, he asked two newspapers to publish a long article that he had written. In the article, he stated the reasons for his actions. One person who read the article was David Kaczynski. He realized that the content and tone of the articles matched the content and tone of letters that he had received from his brother Ted.

Altered Documents Sometimes an expert looks at just one writing sample. The task is to figure out if the writing has been altered in some way. Suppose detectives suspect that a person has changed the amount of a check or forged another person's signature. The expert can use a hand lens or simple microscope to see details of the writing.

The expert may use lighting to reveal other clues. Shining a light on paper from the back may reveal a rough place where writing has been erased. Shining a light from the side can reveal a deep groove in the paper. The groove is where a writer may have pressed down hard while copying a signature.

 **Reading Checkpoint** What clues do experts look for in text messages?

Voice Identification

You answer the phone. You hear, "Hi, it's me." You may not have to ask who "me" is. That's because people's voices have certain distinctive qualities. One person's normal voice is loud and booming. Another person's voice can barely be heard. People may have a voice that is high-pitched like a violin or low-pitched like a tuba. Such differences can be used to identify a voice.

For instance, a woman finds a threatening message in her voice mail. If detectives have a suspect, they can compare the recording to a recording of the suspect's voice. **To compare voice samples, analysts can graph the sounds or listen to the recordings.**

Graphing Sound What does your voice *look* like? A machine called a sound spectrograph can make an image of your voice like the one in Figure 19. The machine changes sound waves to electrical impulses that can be graphed and displayed on a computer screen. The graph, or **voiceprint,** plots the pitch and loudness of sound over time.

What if people try to disguise their voices? There will still be some telltale features that can be used to identify them. Some features will show up in a voiceprint. Some can be recognized by a person listening to a recording.

Listening to Recordings An analyst can compare how sounds are pronounced. She will listen for breathing patterns or the way a voice rises and falls in pitch as a person speaks. She will also note uncommon words or phrases.

The analyst will use what she learns by listening and looking at graphs to draw a conclusion. If she finds 20 or more points in common, she can identify the suspect. If she finds 20 or more differences, she can eliminate the suspect.

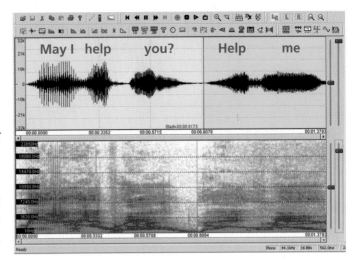

FIGURE 18
Comparing Voiceprints
This graph shows two voiceprints side by side. The voiceprints were made by two different speakers. In the top band, loudness is plotted against time. In the red band below, pitch is plotted against time.
Inferring *What do you think a gap in a voiceprint might represent?*

Lesson 4 Assessment

Target Reading Skill Identifying Main Ideas Use the information in your graphic organizer about handwriting to help answer Question 1.

Reviewing Key Concepts

1. a. **Identifying** What features might an expert look for when examining the letters in a writing sample?
   b. **Describing** What clues do experts use to compare the content of writing samples?
   c. **Making Judgments** Police have two writing samples from a suspect. They have a grocery list and a sample the suspect wrote at the police station. Which sample do you think would be more useful and why?

2. a. **Describing** What methods can analysts use to compare voice samples?
   b. **Explaining** What voice qualities does a voiceprint measure?
   c. **Comparing and Contrasting** What voice features can be heard in a recording that would not show up in a voiceprint?

Writing in Science

Advertisement You want to hire an actor to give news updates during a radio broadcast. Write a help wanted ad for the job. Describe the kind of voice qualities you would want this person to have.

Skills Lab

Measuring Writing

Problem

What measurements can you use to describe a writing sample?

Skills Focus

measuring, calculating, designing experiments

Materials

- ruled paper
- metric ruler
- protractor
- tracing paper

Procedure

1. Write the following words on a sheet of ruled paper: Forensic scientists analyze evidence. They do not convict or clear suspects.

2. Draw a line through each letter in the sample as shown in the photo. The line should have the same slant as the letter.

3. Select a line. Use a protractor to measure the angle the line makes with the ruled line on the paper. Measure the angle for two other lines. Enter your data in a table like the one below.

Data Table				
Feature	Trial 1	Trial 2	Trial 3	Average
Slant (degrees)				
Spacing (mm)				

4. Place tracing paper over your sample. Draw vertical lines between each letter. Select a pair of lines. Use a metric ruler to measure the distance between the lines (the spacing) in millimeters. Repeat the measurement for two other pairs of lines. Record your data.

Analyze and Conclude

1. **Designing Experiments** Why do you think you were asked to make three separate measurements for slant and spacing?

2. **Calculating** Calculate the mean, or average, slant and spacing. Enter the results in your table and record them on your sample.

3. **Designing Experiments** Select another feature of the writing sample that you could measure. Describe the method you would use to measure this feature.

4. **Interpreting Data** Make a class display of the samples. What is the range of data for average slant? For average spacing?

5. **Drawing Conclusions** How could measurements be used to identify a writing sample?

Communicating

Pick two samples to compare. Write a paragraph explaining how an analyst could tell that the samples were written by different people.

Study Guide

🔑 The **BIG Idea** — Fingerprints and DNA can be used to identify an individual. So can handwriting and voiceprints.

① Fingerprints

🔑 **Key Concepts**

- There are three typical patterns of ridge lines—loops, whorls, and arches.
- Methods that are used to reveal and improve latent prints include dusting, chemical reactions, and lighting.
- Fingerprint examiners first try to eliminate some prints. Then they try to match the remaining prints with those of a suspect or with prints in a database.

Key Terms
ridge
visible print
plastic print
latent print

② Evidence From Blood

🔑 **Key Concepts**

- Some chemicals produce light or change color in the presence of hemoglobin. The chemicals can be used to detect or test for blood at a crime scene.
- Scientists can use antibodies to classify blood.
- Investigators analyze patterns of bloodstains to figure out what happened at a crime scene.

Key Terms
hemoglobin
luminol
antibody

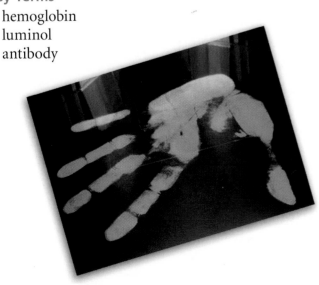

③ DNA Evidence

🔑 **Key Concepts**

- Except for identical twins, no two people have nuclear DNA with the exact same sequence of base pairs.
- To make a profile, scientists must collect, isolate, multiply, and sort DNA.
- As the number of segments tested increases, the probability of two people having the same DNA profile decreases.
- DNA profiles are used to connect a suspect to a crime. They also help solve cold cases, free the innocent, identify human remains, and protect endangered species.

Key Terms
DNA
protein
gene
DNA profile
replication
probability
cold case
endangered species

④ Handwriting and Voice Identification

🔑 **Key Concepts**

- Handwriting experts look at the style of the handwriting and for content clues.
- To compare voice samples, analysts can graph the sounds or listen to the recordings.

Key Terms
voiceprint

Review and Assessment

Organizing Information

Concept Mapping Copy the concept map about fingerprints onto a separate piece of paper. Then complete the map by adding the correct missing words or phrases. (For more on Concept Mapping, see the Skills Handbook.)

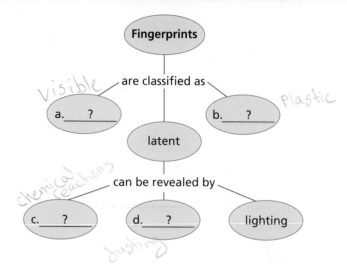

Reviewing Key Terms

Choose the letter of the best answer.

1. A bloody fingerprint on a bathroom tile is an example of
   a. a plastic print.
   b. a latent print.
   c. a visible print.
   d. an impression.

2. To detect traces of blood, investigators depend on chemical reactions with
   a. hemoglobin.
   b. marker molecules.
   c. proteins.
   d. antibodies

3. To classify a sample of blood, scientists test how it reacts with
   a. luminol.
   b. antibodies.
   c. hemoglobin.
   d. the Rh factor.

4. A section of DNA that carries information about the production of a protein is
   a. a DNA profile.
   b. a nitrogen base.
   c. non-coding DNA.
   d. a gene.

If the statement is true, write *true*. If it is false, change the underlined word or words to make the statement true.

5. A fingerprint left in soft material such as wax is called a <u>latent print</u>. impression/plastic

6. An individual's <u>DNA profile</u> is based on a pattern of repeating base sequences.

7. DNA evidence is accepted in court because the <u>probability</u> of its accuracy is so great.

8. An old, unsolved case that is no longer being actively investigated is called a <u>closed case</u>. cold case

9. A visual graph of a person's voice is called a <u>spectrograph</u>. voice print

Writing in Science

News Report A team of forensic scientists holds a press conference. They announce a new method for detecting traces of blood at a crime scene. Pretend you are a science reporter for your local newspaper. Write down four questions you would want to ask the forensic scientists.

Checking Concepts

10. How are fingerprints patterns classified?
11. What three types of fingerprints are found at crime scenes and how is each type produced?
12. How do investigators use fingerprints from a crime scene to lead them to a suspect?
13. Explain what an antibody is and how it can be used to classify blood types.
14. Summarize the steps investigators and scientists use to make a DNA profile.
15. Briefly describe what happens when a DNA molecule makes a copy of itself.
16. What kind of data is stored in a DNA database?
17. When handwriting experts look at writing samples, what two general characteristics do they look at? Give an example of each.
18. What can analysts learn about a voice sample by looking at a voiceprint?

Thinking Critically

19. **Drawing Conclusions** Are fingerprints and blood types equally useful methods for identifying suspects? Why or why not?
20. **Relating Cause and Effect** When a CSI sprays a chemical on a surface, a latent print is revealed. What caused the latent print to become visible?
21. **Comparing and Contrasting** How are nuclear DNA and the DNA found outside the nucleus different?
22. **Problem Solving** Some species of whales are protected. How could a scientist prove that the whale meat being served in a restaurant was from a protected species?
23. **Applying Concepts** A handwriting expert uses style clues to compare two writing samples. But the expert does not use any content clues. What kind of samples might the expert be testing?

Math Practice

24. **Probability** In 1900, about 1 out of every 2 people in the United States had blue eyes. By 2000, only about 1 in 6 people had blue eyes. Express these probabilities as a percentage.

Applying Skills

Use this graph to answer Questions 25–28.

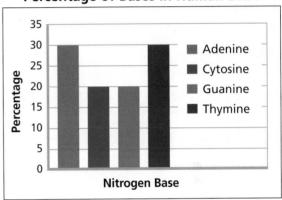

Percentage of Bases in Human DNA

25. **Interpreting Graphs** In human DNA, what percentage of the nitrogen bases are adenine? Cytosine? Guanine? Thymine?
26. **Interpreting Data** How are the amounts of adenine and thymine related? How are the amounts of cytosine and guanine related?
27. **Relating Cause and Effect** Use what you know about the structure of DNA to explain the answer to Question 26.
28. **Predicting** If the percentage of adenine in DNA were 25%, what would the percentage of thymine be?

Chapter **Project**

Performance Assessment Work with your team to decide how best to present the results of the blood tests you did. Then use the results to explain how you identified the person who stole the painting.

Bringing Evidence to Court

Focus on the
BIG Idea

Justice

In the United States, what processes ensure that a person accused of a crime has a fair trial?

Chapter Preview

① **From Arrest to Trial**

② **Presenting Evidence in a Trial**

③ **The Final Stages of a Trial**

Washington County Courthouse, ▶
Jonesborough, Tennessee

▲ Chapter **Project**

Conducting a Trial

You have identified a suspect for the theft of the Missing Masterpiece painting. But your task is not complete. The suspect must be arrested and put on trial.

Your Goal To participate in a mock trial

To successfully complete this part of the unit project, you must

- prepare visual displays of your test results
- decide which witnesses to use to present your evidence
- prepare opening statements and lists of questions for witnesses
- demonstrate appropriate court-room procedures

Plan It! Your team may work with other teams who have identified the same suspect. Brainstorm ways that you can accomplish each task. Then decide who will be responsible for which tasks and what role each person will have in the trial. Be sure to record your plans in your Student Handbook.

From Arrest to Trial

Reading Preview

Key Concepts
- How are a person's rights protected before, during, and after an arrest?
- How are crimes classified?
- What typically happens between an arrest and a trial?

Key Terms
- Bill of Rights
- jury
- bail
- felony
- misdemeanor
- probable cause
- defendant
- judge
- prosecutor
- public defender
- plea bargain

Target Reading Skill
Building Vocabulary After you read this lesson, use what you have learned to write a definition of each Key Term in your own words. Define a term by telling its most important feature or function.

Discover Activity

When Is a Suspect Guilty?
Read the newspaper clipping about the missing books. Look for the word *allegedly*. This word is often used in news reports about crimes. It means "stated but not proven."

Think It Over
Developing Hypotheses Clara was caught with ten rare library books in her car. Why do you think the word *guilty* was not used in the news story?

> **MISSING BOOKS DISCOVERED IN CAR**
> **Local Woman Arrested**
>
> Clara Berle was arrested yesterday afternoon at the car wash on Main Street. Police found ten rare library books on the back seat of her car. Berle allegedly stole the books to pay for a trip around the world.

- *You have the right to remain silent.*
- *Anything you say can and may be used against you.*
- *You have the right to an attorney.*
- *If you cannot afford an attorney, one will be appointed to represent you.*

Why do police have to read words like these before they question a suspect? In 1963, Ernesto Miranda was arrested. While being questioned by the police, he confessed to a crime. But Miranda's lawyer argued that the confession should not be used in court because Miranda was not told that he had the right to remain silent. The U.S. Supreme Court, the highest court in the land, agreed with Miranda's lawyer. The Court decided that police must warn suspects of their rights. The warning that is read is called the *Miranda warning*.

In the United States, the police must balance two tasks. They need to protect society from criminals. They must also protect the rights of people who are accused of crimes. In the United States a person accused of a crime is presumed to be innocent until proven guilty.

The Bill of Rights

Where do the rights listed in the Miranda warning come from? They come from the U.S. Constitution. A constitution describes how a government should be organized and what it can do. The people who wrote the Constitution had fought a war to escape the harsh rule of England's King George III. They wanted a government where ordinary people ruled.

Amendments The framers of the Constitution could not know what issues the country would face in the years ahead. So they agreed on a way to change, or amend, the Constitution. These changes are called amendments. James Madison drafted the first ten amendments, which are known as the Bill of Rights. A right is a freedom that all people have, no matter what their race, religion, or wealth. The **Bill of Rights** is a list of rights that the government promises to protect.

The Bill of Rights protects individual freedoms. These include the right to speak or write freely. The Bill of Rights also protects people from the power of the government. For example, a city can't take a person's land to build a road without paying for the land. The Bill of Rights also ensures that people are not deprived of their liberty without "due process of law." **Four of the amendments in the Bill of Rights protect a person's rights before, during, and after an arrest.**

Forensic Science Video
Bill of Rights

FIGURE 1
James Madison
Madison was a representative to Congress from Virginia and later President of the United States. In 1789, he led the effort to add the first amendments to the Constitution.

Fourth Amendment
Search and Seizure

The Fourth Amendment protects a person against "unreasonable searches and seizures." One way to make sure a search is reasonable is to ask police to obtain a search warrant. Recall that a warrant must list a specific time and place for the search. It must also list what evidence the police expect to find during the search.

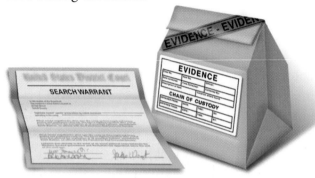

Fifth Amendment
Rights of the Accused

This amendment states that a person can't be forced to be a "witness against himself." This means that people have a right to remain silent when they are asked questions about a crime. In some cases, claiming this protection is called "taking the Fifth."

The Fifth Amendment also says "nor shall any person be subject for the same offense to be twice put in jeopardy." Suppose a person is tried for a crime and found not guilty. That person cannot be tried again for the same crime. To do so would place the person in "double jeopardy."

MIRANDA WARNING
You have the right to remain silent.
Anything you say can and may be used against you.
You have the right to an attorney.
If you cannot afford an attorney, one will be appointed to represent you.

Sixth Amendment
Right to a Jury Trial

In some countries, trials are held in secret or people are kept in prison for a long time without a trial. The Sixth Amendment addresses these and other concerns. It includes rights that help ensure that a person accused of a crime gets a fair trial.

- A person has a right to a speedy and public trial.

- The person has a right to a trial by jury. A **jury** is a group of ordinary citizens who listen to the evidence in a trial. The jury decides whether the person is guilty.

- The person has a right to know what crime he or she is accused of committing and to face the accusers in court.

- A person charged with a crime has the right to a lawyer. Lawyers are trained to offer advice about legal cases and to represent a person in court. If a person cannot afford to hire a lawyer, the government will appoint a lawyer and pay for the lawyer's services.

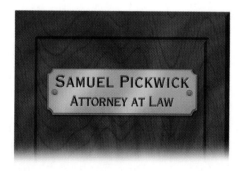

SAMUEL PICKWICK
ATTORNEY AT LAW

Eighth Amendment
Bail and Punishment

Some people who are arrested are released on bail. **Bail** is money or property that is pledged to the court to ensure that a person will appear at trial. The Eighth Amendment states that the amount of bail should be reasonable. For bail to be reasonable, a person must have a fair chance of raising that amount of money. This amendment also states that the punishment a court sets for a crime should not be "cruel and unusual."

Felony

Misdemeanor

FIGURE 2
Felonies and Misdemeanors
An armed robbery is classified as a felony. Painting graffiti is usually a misdemeanor.
Applying Concepts *How did investigators get a photograph of the armed robbery?*

Types of Crimes

Laws are rules that everyone in society is supposed to follow. Some laws define what acts are considered crimes, and how those crimes should be punished. Most crimes are acts that threaten the safety of people or their property. **Crimes are classified as felonies or misdemeanors.**

Felonies A serious crime, such as murder or kidnapping, is classified as a **felony.** People convicted of felonies are called felons. Typically, felons can be sent to prison for more than a year. In addition, felons may lose some rights, such as the right to vote. They may be barred from certain types of jobs, such as teaching. They may not be allowed to serve in the military.

Misdemeanors Crimes that are less serious than felonies are called **misdemeanors** (mis duh MEEN ur). Shoplifting is a misdemeanor. So is spray-painting graffiti on a building. A person convicted of a misdemeanor may pay a fine. The person may be asked to do volunteer work or attend a treatment program. People can be sent to jail for a misdemeanor.

 **Reading Checkpoint** What are laws?

FIGURE 3
Making an Arrest
Local police officers and FBI agents worked together to arrest this member of a Russian mob.
Inferring *What inference can you draw from the location of the defendant's hands?*

Making an Arrest

The events leading up to an arrest can vary, but there are two constants. **Police need probable cause to make an arrest. The person who is arrested is taken into custody and booked.**

Probable Cause A suspect may be caught at or near the scene of a crime. For example, the police may respond to a burglar alarm and see a suspect running from the building. If the police can chase down the suspect, they have probable cause to make an arrest. **Probable cause** is a reasonable belief that a person has committed a crime.

A robber points a gun at a man and steals his watch. The man is able to identify the robber. Or a person who knows the robber tips off the police. If the police trust the identification or the tip, they have probable cause to arrest the suspect.

More often than not, an arrest will not be made right away. The crime scene team will need time to gather evidence, and scientists at the crime lab will need time to test the evidence. If the evidence points to a particular person, police can use the evidence to get an arrest warrant.

Booking The process that takes place at the police station is called a booking. Police record information about the suspect. They usually take mug shots and fingerprints, too. The prints may be compared with prints in a database to see if the suspect is connected to other crimes. Before police question the suspect, they read the Miranda warning.

 **Reading Checkpoint** **What do police need to get an arrest warrant?**

Pretrial Procedures

A person who is accused of a crime is called a **defendant.** A defendant will appear before a judge one or more times before a trial. A **judge** is the person who controls what takes place in a courtroom. **At a pretrial hearing, the defendant is charged. The judge may set bail, assign a lawyer, and review evidence. Before a trial, lawyers may reach a plea bargain.**

Charging the Defendant Crimes are seen as a threat to society. That is why criminal cases are brought in the name of the state, as in *Arizona* v. *Miranda.* The lawyer who represents the state in a criminal case is the **prosecutor.** The prosecutor decides what crime a defendant will be charged with. The charges are read aloud in court. The defendant is then asked to plead guilty or not guilty.

Setting Bail At a pretrial hearing, a defendant may be released. For minor crimes, the defendant may only have to promise to appear at trial. Or the judge may set bail.

Sometimes a judge does not set bail. The crime may be too serious or the judge may be concerned that the defendant will run away. A hearing may be held to decide if a defendant is too dangerous to remain in the community during a trial.

A Lawyer for the Defense If a defendant does not have a lawyer, the judge can assign one. Sometimes the lawyer is a **public defender,** a lawyer who works for the state. Or a lawyer from a private law firm may be assigned to the case.

FIGURE 4
Bail Bonds
Some businesses will guarantee the bail for a defendant, for a fee—often 10 percent of the bail. If a defendant fails to appear in court, the bail bond agent must pay the bail. So the agent will try to track down the defendant.

Four Related Charges	
Charge	Description
Murder, first degree	Planned in advance; intended to harm
Murder, second degree	Not planned in advance; intended to harm
Voluntary manslaughter	Not planned, but intended; "heat of the moment"
Involuntary manslaughter	Not planned or intended; result of reckless behavior

FIGURE 5
Reducing a Charge
When a person kills another person, there are four possible charges. A prosecutor may be able to reduce the charge as part of a plea bargain.
Inferring Which charge would carry the lightest punishment?

Reviewing Evidence A defendant and a lawyer work together as a team. During a pretrial hearing, the defense may ask the judge to dismiss a case for lack of evidence. Then the prosecutor has to persuade the judge that there is enough evidence to go ahead with the case. The defense may also ask to exclude, or keep out, some evidence. They may argue, for example, that a search was not legal.

Plea Bargains Most criminal cases never go to trial. Instead, they are resolved by a **plea bargain,** an agreement between the prosecutor and the defense. The accused person agrees to plead guilty. What does the prosecutor offer in return?

A charge may be changed to a less serious crime. The new charge might be a misdemeanor instead of a felony. The prosecutor may agree to a lighter punishment. This could mean that the defendant serves less time or goes to counseling instead of jail or prison. Some charges against the defendant may be dropped.

Plea bargains help move cases through the courts quickly. But they are controversial. Some people argue that a plea bargain lets a guilty defendant off too lightly. Others say that the threat of a harsh punishment may persuade a defendant to accept a plea bargain even when there is little evidence of guilt.

Lesson 1 Assessment

Target Reading Skill Building Vocabulary Use your definitions to help answer the questions.

Reviewing Key Concepts

1. a. **Identifying** Which Sixth Amendment right is part of the Miranda warning?
   b. **Summarizing** In general, what rights do the Fourth, Fifth, Sixth, and Eighth Amendments protect?
   c. **Applying Concepts** Why is it important that a person accused of a crime has a right to a lawyer?

2. a. **Classifying** What are the two major types of crimes?
   b. **Applying Concepts** Both shoplifting and armed robbery are stealing. Yet these crimes are classified differently. Why?

3. a. **Naming** What four topics can be discussed at a pretrial hearing?
   b. **Identifying** Who controls what takes place at a pretrial hearing?
   c. **Making Generalizations** What is the defendant's role at a pretrial hearing?

In the Community

Comparing Rights Your teacher may invite a few people who were not born in the United State to talk with your class. Prepare some questions in advance. Focus on how the rights people have in the United States compare to the rights people have in other countries.

Presenting Evidence in a Trial

Reading Preview

Key Concepts
- What are the assigned roles of a judge, an impartial jury, and the lawyers at a criminal trial?
- How do lawyers use exhibits in court?
- How do lawyers use witnesses to present evidence?

Key Terms
- bailiff
- exhibit
- testimony
- cross-examination
- expert witness

Target Reading Skill
Previewing Visuals When you preview, you look ahead. Look at Figure 6. Then write two questions you have about the illustration in a graphic organizer like the one below. As you read, answer your questions.

Question	Answer
What does a bailiff do?	A bailiff helps keep order in the court.

Discover Activity

What Makes a Good Juror?
A lawyer often asks potential jurors questions like these.
1. Do you have any personal connection to the defendant or the lawyers in this case? If so, what is that connection?
2. Have you heard or read news reports about this case? If so, have you formed an opinion about the defendant's guilt or innocence?
3. Do you think that people who are charged with crimes are usually guilty of those crimes?

Think It Over
Making Judgments Why would a lawyer want to know the answers to these questions?

Many people like to watch crime shows on television. They enjoy seeing how the detectives and the scientists solve crimes. These shows are designed to entertain the audience. So the writers are drawn to unusual cases. Jurors who watch these shows may come to court with unrealistic expectations. They may, for example, expect to see fingerprints or DNA evidence in every case.

The high expectations of jurors can be a challenge for the lawyers. It helps if the lawyers have a logical story to tell. It also helps if they can present a mix of visual and oral evidence.

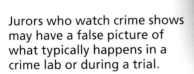
Jurors who watch crime shows may have a false picture of what typically happens in a crime lab or during a trial.

In the Courtroom

Figure 6 shows how a typical courtroom is organized. **In a courtroom, each person has a role and an assigned place.** The roles include a judge, an impartial jury, and the lawyers.

The Judge The judge sits at the front on a raised bench. This arrangement makes it clear who controls what happens in court. **The judge makes sure that everyone behaves and follows the law.** If people fail to follow the rules, the judge can charge them with "contempt of court." The punishment for this crime may be a fine or a jail term.

Lawyers often disagree about what questions a witness can be asked or what evidence can be used. Judges use what they know about the law to decide who is right.

Other Court Employees Three court employees who help a trial run smoothly are the bailiff, the court reporter, and the court clerk. A law enforcement officer called a **bailiff** helps the judge keep order in the court.

A court reporter makes a record of everything that the lawyers, judge, and witnesses say. The reporter types as people talk. Sometimes a reporter is asked to search through and read back part of the record. Court reporters often tape what is said so they can check and correct their typed notes later.

The court clerk keeps the schedule of cases and makes notes summarizing what happens in each case. The clerk has other tasks, too, such as swearing in witnesses.

FIGURE 6
The Courtroom
People have specific roles and assigned places in a courtroom.
Interpreting Diagrams Where do the prosecutor, defense lawyer, and defendant sit?

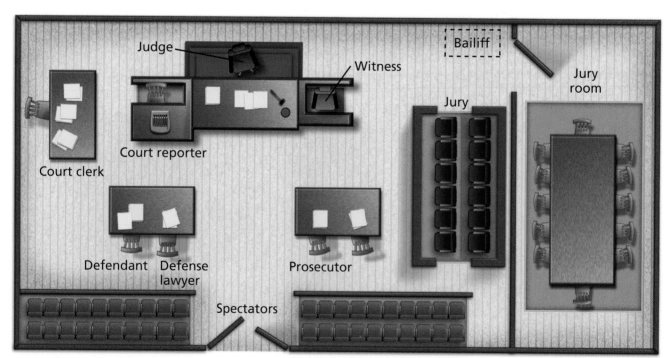

A Jury Is Chosen

A case may be settled before trial. If not, a defendant has the right to a trial by an impartial, or fair, jury. **An impartial jury makes its decision based only on the facts presented in court.** The way a jury is selected can help to ensure a fair jury.

The Jury People who live in the United States have duties as well as rights. One duty is to serve on a jury. To serve on a jury, a person must be a citizen who is age 18 or older. The person must live in the district where the court is located.

In most criminal trials, there are 12 jurors. A jury is likely to have people of different ages. There will be men and women. In many communities, the people will come from different ethnic groups. With a variety of people, the chances are better that the jury will be fair.

The Selection Process Potential jurors are often asked questions by a judge or by the opposing lawyers. The judge and lawyers want to eliminate people who might not make a fair decision. Lawyers also may ask questions to figure out which people are more likely to support their side of the case.

A lawyer can ask the judge to dismiss a juror for cause. For example, a juror might know the defendant. Lawyers often have the right to dismiss a few jurors for no stated reason.

Before the trial begins, the judge gives some instructions to the jury. The jurors may be told not to discuss the case with anyone, not even with other jurors. The jurors may be asked to avoid reading or listening to news reports about the case.

FIGURE 7
The Jury Is Sworn In
A court clerk swears in the jurors. They promise to listen to the evidence and make a fair decision.

Skills **Activity**

Calculating

A person arrives for jury duty. There are a total of 150 people waiting to serve on a jury. At noon, the bailiff announces that a jury will be selected for one trial. What is the probability that any one of the people waiting will end up on the jury?

 **Reading Checkpoint** **Which people can serve on a jury?**

FIGURE 8
Opening Arguments
The prosecutor speaks to the jury first. He begins by stating his hypothesis about the case.
Applying Concepts *Why does the prosecutor direct his arguments to the jury instead of the judge?*

The Lawyers Argue the Case

Now the jury is ready to hear what the lawyers have to say. The American criminal justice system is based on having lawyers who argue for or against a defendant. **The prosecutor tries to convince the jury that the defendant is guilty. The defense needs to give the jury at least one reason to doubt what the prosecutor says.**

The Prosecutor Begins In some ways, prosecutors are like scientists. They start with evidence. The evidence could be photos, interviews, or data from lab tests. Like a scientist, a prosecutor will develop a hypothesis to explain the evidence.

In his opening statement to the jury, the prosecutor will state his hypothesis. He will tell the jury what he thinks the defendant did, and why. The jury may get a preview of the evidence that they will see and hear.

The Defense Responds A lawyer for the defense also makes an opening statement. She will point out places where the prosecutor's case is weak. She may offer a hypothesis of her own that can explain the evidence. Then she may call her witnesses. She may use some of these witnesses to disprove evidence that was presented by the prosecutor.

Closing Arguments Once all the witnesses have spoken, the lawyers make their closing arguments. They review the evidence. Each side tries to use the evidence to persuade the jury to decide in its favor.

 **Reading Checkpoint** How is a prosecutor like a scientist?

Visual Evidence

An **exhibit** (eg zɪʙ it) is a physical object that is used to make a point in court. Each exhibit has a label, such as P102 or D116. The clerk keeps a list of the exhibits. **Lawyers use exhibits to present a crime scene, connect a defendant to a crime, or explain scientific evidence.**

Presenting a Crime Scene Jurors may take a field trip to the crime scene. More often, they are shown enlarged crime scene photos and drawings, or a video of the crime scene. A lawyer may show jurors a three-dimensional (3-D) scale model of the crime scene. Or he may use a computer to give the jury a virtual tour of the crime scene.

Connecting a Defendant to a Crime Lawyers often use exhibits to connect a defendant to a crime. They might show a weapon or enlarged photos of prints. There may be a credit card receipt from a gas station. The jury might even watch a video of the defendant being questioned by the police.

Explaining Scientific Evidence Suppose there is DNA evidence in a case. Before jurors can judge the evidence, they need to learn about DNA. A forensic scientist will likely use diagrams and charts to help explain the scientific concepts.

 **Reading Checkpoint** What are three ways a lawyer can present the crime scene to a jury?

Forensic Science Video
Virtual Crime Scenes

FIGURE 9
Using Exhibits
This witness is using an exhibit to show where she was standing when the crime took place.
Observing *What type of exhibit is the witness using?*

FIGURE 10
Direct Examination
The prosecutor is questioning a witness that he called to testify.
Interpreting Diagrams *How does a lawyer typically behave during direct examination?*

Oral Evidence

Exhibits are never used on their own in a trial. They are used along with the statements of witnesses. **Both eyewitnesses and expert witnesses can provide oral evidence in a trial.** This oral evidence is called **testimony.** Police officers, for example, may testify about what they found at a crime scene.

Before a witness can testify, he or she must take an oath. The witness swears to "tell the truth, the whole truth, and nothing but the truth." People who lie during sworn testimony can be charged with a crime.

No matter what type of witness is called to the stand, the general process is the same. The lawyer who calls a witness does a direct examination. The opposing lawyer may cross-examine the witness.

Direct Examination Before a trial, lawyers prepare their witnesses. They ask questions like the ones they plan to ask in court. They remind witnesses to answer only the questions that are asked and to keep their answers brief and to the point.

Some questions are not allowed during a direct examination. For example, a lawyer cannot ask a leading question—one that contains the answer the lawyer wants. "When you entered the room, was Miss Bell holding this knife?" isn't allowed. "What did you see when you entered the room?" is.

The opposing lawyer may object to a question being asked or to the answer. If the judge agrees with the lawyer, the judge will say, "objection sustained." If the judge does not agree, the judge will say, "objection overruled."

FIGURE 11
Cross-Examination
When the prosecutor is done, the defense lawyer may ask the witness some questions.
Interpreting Diagrams *How does a lawyer typically behave during cross-examination?*

Cross-examination The direct examination is over. Now the opposing lawyer gets a chance to ask questions. The process in which one lawyer asks questions of another lawyer's witness is called **cross-examination.** Each side is given a list of witnesses that the other side plans to call during the trial. This gives the lawyers time to prepare for cross-examination.

There are rules about the questions a lawyer can ask during a cross-examination. The questions must relate to facts that were revealed during the direct examination. The lawyer, however, is allowed to ask leading questions.

A lawyer will try to make the testimony of a witness seem less believable. For example, a woman witnesses a robbery in a store. When she is asked to identify the robber, she points to the defendant. The defense lawyer may ask questions like these. "Wasn't your view blocked by a magazine rack?" "Didn't you accuse my client of stealing your jacket?"

The Defendant as Witness Recall that a person has the right to refuse to be a "witness against himself." This right protects a defendant from having to make statements that prove he is guilty.

Suppose a defendant who is innocent decides not to testify. The jurors may infer that the defendant is guilty. But the judge will explain to the jurors that the law does not allow them to make this inference.

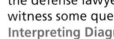

Skills Activity

Posing Questions
You are the defense lawyer for a person on trial for a burglary. A witness states the following. "At around 11 P.M., I saw the defendant cross the street, climb the fire escape, and enter the apartment through a window." Prepare three questions to use when you cross-examine the witness.

Reading Checkpoint What is the goal of cross-examination?

FIGURE 12
Expert Witnesses
This firearms expert is showing the jury a rifle. He will explain how he knows that this rifle was used by the defendant.

Expert Witnesses An **expert witness** is a person who has knowledge of a specific area of study. Forensic scientists may have to testify as expert witnesses. Their role is not to prove a defendant guilty. Their role is to help explain technical evidence to the jury. If they do this job well, the jury will be better able to evaluate the evidence. Unlike other witnesses, expert witnesses can give their opinions. They are also asked to draw conclusions.

The lawyer who calls an expert as a witness starts by asking questions about the expert's education and experience. The goal is to show that the witness is qualified and worthy of trust. The lawyer for the other side may try to show that the expert is not qualified. This lawyer may also question the methods the expert used to test the evidence. The goal is to make the jury doubt the expert's opinion on the test results.

Just knowing the science is not enough. To be a good expert witness, scientists must have good communication skills. They must know how to present technical evidence in a clear way. They must also appear confident.

Lesson 2 Assessment

Target Reading Previewing Visuals Use the graphic organizer you made for Figure 6 to help you answer these questions.

Reviewing Key Concepts

1. a. **Summarizing** What are the roles of a judge, a prosecutor, and a defense lawyer in a trial?
   b. **Defining** What is an impartial jury?
   c. **Posing Questions** A teen is accused of stealing a car. What is a question a lawyer could ask to find out if a juror might have sympathy for the teen?
2. a. **Defining** What is an exhibit?
   b. **Describing** List three reasons that lawyers have for using exhibits during a trial.
   c. **Predicting** Who do you think is more likely to present exhibits, a prosecutor or a defense lawyer? Why?

3. a. **Reviewing** What type of evidence do witnesses provide?
   b. **Identifying** Who does the direct examination of a witness? Who may do the cross-examination?
   c. **Predicting** A judge allows a lawyer to ask a leading question. Is the lawyer doing a direct examination? Why or why not?

 At-Home Activity

Mapping Justice Work with family members to make a map of your community that shows locations where a defendant might be before, during, or after a trial. Include courthouses and police stations. Is there a local jail or a state prison in your community? Use a phone directory or search online to find related locations, such as a legal aid clinic.

Making a Scale Model

Problem

How can you make an accurate scale model of a crime scene?

Skills Focus

making models, measuring, calculating

Materials

- metric ruler
- 2 pieces of graph paper
- 2 pieces of cardboard
- transparent tape

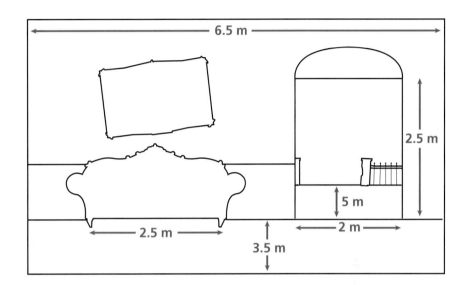

Procedure

Use the measurements in the sketch and the illustration on page 1 to make a scale model of the Missing Masterpiece crime scene.

1. Count the number of squares on the long edge of your graph paper. Divide the width of the crime scene by the number of squares. The result is the scale of your model. For example, one square might represent 0.20 meters.

2. On one piece of graph paper make a floor plan of the crime scene. The plan should show what you would see if you viewed the crime scene from above. Include the drive-way and other objects outside the house.

3. On the second piece of graph paper, make a scale drawing of the wall and doorway.

4. Complete the model by taping each piece of graph paper to cardboard. Then tape the wall to the floor so that the wall is at a right angle to the floor.

Analyze and Conclude

1. **Calculating** What scale did you use for your model? How did you determine this scale?

2. **Making Models** Describe how you used the lines on the graph paper to help you place the objects in your model.

3. **Comparing and Contrasting** How are your scale model and the illustration on page 1 different? How are they similar?

4. **Designing Experiments** Your model is based on an illustration rather than an actual crime scene. How do you think this approach affected the accuracy of your model?

Communicating

Pretend that you are the prosecutor. Write a paragraph explaining how you might use your model during the trial of the Missing Masterpiece thief.

Scanner

Modeling a Crime Scene

One way that lawyers can help a jury picture a crime is to show a model of the crime scene on a computer. The computer model can be used to give a jury a virtual tour of the crime scene.

❶ Laser Scan of a Crime Scene

Light from a laser is reflected off objects at the crime scene back to a scanner. The scanner measures the time it takes the light to travel to an object and back. The farther away an object is from the scanner, the longer it takes for the light to return. The scanner can be rotated or tilted to scan different parts of the scene.

❷ Displaying the Data

The scanner can measure millions of points in a few minutes. The data is stored in a computer and displayed on the screen as a black and white photo. Digital color photos of the scene are used to assign each point a color value.

❸ Wire-Frame Graphic

The millions of individual points are connected to form triangles. A technician will reduce the number of triangles so that the wire-frame graphic will display as an interactive image on a computer.

④ Using the Model

A lawyer can use the final 3-D model to walk the jury through a crime scene while describing what happened. The jury can view the scene from any angle. The lawyer can zoom in on details.

How a Laser Works

A flashlight produces light that spreads out as it travels from the source. A laser produces a narrow beam of coherent light. All the light waves in a coherent beam have the same wavelength.

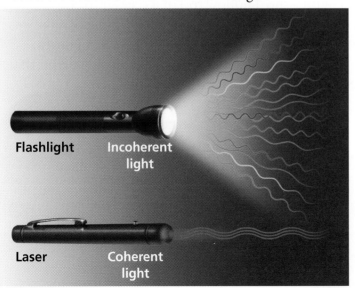

Flashlight   Incoherent light

Laser   Coherent light

You Be the Judge

1. Applying Concepts
Why might a lawyer want to show different views of the same crime scene in court?

2. Comparing and Contrasting
Compare the use of a laser scan to measure a crime scene with the use of sketches and a tape measure to complete the same task.

3. Making Judgments
Do you think laser scanning is a technology that is used in most trials? Why or why not?

For: Links on lasers
Visit: www.SciLinks.org
Web Code: dan-1040

Reading Preview

Key Concepts
- How does a jury reach a verdict?
- What happens after a defendant is found guilty?

Key Terms
- verdict
- foreperson
- probation
- appeal

Target Reading Skill

Relating Cause and Effect As you read, identify three possible effects of a hung jury. Write the information in a graphic organizer like the one below.

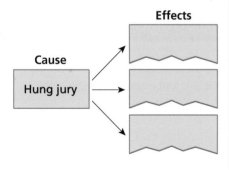

Effects

Cause

Hung jury

Discover Activity

Is the Evidence Persuasive?

A woman is accused of kidnapping a man and collecting a ransom. The following evidence is presented during the trial.

1. A witness claims she saw the woman push the man into a van.
2. The woman has a marked bill from the ransom.
3. A man provides an alibi for the woman. He says she was having dinner with him at the time of the kidnapping.

Think It Over

Posing Questions Work with a partner. Think of at least three questions you would want answered before you decided whether the defendant was guilty.

Greek citizens had key roles in trials in ancient Athens. There was no public prosecutor. Instead, one citizen could bring a charge against another. A public official would decide if there was probable cause to hold a trial.

At the trial of the philosopher Socrates, 500 citizens were chosen to decide the case. They sat on benches in a public square and listened to the arguments. The accusers had three hours to argue their case. Socrates had three hours to respond.

After the arguments, the citizens were asked to vote. They used a flat disk with a short hollow rod in its center to vote guilty. They used a disk with a solid rod to vote not guilty. Socrates was found guilty by a vote of 280 to 220 and sentenced to death.

In a jury trial in the United States, citizens also vote. But that is not all they do.

Not guilty

Guilty

FIGURE 13
The Jury Deliberates
When the jurors meet, they review the evidence. The foreperson encourages all jurors to take part in the discussion.
Developing Hypotheses *Why do you think that the jurors meet in a closed room?*

The Case Goes to the Jury

The jury has listened carefully to the lawyers and witnesses. Now it is time for the jurors to respond to what they have heard. Unlike the citizens of ancient Athens, the jurors will not simply vote guilty or not guilty at the end of the trial. **The jurors must meet and discuss the evidence before they decide a case.** The judge will guide them through the process.

The Judge Instructs the Jury The last words to the jury before it meets come from the judge. The judge will review the charges. She will explain that the jury must follow the law. The decision it reaches, the **verdict,** must be based on the evidence that was presented.

Suppose the prosecutor presents clear proof that a defendant is guilty. Then the verdict should be guilty. But what if the defense has persuaded the jury that there is a good reason to doubt the evidence? Then the verdict should be not guilty.

The Jury Discusses the Case The jurors meet in a closed room. One juror is chosen to be a foreperson. The **foreperson** manages the discussion. He or she should make sure that all jurors have a chance to speak.

Finally, the jurors are free to discuss the case. They will find out whether they tend to agree. The foreperson will ask them to review the evidence in an orderly way. During this process, they may decide that they can't trust what a witness said. Or they may not agree with the inferences that an expert drew from the evidence. They may ask the judge if they can look at an exhibit or have some testimony read to them.

The Jury Makes a Decision When the jurors vote, the foreperson counts the votes and announces the result. On the first vote, jurors may all vote the same way. Often, however, the first vote will be split with some jurors voting guilty and some voting not guilty.

In the end, all 12 jurors must agree; that is, the verdict must be unanimous (yoo NAN uh mus). If the jurors do not agree, they must continue to discuss the case. Suppose the vote is eight to four. The eight voters in the majority may try to convince the four in the minority to change their votes.

Those in the minority may change their votes after further discussion. But sometimes they cannot be persuaded. Then the foreperson will tell the judge that the jury is too divided to make a unanimous decision. A jury that cannot reach a verdict is called a hung jury. Three things can happen when there is a hung jury. The prosecutor may decide not to retry the defendant. The prosecutor may retry the defendant with a new jury. Or the opposing sides may agree on a plea bargain.

✓ Reading Checkpoint **What is a unanimous verdict?**

Math ▶ Analyzing Data

Sentences for Felony Convictions

A defendant who is found guilty of a felony may be sent to a state prison or to a local jail. Or the defendant may be given probation. Use the graph to answer the questions below.

1. **Reading Graphs** About what percentage of felons were sentenced to probation in 1988? In 2002?

2. **Interpreting Graphs** Are more felons sentenced to state prisons or local jails?

3. **Calculating** What percentage of felons went to prison or to jail in 2002?

4. **Predicting** About what percentage of felons were sent to prison or jail in 2005?

5. **Calculating** There were about one million felony convictions in state courts in 2002. About how many felons were sent to state prisons in 2002?

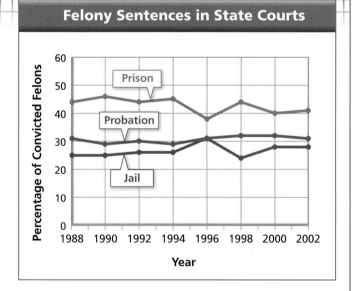

Felony Sentences in State Courts

6. **Inferring** In 2000, 24 new state prisons were opened. Do you think the total number of people in prison increased, decreased, or stayed the same between 1988 and 2002? Explain your answer.

FIGURE 14
The Verdict Is Read
After the jury reaches a verdict, the defendant and the lawyers return to court. The defendant listens as the verdict is read.
Applying Concepts *What will happen if the verdict is not guilty on all charges?*

Sentences and Appeals

If the jury does reach a verdict, the defendant and the lawyers return to court. The defendant hears the verdict read by the foreperson. If the verdict is not guilty, the defendant is freed. The case is over. The state will not be able to try the defendant again for the same crime.

If the foreperson says "guilty," then there is more to do. **When a defendant is found guilty, the judge must decide on a punishment, or sentence. The defense must decide whether to appeal the verdict.**

Sentencing If the crime is a misdemeanor, the judge may announce a sentence right away. If the crime is a felony, the court clerk will likely schedule a date for a hearing.

At a sentencing hearing, the victim of a crime or the family of a victim may speak. They will tell the judge what effect the crime has had on their lives. The defendant or people who support the defendant may also speak.

A judge may not have a choice on the sentence. Lawmakers may decide, for example, that the punishment for murder is life in prison. Sometimes the judge has a range of choices. In Maryland, for example, the maximum sentence for auto theft is five years. A judge could send a convicted auto thief to prison for up to five years or to jail for six months. For a first offense, the sentence might be probation. A person on **probation** stays in the community, where he or she is closely supervised by a probation officer.

FIGURE 15
Making an Appeal
This lawyer is doing research while working on an appeal. She is looking for earlier legal decisions that support her argument.

The Appeal Process In the United States, there are different levels of courts. At the lowest level are the state trial courts. At the highest level is the United States Supreme Court. If a defendant is found guilty, the defense can decide to appeal to a higher court. An **appeal** is a written request that the verdict in a trial be reversed. The lawyer usually has 30 days to file an appeal.

A lawyer cannot present new evidence as part of an appeal. Instead, the lawyer must argue that the trial judge made mistakes that had an effect on the verdict. Perhaps the prosecutor asked to show the jury a video of the defendant confessing to the crime. The defense lawyer objected. She said that the defendant felt forced to confess. But the judge overruled the objection. The lawyer can argue that the judge made a mistake, and that the video had a major effect on the verdict.

During an appeal, the burden of proof belongs to the defense lawyer. If he can prove that there was a serious error, his client may get a new trial. If not, he may appeal to a higher court. Or he may advise his client to accept the sentence.

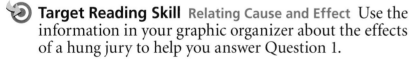

Lesson 3 Assessment

Target Reading Skill Relating Cause and Effect Use the information in your graphic organizer about the effects of a hung jury to help you answer Question 1.

Reviewing Key Concepts

1. a. Describing What do the judge and jury do after the lawyers give their closing arguments?
   b. Summarizing What are two things that might happen if the jury cannot reach a verdict?
   c. Drawing Conclusions Why do you think that there is a foreperson on a jury?

2. a. Reviewing What must the trial judge do after a guilty verdict? What must the defense do?
   b. Inferring Why do you think a victim of a crime might want to speak at a sentencing hearing?
   c. Applying Concepts After the verdict, a lawyer finds some new evidence that could help the defendant. Can the lawyer use this new evidence during an appeal? Why or why not?

Writing in Science

Summary Interview an adult family member or friend who received a notice to report for jury duty. Ask the person to describe what happened when he or she arrived at the courthouse. If the person was selected to serve on a jury, also ask questions about what happened in the courtroom and the jury room. Write a paragraph summarizing what you learned.

Study Guide

The BIG Idea The right to a defense lawyer and an impartial jury ensure that a person accused of a crime has a fair trial.

1 From Arrest to Trial

Key Concepts

- Four of the amendments in the Bill of Rights protect a person's rights before, during, and after an arrest.

- Crimes are classified as felonies or misdemeanors.

- Police need probable cause to make an arrest. The person who is arrested will be taken into custody and booked.

- At a pretrial hearing, the defendant is charged. The judge may set bail, assign a lawyer, and review evidence. Before a trial, lawyers may reach a plea bargain.

Key Terms

Bill of Rights
jury
bail
felony
misdemeanor
probable cause
defendant
judge
prosecutor
public defender
plea bargain

2 Presenting Evidence in a Trial

Key Concepts

- In a courtroom, each person has a role and an assigned place.

- The judge makes sure that everyone behaves and follows the law.

- An impartial jury makes its decisions based only on the facts presented in court.

- The prosecutor tries to convince the jury that the defendant is guilty. The defense needs to give the jury at least one reason to doubt what the prosecutor says.

- Lawyers use exhibits to present a crime scene, connect a defendant to a crime, or explain scientific evidence. Both eyewitnesses and expert witnesses can provide oral evidence in a trial.

Key Terms

bailiff
exhibit
testimony
cross-examination
expert witness

3 The Final Stages of a Trial

Key Concepts

- The jurors must meet and discuss the evidence before they decide a case.

- When a defendant is found guilty, the judge must decide on a punishment, or sentence. The defense must decide whether to appeal the verdict.

Key Terms

verdict
foreperson
probation
appeal

Review and Assessment

Organizing Information

Identifying Main Ideas Copy the graphic organizer about main ideas onto a separate piece of paper. Then complete it and add a title. (For more on Identifying Main Ideas, see the Skills Handbook.)

Amendment	Description	Protects against or provides for
a.___?___	Search and Seizure	Unreasonable search
Fifth	b.___?___	c.___?___ Double jeopardy
Sixth	d.___?___	Speedy, public trial Trial by jury Facing accusers in court e.___?___
Eighth	Bail and Punishment	Unreasonable bail f.___?___

Reviewing Key Terms

Choose the letter of the best answer.

1. Before a trial, the prosecutor and defense lawyer may negotiate
   a. a verdict.
   b. a probable cause.
   c. an appeal.
   d. a plea bargain.

2. One person in a courtroom who must be impartial is
   a. a public defender.
   b. a prosecutor.
   c. a juror.
   d. the defendant.

3. The decision that a jury makes is called
   a. a plea bargain.
   b. a verdict.
   c. a sentence.
   d. an appeal.

4. An appeal is a request to
   a. have a higher court review a case.
   b. have a case dismissed.
   c. introduce new evidence in a case.
   d. move the trial to a different court.

If the statement is true, write *true*. If it is false, change the underlined word or words to make the statement true.

5. A bailiff is the person who sets the amount of bail at a pretrial hearing.

6. An exhibit may be a scale model or a video taken at the crime scene.

7. After the prosecutor questioned the witness, the defense lawyer began direct examination.

8. The forensic scientist offered testimony about the defendant's DNA.

9. The judge gave the first-time offender probable cause, so he could stay in the community.

Writing in Science

Debate Some people think that lawyers should not defend people who are accused of horrible crimes. You have been assigned to debate this topic. Write down three points you could make to argue that every person accused of a crime deserves a strong defense.

Checking Concepts

10. What role does the Bill of Rights play in the criminal justice system?

11. What is the main difference between a felony and a misdemeanor?

12. Describe three things that might happen when a suspect is booked.

13. Describe briefly what a court reporter and a court clerk do.

14. Why is it important to have a variety of ages, genders, and ethnic backgrounds on a jury?

15. Explain how lawyers use visual and oral evidence during a trial.

Thinking Critically

16. **Drawing Conclusions** The Bill of Rights protects a suspect's right to remain silent and speak with a lawyer. So why is the Miranda warning needed?

17. **Comparing and Contrasting** How are search warrants and arrest warrants similar?

18. **Classifying** Which of these is a leading question, and why? (a) "What did you see the defendant do?" (b) "Did you see the defendant put the watch in his pocket?"

19. **Comparing and Contrasting** Compare the roles of the judge and the jury in the final stages of a trial.

20. **Inferring** When a jury is having trouble reaching a verdict, a judge will usually urge the jurors to keep trying. Why do you think the judge would want to avoid a hung jury?

21. **Interpreting Diagrams** A defendant is found guilty in a state trial court. The defendant's lawyer appeals the case and loses the appeal. What can the lawyer do next?

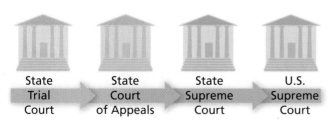

Applying Skills

Use the data table below to answer Questions 22–24.

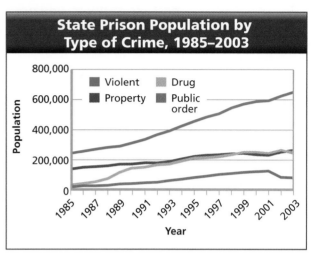

State Prison Population by Type of Crime, 1985–2003

Robbery is a violent crime. Auto theft is a property crime. Drug offenses include possession and sales. Driving without a license is a public order crime.

22. **Interpreting Graphs** What happened to the state prison population from 1985 to 2003? Which type of crime was most responsible for this change?

23. **Calculating** About how many people were in state prisons in 2003? About what percentage of these people had committed drug crimes?

24. **Relating Cause and Effect** In most states, lawmakers pass more and more sentencing guidelines, or rules, each year. Judges must follow these rules. How do you think these rules affect the size of the prison population?

Chapter Project

Performance Assessment After your mock trial, meet with your team to discuss the process. Use questions like the following to guide the discussion. Which parts of your presentation were most persuasive? How could you have improved your presentation?

Think Like a Scientist

Scientists have a particular way of looking at the world, or scientific habits of mind. Whenever you ask a question and explore possible answers, you use many of the same skills that scientists do. Some of these skills are described on this page.

Observing

When you use one or more of your five senses to gather information about the world, you are **observing.** Hearing a dog bark, counting twelve green seeds, and smelling smoke are all observations. To increase the power of their senses, scientists sometimes use microscopes, telescopes, or other instruments that help them make more detailed observations.

An observation must be an accurate report of what your senses detect. It is important to keep careful records of your observations in science class by writing or drawing in a notebook. The information collected through observations is called evidence, or data.

Inferring

When you interpret an observation, you are **inferring,** or making an inference. For example, if you hear your dog barking, you may infer that someone is at your front door. To make this inference, you combine the evidence— the barking dog—and your experience or knowledge—you know that your dog barks when strangers approach—to reach a logical conclusion.

Notice that an inference is not a fact; it is only one of many possible interpretations for an observation. For example, your dog may be barking because it wants to go for a walk. An inference may turn out to be incorrect even if it is based on accurate observations and logical reasoning. The only way to find out if an inference is correct is to investigate further.

Predicting

When you listen to the weather forecast, you hear many predictions about the next day's weather—what the temperature will be, whether it will rain, and how windy it will be. Weather forecasters use observations and knowledge of weather patterns to predict the weather. The skill of **predicting** involves making an inference about a future event based on current evidence or past experience.

Because a prediction is an inference, it may prove to be false. In science class, you can test some of your predictions by doing experiments. For example, suppose you predict that larger paper airplanes can fly farther than smaller airplanes. How could you test your prediction?

Activity

Use the photograph to answer the questions below.

Observing Look closely at the photograph. List at least three observations.

Inferring Use your observations to make an inference about what has happened. What experience or knowledge did you use to make the inference?

Predicting Predict what will happen next. On what evidence or experience do you base your prediction?

Classifying

Could you imagine searching for a book in the library if the books were shelved in no particular order? Your trip to the library would be an all-day event! Luckily, librarians group together books on similar topics or by the same author. Grouping together items that are alike in some way is called **classifying**. You can classify items in many ways: by size, by shape, by use, and by other important characteristics.

Like librarians, scientists use the skill of classifying to organize information and objects. When things are sorted into groups, the relationships among them become easier to understand.

> **Activity**
>
> Classify the objects in the photograph into two groups based on any characteristic you choose. Then use another characteristic to classify the objects into three groups.

> **Activity**
>
> This student is using a model to demonstrate what causes day and night on Earth. What do the flashlight and the tennis ball in the model represent?

Making Models

Have you ever drawn a picture to help someone understand what you were saying? Such a drawing is one type of model. A model is a picture, diagram, computer image, or other representation of a complex object or process. **Making models** helps people understand things that they cannot observe directly.

Scientists often use models to represent things that are either very large or very small, such as the planets in the solar system, or the parts of a cell. Such models are physical models—drawings or three-dimensional structures that look like the real thing. Other models are mental models—mathematical equations or words that describe how something works.

Communicating

Whenever you talk on the phone, write a report, or listen to your teacher at school, you are communicating. **Communicating** is the process of sharing ideas and information with other people. Communicating effectively requires many skills, including writing, reading, speaking, listening, and making models.

Scientists communicate to share results, information, and opinions. Scientists often communicate about their work in journals, over the telephone, in letters, and on the Internet.

They also attend scientific meetings where they share their ideas with one another in person.

> **Activity**
>
> On a sheet of paper, write out clear, detailed directions for tying your shoe. Then exchange directions with a partner. Follow your partner's directions exactly. How successful were you at tying your shoe? How could your partner have communicated more clearly?

Making Measurements

By measuring, scientists can express their observations more precisely and communicate more information about what they observe.

Measuring in SI

The standard system of measurement used by scientists around the world is known as the International System of Units, which is abbreviated as SI (**Système International d'Unités,** in French). SI units are easy to use because they are based on multiples of 10. Each unit is ten times larger than the next smallest unit and one tenth the size of the next largest unit. The table lists the prefixes used to name the most common SI units.

Length To measure length, or the distance between two points, the unit of measure is the **meter (m).** The distance from the floor to a doorknob is approximately one meter. Long distances, such as the distance between two cities, are measured in kilometers (km). Small lengths are measured in centimeters (cm) or millimeters (mm). Scientists use metric rulers and meter sticks to measure length.

Common Conversions
1 km = 1,000 m
1 m = 100 cm
1 m = 1,000 mm
1 cm = 10 mm

Common SI Prefixes		
Prefix	**Symbol**	**Meaning**
kilo-	k	1,000
hecto-	h	100
deka-	da	10
deci-	d	0.1 (one tenth)
centi-	c	0.01 (one hundredth)
milli-	m	0.001 (one thousandth)

Liquid Volume To measure the volume of a liquid, or the amount of space it takes up, you will use a unit of measure known as the **liter (L).** One liter is the approximate volume of a medium-size carton of milk. Smaller volumes are measured in milliliters (mL). Scientists use graduated cylinders to measure liquid volume.

Activity

The larger lines on the metric ruler in the picture show centimeter divisions, while the smaller, unnumbered lines show millimeter divisions. How many centimeters long is the shell? How many millimeters long is it?

Activity

The graduated cylinder in the picture is marked in milliliter divisions. Notice that the water in the cylinder has a curved surface. This curved surface is called the *meniscus*. To measure the volume, you must read the level at the lowest point of the meniscus. What is the volume of water in this graduated cylinder?

Common Conversions
1 L = 1,000 mL

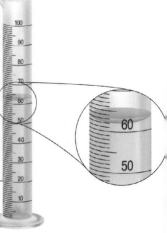

Mass To measure mass, or the amount of matter in an object, you will use a unit of measure known as the **gram (g).** One gram is approximately the mass of a paper clip. Larger masses are measured in kilograms (kg). Scientists use a balance to find the mass of an object.

Common Conversion
1 kg = 1,000 g

Activity

The mass of the potato in the picture is measured in kilograms. What is the mass of the potato? Suppose a recipe for potato salad called for one kilogram of potatoes. About how many potatoes would you need?

Temperature To measure the temperature of a substance, you will use the **Celsius scale.** Temperature is measured in degrees Celsius (°C) using a Celsius thermometer. Water freezes at 0°C and boils at 100°C.

Time The unit scientists use to measure time is the **second (s).**

Activity

What is the temperature of the liquid in degrees Celsius?

Converting SI Units

To use the SI system, you must know how to convert between units. Converting from one unit to another involves the skill of **calculating,** or using mathematical operations. Converting between SI units is similar to converting between dollars and dimes because both systems are based on multiples of ten.

Suppose you want to convert a length of 80 centimeters to meters. Follow these steps to convert between units.

1. Begin by writing down the measurement you want to convert—in this example, 80 centimeters.

2. Write a conversion factor that represents the relationship between the two units you are converting. In this example, the relationship is 1 meter = 100 centimeters. Write this conversion factor as a fraction, making sure to place the units you are converting from (centimeters, in this example) in the denominator.

3. Multiply the measurement you want to convert by the fraction. When you do this, the units in the measurement will cancel out with the units in the denominator. Your answer will be in the units you are converting to (meters, in this example).

Example

$$80 \text{ centimeters} = \blacksquare \text{ meters}$$

$$80 \text{ centimeters} \times \frac{1 \text{ meter}}{100 \text{ centimeters}} = \frac{80 \text{ meters}}{100}$$

$$= 0.8 \text{ meters}$$

Activity

Convert between the following units.
1. 600 millimeters = ■ meters
2. 0.35 liters = ■ milliliters
3. 1,050 grams = ■ kilograms

Conducting a Scientific Investigation

In some ways, scientists are like detectives, piecing together clues to learn about a process or event. One way that scientists gather clues is by carrying out experiments. An experiment tests an idea in a careful, orderly manner. Although experiments do not all follow the same steps in the same order, many follow a pattern similar to the one described here.

Posing Questions

Experiments begin by asking a scientific question. A scientific question is one that can be answered by gathering evidence. For example, the question "Which freezes faster—fresh water or salt water?" is a scientific question because you can carry out an investigation and gather information to answer the question.

Developing a Hypothesis

The next step is to form a hypothesis. A **hypothesis** is a possible explanation for a set of observations or answer to a scientific question. In science, a hypothesis must be something that can be tested. A hypothesis can be worded as an *If . . . then . . .* statement. For example, a hypothesis might be "*If I add salt to fresh water, then the water will take longer to freeze.*" A hypothesis worded this way serves as a rough outline of the experiment you should perform.

Designing an Experiment

Next you need to plan a way to test your hypothesis. Your plan should be written out as a step-by-step procedure and should describe the observations or measurements you will make.

Two important steps involved in designing an experiment are controlling variables and forming operational definitions.

Controlling Variables In a well-designed experiment, you need to keep all variables the same except for one. A **variable** is any factor that can change in an experiment. The factor that you change is called the **manipulated variable.** In this experiment, the manipulated variable is the amount of salt added to the water. Other factors, such as the amount of water or the starting temperature, are kept constant.

The factor that changes as a result of the manipulated variable is called the **responding variable.** The responding variable is what you measure or observe to obtain your results. In this experiment, the responding variable is how long the water takes to freeze.

An experiment in which all factors except one are kept constant is called a **controlled experiment.** Most controlled experiments include a test called the control. In this experiment, Container 3 is the control. Because no salt is added to Container 3, you can compare the results from the other containers to it. Any difference in results must be due to the addition of salt alone.

Forming Operational Definitions Another important aspect of a well-designed experiment is having clear operational definitions. An **operational definition** is a statement that describes how a particular variable is to be measured or how a term is to be defined. For example, in this experiment, how will you determine if the water has frozen? You might decide to insert a stick in each container at the start of the experiment. Your operational definition of "frozen" would be the time at which the stick can no longer move.

Experimental Procedure
1. Fill 3 containers with 300 milliliters of cold tap water.
2. Add 10 grams of salt to Container 1; stir. Add 20 grams of salt to Container 2; stir. Add no salt to Container 3.
3. Place the 3 containers in a freezer.
4. Check the containers every 15 minutes. Record your observations.

Interpreting Data

The observations and measurements you make in an experiment are called **data**. At the end of an experiment, you need to analyze the data to look for any patterns or trends. Patterns often become clear if you organize your data in a data table or graph. Then think through what the data reveal. Do they support your hypothesis? Do they point out a flaw in your experiment? Do you need to collect more data?

Drawing Conclusions

A **conclusion** is a statement that sums up what you have learned from an experiment. When you draw a conclusion, you need to decide whether the data you collected support your hypothesis or not. You may need to repeat an experiment several times before you can draw any conclusions from it. Conclusions often lead you to pose new questions and plan new experiments to answer them.

Activity

Is a ball's bounce affected by the height from which it is dropped? Using the steps just described, plan a controlled experiment to investigate this problem.

Creating Data Tables and Graphs

How can you make sense of the data in a science experiment?
The first step is to organize the data to help you understand them.
Data tables and graphs are helpful tools for organizing data.

Data Tables

You have gathered your materials and set up your experiment. But before you start, you need to plan a way to record what happens during the experiment. By creating a data table, you can record your observations and measurements in an orderly way.

Suppose, for example, that a scientist conducted an experiment to find out how many Calories people of different body masses burn while doing various activities. The data table shows the results.

Notice in this data table that the manipulated variable (body mass) is the heading of one column. The responding variable (for

Calories Burned in 30 Minutes			
Body Mass	Experiment 1: Bicycling	Experiment 2: Playing Basketball	Experiment 3: Watching Television
30 kg	60 Calories	120 Calories	21 Calories
40 kg	77 Calories	164 Calories	27 Calories
50 kg	95 Calories	206 Calories	33 Calories
60 kg	114 Calories	248 Calories	38 Calories

Experiment 1, the number of Calories burned while bicycling) is the heading of the next column. Additional columns were added for related experiments.

Bar Graphs

To compare how many Calories a person burns doing various activities, you could create a bar graph. A bar graph is used to display data in a number of separate, or distinct, categories. In this example, bicycling, playing basketball, and watching television are the three categories.

To create a bar graph, follow these steps.

1. On graph paper, draw a horizontal axis, or *x*-axis, and a vertical axis, or *y*-axis.

2. Write the names of the categories to be graphed along the horizontal axis. Include an overall label for the axis as well.

3. Label the vertical axis with the name of the responding variable. Include units of measurement. Then create a scale along the axis by marking off equally spaced numbers that cover the range of the data collected.

4. For each category, draw a solid bar using the scale on the vertical axis to determine the height. Make all the bars the same width.

5. Add a title that describes the graph.

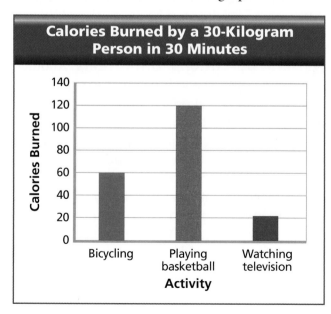

Calories Burned by a 30-Kilogram Person in 30 Minutes

Line Graphs

To see whether a relationship exists between body mass and the number of Calories burned while bicycling, you could create a line graph. A line graph is used to display data that show how one variable (the responding variable) changes in response to another variable (the manipulated variable). You can use a line graph when your manipulated variable is continuous, that is, when there are other points between the ones that you tested. In this example, body mass is a continuous variable because there are other body masses between 30 and 40 kilograms (for example, 31 kilograms). Time is another example of a continuous variable.

Line graphs are powerful tools because they allow you to estimate values for conditions that you did not test in the experiment. For example, you can use the line graph to estimate that a 35-kilogram person would burn 68 Calories while bicycling.

To create a line graph, follow these steps.

1. On graph paper, draw a horizontal axis, or x-axis, and a vertical axis, or y-axis.

2. Label the horizontal axis with the name of the manipulated variable. Label the vertical axis with the name of the responding variable. Include units of measurement.

3. Create a scale on each axis by marking off equally spaced numbers that cover the range of the data collected.

4. Plot a point on the graph for each piece of data. In the line graph above, the dotted lines show how to plot the first data point (30 kilograms and 60 Calories). Follow an imaginary vertical line extending up from the horizontal axis at the 30-kilogram mark. Then follow an imaginary horizontal line extending across from the vertical axis at the 60-Calorie mark. Plot the point where the two lines intersect.

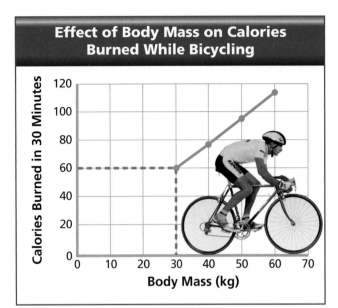

Effect of Body Mass on Calories Burned While Bicycling

5. Connect the plotted points with a solid line. (In some cases, it may be more appropriate to draw a line that shows the general trend of the plotted points. In those cases, some of the points may fall above or below the line. Also, not all graphs are linear. It may be more appropriate to draw a curve to connect the points.)

6. Add a title that identifies the variables or relationship in the graph.

Activity

Create line graphs to display the data from Experiment 2 and Experiment 3 in the data table.

Activity

You read in the newspaper that a total of 4 centimeters of rain fell in your area in June, 2.5 centimeters fell in July, and 1.5 centimeters fell in August. What type of graph would you use to display these data? Use graph paper to create the graph.

Circle Graphs

Like bar graphs, circle graphs can be used to display data in a number of separate categories. Unlike bar graphs, however, circle graphs can only be used when you have data for *all* the categories that make up a given topic. A circle graph is sometimes called a pie chart. The pie represents the entire topic, while the slices represent the individual categories. The size of a slice indicates what percentage of the whole a particular category makes up.

The data table below shows the results of a survey in which 24 teenagers were asked to identify their favorite sport. The data were then used to create the circle graph at the right.

Favorite Sports	
Sport	Students
Soccer	8
Basketball	6
Bicycling	6
Swimming	4

To create a circle graph, follow these steps.

1. Use a compass to draw a circle. Mark the center with a point. Then draw a line from the center point to the top of the circle.

2. Determine the size of each "slice" by setting up a proportion where x equals the number of degrees in a slice. (Note: A circle contains 360 degrees.) For example, to find the number of degrees in the "soccer" slice, set up the following proportion:

$$\frac{\text{Students who prefer soccer}}{\text{Total number of students}} = \frac{x}{\text{Total number of degrees in a circle}}$$

$$\frac{8}{24} = \frac{x}{360}$$

Cross-multiply and solve for x.

$$24x = 8 \times 360$$
$$x = 120$$

The "soccer" slice should contain 120 degrees.

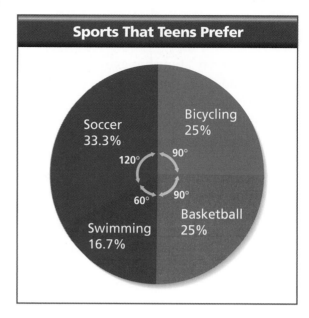

Sports That Teens Prefer

3. Use a protractor to measure the angle of the first slice, using the line you drew to the top of the circle as the 0° line. Draw a line from the center of the circle to the edge for the angle you measured.

4. Continue around the circle by measuring the size of each slice with the protractor. Start measuring from the edge of the previous slice so the wedges do not overlap. When you are done, the entire circle should be filled in.

5. Determine the percentage of the whole circle that each slice represents. To do this, divide the number of degrees in a slice by the total number of degrees in a circle (360), and multiply by 100%. For the "soccer" slice, you can find the percentage as follows:

$$\frac{120}{360} \times 100\% = 33.3\%$$

6. Use a different color for each slice. Label each slice with the category and with the percentage of the whole it represents.

7. Add a title to the circle graph.

Activity

In a class of 28 students, 12 students take the bus to school, 10 students walk, and 6 students ride their bicycles. Create a circle graph to display these data.

Math Review

Scientists use math to organize, analyze, and present data.
This section will help you review some basic math skills.

Mean, Median, and Mode

The **mean** is the average, or the sum of the data divided by the number of data items. The middle number in a set of ordered data is called the **median.** The **mode** is the number that appears most often in a set of data.

Example

A scientist counted the number of distinct songs sung by seven different male birds and collected the data shown below.

Male Bird Songs							
Bird	A	B	C	D	E	F	G
Number of Songs	36	29	40	35	28	36	27

To determine the mean number of songs, add the total number of songs and divide by the number of data items—in this case, the number of male birds.

$$\text{Mean} = \frac{231}{7} = 33 \text{ songs}$$

To find the median number of songs, arrange the data in numerical order and find the number in the middle of the series.

27 28 29 35 36 36 40

The number in the middle is 35, so the median number of songs is 35.

The mode is the value that appears most frequently. In the data, 36 appears twice, while each other item appears only once. Therefore, 36 songs is the mode.

Practice

Find out how many minutes it takes each student in your class to get to school. Then find the mean, median, and mode for the data.

Probability

Probability is the chance that an event will occur. Probability can be expressed as a ratio, a fraction, or a percentage. For example, when you flip a coin, the probability that the coin will land heads up is 1 in 2, or $\frac{1}{2}$, or 50 percent.

The probability that an event will happen can be expressed in the following formula.

$$P(\text{event}) = \frac{\text{Number of times the event can occur}}{\text{Total number of possible events}}$$

Example

A paper bag contains 25 blue marbles, 5 green marbles, 5 orange marbles, and 15 yellow marbles. If you close your eyes and pick a marble from the bag, what is the probability that it will be yellow?

$$P(\text{yellow marbles}) = \frac{15 \text{ yellow marbles}}{50 \text{ marbles total}}$$

$$P = \frac{15}{50}, \text{ or } \frac{3}{10}, \text{ or } 30\%$$

Practice

Each side of a cube has a letter on it. Two sides have *A*, three sides have *B*, and one side has *C*. If you roll the cube, what is the probability that A will land on top?

Area

The **area** of a surface is the number of square units that cover it. The front cover of your textbook has an area of about 600 cm².

Area of a Rectangle and a Square To find the area of a rectangle, multiply its length times its width. The formula for the area of a rectangle is

$$A = \ell \times w, \text{ or } A = \ell w$$

Since all four sides of a square have the same length, the area of a square is the length of one side multiplied by itself, or squared.

$$A = s \times s, \text{ or } A = s^2$$

Example

A scientist is studying the plants in a field that measures 75 m × 45 m. What is the area of the field?

$$A = \ell \times w$$
$$A = 75 \text{ m} \times 45 \text{ m}$$
$$A = 3,375 \text{ m}^2$$

Area of a Circle The formula for the area of a circle is

$$A = \pi \times r \times r, \text{ or } A = \pi r^2$$

The length of the radius is represented by r, and the value of π is approximately $\frac{22}{7}$.

Example

Find the area of a circle with a radius of 14 cm.

$$A = \pi r^2$$
$$A = 14 \times 14 \times \frac{22}{7}$$
$$A = 616 \text{ cm}^2$$

Practice

Find the area of a circle that has a radius of 21 m.

Circumference

The distance around a circle is called the circumference. The formula for finding the circumference of a circle is

$$C = 2 \times \pi \times r, \text{ or } C = 2\pi r$$

Example

The radius of a circle is 35 cm. What is its circumference?

$$C = 2\pi r$$
$$C = 2 \times 35 \times \frac{22}{7}$$
$$C = 220 \text{ cm}$$

Practice

What is the circumference of a circle with a radius of 28 m?

Volume

The volume of an object is the number of cubic units it contains. The volume of a wastebasket, for example, might be about 26,000 cm³.

Volume of a Rectangular Object To find the volume of a rectangular object, multiply the object's length times its width times its height.

$$V = \ell \times w \times h, \text{ or } V = \ell w h$$

Example

Find the volume of a box with length 24 cm, width 12 cm, and height 9 cm.

$$V = \ell w h$$
$$V = 24 \text{ cm} \times 12 \text{ cm} \times 9 \text{ cm}$$
$$V = 2,592 \text{ cm}^3$$

Practice

What is the volume of a rectangular object with length 17 cm, width 11 cm, and height 6 cm?

Fractions

A **fraction** is a way to express a part of a whole. In the fraction $\frac{4}{7}$, 4 is the numerator and 7 is the denominator.

Adding and Subtracting Fractions To add or subtract two or more fractions that have a common denominator, first add or subtract the numerators. Then write the sum or difference over the common denominator.

To find the sum or difference of fractions with different denominators, first find the least common multiple of the denominators. This is known as the least common denominator. Then convert each fraction to equivalent fractions with the least common denominator. Add or subtract the numerators. Then write the sum or difference over the common denominator.

Example

$$\frac{5}{6} - \frac{3}{4} = \frac{10}{12} - \frac{9}{12} = \frac{10-9}{12} = \frac{1}{12}$$

Multiplying Fractions To multiply two fractions, first multiply the two numerators, then multiply the two denominators.

Example

$$\frac{5}{6} \times \frac{2}{3} = \frac{5 \times 2}{6 \times 3} = \frac{10}{18} = \frac{5}{9}$$

Dividing Fractions Dividing by a fraction is the same as multiplying by its reciprocal. Reciprocals are numbers whose numerators and denominators have been switched. To divide one fraction by another, first invert the fraction you are dividing by—in other words, turn it upside down. Then multiply the two fractions.

Example

$$\frac{2}{5} \div \frac{7}{8} = \frac{2}{5} \times \frac{8}{7} = \frac{2 \times 8}{5 \times 7} = \frac{16}{35}$$

Practice

Solve the following: $\frac{3}{7} \div \frac{4}{5}$.

Decimals

Fractions whose denominators are 10, 100, or some other power of 10 are often expressed as decimals. For example, the fraction $\frac{9}{10}$ can be expressed as the decimal 0.9, and the fraction $\frac{7}{100}$ can be written as 0.07.

Adding and Subtracting With Decimals To add or subtract decimals, line up the decimal points before you carry out the operation.

Example

$$\begin{array}{r} 27.4 \\ + 6.19 \\ \hline 33.59 \end{array} \qquad \begin{array}{r} 278.635 \\ - 191.4 \\ \hline 87.235 \end{array}$$

Multiplying With Decimals When you multiply two numbers with decimals, the number of decimal places in the product is equal to the total number of decimal places in each number being multiplied.

Example

$$\begin{array}{rl} 46.2 & \text{(one decimal place)} \\ \times 2.37 & \text{(two decimal places)} \\ \hline 109.494 & \text{(three decimal places)} \end{array}$$

Dividing With Decimals To divide a decimal by a whole number, put the decimal point in the quotient above the decimal point in the dividend.

Example

$$15.5 \div 5$$
$$\begin{array}{r} 3.1 \\ 5\overline{)15.5} \end{array}$$

To divide a decimal by a decimal, you need to rewrite the divisor as a whole number. Do this by multiplying both the divisor and dividend by the same multiple of 10.

Example

$$1.68 \div 4.2 = 16.8 \div 42$$
$$\begin{array}{r} 0.4 \\ 42\overline{)16.8} \end{array}$$

Practice

Multiply 6.21 by 8.5.

Ratio and Proportion

A **ratio** compares two numbers by division. For example, suppose a scientist counts 800 wolves and 1,200 moose on an island. The ratio of wolves to moose can be written as a fraction, $\frac{800}{1,200}$, which can be reduced to $\frac{2}{3}$. The same ratio can also be expressed as 2 to 3 or 2 : 3.

A **proportion** is a mathematical sentence saying that two ratios are equivalent. For example, a proportion could state that $\frac{800 \text{ wolves}}{1,200 \text{ moose}} = \frac{2 \text{ wolves}}{3 \text{ moose}}$. You can sometimes set up a proportion to determine or estimate an unknown quantity. For example, suppose a scientist counts 25 beetles in an area of 10 square meters. The scientist wants to estimate the number of beetles in 100 square meters.

Example

1. Express the relationship between beetles and area as a ratio: $\frac{25}{10}$, simplified to $\frac{5}{2}$.
2. Set up a proportion, with x representing the number of beetles. The proportion can be stated as $\frac{5}{2} = \frac{x}{100}$.
3. Begin by cross-multiplying. In other words, multiply each fraction's numerator by the other fraction's denominator.

$$5 \times 100 = 2 \times x, \text{ or } 500 = 2x$$

4. To find the value of x, divide both sides by 2. The result is 250, or 250 beetles in 100 square meters.

Practice

Find the value of x in the following proportion: $\frac{6}{7} = \frac{x}{49}$.

Percentage

A **percentage** is a ratio that compares a number to 100. For example, there are 37 granite rocks in a collection that consists of 100 rocks. The ratio $\frac{37}{100}$ can be written as 37%. Granite rocks make up 37% of the rock collection.

You can calculate percentages of numbers other than 100 by setting up a proportion.

Example

Rain falls on 9 days out of 30 in June. What percentage of the days in June were rainy?

$$\frac{9 \text{ days}}{30 \text{ days}} = \frac{d\%}{100\%}$$

To find the value of d, begin by cross-multiplying, as for any proportion:

$$9 \times 100 = 30 \times d \quad d = \frac{900}{30} \quad d = 30$$

Practice

There are 300 marbles in a jar, and 42 of those marbles are blue. What percentage of the marbles are blue?

Significant Figures

The **precision** of a measurement depends on the instrument you use to take the measurement. For example, if the smallest unit on the ruler is millimeters, then the most precise measurement you can make will be in millimeters.

The sum or difference of measurements can only be as precise as the least precise measurement being added or subtracted. Round your answer so that it has the same number of digits after the decimal as the least precise measurement. Round up if the last digit is 5 or more, and round down if the last digit is 4 or less.

> **Example**
> Subtract a temperature of 5.2°C from the temperature 75.46°C.
>
> **75.46 − 5.2 = 70.26**
>
> 5.2 has the fewest digits after the decimal, so it is the least precise measurement. Since the last digit of the answer is 6, round up to 3. The most precise difference between the measurements is 70.3°C.

> **Practice**
> Add 26.4 m to 8.37 m. Round your answer according to the precision of the measurements.

Significant figures are the number of nonzero digits in a measurement. Zeroes between non-zero digits are also significant. For example, the measurements 12,500 L, 0.125 cm, and 2.05 kg all have three significant figures. When you multiply and divide measurements, the one with the fewest significant figures determines the number of significant figures in your answer.

> **Example**
> Multiply 110 g by 5.75 g.
>
> **110 × 5.75 = 632.5**
>
> Because 110 has only two significant figures, round the answer to 630 g.

Scientific Notation

A **factor** is a number that divides into another number with no remainder. In the example, the number 3 is used as a factor four times.

An **exponent** tells how many times a number is used as a factor. For example, $3 \times 3 \times 3 \times 3$ can be written as 3^4. The exponent 4 indicates that the number 3 is used as a factor four times. Another way of expressing this is to say that 81 is equal to 3 to the fourth power.

> **Example**
> $3^4 = 3 \times 3 \times 3 \times 3 = 81$

Scientific notation uses exponents and powers of ten to write very large or very small numbers in shorter form. When you write a number in scientific notation, you write the number as two factors. The first factor is any number between 1 and 10. The second factor is a power of 10, such as 10^3 or 10^6.

> **Example**
> The average distance between the planet Mercury and the sun is 58,000,000 km. To write the first factor in scientific notation, insert a decimal point in the original number so that you have a number between 1 and 10. In the case of 58,000,000, the number is 5.8.
>
> To determine the power of 10, count the number of places that the decimal point moved. In this case, it moved 7 places.
>
> **58,000,000 km = 5.8×10^7 km**

> **Practice**
> Express 6,590,000 in scientific notation.

Reading Comprehension Skills

You will improve your reading comprehension by using the Target Reading Skills described below.

Using Prior Knowledge

Your prior knowledge is what you already know before you begin to read about a topic. Building on what you already know gives you a head start on learning new information. Before you begin a new assignment, think about what you know. You might look at the headings and the visuals to spark your memory. You can list what you know. Then, as you read, consider questions like these.

- How does what you learn relate to what you know?

- How did something you already know help you learn something new?

- Did your original ideas agree with what you have just learned?

Asking Questions

Asking yourself questions is an excellent way to focus on and remember new information in your textbook. For example, you can turn the text headings into questions. Then your questions can guide you to identify the important information as you read. Look at these examples:

Heading: Using Seismographic Data

Question: How are seismographic data used?

Heading: Kinds of Faults

Question: What are the kinds of faults?

You do not have to limit your questions to text headings. Ask questions about anything that you need to clarify or that will help you understand the content. *What* and *how* are probably the most common question words, but you may also ask *why, who, when,* or *where* questions.

Previewing Visuals

Visuals are photographs, graphs, tables, diagrams, and illustrations. Visuals contain important information. Before you read, look at visuals and their labels and captions. This preview will help you prepare for what you will be reading.

Often you will be asked what you want to learn about a visual. For example, after you look at the normal fault diagram below, you might ask: What is the movement along a normal fault? Questions about visuals give you a purpose for reading—to answer your questions.

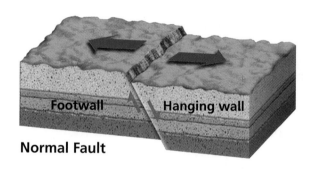

Footwall   **Hanging wall**

Normal Fault

Outlining

An outline shows the relationship between main ideas and supporting ideas. An outline has a formal structure. You write the main ideas, called topics, next to Roman numerals. The supporting ideas, called subtopics, are written under the main ideas and labeled A, B, C, and so on. An outline looks like this:

Technology and Society
I. Technology through history
II. The impact of technology on society
A.
B.

Identifying Main Ideas

When you are reading science material, it is important to try to understand the ideas and concepts that are in a passage. Each paragraph has a lot of information and detail. Good readers try to identify the most important—or biggest—idea in every paragraph or section. That's the main idea. The other information in the paragraph supports or further explains the main idea.

Sometimes main ideas are stated directly. In this book, some main ideas are identified for you as key concepts. These are printed in bold-face type. However, you must identify other main ideas yourself. In order to do this, you must identify all the ideas within a paragraph or section. Then ask yourself which idea is big enough to include all the other ideas.

Comparing and Contrasting

When you compare and contrast, you examine the similarities and differences between things. You can compare and contrast in a Venn diagram or in a table.

Venn Diagram A Venn diagram consists of two overlapping circles. In the space where the circles overlap, you write the characteristics that the two items have in common. In one of the circles outside the area of overlap, you write the differing features or characteristics of one of the items. In the other circle outside the area of overlap, you write the differing characteristics of the other item.

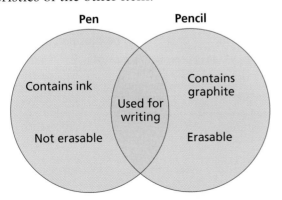

Pen — Pencil

Contains ink

Not erasable

Used for writing

Contains graphite

Erasable

Table In a compare/contrast table, you list the characteristics or features to be compared across the top of the table. Then list the items to be compared in the left column. Complete the table by filling in information about each characteristic or feature.

Blood Vessel	Function	Structure of Wall
Artery	Carries blood away from heart	
Capillary		
Vein		

Identifying Supporting Evidence

A hypothesis is a possible explanation for observations made by scientists or an answer to a scientific question. Scientists must carry out investigations and gather evidence that either supports or disproves the hypothesis.

Identifying the supporting evidence for a hypothesis or theory can help you understand the hypothesis or theory. Evidence consists of facts—information whose accuracy can be confirmed by testing or observation.

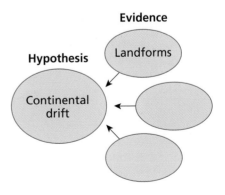

Evidence

Hypothesis — Landforms

Continental drift

Sequencing

A sequence is the order in which a series of events occurs. A flowchart or a cycle diagram can help you visualize a sequence.

Flowchart To make a flowchart, write a brief description of each step or event in a box. Place the boxes in order, with the first event at the top of the chart. Then draw an arrow to connect each step or event to the next.

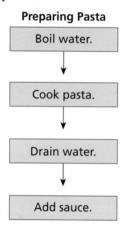

Preparing Pasta

Boil water.

Cook pasta.

Drain water.

Add sauce.

Cycle Diagram A cycle diagram shows a sequence that is continuous, or cyclical. A continuous sequence does not have an end because when the final event is over, the first event begins again. To create a cycle diagram, write the starting event in a box placed at the top of a page in the center. Then, moving in a clockwise direction, write each event in a box in its proper sequence. Draw arrows that connect each event to the one that occurs next.

Seasons of the Year

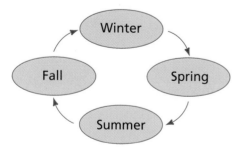

Relating Cause and Effect

Science involves many cause-and-effect relationships. A cause makes something happen. An effect is what happens. When you recognize that one event causes another, you are relating cause and effect.

Words like *cause*, *because*, *effect*, *affect*, and *result* often signal a cause or an effect. Sometimes an effect can have more than one cause, or a cause can produce several effects.

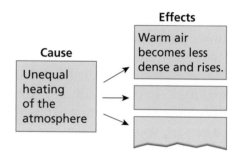

Cause

Unequal heating of the atmosphere

Effects

Warm air becomes less dense and rises.

Concept Mapping

Concept maps are useful tools for organizing information on any topic. A concept map begins with a main idea or core concept and shows how the idea can be subdivided into related subconcepts or smaller ideas.

You construct a concept map by placing concepts (usually nouns) in ovals and connecting them with linking words (usually verbs). The biggest concept or idea is placed in an oval at the top of the map. Related concepts are arranged in ovals below the big idea. The linking words connect the ovals.

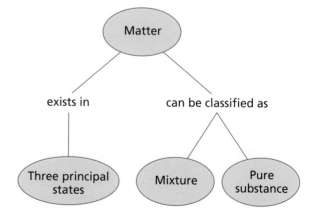

Matter

exists in

can be classified as

Three principal states

Mixture

Pure substance

Building Vocabulary

Knowing the meaning of these prefixes, suffixes, and roots will help you understand the meaning of words you do not recognize.

Word Origins Many science words come to English from other languages, such as Greek and Latin. By learning the meaning of a few common Greek and Latin roots, you can determine the meaning of unfamiliar science words.

Prefixes A prefix is a word part that is added at the beginning of a root or base word to change its meaning.

Suffixes A suffix is a word part that is added at the end of a root word to change the meaning.

Greek and Latin Roots		
Greek Roots	**Meaning**	**Example**
ast-	star	astronaut
geo-	Earth	geology
metron-	measure	kilometer
opt-	eye	optician
photo-	light	photograph
scop-	see	microscope
therm-	heat	thermostat
Latin Roots	**Meaning**	**Example**
aqua-	water	aquarium
aud-	hear	auditorium
duc-, duct-	lead	conduct
flect-	bend	reflect
fract-, frag-	break	fracture
ject-	throw	reject
luc-	light	lucid
spec-	see	inspect

Prefixes and Suffixes		
Prefix	**Meaning**	**Example**
com-, con-	with	communicate, concert
de-	from; down	decay
di-	two	divide
ex-, exo-	out	exhaust
in-, im-	in, into; not	inject, impossible
re-	again; back	reflect, recall
trans-	across	transfer
Suffix	**Meaning**	**Example**
-al	relating to	natural
-er, -or	one who	teacher, doctor
-ist	one who practices	scientist
-ity	state of	equality
-ology	study of	biology
-tion, -sion	state or quality of	reaction, tension

Safety Symbols

These symbols warn of possible dangers in the laboratory and remind you to work carefully.

 Safety Goggles Wear safety goggles to protect your eyes in any activity involving chemicals, flames or heating, or glassware.

 Lab Apron Wear a laboratory apron to protect your skin and clothing from damage.

 Breakage Handle breakable materials, such as glassware, with care. Do not touch broken glassware.

 Heat-Resistant Gloves Use an oven mitt or other hand protection when handling hot materials such as hot plates or hot glassware.

 Plastic Gloves Wear disposable plastic gloves when working with harmful chemicals and organisms. Keep your hands away from your face, and dispose of the gloves according to your teacher's instructions.

 Heating Use a clamp or tongs to pick up hot glassware. Do not touch hot objects with your bare hands.

 Flames Before you work with flames, tie back loose hair and clothing. Follow instructions from your teacher about lighting and extinguishing flames.

 No Flames When using flammable materials, make sure there are no flames, sparks, or other exposed heat sources present.

 Corrosive Chemical Avoid getting acid or other corrosive chemicals on your skin or clothing or in your eyes. Do not inhale the vapors. Wash your hands after the activity.

 Poison Do not let any poisonous chemical come into contact with your skin, and do not inhale its vapors. Wash your hands when you are finished with the activity.

 Fumes Work in a ventilated area when harmful vapors may be involved. Avoid inhaling vapors directly. Only test an odor when directed to do so by your teacher, and use a wafting motion to direct the vapor toward your nose.

 Sharp Object Scissors, scalpels, knives, needles, pins, and tacks can cut your skin. Always direct a sharp edge or point away from yourself and others.

 Animal Safety Treat live or preserved animals or animal parts with care to avoid harming the animals or yourself. Wash your hands when you are finished with the activity.

 Plant Safety Handle plants only as directed by your teacher. If you are allergic to certain plants, tell your teacher; do not do an activity involving those plants. Avoid touching harmful plants such as poison ivy. Wash your hands when you are finished with the activity.

 Electric Shock To avoid electric shock, never use electrical equipment around water, or when the equipment is wet or your hands are wet. Be sure cords are untangled and cannot trip anyone. Unplug equipment not in use.

 Physical Safety When an experiment involves physical activity, avoid injuring yourself or others. Alert your teacher if there is any reason you should not participate.

 Disposal Dispose of chemicals and other laboratory materials safely. Follow the instructions from your teacher.

 Hand Washing Wash your hands thoroughly when finished with the activity. Use antibacterial soap and warm water. Rinse well.

 General Safety Awareness When this symbol appears, follow the instructions provided. When you are asked to develop your own procedure in a lab, have your teacher approve your plan before you go further.

Science Safety Rules

General Precautions

Follow all instructions. Never perform activities without the approval and supervision of your teacher. Do not engage in horseplay. Never eat or drink in the laboratory. Keep work areas clean and uncluttered.

Dress Code

Wear safety goggles whenever you work with chemicals, glassware, heat sources such as burners, or any substance that might get into your eyes. If you wear contact lenses, notify your teacher.

Wear a lab apron and disposable plastic gloves whenever you work with corrosive chemicals or substances that can stain. Tie back long hair. Remove or tie back any article of clothing or jewelry that can hang down and touch chemicals, flames, or equipment. Roll up long sleeves. Never wear open shoes or sandals.

First Aid

Report all accidents, injuries, or fires to your teacher, no matter how minor. Be aware of the location of the first-aid kit, emergency equipment such as the fire extinguisher and fire blanket, and the nearest telephone. Know whom to contact in an emergency.

Heating and Fire Safety

Keep all combustible materials away from flames. When heating a substance in a test tube, make sure that the mouth of the tube is not pointed at you or anyone else. Never heat a liquid in a closed container. Use an oven mitt to pick up a container that has been heated.

Using Chemicals Safely

Never put your face near the mouth of a container that holds chemicals. Never touch, taste, or smell a chemical unless your teacher tells you to.

Use only those chemicals needed in the activity. Keep all containers closed when chemicals are not being used. Pour all chemicals over the sink or a container, not over your work surface. Dispose of excess chemicals as instructed by your teacher.

Be extra careful when working with acids or bases. When mixing an acid and water, always pour the water into the container first and then add the acid to the water. Never pour water into an acid. Wash chemical spills and splashes immediately with plenty of water.

Using Glassware Safely

If glassware is broken or chipped, notify your teacher immediately. Never handle broken or chipped glass with your bare hands.

Never force glass tubing or thermometers into a rubber stopper or rubber tubing. Have your teacher insert the glass tubing or thermometer if required for an activity.

Using Sharp Instruments

Handle sharp instruments with extreme care. Never cut material toward you; cut away from you.

Animal and Plant Safety

Never perform experiments that cause pain, discomfort, or harm to animals. Only handle animals if absolutely necessary. If you know that you are allergic to certain plants, molds, or animals, tell your teacher before doing an activity in which these are used. Wash your hands thoroughly after any activity involving animals, animal parts, plants, plant parts, or soil.

During field work, wear long pants, long sleeves, socks, and closed shoes. Avoid poisonous plants and fungi as well as plants with thorns.

End-of-Experiment Rules

Unplug all electrical equipment. Clean up your work area. Dispose of waste materials as instructed by your teacher. Wash your hands after every experiment.

The microscope is an essential tool in the study of life science. It allows you to see things that are too small to be seen with the unaided eye.

You will probably use a compound microscope like the one you see here. The compound microscope has more than one lens that magnifies the object you view.

Typically, a compound microscope has one lens in the eyepiece, the part you look through. The eyepiece lens usually magnifies 10×. Any object you view through this lens would appear 10 times larger than it is.

The compound microscope may contain one or two other lenses called objective lenses. If there are two objective lenses, they are called the low-power and high-power objective lenses. The low-power objective lens usually magnifies 10×. The high-power objective lens usually magnifies 40×.

To calculate the total magnification with which you are viewing an object, multiply the magnification of the eyepiece lens by the magnification of the objective lens you are using. For example, the eyepiece's magnification of 10× multiplied by the low-power objective's magnification of 10× equals a total magnification of 100×.

Use the photo of the compound microscope to become familiar with the parts of the microscope and their functions.

The Parts of a Compound Microscope

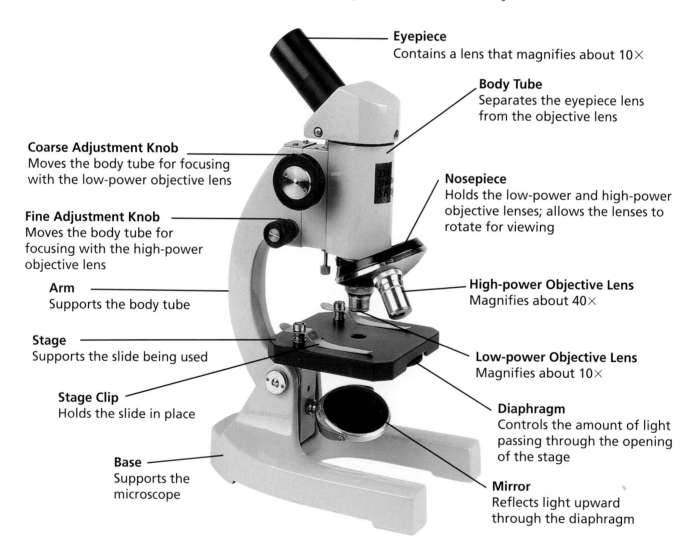

Eyepiece
Contains a lens that magnifies about 10×

Body Tube
Separates the eyepiece lens from the objective lens

Coarse Adjustment Knob
Moves the body tube for focusing with the low-power objective lens

Nosepiece
Holds the low-power and high-power objective lenses; allows the lenses to rotate for viewing

Fine Adjustment Knob
Moves the body tube for focusing with the high-power objective lens

Arm
Supports the body tube

High-power Objective Lens
Magnifies about 40×

Stage
Supports the slide being used

Low-power Objective Lens
Magnifies about 10×

Stage Clip
Holds the slide in place

Diaphragm
Controls the amount of light passing through the opening of the stage

Base
Supports the microscope

Mirror
Reflects light upward through the diaphragm

Using the Microscope

Use the following procedures when you are working with a microscope.

1. To carry the microscope, grasp the microscope's arm with one hand. Place your other hand under the base.
2. Place the microscope on a table with the arm toward you.
3. Turn the coarse adjustment knob to raise the body tube.
4. Revolve the nosepiece until the low-power objective lens clicks into place.
5. Adjust the diaphragm. While looking through the eyepiece, also adjust the mirror until you see a bright white circle of light. **CAUTION:** *Never use direct sunlight as a light source.*
6. Place a slide on the stage. Center the specimen over the opening on the stage. Use the stage clips to hold the slide in place. **CAUTION:** *Glass slides are fragile.*
7. Look at the stage from the side. Carefully turn the coarse adjustment knob to lower the body tube until the low-power objective almost touches the slide.
8. Looking through the eyepiece, very slowly turn the coarse adjustment knob until the specimen comes into focus.
9. To switch to the high-power objective lens, look at the microscope from the side. Carefully revolve the nosepiece until the high-power objective lens clicks into place. Make sure the lens does not hit the slide.
10. Looking through the eyepiece, turn the fine adjustment knob until the specimen comes into focus.

Making a Wet-Mount Slide

Use the following procedures to make a wet-mount slide of a specimen.

1. Obtain a clean microscope slide and a coverslip. **CAUTION:** *Glass slides and coverslips are fragile.*
2. Place the specimen on the slide. The specimen must be thin enough for light to pass through it.
3. Using a plastic dropper, place a drop of water on the specimen.
4. Gently place one edge of the coverslip against the slide so that it touches the edge of the water drop at a 45° angle. Slowly lower the coverslip over the specimen. If air bubbles are trapped beneath the coverslip, tap the coverslip gently with the eraser end of a pencil.
5. Remove any excess water at the edge of the coverslip with a paper towel.

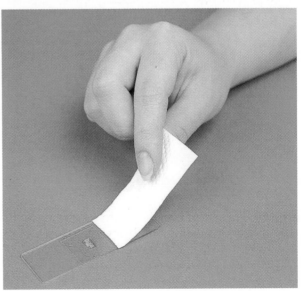

English and Spanish Glossary

antibody A molecule that binds to a specific marker molecule. (p. 82)
anticuerpo Molécula que se adhiere a una molécula específica.

appeal A written request submitted to a higher court asking that the verdict in a trial be reversed. (p. 128)
apelar Petición escrita presentada a la corte pidiendo revocar el veredicto del jurado.

autopsy A detailed exam of a dead body. (p. 11)
autopsia Examen detallado de un cadáver.

bail Money or property that is pledged to the court to ensure that a person will appear at trial. (p. 108)
fianza Dinero o propiedad que se presenta a la corte para asegurar que la persona se presente a juicio.

bailiff A law enforcement officer who helps the judge keep order in the court. (p. 114)
alguacil de la corte Oficial de la justicia que ayuda al juez a mantener orden en la corte.

Bill of Rights A list of individual rights that the government promises to protect; the first ten amendments of the U.S. Constitution. (p. 107)
Carta de Derechos Lista de derechos bajo la protección del gobierno; las primeras diez enmiendas de la Constitución de los Estados Unidos.

burglary The act of breaking into a building with the intent of stealing an object. (p. 6)
allanamiento de morada Entrar sin autorización a un domicilio con intento de robo.

cartridge The metal case that contains a bullet, gunpowder, and primer. (p. 65)
cartucho Recipiente metálico que contiene una bala, pólvora y fulminante.

cast An object made by filling a mold with a liquid that takes the shape of the mold as it changes to a solid. (p. 49)
yeso Objeto creado al introducir un líquido en un molde que toma la horma del molde al tornarse en un sólido.

chain of custody A written record of who had control of a piece of evidence from the time it was collected. (p. 37)
cadena de custodia Seguimiento escrito del control de la evidencia desde el momento en que se recolecta.

chromatography One way to separate a mixture based on the properties of its components. (p. 60)
cromatografía Una manera de separar una mezcla basada en las propiedades de sus componentes.

classifying Grouping objects together that are alike in some way. (p. 56)
clasificar Agrupar objetos que se asemejan de alguna manera.

cold case An old, unsolved criminal case. (p. 93)
caso cerrado Caso criminal antiguo y sin resolver.

communicating The sharing of ideas with other people. The ideas may be written or spoken. (p. 21)
comunicar Compartir ideas con otra gente. Estas ideas pueden ser escritas o habladas.

concentration The amount of one substance in a given mass or volume of a mixture. (p. 59)
concentración La cantidad de una sustancia en cierta determinada masa o volumen de una mezcla.

contamination The adding of unwanted material to an object. (p. 34)
contaminación Agregar material no deseado a un objeto.

crime scene investigator (CSI) A person who is trained to record, collect, and test evidence from a crime scene. (p. 10)
Investigador de la escena del crimen Persona entrenada para grabar, recolectar y examinar la evidencia de la escena de un crimen.

cross-examination The process in which one lawyer asks questions of another lawyer's witness. (p. 119)
contrainterrogación Preguntas hechas por un abogado a un testigo de la contraparte.

D

defendant A person who is charged with a crime. (p. 111)
acusado Persona a la que se le culpa de un crimen.

density The ratio of the mass of a substance to its volume. (p. 12)
densidad Relación entre el peso de una sustancia y su volumen.

direct evidence A firsthand observation made by an eyewitness. (p. 25)
evidencia directa Observación directa hecha por un testigo ocular.

DNA The deoxyribonucleic acid molecules that control the production of proteins in the human body. (p. 89)
ADN Las moléculas de ácido desoxirribonucleico que controlan la producción de proteínas en el cuerpo humano.

DNA profile A distinctive pattern of DNA fragments that can be used to match a biological sample to an individual. (p. 90)
Pérfil de ADN Patrón distintivo de fragmentos del ADN que se pueden usar para emparejar una muestra biológica a un individuo.

E

endangered species A species whose numbers are so small that it may disappear from the world. (p. 95)
especies en vía de extinción Especies cuyo número en existencia es tan pequeño que pueden desaparecer de la Tierra.

evidence In the legal system, something that can be presented in court to make a point during a trial. (p. 7)
evidencia En el sistema legal, lo que se presenta en corte para reforzar un punto ante el juzgado.

exhibit A physical object that is used to make a point in court. (p. 117)
prueba Objeto que se usa en corte para fundamentar un punto.

expert witness A person who has knowledge of a specific area of study. (p. 120)
testigo pericial Persona con conocimiento específico en un área de estudio.

eyewitness A person who directly observes an event. (p. 25)
testigo ocular Persona que observa un acontecimiento directamente.

F

felony A serious crime, such as murder or kidnapping. (p. 109)
delito mayor Un crimen grave, tal como un asesinato o un secuestro.

forensic science The use of scientific knowledge and methods to answer legal questions. (p. 7)
ciencia forense El uso de conocimientos y métodos científicos para responder cuestiones legales.

foreperson The juror who manages the discussion in the jury room. (p. 125)
presidente del jurado miembro del jurado que modera la discusión en la sala de deliberación.

gene A section of DNA that contains information that cells need to make a protein. (p. 89)
gen Sección del ADN que contiene la información que necesitan las células para producir una proteína.

gunshot residue The unburned gunpowder and primer that sprays out of a gun barrel and trigger hole. (p. 66)
residuo de disparo La pólvora y el fulminante que se rocea fuera del cañon y del hueco del gatillo de un arma de fuego.

hemoglobin The molecule in red blood cells that carries oxygen to cells in the body. (p. 81)
hemoglobina Molécula en las células rojas que transporta oxígeno a las células del cuerpo.

hypothesis A possible explanation for a set of observations. (p. 9)
hipótesis Explicación posible para un grupo de observaciones.

impression The pattern left when an object is pressed into a surface. An impression has three dimensions—length, width, and depth. (p. 44)
impresión Marca o huella que deja un objeto al apretarse contra una superficie. Una impresión tiene tres dimensiones: longitud, anchura y profundidad.

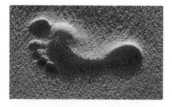

imprint A print that is flat and has only two dimensions. (p. 44)
huella Impresión plana de solo dos dimensiones.

inferring Offering a reasoned opinion based on observations and experience. (p. 8)
inferir Ofrecer una interpretación basada en observaciones y en conocimiento previo.

judge The person who controls what takes place in a courtroom; the person who applies the law to decide who is right when the lawyers disagree. (p. 111; p. 114)
juez Persona que controla lo que ocurre en la sala de justicia; esta persona aplica la ley para decidir quien tiene la razón cuando los abogados están en desacuerdo.

jury A group of ordinary citizens who listen to the evidence in a trial and decide whether the defendant is guilty. (p. 108)
jurado Grupo de ciudadanos comunes y corrientes que observan la evidencia de un juicio y deciden si el acusado es culpable.

latent print A hidden print made when sweat or oil is transferred from the ridges of a finger to the surface of an object. (p. 76)
huella latente Huella oculta que se crea cuando sudor o aceite se transfiere de la cresta de los dedos a la superficie de un objeto.

luminol A chemical that emits a blue glow when it comes in contact with blood. (p. 81)
luminol Sustancia química que emite un brillo de color azul cuando entra en contacto con la sangre.

medical examiner A medical doctor who will come to observe a body when there is a sudden or suspicious death. (p. 11)
médico forense Médico que analiza un cadáver cuando ocurre una muerte repentina o sospechosa.

microscope An instrument that makes very small objects look larger. (p. 61)
microscopio Instrumento que permite ver objetos pequeños a una escala más grande.

misdemeanor A crime, such as shoplifting, that is less serious than a felony. (p. 109)
delito menor Crimen, tal como el hurto en tiendas, de menor gravedad que un delito mayor.

modus operandi The way a person approaches a task; often abbreviated as MO. (p. 27)
modus operandi o modo de operar La manera en que una persona aborda una tarea; se abrevia como MO.

observing Using one or more of your senses to gather information. (p. 7)
observar El uso de uno o más de tus sentidos para reunir información.

physical evidence In the legal system, any object that can be used to prove that a fact is true. (p. 30)
evidencia física Bajo el sistema legal, cualquier objeto que se pueda usar para comprobar la veracidad de un hecho.

plastic print An impression of a fingertip left in a soft surface. (p. 76)
huella dactilar La impresión que deja la yema del dedo en una superficie suave.

plea bargain An agreement between the prosecutor and the defense in which the accused pleads guilty in return for a lesser charge or a lighter punishment. (p. 112)
trato declaratorio Acuerdo entre el fiscal y el abogado defensor en el que el acusado se confiesa culpable a cambio de una pena o un castigo más noble.

predicting Stating an opinion about what will happen in the future. (p. 8)
predecir Dar una opinión sobre lo que va a suceder en el futuro.

print A mark left when an object is pressed against the surface of another object. (p. 44)
imprimir Marca que se obtiene al sujetar un objeto contra la superficie de otro objeto.

probability A measure of the chance that an event will happen. (p. 92)
probabilidad Cálculo cuantitativo de la posibilidad de que ocurra un evento.

probable cause A reasonable belief that a person has committed a crime. (p. 110)
motivos fundados Información o conocimiento que da a creer que una persona ha cometido un delito.

probation A sentence which allows a person convicted of a crime to remain in the community under the close supervision of a probation officer. (p. 127)
libertad condicional Sentencia que permite a la persona condenada por un crimen permanecer en la comunidad bajo la supervisión de un funcionario de la ley.

prosecutor The lawyer who represents the state in a criminal case. (p. 111)
fiscal Abogado que representa al estado en un caso criminal.

protein A molecule that your body uses to build tissues and organs. Some proteins control the chemical reactions that take place in cells. (p. 89)
proteína Molécula que usa el cuerpo para crear tejidos y órganos. Algunas proteínas controlan las reacciones químicas que ocurren dentro de las células.

public defender A lawyer who works for the state and represents defendants in criminal cases. (p. 111)
defensor del pueblo Abogado empleado por el estado que representa a los acusados en casos criminales.

replication The process by which a DNA molecule makes a copy of itself. (p. 91)
replicación Proceso en el que una molécula de ADN se copia a si misma.

ridge A raised line on a fingertip that corresponds to a line on a fingerprint. (p. 75)
cresta Línea en relieve en la punta del dedo que corresponde a una línea en una huella digital.

rifling The spiral grooves inside a gun barrel and the marks left on a bullet by the grooves. (p. 66)
estriado Marcas u ondulaciones que se encuentran dentro del cañón de un arma de fuego y que éstas dejan en la bala.

English and Spanish Glossary

S

scale The ratio of a model to the actual size of an object. (p. 20)
escala La proporción de un modelo en comparación a su tamaño real.

search warrant A written court order that allows police to search for specific objects at a given place and time. (p. 51)
orden de registro Orden escrita por la corte que permite que la policía busque objetos específicos en un tiempo y lugar determinado.

sketch A rough drawing that is done quickly and without much detail. (p. 20)
bosquejo Dibujo hecho con rapidez y sin mucho detalle.

skid mark The mark left when a vehicle with locked wheels slides along a road surface. (p. 46)
huella de resbalón Marca que deja las llantas de un vehículo al bloquearse y deslizarse en la superficie de la carretera.

surveillance camera A camera that watches over and records what occurs in or around banks, stores, and other public spaces. (p. 29)
cámara de vigilancia Cámara que monitorea y graba lo que ocurre en bancos, almacenes, espacios públicos a sus alrededores.

T

testimony Statements made by a sworn witness in a court of law. (p. 118)
testimonio Declaración hecha bajo juramento por un testigo en la corte de justicia.

trace evidence Tiny amounts of physical evidence that are transferred at a crime scene. (p. 54)
evidencia de rastro Pequeñas cantidades de evidencia física encontradas en una escena de crimen.

V

verdict The decision a jury makes after they review the evidence. (p. 125)
veredicto Decisión del jurado después de deliberar sobre la evidencia.

visible print A fingerprint that can be seen. (p. 76)
huella visible Huella dactilar que se puede ver.

voiceprint A graph that plots the pitch and loudness of sound over time. (p. 99)
impresión vocal Una gráfica que graba y demuestra el tono y volumen del sonido por un tiempo determinado.

Page numbers for key terms are printed in **boldface** type.
Page numbers for illustrations, maps, and charts are printed in *italics*.

Index

A

ABO blood groups 82
accelerants 63
accused, rights of the. *See* **Bill of Rights**
AFIS (automated fingerprint identification system) 79
altered documents, identifying 98
amendments to U.S. Constitution 107–108
anthropologist, forensic *11*
antibodies 82
appeal **128**
arch (fingerprint pattern) *75*
Archimedes 12
arrest
 making 110
 person's rights before, during, and after 107–108
arson investigations 62–63
art, detecting fake 13
artist, forensic 28, 86–87
autopsy **11**

B

bail **108**
 setting 111
bail bonds *111*
bailiff **114**
base pairs in DNA 89, 91, 92
biathlon *64*
Bill of Rights **107**–108
blood
 classifying 82–83
 isolating DNA from 90
 searching for 81
 testing for 81
bloodstain patterns, analyzing *84*–85
blood types 82–83
booking a suspect 110
bullet 65
 evidence from 66
 testing firearm with 67
burden of proof
 at trial 125
 during appeal 128
burglary **6**
 investigating scene of 7–9

C

CAD software 20
cameras
 recording crime scene with 19
 surveillance **29**
cartridges 65
 comparing 67
cast **49**
 comparing tire to *50*
chain of custody **37**
charging the defendant 111
chromatography **60**
classifying *9*, **56**, 133
clerk, court 114, *115*, 117
closing arguments 116
clothing, CSI
 to prevent contamination 34
 protective 38
clues vs. evidence 7
coding crime data 22
CODIS (Combined DNA Index System) 93
cold cases 93
combustion 62
communicating *9*, **21**, 133
comparison microscope *61*
 analyzing firearms evidence with 67
computer(s). *See also* **database**
 bloodstain pattern analysis by 85
 facial recognition software for 29
 fingerprint identification systems 79
 making scale drawings on 20
 mapping crime with 22–23
 modeling crime scene on 122–123
 sketching criminal on 28
computer-aided drafting (CAD) software 20
concentration **59**
constitution 107
 U.S. Constitution 51, 107–108
contamination **34**
content clues in writing samples 98
court(s)
 bringing evidence to. *See* **trial**
 contempt of 114
 employees of 114
 levels of 128
 organization of courtroom *114*

court clerk 114
 list of exhibits kept by 117
 swearing in jury *115*
court reporter 114
crimes, types of 109
crime scene investigation 4–38
 eyewitnesses and 24–28
 forensic science methods 12–13
 inquiry skills used in 7–9
 keeping evidence useful 34–37
 making model of crime scene 122–123
 recording a crime scene 18–21
 organizing a search 33
 securing a crime scene 17
 teamwork and 10–11
 transfer of physical evidence 30
crime scene investigator (CSI) **10**
 protecting 38
cross-examination **119**
custody, chain of 37

D

database
 comparing prints using 50
 DNA 93
 fingerprint identification using 79
 of firearms evidence 68
 Paint Data Query (PDQ) 58
decision of jury. *See* **verdict**
defendant **111**
 charging 111, 112
 sentencing of 127
 as witness 119
defense, lawyer for 111
 appeal by **128**
 case argued by 116
 in pretrial hearing 112
density **12**
dental stone 49
deoxyribonucleic acid. *See* **DNA**
detectives 10
dictating notes 21
Dillinger, John *74*
direct evidence 24–25
 problems with 25
direct examination **118**
DNA 88–**89**, 90–95
 collecting and isolating *90*
 replication of **91**
 structure of *89*

Index

Page numbers for key terms are printed in **boldface** type.
Page numbers for illustrations, maps, and charts are printed in *italics*.

Index

Page numbers for key terms are printed in **boldface** type.
Page numbers for illustrations, maps, and charts are printed in *italics*.

Acknowledgments

Staff Credits

The people who made up the **Prentice Hall** *Forensic Science* team—representing design services, editorial, editorial services, image services, marketing services, planning and budgeting, product planning, production services, and publishing processes—are listed below. Boldface type denotes the core team members.

Leann Davis Alspaugh, Suzanne Biron, Peggy Bliss, Jim Brady, **Diane Braff,** Kerry Cashman, Thomas Ferreira, **Jonathan Fisher,** Paula Gogan-Porter, Louise Gachet, **Sandra Graff,** Susan Hutchinson, Etta Jacobs, **Greg Lam,** Russ Lappa, John McClure, Brent McKenzie, Rich McMahon, Julia F. Osborne, Cyndy Patrick, Linda Punskovsky, **Paul M. Ramos,** Rashid Ross, **Siri Schwartzman, Malti Sharma,** Laurel Smith, Nancy Smith, Ted Smykal, Emily Soltanoff, Kira Thaler, Adam Velthaus, Ana Sofia Villaveces, Roberta Warshaw, **Merce Wilczek,** Jenny Wong, John Wong

Additional Credits

Karen Beck, Carey Ann Gallini, Steve McEntee

Cover Design

Robert Brook Allen

Photography

Front cover, background, Comstock Premium/Alamy; **magnifying lens,** Mikael Karlsson/Alamy; **all others,** iStockphoto.

Back cover, background, Comstock Premium/Alamy; **magnifying lens,** Mikael Karlsson/Alamy; **footprint,** iStockphoto.

Page iv m, Jim Brady; **v,** AP Photo/Peoria Journal Star, Matt Dayhoff; **v inset t,** Dr. Dennis Kunkel/Visuals Unlimited; **v inset b,** Andrew Syred/SPL/Photo Researchers, Inc.; **vi t,** Jim Brady; **vi b,** Siri Schwartzman.

Chapter 1
Pages 4–5, AP Photo/Steve Miller; **5,** Richard Haynes; **7,** Cyril Laubscher/Dorling Kindersley; **10,** Patrick Schneider/The Charlotte Oberserver/Polaris; **11 l,** Patrick Zachmann/Magnum Photos; **11 r,** Horacio Villalobos/Corbis; **13,** Museum Conservation Institute/Smithsonian Institution; **17,** Reuters/Corbis; **18 both,** Bob Krist/Corbis; **19 l,** Bill Ross/Corbis; **19 r,** Siri Schwartzman; **21,** Siri Schwartzman; **23,** A. Ramey/PhotoEdit; **25 both,** Richard Haynes; **26–27,** Russ Lappa; **27,** Courtesy of San Matteo Sheriff's Department; **28 t,** Brad Markel/Liaison/Getty Images, Inc.; **28 m,** AP Photo/David Longstreath; **28 b all,** Geoff Dann/Dorling Kindersley; **29,** Shmuel Thaler/Index Stock Imagery, Inc.; **30,** AP Photo/Peoria Journal Star, Matt Dayhoff; **30 inset t,** Dr. Dennis Kunkel/Visuals Unlimited; **30 inset b,** Andrew Syred/SPL/Photo Researchers, Inc.; **31 l,** Collection Roger-Viollet/The Image Works; **31 r,** AP Photo/Al Goldis; **32–33,** John Giles/PA; **35,** Siri Schwartzman; **36,** Bruce Cotler/911 Pictures; **38,** AP Photo/Potomac News, Dave Ellis; **39,** John Giles/PA; **41,** AP photo/The Bakersfield Californian, Casey Christie.

Chapter 2
Pages 42–43, Paul J. Penders, Connecticut Department of Public Safety, Forensic Photo Unit; **43,** Russ Lappa; **44 l,** imagestopshop/Alamy; **44 r,** A ET E LAPIED/Peter Arnold; **45 t,** Sean Justice/Getty Images, Inc.; **45 b,** Jess Alford/Getty Images, Inc.; **46,** Robert Stolarik/Polaris Images; **47 all,** Jim Brady; **49 all,** Sirchie Finger Print Laboratories; **50,** Alain Nogues/Corbis; **51,** James Messerschmidt/Polaris Images; **53,** Russ Lappa; **54,** Michael Sofronski/Polaris Images; **55,** Jim Brady; **56,** Ron Kimball/Ron Kimball Stock; **56 insets,** Reprinted from *Criminalistics: An Introduction to Forensic Science,* 9th Edition; **57 l,** Richard Haynes; **57 r,** Eric Glenn/Getty Images, Inc.; **57 inset tr,** © 2004 Richard Megna/Fundamental Photographs; **57 inset tl,** Dennis Kunkel; **57 inset b,** Jim Zuckerman/Corbis; **58,** Eye of Science/Photo Researchers, Inc.; **59 t,** J. Burgess/Photo Researchers, Inc.; **59 b,** George Diebold Photography/Getty Images, Inc.; **61,** Spencer Grant/Photo Researchers, Inc.; **62,** Robert Stolarik/Polaris Images; **63 t,** Billy Hustace/Getty Images, Inc.; **63 b,** New Jersey State Police; **64,** Martin Schutt/epa/Corbis; **65 l,** Dorling Kindersley; **65 r,** Jim Brady; **66 all,** Jim Brady; **67 l,** John Nixon; **67 m,** John Nixon; **67 r,** Courtesy of Ronald Welsh, Bureau of Forensic Services, Central Valley Laboratory, Ripon, California; **68,** Brooks Kraft/Corbis.

Chapter 3
Pages 72–73, N.R. Rowan/ Custom Medical Stock Photo; **73,** Jim Brady; **74,** Hulton Archive/Getty Images, Inc.; **75 all,** Dorling Kindersley; **76 l, m,** James King-Holmes/Photo Researchers, Inc.; **76 r,** John Berry/Syracuse Newspapers/The Image Works; **77 tl,** Katz/FSP; **77 tr,** Courtesy of the ATF taken with the Coherent TracER; **77 b,** Jochen Tack/Das Fotoarchiv/Peter Arnold; **78 t,** James King-Holmes/Photo Researchers, Inc.; **78 b both,** iStockphoto; **80,** Bettmann/Corbis; **81 l,** Jochen Tack/Das Fotoarchiv/Peter Arnold; **81 r,** Andrew Syred/Getty Images, Inc.; **82,** Jean Claude Revy/ISM/Phototake USA; **84 all,** Courtesy, A.Y. Wonder; **86–87 all,** Michael Donne, University of Manchester/Photo Researchers, Inc.; **88,** AP Photo/Keith Srakocic; **90 l,** Courtesy of Tri-tech Inc., Southport, NC, www.tritechusa.com; **90 r,** Tek Image/Photo Researchers, Inc.; **91,** Courtesy: Pacific Northwest National Laboratory; **94,** Bettmann/Corbis; **94 inset,** Alain Pol, ISM/SPL/Photo Researchers, Inc.; **95,** Tom Brakefield/Corbis; **96,** Prentice Hall; **97,** Allan Tannenbaum//Time Life Pictures/Getty Images, Inc.; **98,** DC LIVE/Forensics from Enhancedaudio.com, Courtesy of Tracer Technology; **100,** Russ Lappa; **101 t,** Alain Pol, ISM/SPL/Photo Researchers, Inc.; **101 b,** Katz/FSP.

Chapter 4
Pages 104–105, Jerry Whaley/Alamy; **105,** Jim Brady; **107 l,** Roger-Viollet/The Image Works; **107 r,** SuperStock, Inc./SuperStock; **109 l,** AP Photo; **109 r,** Royalty-Free/Corbis; **110,** AP Photo/Akira Ono; **111,** Peter Horree/Alamy; **113,** Supplied by Capital Pictures; **113 television,** iStockphoto; **117,** Photo by Rex USA; **120,** Photo by Rex USA; **122–123 all,** Courtesy of 3rdTech, Inc.; **124,** Agora Museum, Athens; **128,** Michelangelo Gratton/Getty Images, Inc.

Page 132, Tony Freeman/PhotoEdit; **133 t,** Russ Lappa; **133 m,** Richard Haynes; **133 b,** Russ Lappa; **134,** Richard Haynes; **136,** Richard Haynes; **169t,** Dorling Kindersley; **169 b,** Richard Haynes; **141,** Imagestop/Phototake; **144,** Richard Haynes; **151,** Richard Haynes; **152,** Russ Lappa; **153 both,** Russ Lappa; **154 t,** A ET E LAPIED/Peter Arnold; **154 b,** Spencer Grant/Photo Researchers, Inc.; **156 t,** Jim Brady; **156 m,** Peter Horree/Alamy; **156 b,** SuperStock, Inc./SuperStock.

TAPAS, WINES & GOOD TIMES

DON AND MARGE FOSTER

CONTEMPORARY
BOOKS, INC.
CHICAGO ▪ NEW YORK

CONTENTS

INTRODUCTION

This book is more than a collection of recipes, more than just an introduction to Spain's "little foods" or to Spanish cookery. It's a visit to Spain—her sights, sounds, smells, tastes—and it's a visit you can enjoy right in your own kitchen. Sharing tapas with family and friends is the best possible way to visit Spain without being there, even better than a stack of travel brochures or Uncle Ned's slide show. Why? Because all your senses are involved. While you prepare, eat, inhale, observe, and talk about tapas, you'll be conjuring up flavors (gastronomic and otherwise) that would be impossible to duplicate in any other way.

If you've just returned from the Iberian Peninsula, use this book to recapture those moments spent in the cafés, restaurants, and other gathering places of Spain. If you're planning your first visit (or your first revisit) use these recipes to savor what's in store. Discovering tapas—how they're made, who eats them, where, when, and why—is your best guarantee of a self-confident enjoyment of Spain and her people. As any Hispanophile will tell you, tapas and drinks at a sidewalk café are as revealing and as thorough an exposure to Spain as a museum or castle tour. A lot more fun, too.

One of the things you'll learn from this book is that you can go as far as you like with tapas. Use them as appetizers or snacks, as a party food or side dish, as a quick no-fuss, no-fail meal or a leisurely gourmet buffet. All this with a minimum of effort. America's leading authority on snack foods, the late James Beard, put it as succinctly as anyone could when he pronounced Spanish tapas "marvelous, absolutely delicious. So easy to serve and to eat."

Just as important, you can go as far as you like with the ambience of tapas. Convert your den into a tapa bar; set up a sidewalk café in your backyard or on your patio; summon friends around the kitchen table for a *tertulia*—all, of course, accompanied by the dynamic duo of tapas and drinks. This book will show you how and, in the process, involve you in the excitement and cheer that is the tapa way of life.

In short, you're about to embark upon the culinary adventure of your life. Hemingway wrote of the "moveable feast" that was Paris in the twenties. Tapas are moveable Hispanic feasts in miniature—expressions of the moment, remembrances of things past, anticipations of the future—to be enjoyed wherever you are: in a tapa bar, sidewalk café, restaurant, or *en casa*.

A word about the arrangement of your Spanish adventure book. In Part I we will be discussing the what, where, when, and how-to of tapas. Specifically, Chapter 1 answers the question "What *is* a tapa?" Chapter 2 emphasizes the where and when of tapa consumption in Spain, including such "wheres" as *tascas*, sidewalk cafés, and restaurants and "whens" like the tertulia and *paseo*. Chapter 3 explains how to bring the tapa way of life into the home and outlines the

1

hardware and software requirements of tapa entertaining. Chapters 4 and 5 expose the two best-kept secrets of the tapa way of life: Spanish wines and seasonings.

In Part II, Tapa Parties, we'll explore ways to entertain with tapas, including how to bring tapas into your home as appetizers, snacks, and meals in parties, buffets, holiday get-togethers, and more. We'll include recipes, provide drink suggestions, and offer hints on ambience. After a party or two, you're ready to move on to Part III, a multifarious collection of authentic recipes gathered from tapa bars throughout Spain.

More or less, we have grouped the tapa recipes in Part III according to the traditional order of serving and eating in Spain, which is the same sequence many Spaniards choose to consume tapas. In Chapter 13 we feature salads and finger-foods (*ensaladas y entremeses*). Chapter 14 covers eggs and cheeses (*huevos y quesos*), Chapter 15 contains vegetable (*verdura*) recipes, and Chapter 16 focuses on rice (*arroces*). Then come fish and seafood (*pescados y mariscos*) in Chapter 17; pork, beef, and sausage (*carnes*) in Chapter 18; then poultry and game (*aves y caza*) in Chapter 19; and, finally, for the more adventurous Hispanophile, exotic tapas.

PART ONE
ABOUT TAPAS

CHAPTER ONE
THE TAPA ADVENTURE

What's a tapa? Tapas are bite-size snacks served in cafés, bars, restaurants, and just about every other eating and drinking place in Spain. A tapa can be hot, cold, or room temperature; fried, broiled, grilled, roasted, smoked, cured, baked, sautéed, raw, or marinated; made of meat, fish, shellfish, vegetables, whatever; eaten with a miniature fork, toothpicks, or out of hand.

As legend has it, the tapa—the word means "lid"—was a piece of bread placed on a wine glass to keep out the flies. Spaniards, a frugal people who love to eat as they drink, soon began nibbling their edible lids as they sipped their *vinos*. Nibbling increased as scraps of ham, cheese, and other edibles were used to cover the glasses. The next step was inevitable: tapas became a Spanish "free lunch."

Nowadays seldom free, these edible "lids" have evolved through centuries of continuous nibbling into bite-size snacks served throughout Spain—in the sidewalk cafés of Madrid, *bodegas* of Jerez, gourmet eating clubs of the Basque country, and beach bars that line the Costa del Sol. In hotel bars, restaurants, airport snack counters, bus terminals, department-store cafeterias. Walk into the humblest bar in Extremadura, and on the counter you'll find a plate of marinated olives or live mussels or a tortilla cut into strips; in the five-fork restaurants of Madrid, you'll find the very same olives, mussels, and tortilla strips, and more.

How do Spanish tapas differ from French *hors d'oeuvres*, Italian *antipasto*, Chinese *dim sum*, Swedish *smorgasbord*, German *Vorspeise*, Russian *azkuska*, Greek *mezze*, and American bar snacks? Variety, for one thing. In a typical Spanish bar that specializes in tapas, called a tasca, you will find up to fifty and sometimes more different snacks, many of which change from week to week. It has been said that you could spend a month rambling through the tascas of Madrid or any other large Spanish city and not taste the same tapa twice.

But certainly the one thing that separates tapas from all other ethnic snacks is their *españolismo*. Being Spanish, tapas are hardy, robust, rugged, earthy, yet never uncouth. Although served in small portions, tapas are substantial, not flimsy, dainty, fussy, or superficial. You would never, for example, call tapas "tidbits."

Tapas reflect Spain and her people: individualistic, assertive, spirited. Like the Spaniards who consume thousands—perhaps millions—of these hardy snacks each day, tapas have *pundonor*. Honor! Pride! They are what they are. There's nothing phony about them. Tapas are down-to-earth, no-nonsense foods, eaten because of their robust flavors and their ability to stand up to robust drinks. Eaten, in other words, deliberately, never out of habit. Tapas are a *macho* (and *macha*) food for both genders, all seasons, and any occasion.

But can Spanish tapas be accepted in America? The answer is an unqualified yes! More important, the proud tapa can find acceptance without compromising its Hispanic heritage—without, in other words, ending up on buy-one-get-one-free coupons redeemable at the local Tapa Bell or Hut. True, tapa bars are snack bars, which to Americans means fast food, which spells junk food. But there's a difference, both in the foods themselves and in the reasons Spaniards are so determined to eat them.

Spaniards congregate where tapas are served to relax and to enjoy themselves, not because they are in a hurry to go somewhere else. They squeeze into tapa bars and cafés out of desire, not necessity. Tapas serve one end: the honest, unaffected enjoyment of life. They are made to be consumed by good-humored congenial people, under friendly, informal circumstances, in stimulating surroundings. They are a democratic food—or, better, a *soul* food—for peoples of all classes and backgrounds. In short, tapas are potentially as enjoyable in America as they are habitually enjoyable in Spain.

CHAPTER TWO
TAPAS AND THE SPANISH WAY OF LIFE

THE TAPAS DAY

To best entertain Spanish style, it helps to understand how tapas fit into the Spanish way of life. First off, tapas are not just snacks or "small foods." They are a way of life, an all-day-and-night institution. Tapa eating begins around mid-morning in most Spanish communities, continuing on till lunch (about 2:00 P.M.), subsiding only somewhat during the afternoon *siesta*. Tapa consumption picks up around 6:00 (the beginning of the Spanish happy hour) and roars on till the 10:00 P.M. dinner hour. Around midnight, after a couple of hours off for a leisurely evening meal, tapa-ing again intensifies until 2:00 or 3:00 in the morning. Only then do the Spanish bars and cafés begin to close, one by one, leaving just enough time for the haggard tapa cooks to catch a few hours of sleep before scampering off to the early-morning markets for the next day's ingredients.

Although tapas are served *everywhere* in Spain, they are the most bountiful in the tascas, or "tapa bars." From the outside, a Spanish tasca looks like any other neighborhood bar in any other Mediterranean country. Once inside, however, there's no mistaking the sights, sounds, and smells.

First off, as you enter you'll see the tattered bullfight posters peeling off the walls, a stuffed bull's head glaring down at you, and perhaps several pairs of matador swords. If not bullfight memorabilia, then wall-mounted jai alai gear or *fútbol* posters along with some team pictures and maybe a row of trophies perched high up on the wall. Behind the bar, a dozen or more wine casks and several goatskin wine bags dangle above the bartender's head. Also suspended from the hand-hewn rafters are bunches of onions, ropes of *chorizo* (sausage), loops of twisted strands of garlic, and plump *serrano* hams.

The sounds, too, are unmistakable: the rumble of voices punctuated by shouts from white-aproned bartenders and the cadenced call of a lottery seller; and in the background, the clatter of tapa saucers and the hissing of an espresso machine, accompanied by the eerie sounds of a musical slot machine. Through the open door (it's always open) comes the occasional roar of a motorbike negotiating the narrow street.

The smells? As you wade through the debris—cigar butts, mussel shells, sugar wrappers, shrimp heads, bottle tops, crumpled napkins, broken toothpicks—your nostrils fill with cigarette smoke and the unmistakable whiffs of garlic, wine, and fish sizzling in olive oil.

Don't be put off; you're in the right place. The fact is, you're in one of the better places. As any *tinto*-blooded tapa aficionado will tell you, the level of debris, noise, and smells is in direct ratio to the quantity and quality of the tapas.

To partake, simply call out your preferences (or point if you don't speak the language), and

7

one of the bustling bartenders will ladle each of your orders onto a small oval saucer called a *concha* (shell). With every savory selection, you'll find a miniature fork to facilitate eating and two or three hunks of crusty Spanish bread to sop up the sauce. Stationed here and there along the bar will be glasses crammed with toothpicks (both for spearing tapas and for tooth-picking) and piles of thin paper squares that serve as napkins. While you browse, point, munch, and sip, the harried bartender will be adding up your bill on a scrap of paper kept next to the cash register, or he'll simply chalk up your tab on the bar in front of you. In the neighborhood tascas, you keep your own score, which you're expected to recite at the end of the evening.

If you should nibble a tapa that you'd like to expand into a meal, you can order a *ración* (or *media ración*) and receive your very own heaping platter. If you'd like to try a house assortment, ask for *tapas variados*.

Being a novice at all this you'll probably start your gastronomic exploits with the more identifiable items—fried shrimp, sliced ham, hard-boiled eggs, chicken wings—working your way into the stews, salads, and other unrecognizable dishes. What happens if you overindulge? No problem. Every bar and café in Spain provides free *bicarbonato*, bicarbonate of soda, for its customers.

The only problem comes in choosing from the infinite variety of tasty dishes. To complicate your dilemma, you will seldom find tapas listed on menus, even in restaurants. You might be able to make out a few names scrawled on the glass cases that sometimes enclose the platters, or a few house specialties will be scribbled on chalkboards nailed to the pillars. Sometimes the *especialidades de la casa* are listed outside on the plate-glass window or printed on the mirror behind the bar. Usually, though, you point and take your chances.

Again, no problem. You can't go wrong. At the very least, you'll be rewarded with the gastronomic adventure of your life. And since the helpings are small, you'll be experiencing these adventures over and over without committing yourself to a meal each time you place an order.

Madrid's tascas are the most famous, but tapa bars of one kind or another (variously called *tabernas, mesónes, cantinas, bodegas,* or just plain *bars*) exist in every village in Spain. According to many tapa addicts, the tapa bars of Andalusia have the choicest selections, and surely the Andalusians are some of the most dedicated consumers. "The variety of Spanish tapas," wrote Fernando Diaz-Plaja, a popular Spanish writer and social commentator, "especially Andalusian ones, is incredible, and the sum of those squids, hard-boiled eggs, octopuses, sardines, and dishes of this and that would constitute a normal meal in many European and American countries."

The Spaniard frequently *does* make a meal of tapas. But as James Michener points out in his *Iberia*, this is not "the traditional way to enjoy the tapa bar." The way to go about it, explains Michener, is "to gather a group of friends and wander leisurely from one bar to the next, taking from each the one dish for which it is famous." One bar might specialize in squid prepared in different ways, another in meat casseroles, another in shellfish, while still others will offer tempting displays of every conceivable combination of foods imaginable.

The point is that whether you're on the prowl for predinner appetizers or a megameal, you will be enjoying, as you tasca-hop through the narrow streets, along the waterfront, and around the square, the very best eating in town. Tapa aficionados will tell you it's the very best in the world.

If you prefer to sample tapas in an atmosphere that's more sedate than you're likely to find in the earthy, often turbulent tasca, head for a Spanish café. "In no country," wrote the Nordic Hispanophile, Hans Christian Andersen, "have I seen such splendid cafés as in Spain; cafés so beautifully and tastefully decorated." This is as true today as it was a century ago. A devastating civil war followed by the onslaught of tens of thousands of skyscrapers and apartment blocks have completely transformed large portions of Spain's cities and most of her fishing villages as well. But through it all the cafés live on, many as splendid as ever and all as charming as ever.

Spanish cafés feature the more standard tapas—meatballs, shrimp, potato salad, sliced ham—and if multicourse meals are also served at the café, you'll find listed on the menu a first course called *entremeses variados*, consisting of a plate of assorted cold tapas: hard-boiled eggs, marinated mushrooms, *Manchego* cheese, asparagus vinaigrette.

The fact is, if you've encountered tapas before, it was probably in a sidewalk café. The scenario went something like this: You're sitting in a café recovering from a morning of rigorous sightseeing when you spot someone at the next table eating a small dish of what looks like fried onion rings. Catching the waiter's eye, you point to your neighbor's rings. The waiter smiles, nods, glides off, and in a minute or two you receive your own saucerful. You bite into one of your golden brown rings and *magnífico*!

It's not until you're back in the States dining in your favorite Italian restaurant that you realize that those delectable rings (called *calamari* on the Italian menu and *calamares* by your waiter back at the *Café del Prado*) were a tapa of fried squid, not a dish of onion rings.

More than a place to discover tapas, however, the café is where you discover Spain. It's the hub of Spanish life: the Spaniard's social center, extra living room, office conference room, communications center. It's where the Spaniard, female as well as male, entertains, meets friends, conducts business, receives messages, eats, drinks, and relaxes. The café is to the Spaniard "what the Agora was to the Athenians," John Dos Passos wrote.

Café living is nonstop living. Along with the tasca, it's one of the very few institutions in Spain that is uninterrupted by siestas and doesn't have days off. More important, it's real value for your *pesetas*. The price you pay for your tapas and drink is simply a modest rental fee that allows you to sit at a table as long as you wish, sipping your favorite beverage, sampling tapas, watching life unfolding around you—a comfortable, relaxing blend of eating, drinking, and sightseeing. Your bill, or entrance ticket, will depend as much on your view of the traffic, harbor, mountains, or paseo as it does on what you eat and drink.

You are free to read newspapers, write postcards, or chat with your neighbors. Or you can lean back and join the Spanish "listening to themselves living," as the English writer, Gerald Brenan, put it; or make yourself "an unwanted fifth leg to a café table," as the Spanish like to say.

The cafés and tapa bars being the center of Spanish life, it's natural that they would also be the center of a uniquely Iberian ritual called a tertulia ("group"). Tertulias are clubs within clubs, but with no rules, dues, or anything else to bind the members together. The only "rule" is an agreed-upon hour when the five to ten select friends meet to discuss common interests. Black coffee replaces wine as the chief beverage, accompanied, of course, by tapas.

Visitors come and go, but the core of friends (often from the same profession) remains the same, sometimes for decades. Tertulias are usually in cafés, coffee houses, and tascas, but the habitual meeting place can be anywhere. During the eighteenth century, tertulias were held in the home—"a species of salon," according to William Dean Howells.

But don't get the wrong idea. The tertulia is not a coffee klatch. Serious discussions take place. "Spanish culture," according to the Spanish philosopher, Miguel de Unamuno, "is to be found more in the cafés than in the universities." Whatever it is you might want to learn about Spain and her people, chances are the place to learn is in a café tertulia. Ernest Hemingway picked up the finer points of the *corrida de toros* at a bullfighters' tertulia held in Madrid's Café Gijón, and during the Spanish Civil War, a good deal of what appeared in Hemingway's newspaper dispatches was based on stories swapped over tapas and sherry at the Chicote Café: "One might say I cut my wisdom teeth nibbling on olives in the Chicote." Years later, James Michener researched his best-seller, *Iberia*—again, over tapas and sherry—while a guest at a 4:30 tertulia at the Café Leon. "My life in the tertulia," he wrote in *Iberia*, "was one of the most instructive things that happened to me."

After coffee and tapas, seasoned with an animated discussion, the afternoon tertulia is free to join the early evening promenade or paseo ("walk"). Around 6:00 P.M., weather permitting, paseo streets and squares all over Spain become hives of people. Couples, families, and tertulias stroll slowly up and down the streets or circulate in the squares, arm in arm, up to six or more abreast, chatting and greeting friends. At some point during the stroll, most will drift into nearby bars for more tapas and drinks or settle into one of the sidewalk cafés that line the paseo streets. An American journalist once said that Madrid's paseos gave him the impression of a city divided into two groups: "The first sit in the sidewalk cafés watching those who circulate, and the second circulate while watching those seated in the cafés." Early evening promenades are a tradition throughout the Mediterranean, but only Spain combines them with a tradition of tapas.

CHAPTER THREE
ENTERTAINING WITH TAPAS

Tapas are a convenience food, but not in the prepackaged sense. They are a convenience to prepare. Your starter kit is a handful of fresh ingredients—just about *any* ingredients will do—a few basic seasonings, a top-quality cooking oil (preferably extracted from the olive), and a skillet. Unlike many other national cuisines, tapa cookery is not based on elaborate recipes gleaned from five-star restaurants or *haute-cuisine* cooking schools. You won't need a battery of utensils, fancy cuts of meat, or elaborate sauces. Tapa cookery is a practical, wholesome, economical, low-calorie, no-nonsense style of cooking from scratch. Although usually prepared for large numbers of people, the proportions are small enough to make ingredients manageable and the utensils basic.

Tapa cookery begins with fresh ingredients. For centuries, the lack of refrigeration has forced Spanish cooks to think fresh and cook seasonally, and they still do. Although freezers are available today even in the remotest parts of Spain, the freshness habit dies hard; when it comes to food preservation, tapa cooks still prefer the creative methods of drying, seasoning, smoking, and marinating. Of course not every ingredient will be available fresh in America. You may have to use frozen or canned foods, at least during certain times of the year. And for those ingredients unavailable in any form, we have suggested substitutes, but ones that will retain the Spanishness of the original dishes.

When making a substitution, remember that integrity of ingredients is essential, even with stews, salads, and other dishes that contain a variety of foods and seasonings. Don't, in other words, mask flavors. If you're unhappy with an ingredient or a seasoning, omit it or make a substitution—boldly, but without destroying the *particularismo*, or individuality, of the dish.

Aromas and textures are important, and so is appearance. To be orthodox, a tapa must not only be taste-tempting; it must look, smell, and feel inviting to the palate.

Besides one or more favorite beverages, the only other accompaniment would be small hunks of Spanish bread (two or three to a saucer), but there should be no butter, margarine, or other spread to mar the palate. American versions of Italian or French bread would be fine as long as they're freshly baked and sturdy enough to sop up the sauces.

TYPICAL TAPA GATHERINGS

One of the more attractive features of tapas is that they are consumable just about anywhere, anytime, and any way. You could, for example, prepare a half-dozen tapas as a prelude to a dinner, as the Spanish often do. The emphasis would be on a few cold items (*tapas naturales*) that are simple, honest, and natural: cold meats and cheese, shrimp, asparagus, tomatoes.

Another possibility would be a buffet of tapas. Here you would want a variety of cold and hot items with a balance of flavors, colors, and textures. Either provide dinner plates, American-style, so that guests can pile everything on together (returning, of course, for refills) or suggest that they put each item on a separate saucer, tasca-style.

You could even enlarge three or four tapa recipes into a sit-down, multicourse Spanish dinner. An especially attractive part of tapa cookery is that it is a cross section of Spanish cuisines in miniature. Many tapas have evolved from regional Spanish dishes, and by simply adding potatoes, rice, or a vegetable—presto!—you have an authentic Spanish meal. Be careful, though. Some tapa recipes are too rich to expand into meals, just as many tapa drinks (Spanish brandy, for example) are too strong for continual table drinking.

A singularly congenial setting would be a stand-up tapa party where you present a wide selection of foods and drinks and where you fix on demand—that is to say, where you prepare dishes to the point where they are ready to cook when requested. For the sake of convenience, you can fix many tapas the day before, refrigerate, and serve either chilled or reheated; tapa casseroles are usually enhanced by reheating. And you can prepare still other dishes a few hours ahead, keeping them warm on hot plates or in chafing dishes.

The question remains: How do you bring the tapa way of life into the home? Much will depend on what you want out of your tapas, which can be anything from a few cold snacks for a casual twosome to a formal buffet for a ballroom full of wedding guests. A good deal will depend on the ambience you want: tapa bar, sidewalk café, kitchen-table tertulia. Certainly you'll have to consider the availability of ingredients. If you have instant access to fresh seafood, your emphasis should be on *frutas del mar*. If you have a backyard of ripening vegetables, you possess all the fixings for a delicious, nutritious vegetarian spread. The blessing of tapa cookery is that any combination of guests, ingredients, and occasions provides the perfect excuse for a party.

The Tapas Team

A beverage always accompanies tapas. The operative word is *accompany*. Tapa and drink complement each other; neither dominates. In most parts of Spain, the traditional beverage has been a small glass of house wine (called a *chato*); nowadays, it is often a glass of sherry, a small bottle of beer, or a demitasse of espresso coffee. Brandy, vermouth, and cider are also popular, and almost any other drink is acceptable, including soft and mixed drinks. Lhardy, a 145-year-old Madrid restaurant, continues to offer a cup of soup as the accompanying "drink" with its canapé tapas.

Tapa Customs and Etiquette

Tapas, like their beverage teammates, are a matter of personal preference. Most Spaniards will avoid a careless mixture, but all insist on following their own tastes. Many like to start with salads and vegetables, while others begin with the simpler items, like marinated olives and sliced red peppers. Aficionados prefer to eat cold items first, including cold fish and seafood, followed by meat casseroles and other hot dishes, ending with cheeses and perhaps a brief return to some of the lighter tapas missed during the first go-around. The only point of tapa etiquette that everyone seems to agree upon is to eat and drink Spanish style: slowly, leisurely, enjoyably, socially.

What is a tapa portion? Traditionally it's a heaping ladleful or, in other words, enough to fill an oval tapa saucer (usually about three inches wide and six inches long) or an individual earthenware casserole (four or five inches in diameter and an inch or so deep). A portion might be, depending on size, two or three canapés or a good-size turnover. A portion might equal, again depending on size, three to five sardines; four or five good-size mussels, oysters, or other shellfish; perhaps four to six average-size shrimp; one large sausage or several tiny ones; three or four small fish sticks; five to seven small meatballs. The more pungent or hearty the flavor, the less will be served per portion, and a bit less will be offered of a hot tapa than a cold one.

Utensils and Other Paraphernalia

Whether you're throwing a stand-up party or a sit-down buffet, you will need one large serving platter and a serving spoon for each dish, stacks of saucers, containers of toothpicks, and a goodly supply of small dessert-type forks, one fork for each saucer. You might also keep handy a few eight-inch plates for anyone who wants a ración. If you don't want to be continually darting back and forth to the dishwasher, use paper plates and plastic forks.

Although most tapa cooking is done in Spain on the equivalent of butane campstoves, don't turn your back on New World culinary innovations. Tapas adapt admirably to the latest in cooking fads. Steamers and woks are ideal for vegetables, and nonstick skillets are perfect for the elusive Spanish omelet. Backyard grills are great for grilling, and so are hibachis and braziers. Electric fry pans, food processors, crockpots, and blenders all have a part to play, if you want them to. Tapa cooks have been quick to take advantage of modern conveniences, as long as these conveniences don't detract from freshness, flavor, and gusto. In the last few years, hotel bars throughout Spain have installed microwave ovens into which bartenders plunk individual earthenware casseroles served, seconds later, piping hot; you can do the same.

But to do an authentic job of tapa entertaining, you should be familiar with not only the hardware of tapa preparation, but with accompanying wines and other beverages and with Spanish seasonings and other ingredients. All these—ingredients, seasonings, and beverages—are the foundation of tapa preparation and presentation, which, in turn, is the foundation of Spanish-style entertaining.

CHAPTER FOUR
THE BEST WINES AND DRINKS FOR TAPA-TASTING

Spain is one of the world's leading wine-producing countries, boasting the most vineyard acreage in all of Europe. Spanish vineyards yield many excellent table wines, the world's finest sherries, several superb brandies, more champagnes than are produced in the champagne district of France, and some truly great dinner wines. Yet, except for the sherries, many Spanish wines remain unappreciated outside the peninsula. One reason is that most do not travel well; according to a Spanish saying, not even across the river and into the next province. Two exceptions are the remarkable Rioja wines of northern Spain and the excellent Catalonian wines, both readily available in America.

RIOJA WINES

The vineyards of Spain are divided into three main growing regions—northern, central, and southern—each producing its own characteristic wines. The fertile north, with its hot summers, cold winters, and fairly consistent rainfalls, offers what connoisseurs consider Spain's finest dinner wines. The best known, and most prestigious are from the Rioja region; the name *Rioja* comes from the Río (river) Oja. The white and especially the red wines of Rioja have been compared favorably to those from Bordeaux, whose vineyards lie barely 100 miles to the north.

The red Riojas are robust and full-bodied, vivid in color, with a solid, oaky flavor that smacks of the rugged terrain of northern Spain. The grapes are allowed to mature longer than most other varieties, both in the barrel and in the bottle. This careful aging process, coupled with rigid performance standards and a relatively stable amount of sun and rain, help to ensure high-quality Riojas, vintage after vintage.

PENEDÉS WINES

The Penedés area of Catalonia, just southwest of Barcelona, produces another group of superb red and white wines. Penedés wines are younger than the Riojas, aged less in the barrel but more in the bottle. They are lighter than the Riojas and have less of the traditional Spanish fullness. Penedés wines (notably the red *Coronas* and *Sangre de Toros* and the white *Viña Sols* of the Miguel Torres vineyards) have become one of Spain's most popular exports, mainly because of the creative blending techniques developed by the Torres and other Catalonian wine makers.

VALDEPEÑAS WINES

The bulk of the honest, everyday carafe wines (*vinos corriente*) are produced in the central region, principally in the vineyards of Valdepeñas. Midway between Madrid and Granada is the region called La Mancha, Don Quixote's homeland and the home of the Valdepeñas wines. The Valdepeñas area is rocky and semiarid (the phrase *Val-de-Peñas* means "Vale-of-Stones"), and the climate is much hotter than in the north. The result is a hearty wine that is fuller, heavier, and stronger even than the Riojas, yet smooth, fruity, light tasting, and well balanced.

As is often the case with anyone switching from the lighter hors d'oeuvres to the robust tapas, those accustomed to the more delicate French wines sometimes find Valdepeñas a bit heavy on the palate. "Thick enough to cut with a knife" was the exaggerated judgment of the French writer, Théophile Gautier. "A strong wine," according to Henry Wadsworth Longfellow, "that readily ascends one into the brain." Valdepeñas were Ernest Hemingway's favorite: "It cools you and then lights the fire that you need," was his assessment. "Ernesto" would drink four or five bottles at a meal, although he much preferred a dry sherry, manzanilla, with his tapas.

Valdepeñas wines go well with the tapas of La Mancha, especially with the hardy stews. But like so many of Spain's table wines, Valdepeñas are not a consistent wine and do not travel well. Some actually begin to lose their fullness after only a few months in the bottle.

SHERRY

Although the chalky soil and scorching sun of southern Spain is unsuitable for quality table wines, the area does produce superb sherries, strong in alcohol and with a high sugar content. The name sherry is the Anglicized version of the Spanish town Jerez, which has been the center of the sherry-producing region since the English began exporting this special wine in the early 1600s. Today, the British drink over 60 million bottles of Spanish sherry each year.

Sherry must be produced in a legally defined area surrounding the three Andalusian towns of Jerez de la Frontera, El Puerto de Santa María, and Sanlucar de Barrameda—the so-called "sherry triangle." The law aside, it is impossible to produce quality sherry anywhere else in the world, although several wineries in California and elsewhere continue to try. The special grapes, called Palamino, and the chalky soil, blazing sun, and sparse rainfall coupled with complex sherry production methods work together to create a wine that has been impossible to duplicate outside of the Jerez triangle.

Sherry production is based on a blending and aging process called *solera*, which is responsible both for the unique sherry taste and for top-quality wines year after year. The solera process consists of pouring each year's harvest into oaken barrels already partially filled with wine from previous years. Every year a portion of the wine is poured out, transferred to other barrels, and replaced by new wine. Depending on the quality desired, it can take 3 to 20 or more years of blending (or "fortifying") before a year's harvest is ready for bottling.

Each *bodega*, or wine producer, blends many different sherries, ranging from the crisp, very light and dry finos to the heavy sweet creams, with dozens of gradations in between. The four most popular sherries (from which many derivatives are made) are fino, amontillado, oloroso, and manzanilla.

Fino is a sharp-tasting sherry, pale, light in color, and very dry, with a penetrating bouquet. It is an ideal drink with before-dinner tapas and an excellent cooking wine.

Amontillado (the sherry immortalized by Edgar Allan Poe) is a richer, darker, stronger-tasting version of fino, with a "nutty" taste that stands up well to most tapas. Amontillado is dry, but like most dry sherries, it is usually sweetened for export, especially when exported by English firms. Spaniards prefer their sherries crisp, dry, and very young (even raw-tasting); most Americans, like the English, are attracted to the sweeter blends.

Oloroso is one of the two basic wines of the sherry district; fino is the other. Oloroso is a heavier, stronger wine than the fino, darker and golden in color with more body, but still a dry wine. It leaves more of an aftertaste than most other sherries. Olorosos are also usually sweetened for export, which in America classifies them as medium sherries. They stand up best with after-dinner tapas and are excellent as dessert wines.

It is from the oloroso sherries that we make the Bristol Cream and other sweet blends. In Spain, olorosos are a favorite with *meriendas* (afternoon teas) and as an accompaniment to pastries; they also go well with cheese tapas and with fruit.

Manzanilla is the lightest and driest of the sherries—said, in fact, to be the driest wine in the world—clearly the favorite of most tapa aficionados. Manzanilla is an excellent sherry for tapa cooking and the basis of numerous sauces, especially seafood sauces

Manzanilla is produced exclusively in the area around Sanlucar de Barrameda, where the wine is aged in oaken barrels exposed to the Atlantic breezes. The sea breezes are said to be responsible for manzanilla's characteristic salty, essence-of-the-sea flavor, making it an ideal companion to shellfish tapas.

Also from Andalusia come the dark sweet aperitif wines produced in the province of Málaga. Although no longer as fashionable as they once were, sweet Málaga wines still have many ardent followers, both in Spain and abroad.

CIDER

In the Asturias region of northern Spain, the wine of the apple rivals the wine of the grape as the favorite tapa accompaniment. This foaming, power-packed apple drink exudes the cool, clean taste of Spain's northern mountains and valleys. It is an excellent match for the food harvested on land and offshore; local aficionados consider it the ideal partner for shellfish from the Bay of Biscay.

BRANDY

Employing the same solera system used for sherry (although usually not the same grapes), the bodegas of Jerez produce a wide range of excellent brandies. Most are heavier, slightly sweeter, and taste more of the grape than do their French or Californian counterparts; most also have a fullness that the others lack.

Dr. Samuel Johnson put it best: "Claret is the liquor for boys, port for men; but he who aspires to be a hero must drink brandy." Spaniards—the males, anyway—like that kind of talk. Spanish men not only aspire to be heroes; each knows beyond any doubt that he *is* a hero. At any rate, Spanish brandies fit perfectly the Spaniard's *viva yo* outlook on life and can stand up exceedingly well to just about any tapa.

CHAMPAGNE

Spanish sparkling wines, especially the "champagnes," are becoming more and more popular at tapa gatherings. The champagnes of Spain, favorably compared with French champagnes, come from the Penedés area of Catalonia where today more sparkling wines are produced than in the French champagne region.

Spanish champagnes may be a bit sweeter than those from France, although both are made by the same process. Champagne (whether from Spain, France, or New York) is an excellent accompaniment to seafoods and the lighter tapas. It is a festive drink in Spain, as in America, often served with platters of before-dinner tapas.

SANGRIA

When Spaniards want a cool, refreshing fiesta drink to go with platters of fiesta tapas, they instinctively pour a bottle of dry red wine into a large pitcher, add slices of lemon, orange, and whatever other in-season fruits they have on hand, add sugar to taste, sprinkle with cinnamon, and fill to the top with carbonated water and cracked ice. They call it *sangria* and so do we.

Over the decades, sangria has been the Spaniard's idea of punch; recently, it's become many Americans' idea of Spanish wine, all of which probably accounts for much of the popularity of this cool crisp beverage, both in Spain and here. Enterprising American importers have even gone so far as to bottle it. For a refreshing compromise, place a block of ice in a large punch bowl, fill with chilled bottled sangria, and float slices of fresh lemons, oranges, bananas, peaches, and pears to cover.

BEER

Spanish brewing techniques have come a long way since the turn of the century when Baedeker warned his readers that "Spanish beer is almost certain to produce diarrhea in the unacclimated foreigner." Today, beer is second only to wine as the most popular alcoholic tapa companion and is fast gaining ground.

Spain produces over a dozen excellent regional brands and has several of Europe's most famous breweries under license, not to mention scores of imports. The most popular beer in Spanish tapa bars is San Miguel, an international beer that got its start in the former Spanish colony of the Philippines. The Spanish version, now brewed throughout the peninsula (and the world), is a light, dry pilsner and an excellent tapa accompaniment.

COFFEE

The leading nonalcoholic tapa companion is strong black espresso coffee. The Spanish have a saying that the Italians make the best espresso machines but the Spanish know best how to use them. Most Spaniards, at some point in the day, will select a *café con leche* (espresso coffee with milk) or, more likely, a *café solo* (black espresso coffee) to accompany one or more of their tapas.

MIXING AND MATCHING DRINKS WITH TAPAS

Which drinks go with which tapas? It's up to you, which is both the joy and the adventure of tapa consumption. You are expected to follow your own tastes when it comes to tapa-ing. There are no hard-and-fast rules, only personal prejudices, and each tapa consumer is entitled to his or her own; the fact is that each, in the true Spanish tradition, is expected to *insist* on his or her own prejudices.

There is, of course, the rule of thumb that red wines go best with meats and white wines with fish and poultry. But this, too, is a matter of preference. Generalizations like this are, in fact, impossible to follow, since tapas often include unorthodox combinations of ingredients. Actually, it is not so much a question of red, white, or rosé, but of full-bodied, light, sweet, or dry. Robust wines, regardless of color, seem to go best with robust tapas and light wines with the lighter tapas. But you will discover this for yourself. And if wines are not to your taste, that's fine too. Any beverage will do—alcoholic or not—as long as it's *your* choice. Don't, however, use the excuse that wine is bad for you, at least not when consumed tapa-style—that is, in moderation and while eating. Remember Louis Pasteur's prescription for wine: "The most healthful and most hygienic of beverages."

Although there may not be a consensus on what drinks go with what tapas, there is on how you drink. Never swill or guzzle. You sip, leisurely and deliberately.

Temperature is important. Beer should be cold, coffee hot. As for table wines, most tapa enthusiasts prefer their full-bodied reds at room temperature and their whites and rosés slightly chilled. The higher the quality of the wine, the less chilling needed.

A dry fino or manzanilla is at its best when a bit on the cool side, although some people prefer all sherries at room temperature. In any case, never serve sherry on the rocks, which both dilutes flavor and masks character. Sweet sherries and Malaga dessert wines are best at room temperature. According to most connoisseurs, chilling interferes with the distinctive bouquet of dessert wines.

Don't be afraid to switch drinks as you tiptoe back and forth among the tapas. You might, for example, start out by sipping a dry sherry with one or two salad tapas (sherry is ideal for clearing the palate at any point in tapa sampling), then switch to a white wine for seafood, move on to a hearty red for meat casseroles, and end the evening with a brandy or black coffee, or both.

Local customs, regional specialities, and seasons of the year have as much as anything else to do with tapa and beverage combinations. Some bars in Spain will automatically serve two or three jumbo shrimp just snatched from the Mediterranean or a thick slice of local cheese or a homemade sausage with each drink ordered. On a trip to Seville, the English writer, Evelyn Waugh, made a point of sampling manzanillas in the cafés and bars surrounding his hotel, "served as a rule," he later reported, "with a little piece of smoked boar's-head."

CHAPTER FIVE
UNDERSTANDING SPANISH SEASONINGS AND OTHER INGREDIENTS

In learning tapa cookery, it's important to understand something about what makes tapas unique, or, more to the point, what makes tapas different from traditional snack foods. One difference, of course, is the ingredients, especially the seasonings.

SEASONINGS

Creative seasoning is the backbone of tapa cookery. Spanish cooks use herbs (mainly the leaves of plants) and spices (the roots, seeds, and other parts) to enhance and accent flavor, add color and texture, create enticing aromas, and support tapas in stimulating the appetite and complementing drinks.

Saffron, thyme, oregano, bay leaves, paprika, and basil are favorites; garlic is indispensable. Parsley, lemons, almonds, olives, and other so-called garnishes are basic flavoring agents, never simply decorations; olive oil is for seasoning as well as for cooking and marinating. Tomatoes, ham, eggs, onions, carrots, sweet peppers, chocolate, cheeses, among other popular ingredients, are both foods and flavoring agents. Wines are for drinking, cooking, marinating, seasoning, and more. In short, tapa cooks make very little distinction among seasonings, condiments, flavoring agents, ingredients, sauces, garnishes, beverages, and cooking agents.

Most tapa seasonings will be familiar to you, a few perhaps unfamiliar, and you may find some of your favorites missing. Ground pepper, for example, is not widely used in Spain; in most parts of the country it is absent from tapa bars and even from restaurant and home dining tables. Spanish cooks prefer paprika, whole peppercorns, and other more distinctive seasonings. Salt is just as popular in Spain as it is in America, but as you become more inventive with other seasonings you'll find that you are using much less of it. We have, therefore, left it up to you to add salt and pepper to taste. When you do use salt and pepper, be sure to use only freshly ground pepper. Coarse salt will give you more of the classic flavor of Spain.

Herbs and spices should complement each other, working as a team to enhance flavors and reveal taste potentials. Never let one disguise or abuse another. Even when one seasoning (garlic, for example) seems to dominate a dish, it should never overpower.

Although quite pungent at times, Spanish cookery is not "hot" as is Mexican cooking. Hot spices are seldom used in Spain, and when they are, it is only to provide a little bite.

Feel free to adjust amounts to suit your palate. But try to do so without changing the character of the tapa or destroying its españolismo. If in doubt about a seasoning, use it sparingly (perhaps in half-quantities), then wait a few minutes and taste; season a bit more and taste again. It is easy to add more of an herb or spice, but impossible to subtract.

We have called for dried herbs in the recipes, even though fresh herbs are always better and

19

should be used in season. Remember, however, that dried herbs are stronger than an equal amount of fresh ones, so if you are fortunate enough to have fresh on hand, you will have to use up to three times as much as is called for in the recipe. For example, if 1 teaspoon of dried oregano is requested in the recipe, use 3 teaspoons of fresh oregano. The bay leaf is an exception. A fresh bay leaf is about twice as strong as a dried one.

Remember also that prolonged cooking can change the character of a seasoning, sometimes strengthening and at other times diminishing flavor, often leaving a bitter taste.

Almonds (Almendras)

The almond is Spain's—and the world's—most important nut for cooking. It provides a subtle taste and a distinctive texture to foods and especially to sauces. Depending on the tapa, you can use almonds whole, diced, or ground to form a paste. Two other nuts frequently used in tapa seasoning (as well as eaten out of hand) are piñones (pine nuts) and hazelnuts.

Almonds are popular in tapa bars roasted and eaten whole. You can serve them right from the can or prepare them in one of several traditional ways. The simplest method is to toast unshelled almonds in a preheated oven at 275°F for 30-40 minutes or until the nuts are toasted through. Serve in the shell with a nutcracker.

Another technique is to shell the almonds (or buy them shelled) and bake in their skins in a preheated 275°F oven. Toast for 30-40 minutes (shaking occasionally) or until the nuts are dark brown and the skins slip off easily. Salt and serve.

A tastier and more popular method is to toast blanched almonds in a preheated oven at 275°F for 30-40 minutes, remove, and sprinkle with olive oil and salt. You can do the blanching yourself by putting shelled almonds in boiling water for 30-60 seconds or until you can squeeze off the skins. Drain, bake, and sprinkle with olive oil and salt.

Instead of baking, you can fry blanched almonds in olive oil, drain, and salt. Tapa cooks like to fry piñones the same way. Both pine nuts and almonds make perfect sherry partners.

Basil (Albahaca)

This pungent herb is grown throughout Spain. Basil blends well with other Spanish seasonings, including garlic and olive oil. It is used in sauces and salads and in various seafood, pork, and vegetable tapas. It also combines well with tomatoes.

Bay Leaf (Laurel)

The bay leaf is one of the oldest seasonings in Spain, where it still grows wild. It is strongly aromatic; a single leaf is enough for just about any tapa recipe. It is best when fresh, but you will probably have to settle for dried leaves. In any case, the bay leaf preserves its flavor well when dried. It is always used in combination with other seasonings, notably with parsley and thyme, and is essential in many marinades and sauces. It complements most meats, fish, and fowl and blends well with Spanish wines.

Garlic (Ajo)

Since its introduction by the early Romans, garlic has been greatly admired in Spain as both a seasoning and a food. It has also, over the centuries, been used as a disinfectant, an antiseptic, a cold and flu remedy, an antidote for poison, a defense against the plague, and an instrument to ward off evil. It is popular in America as a health food, available in liquid, capsule, and tablet forms. Besides taste, the two other gastronomic features that enhance its use in tapa cookery are its ability to heighten appetite and to aid digestion.

Chefs throughout the world agree that when cooked properly, used discriminatingly, and combined in the right way with the right ingredients, garlic will produce a flavor that can enhance just about any dish, including, of course, tapa dishes. "The honest flavor of garlic," insisted James Beard, "is something I can never have enough of."

Garlic comes in many varieties and sizes. The smaller the cloves, the milder the taste. The traditional way to crush a clove (the flavor comes from the oil) is by placing the flat of a wide-blade kitchen knife over a clove and banging the blade with your fist. Tapa cooks prefer to use a mortar and pestle, which extracts more of the oil, but this will also leave an odor in a wooden mortar, so you might want to use a porcelain or marble mortar and pestle. A garlic press is perhaps the handiest way to crush garlic, and an electric blender is best if liquifying.

You can diminish the aftertaste (and afterbreath) of garlic with the addition of leafy greens rich in chlorophyll: parsley, watercress, celery leaves. Sautéing also tames garlic. To help seal in the underlying sweetness (and vitamins) and eliminate the bitterness that sometimes develops from prolonged cooking, you can fry the cloves in olive oil and then discard the garlic.

Garlic, usually combined with onions (the world's two oldest seasonings), is associated in tapa cookery with most meats, fish, and poultry; it is indispensable in tapas containing lamb or kidneys.

Olive Oil (*Aceite*)

"Except the vine," wrote the early Roman historian, Pliny, "there is no plant which bears a fruit of as great importance as the olive." Tapa cooks agree. Spain is the world's largest producer of olive oil and one of its chief users. Besides cooking, oil from the olive is used in Spain as fuel for lamps; as a weed killer; as a lubricant and body rub; and as a preservative, medicine, perfume, and cleanser. Most important, of course, olive oil is an indispensable tapa seasoning and Spain's chief cooking oil. It is flavorful and nutritious, contains no cholesterol or additives, has 100-percent usable fat, and is one of the very few oils that can be used in its pure, unrefined state. It is easy to digest and aids in the digestion of other foods. Olive oil does not produce greasy cooking, nor does it leave a residue on foods. It is perfect for cooking tapas and even more perfect for eating them, whether sizzling hot, reheated, or chilled.

The high burning temperature of olive oil permits foods to cook quickly, which ensures a crisp outside and juicy inside and prevents foods from absorbing the oil. When pan- or deep-frying, always be sure to get the oil sizzling hot, but not smoking, before cooking; a temperature of 375°F is generally about right.

You can use olive oil again and again, as long as it has never been burned. Of course, keep the oil for fish separate. You can store a good-quality olive oil at room temperature indefinitely, preferably in a glass container and in a dark place. Olive oil is sensitive to light, and prolonged heat can turn it rancid.

Vegetable oil would be an adequate substitute for cooking most (but not all!) tapas (see individual recipes for specific recommendations). Because of the relatively high cost of top-quality virgin olive oil (the only kind you should use with tapas), Spanish cooks often fry with the blander-tasting vegetable oils but also add a few tablespoons of pure olive oil to preserve the fragrance and flavor that only virgin oil from the olive offers. Butter is used for some seafood, fowl, and especially pastries; in northern Spain, lard is the chief cooking agent, at least for nontapa cooking.

Oregano (*Amáraco*)

Oregano is a pungent, fragrant herb, popular throughout the Mediterranean. Although at its best when fresh, oregano dries well and is effective in this form. It combines well with basil, another strong herb. Oregano enhances tomato sauces and goes well with eggplant, zucchini, and other vegetable tapas; it's essential with grilled meats.

Paprika (*Pimentón*)

An aromatic spice that is applied in many tapa bars the same way black pepper is in America. Use paprika in your tapas even when not called for to add flavor, color, and character.

Parsley (*Perejil*)

Parsley is a Spanish favorite, not to mention the most commonly used herb in America, yet seldom is it a dominating seasoning on its own. The delicate flavor of parsley enhances sauces and many fish, meat, and salad tapas. Don't take it for granted and never think of it as a decoration. Parsley is a necessary part of most fried tapas and is often used to mellow the taste of stronger seasonings such as garlic.

Saffron (*Azafrán*)

The Moors introduced this colorful spice to Spain (the Arabic word *safran* means "yellow"); it is now the world's most expensive spice. Fortunately, a little goes a long way. You need only a pinch to flavor and color a recipe.

Saffron is the dried stigmas, and usually part of the styles, of a flower called *saffron crocus*. The saffron must be picked painstakingly out of each blossom, flower by flower. One gram requires the stigmas and styles of about 150 flowers.

Saffron is sold in Spain unpulverized in individual stigmas; in America it comes either in stigmas or in powdered form. Because of the high cost, you may want to use turmeric or some other substitute. Turmeric colors food yellow and blends well with Spanish foods, but it has its own taste and does not give saffron's subtle flavor and fragrance. Due to saffron's expense, even tapa cooks use substitutes, usually a combination of saffron and a Spanish food coloring called *azafrán de color*.

In any case, inexpensive saffron does not exist, so be aware of substitutes, especially inferior ones. Many "saffrons," including those from Mexico, contain additives.

The way most tapa cooks incorporate this precious seasoning into a dish is to dissolve a pinch in a little liquid (wine, for example, or in olive oil, warm water, or cooking juices) and stir into the dish.

Thyme (*Tomillo*)

Thyme, aromatic and pungent, is a popular herb in Spain. A small amount will affect the taste of just about any dish. Thyme goes well with Spanish wines and is often used with bay leaves and parsley (bouquet garni). Thyme adds zest to stews and sauces (especially where long, slow cooking is required) and is popular in poultry, fish, and many meat tapas, including lamb and pork; it is seldom used with veal.

Wine (*Vino*)

Wine has been used for cooking and seasoning almost as long as it has for drinking. Wine, including sherry and brandy, is also the basis for nearly all tapa marinades. Whether for cooking or marinating, be sure to use a good-quality wine and avoid "cooking wines." The better the wine, the better the flavor.

For most tapa cooking, the wine (traditionally white for fish and poultry and a full-bodied red for meats) should be dry, except in those few recipes that call specifically for a sweet wine. Cook the foods in the wine at a moderate or low heat and long enough to evaporate the alcohol and remove any acidity. Prolonged cooking also allows the remnants to permeate the dish and blend with the other seasonings.

But don't use wine indiscriminately and never permit the flavor to overpower a dish. Strive for balance. Also, be aware of possible coloring effects. Red wines, for instance, tend to discolor fish, chicken, and other light-colored tapas.

CHEESES

Spain produces some three dozen varieties of cheese. Most have a richer flavor and a bit more bite than our North American varieties. A few Spanish cheeses are available year round in American specialty shops; most are not. In any case, throughout the book we have suggested substitutes, usually American, French, or Dutch varieties. The better-known Spanish cheeses include the following types:

Queso de Manchego

Manchego is Spain's most famous and popular cheese. Like so many Spanish foods and drinks, it gets its name from the region where it originated, La Mancha. Manchego is traditionally the product of sheep's milk, but in the northern provinces it is now being made from cow's milk. Depending on the variety (there are over a dozen kinds produced throughout the country), Manchego will range from a white, semisoft cheese with a creamy consistency to a dry cheese, hard and a bit crumbly, straw-yellow in color. When well aged, it can be very rich ("rich as manure," according to Waldo Frank) and sharp-tasting; in its milder versions, the taste is more like an Italian Parmesan or a mild Swiss. Like Swiss cheese, Manchego usually has tiny holes, called "eyes" (*ojos*), throughout the inside.

Most Americans prefer to eat Manchego fresh, soft, and mellow; the Spanish like it hard, dry, and aged. Manchego, served in thick slices, goes well with other cold tapas, especially with Spanish hams and sausages. The sharp-tasting versions are excellent when accompanied by a crisp, dry sherry. Either a Parmesan or Swiss cheese would be an acceptable substitute for Manchego.

Queso de Cabrales

A gourmet delicacy, Cabrales is usually made from a combination of cow's, sheep's, and goat's milk in the lush valleys surrounding the town of Cabrales in Asturias. It is cured in special mountain caves for two to three months, where it acquires a blue-green mold, creamy consistency, and tangy flavor. The taste is not quite as strong as that of French Roquefort, with which it is often compared. Cabrales goes well with the cider of Asturias and with the hardy wines of northern Spain. It is a popular tapa spread. A French Roquefort would be the best substitute.

Queso de bola

Bola is Spain's version of the ball-shaped Dutch Edam and the most popular of the foreign-type cheeses. Because of its familiar Edam flavor, it is a favorite with tourists. Thick slices of bola stand up well to red wines. A good Dutch Edam would be an excellent substitute.

Queso de Burgos

Burgos is a soft, very mild sheep's-milk cheese from the city of the same name. It has a texture and flavor similar to those of a soft mozzarella. Burgos is popular both as a tapa and as a dessert cheese, served in Spanish restaurants as a last course accompanied by fruit, nuts, or honey. Mozzarella might be the closest substitute for Burgos.

Queso de tetilla

Tetilla is a Galician cheese made from cow's milk, but sometimes produced from sheep's or goat's milk. It is one of the few regional cheeses not named after the area where it was first produced. It's name, tetilla ("nipple"), comes from its cone shape, which is said by the Spanish to resemble a female breast. It has a smooth, creamy texture with a slightly tangy flavor. A good Monterey Jack would be a mild-tasting version of tetilla.

SEAFOOD

Seafood is the basis for some of Spain's most popular tapas. Although some Mediterranean varieties may be unavailable in America, at least during certain times of the year, substitutes abound, and we have noted specific exchanges throughout Chapter 17. Generally, most white fish (sole and flounder, for example) will conveniently substitute for most Mediterranean white fish, such as *rape* and *merluza*. You can also successfully interchange most of the richer fish with salmon, tuna, and mackerel, although certainly the result will be a different tasting dish. Shellfish provide delicious interchanges. Shrimp and lobster, for example, offer pleasant and authentic-tasting tapas when incorporated into just about any shellfish recipe. The fact is that to maintain both the unique flavor and the authenticity of a tapa dish it is often more important to follow strictly the seasoning and cooking requirements than to use a specific variety of fish or shellfish. Freshness is important; however, if obtaining fresh fish or shellfish is impossible, quick-frozen will suffice.

MEATS, POULTRY, AND GAME

Chicken, veal, pork, and lamb are traditional tapa ingredients; beef is reserved mainly for casserole tapas. Most tapa meats and poultry are available in American markets, but you should feel free to interchange, if only to exercise your culinary creativity. But when you do, be sure to adjust cooking, seasoning, and marinating instructions. All things being equal, you would need to marinate and cook a chunk of beef longer than you would an equal amount of sliced veal.

Game is popular throughout Spain. Where a particular bird or animal is unavailable, the versatile chicken will often provide an adequate, albeit milder-tasting, substitute. You can also substitute local sausages and cured hams for the Spanish varieties, as we have noted throughout the recipes: Italian prosciutto is usually a suitable substitute for *serrano* and pepperoni can be used for *chorizo*; many good pork sausages work well in *butifarra* recipes; most blood sausages can take the place of *morcilla*; and so on. Again, specific substitute possibilities are noted in the recipes. Remember also that when mixing, matching, and substituting, one of your first considerations should be the sauces. Spanish tapa cooks rely on sauces to create original dishes, not just for flavor but for added color and texture and also to help in stimulating the appetite. Spanish meatballs, for example, are not only made with different combinations of meats, but with various sauces, including tomato, almond, and sherry.

EXOTICS

The exoticness of a tapa is in the mind of the tapa cook. What is exotic to one person is a gourmet delicacy to another and everyday fare to still others. Tastes, economics, availability, habit, and nationality are, among many other things, what determines the degree of exoticness of a particular tapa. Suffice it to say that one of the unique features of tapas is that they can be made from just about any ingredient or combination of ingredients. Nothing that is at all edible is neglected by the imaginative tapa cook. In any case, you have nothing to fear. Tapas are time-honored foods that have evolved over the centuries; today, they are being cooked and eaten by discriminating aficionados in every corner of the Iberian Peninsula. The catch is that some ingredients will be difficult or perhaps even impossible to find in North America. And although you are free to make substitutions, the elimination or substitution of many of the so-called exotic ingredients can cause the dish to lose much of its Spanishness. You may have to visit Spain to enjoy such tapas as *chanquetes* and *percebes*. But take comfort in the fact that as you read through these back-of-the-tapa-book exotics you will be receiving just about as thorough an understanding of Spanish-style cookery as you would in any other way.

PART TWO
TAPA PARTIES

To help you prepare perfect parties, we have put together in Part II an assortment of enticing entertainment ideas. Included are chapters on tapas as appetizers, tapas for two, and tapas for all kinds of small, medium, and mob-size gatherings. Remember, however, that the recipes presented here are only suggestions. We encourage you—or, better, we *urge* you—to do your own matching of recipes and parties, especially where recipe suggestions might contain out-of-season or hard-to-find ingredients. With each party idea we have also included tips on beverages, table settings, and decorations.

CHAPTER SIX
BRILLIANT BEGINNINGS

Tapas are ideal before-dinner appetizers. Just be sure to keep your dinner in mind when making your selections. If your main course is heavy, keep the tapas light. If the meal is light, you can start with the more earthy tapas, including a hot stew. For example, an entree of beef stroganoff might be accompanied by a white asparagus or celery tapa and a light fish main course by a tapa of kidneys in sherry or cheese and ham rolls. The idea is to offer contrasts.

Keep the quantity of food down so that the tapas tease, not ruin, the appetite; you want to satisfy the appetite with tastes rather than with bulk. Four or five well-chosen items will suffice: maybe a cheese, a salad, a vegetable, and a meat or fish tapa; perhaps one of them hot. But don't overgarnish. Let the ingredients do the decorating. Either arrange your before-dinner tapas, called *entremeses variados*, on large platters to pass around the table (or around the living room) or provide individual assortments. Champagne, sherry, mixed drinks, or a choice of light wines would be the best accompaniment.

If you're inviting the gang over for appetizers *only*, the tapas can be heavier, more varied, more numerous, and include two or three hot dishes. The rule of diversification still holds: don't bore your guests with look-alikes or taste-alikes.

For a brilliant beginning to your next multi- or mini-course meal, present your guests with the following pre-dinnertime tapas.

MENU

FLAMENQUINES
(Cheese and Ham Rolls)

HUEVOS DUROS CON QUESO
(Hard-boiled Eggs with Cheese)

ENSALADA DE JUDIAS VERDES
(Green Bean Salad)

ESPARRAGOS AL JAMON
(Asparagus with Ham)

GAMBAS AL AJILLO
(Garlic Shrimp)

FLAMENQUINES
(CHEESE AND HAM ROLLS)

Flamenquines, a popular "flamenco" (or gypsy) tapa from Andalusia, vary from tapa bar to tapa bar. Usually they consist of cheese wrapped in ham and then deep-fried, but fish is another popular stuffing. Excellent with a white wine, sherry, or crisp beer.

1 **pound Manchego, Swiss, or other cheese**

¼ **pound boiled ham, sliced thin**

1 **cup White Sauce (see index for recipe)**

1 **egg, beaten**

1 **cup bread crumbs**

2 **tablespoons chopped fresh parsley**

Salt and pepper to taste

Oil for deep-frying

Cut cheese into 2-inch strips ½-¾ inch thick. Roll a small strip of sliced ham 1½ or 2 turns around each cheese stick to cover the cheese and fasten with toothpicks. Dip sticks in White Sauce and refrigerate until sauce hardens. Dip each in beaten egg and roll in bread crumbs seasoned with parsley, salt, and pepper. Deep-fry at 370°F in hot oil (or pan-fry on all sides) 4 minutes, or until golden. Drain and serve hot.

Serves 8–10 (3 or 4 sticks per portion)

HUEVOS DUROS CON QUESO
(HARD-BOILED EGGS WITH CHEESE)

An ideal tapa with cold beer.

3 **tablespoons butter**

3 **tablespoons flour**

1 **cup milk**

2 **ounces Manchego or other favorite cheese, grated**

Salt and pepper to taste

6 **hard-boiled eggs**

1 **cup bread crumbs**

2 **eggs, beaten**

Oil for deep-frying

Melt butter in a skillet, add flour, and simmer lightly. Slowly pour in milk, stirring constantly. Sprinkle in cheese, again stirring constantly; season with salt and pepper, and continue to simmer until a smooth, creamy sauce forms. Peel hard-boiled eggs and carefully roll each in the cheese sauce and then in bread crumbs. Dip coated eggs in beaten eggs, again in cheese sauce, and again in bread crumbs. Deep-fry at 370°F, 3-4 minutes, or until golden brown. Drain and serve hot.

Serves 6

ENSALADA DE JUDIAS VERDES
(GREEN BEAN SALAD)

Excellent with a good red wine.

1 pound fresh green beans
6 tablespoons olive oil
2 tablespoons vinegar
3 cloves garlic, chopped
2 tablespoons chopped onion
2 tablespoons chopped pimientos
  Salt to taste
1 hard-boiled egg, sliced

Wash beans, trim off the ends, and cut into 1-inch lengths. Boil beans in salted water for about 5 minutes, or until barely tender. Remove, drain, and let cool. Mix oil and vinegar with chopped garlic, onion, and pimientos; sprinkle over the beans. Salt to taste and top with egg slices.

Serves 8

ESPARRAGOS AL JAMON
(ASPARAGUS WITH HAM)

Serve with a dry white wine.

1 pound canned cooked white asparagus
¼ cup mayonnaise
¼ pound boiled ham, sliced thin
2 hard-boiled eggs, chopped
1 small can red pimientos

Place a dab of mayonnaise on each asparagus stalk. Wrap a slice of ham (1½ or 2 turns) around 1-3 asparagus, depending on size. Sprinkle with chopped hard-boiled eggs and lay a strip of pimiento on each.

Serves 4–5 (2 or 3 wrapped asparagus each)

GAMBAS AL AJILLO
(GARLIC SHRIMP)

This four-olé tapa is a favorite throughout Spain. As with many other tapas, this works best if you can cook on demand. It stands up well to any brandy drink—the hardier the better.

1 **pound shrimp**
1 **cup olive oil**
4 **cloves garlic, chopped**
1 **small dried chili pepper,
 chopped and seeded,** *or*
 2 tablespoons paprika

Peel and devein shrimp. Heat olive oil in a skillet or in small individual earthenware skillets, and sauté garlic and chili pepper until garlic is golden. Add shrimp and simmer for 5 minutes, or until shrimp are pink, turning once. Spear shrimp with toothpicks and serve hot in the oil-chili-garlic sauce.

VARIATIONS

1. If you double the amount of chili pepper or paprika and add still more garlic to taste, you'll have the Basque version called *Gambas al Pil Pil*.

2. Local house versions often add 2 tablespoons sherry or lemon juice (sometimes also a bay leaf) and sprinkle with parsley.

Serves 4 (6–8 small shrimp each)

CHAPTER SEVEN
TAPAS FOR TWO OR THREE

The simplest to prepare, tapas for two (or three or four) is, nevertheless, an exciting way to top off an evening at a Picasso exhibit or Segovia concert. Either center your tapas around one large helping (called a ración) or present four or more traditional tapa portions. You can cook one or two dishes in the morning (or even the day before) to reheat just before tapa time. Put the wine in the refrigerator, set the table, and place the espresso pot on the stove. Then, back home after the flamenco concert, pop the tapa dish into the oven. When the timer bell rings, take out your hot dish, assemble your cold tapas, bring the cooled wine to the table, light the candles, and, *salud*, you're ready to start your Spanish adventure.

To get your next adventure for two off to a delicious start, center the evening around the following tapas menu.

MENU

TARTALETAS DE ANCHOAS
(Anchovy Tartlets)

BOLAS DE QUESO Y PATATA
(Cheese and Potato Balls)

HUEVOS RELLENOS
(Stuffed Eggs)

PASTELILLO DE HIGADILLOS
(Chicken Liver Pâté)

ENSALADA DE CALAMARES
(Squid Salad)

POLLO AL AJILLO
(Garlic Chicken)

TARTALETAS DE ANCHOAS
(ANCHOVY TARTLETS)

Cold, crisp beer is an especially compatible partner for these tartlets.

Tartlet Shells (see recipe below)

1 7-ounce can anchovy fillets, chopped

1 2-ounce jar chopped pimientos

Mayonnaise

2 chopped hard-boiled egg yolks

Rolled anchovies or hard-boiled egg slices for garnish

Prepare and bake Tartlet Shells as directed. Mix together anchovies, pimientos, and enough mayonnaise to bind. Fill Tartlet Shells with the mixture and sprinkle with chopped hard-boiled egg yolks. Top each with a rolled anchovy or a slice of hard-boiled egg.

Note: Any tartaleta filling can be substituted for this recipe. Concoct your own or try the Ham and Cheese Tartlets in Chapter 13 (see index for recipe).

Serves 6–8 (1–2 tartlets each)

1¼ cups flour

½ cup lard

½ teaspoon salt

½ teaspoon baking powder

½ beaten egg

¼ cup cold water

1½ teaspoon lemon juice

TARTLET SHELLS

The handiest way to shape the *barcos* (boats) is with special tartlet forms, or you can use ordinary muffin tins. Mix all ingredients and leave for 1 hour at room temperature. Roll out the dough about ⅛ inch thick and line the molds with it; or you can shape the boats with your fingers and place on flat baking sheets. Refrigerate until firm and bake in preheated 475°F oven for 8 to 10 minutes. Cool the shells, remove from the molds, and spoon in a filling. You can bake the tartlet shells in advance and add the filling just before serving.

YIELD: 8 shells

BOLAS DE QUESO Y PATATA
(CHEESE AND POTATO BALLS)

A dry white wine or ice-cold beer would be the ideal companion.

½ cup flour
1 teaspoon double-acting
    baking powder
1 egg, beaten
2 cups mashed potatoes
    (leftover or freshly
    made)
1 cup young Manchego or
    other soft cheese, grated
  Oil for deep-frying

Add flour, baking powder, and beaten egg to mashed potatoes and mix well. Stir in the cheese and form into 1-inch balls. Drop each ball into hot oil and deep-fry at 375°F, turning once, for 4 minutes or until golden and puffy. Drain and serve warm or cold, several balls on each tapa saucer.

VARIATION
For added texture, roll cheese balls in fine bread crumbs before frying.

Serves 8

HUEVOS RELLENOS
(STUFFED EGGS)

Just about any drink would be an appropriate partner.

6 hard-boiled eggs
1 2-ounce jar pimientos
½ cup chopped tuna, shrimp,
    or anchovies
6 green olives, pitted and
    chopped
1 teaspoon fresh lemon juice
1 tablespoon chopped fresh
    parsley
  Salt to taste
¼ cup mayonnaise

Peel hard-boiled eggs, cut in half lengthwise, and remove yolks. Chop half the pimientos into pieces and mix together with chopped tuna, olives, lemon juice, and parsley. Salt to taste. Refill egg halves with the mixture. Top each egg with a spoonful of mayonnaise and lay on a strip of pimiento. Crumble egg yolks and sprinkle over the stuffed eggs.

VARIATION
For an Anglicized version, mix mayonnaise and egg yolks in with the stuffing.

Serves 6 (2 halves each)

PASTELILLO DE HIGADILLOS
(CHICKEN LIVER PATE)

Delicious with a dry sherry.

3 tablespoons butter

1 pound chicken livers, trimmed

2 hard-boiled eggs, chopped

1 tablespoon chopped fresh parsley

2 tablespoons Spanish brandy

Approximately ½ cup medium-dry sherry (oloroso, for example)

Salt and pepper to taste

Melt butter in a skillet, add livers, and sauté 10 minutes or until barely cooked. Remove and drain. In an electric blender, or with a mortar and pestle, mix together livers and hard-boiled eggs until pureed. Add parsley. Pour in brandy and enough sherry to form a smooth paste, add salt and pepper to taste, and blend well. Serve on squares of thin-sliced bread, toasted, or on crackers.

Serves 6

ENSALADA DE CALAMARES
(SQUID SALAD)

Accompany with a light beer.

2 pounds squid

Water for boiling, lightly salted

1 onion, chopped

2 cloves garlic, chopped

2 green peppers, chopped

2 tomatoes, chopped

1 tablespoon chopped fresh parsley

¼ cup olive oil

1 tablespoon fresh lemon juice

Clean and wash squid. Remove ink sacs, heads, and insides and peel off the skins. Boil salted water in a kettle and quickly cook squid until barely tender, about 2-3 minutes. Remove, drain, and cut bodies into rings and tentacles into pieces. Add chopped onion, garlic, peppers, tomatoes, and parsley. Drizzle with olive oil and lemon juice and toss. Refrigerate and serve chilled.

VARIATION
In Galicia, octopus is used in place of squid.

Serves 8

POLLO AL AJILLO
(GARLIC CHICKEN)

A garlic lover's delight, excellent accompanied by a good red wine. If you're apprehensive about using this much garlic, skip the recipe. Don't cut back on the garlic (you can, of course, add more) or you'll miss the whole point of al ajillo. Garlic chicken without plenty of garlic is like Mexican chili without plenty of chili.

1	chicken or 2 large whole chicken breasts
	Salt, pepper, and paprika to taste
½	cup olive oil for frying
1	large bulb garlic, peeled and chopped
1	bay leaf
⅓	cup brandy or dry sherry

Skin, bone, and cut chicken into bite-size pieces and season with salt, pepper, and a little paprika. Heat ½ cup olive oil in a large skillet or a large earthenware casserole, and fry chicken pieces on all sides until golden. Add garlic and bay leaf, and simmer until garlic is browned. Pour in brandy, cover, and continue to simmer over low heat for about 15 minutes or until chicken pieces are tender. Taste for salt and serve hot in the garlic juices. For a main course, cut the chicken into large serving pieces with bones intact; add french fries or rice and spoon on the garlic juices.

Serves 6–8

CHAPTER EIGHT
TAPAS AMONG FRIENDS

For a larger gathering of, say, six to eight guests, you might want to take time to interject a touch of Spain into your den or patio. Tack up a bullfight poster, hang a couple of *botas* or wine bottles, perhaps dangle a string of red peppers or garlic. If this is a patio happening, and you want to make the party truly authentic, you can forget about ashtrays, wastebaskets, and other receptacles. The debris goes on the ground, just as it does in any self-respecting tapa bar.

Although parties offer the temptation to show off your best table settings, you should keep it simple. Generally speaking, less is more when it comes to tapa tableware. Platters for food, serving spoons, napkins, toothpicks, tapa plates, and forks are enough.

Two or three hot tapas will probably suffice. At least one should be something that can be kept hot in a chafing dish and that can stand constant heat throughout the evening. One of the advantages of casserole tapas is that sauces help insulate the food against burning. Hardy casserole tapas also have the ability to coat the stomachs of guests who might have already had a bit too much to drink and who forgot to eat before arriving. Remember also that the uniqueness of tapas will help divert the attention of overimbibing guests away from the drinks.

An excellent icebreaker for a small group like this is for everyone to share in assembling and cooking the tapas. You could have small individual kabobs displayed on platters, skewered but uncooked, ready for the grill the moment a guest wants to partake. Likewise, mussels, clams, oysters, or other shellfish should be allowed to lounge on platters, alive and well, waiting to be steamed or fried. As a souvenir of the evening *español*, everyone can take home a door prize of adventuresome recipes.

The following menu offers both a representative and a diverse tapa presentation, and is one guaranteed to enchant friends and family.

MENU

EMPANADILLAS DE LOMO
(Pork Turnovers)

PINCHITOS DE CARNE
(Shish Kabobs)

QUESO FRITO
(Fried Cheese)

MEJILLONES EN SALSA VERDE
(Mussels in Green Sauce)

PIPIRRANA ANDALUZ CON ATUN
(Andalusian Salad with Tuna)

ESTOFADO DE BUEY
(Beef Stew)

37

EMPANADILLAS DE LOMO
(PORK TURNOVERS)

Perfect with a chilled white or rosé wine.

Empanadilla Dough (see recipe below)
2   cloves garlic, chopped
1   onion, chopped
2   green peppers, chopped
¼   pound pork, diced
¼   pound veal (or beef), diced
½   cup dry white wine
¼   teaspoon oregano
½   teaspoon paprika
    Pinch thyme
    Salt to taste
    Oil for frying

Heat oil in a skillet and sauté garlic and onion until onion is soft. Stir in peppers and cook until tender. In a separate skillet, heat a little more oil and fry pork and veal until well-browned. Pour in white wine and continue cooking for 10 minutes or until liquid is reduced. Add peppers, garlic, and onion along with oregano, paprika, and thyme. Continue to cook until just enough liquid remains for binding. Salt to taste and fill each turnover with 1 rounded tablespoon of the mixture.

VARIATIONS

Other possible empanadilla combinations include: chopped ham, onion, and pickles, with mustard to bind. Chopped beef or veal, onion, garlic, and pimientos, with tomato or red wine (or both) for binding. Thinly sliced chorizo or other sausage with a raw egg yolk or tomato to bind. Chicken with chopped celery, olives, and pimientos, with a mayonnaise binding. Create your own combinations!

Serves 6

EMPANADILLA DOUGH

1   tablespoon (1 package) active dry yeast
    Warm water
3½ cups flour
1   egg, beaten
1   cup warm milk
2   tablespoons butter
¼   teaspoon salt

In a large bowl, dissolve dry yeast in a little warm water. Mix in flour, beaten egg, milk, butter, and salt. Slowly add more warm water (about ¼ cup) until dough is smooth. Knead dough, cover with a towel, and leave in a warm place for 1 hour or until dough has risen.

Roll out dough on a lightly floured surface until thin. Cut into equal circles, squares, or rectangles, about 3-4 inches across. Fill the center of each with the ingredients, fold up the sides, and pinch together to seal. For larger turnovers, you can fill one circle and cover with another of equal size, again pinching the sides together. Leave in a warm place for 15 minutes and then bake at 400°F, 10-15 minutes, or fry as directed.

Yield: 24 empanadillas

VARIATIONS

1. If you want a glaze on your turnovers, brush with beaten egg before baking.

2. You can also, after baking, top with pimientos, crumbled hard-boiled egg, parsley, etc.

3. Instead of baking, many tapa cooks prefer to pan-fry or deep-fry in enough oil to cover (4-5 minutes at 375°F) on demand.

QUESO FRITO
(FRIED CHEESE)

A cold, crisp beer would stand up best to these fried cheese squares.

½   **pound aged Manchego, gouda, bola, mozzarella, or other firm cheese**
1   **egg, beaten**
1   **cup bread crumbs**
   Salt and pepper to taste
   Oil for deep-frying

Cut cheese into bite-size squares or wedges. With toothpicks or a fork, dip cheese squares in beaten egg and then into bread crumbs seasoned with salt and pepper. Deep-fry the squares in hot oil only long enough for the crumbs to turn golden.

Serves 6–8

PIPIRRANA ANDALUZ CON ATUN
(ANDALUSIAN SALAD WITH TUNA)

In the tapa bars of Andalusia, pipirrana *has become synonymous with* ensalada. *It is prepared in numerous local varieties, but always with tomatoes and green peppers. On Andalusian restaurant menus, it is often listed as the* ensalada de casa. *Excellent with a chilled white wine.*

2   **green peppers, chopped**
3   **medium tomatoes, chopped**
1   **small onion, chopped**
1   **clove garlic, minced**
3   **tablespoons olive oil**
2   **tablespoons vinegar**
   Salt to taste
1   **7-ounce can oil-packed tuna**

Mix together green peppers, tomatoes, and onion. Add garlic and sprinkle with olive oil and vinegar. Add salt to taste and toss. Flake tuna into chunks and place the chunks on top.

VARIATIONS
   1. You can also add sliced hard-boiled eggs or slices of cucumbers to the salad.
   2. If you wish, substitute cod, sardines, ham, shrimp, or other meat or seafood for the tuna.

Serves 6–8

PINCHITOS DE CARNE
(SHISH KABOBS)

Pinchitos are small skewers threaded with cubes of meat, sometimes alternating with mushrooms, green olives, onions, red peppers, or other vegetables. Kabobs in one form or another are popular throughout the Mediterranean; Spanish pinchitos evolved from the brochettes of Morocco. In Spain, special pinchito spice mixtures are sold prepackaged in supermarkets and in bulk form by "spice ladies" in the village markets. Perfect with a full-bodied red wine.

2 pounds pork, lamb, or beef
¼ cup fresh lemon or lime juice
¾ cup olive oil
5 cloves garlic, chopped
¼ teaspoon ground cumin
¼ teaspoon crushed red pepper
2 tablespoons chopped fresh parsley
Salt to taste

Cut meat into ¾-inch cubes. In a bowl, stir together lemon juice, olive oil, garlic, cumin, pepper, parsley, and salt to taste. Add meat cubes and marinate for several hours. Thread 5 or 6 cubes of meat on thin individual metal or wooden skewers. Arrange skewers on a broiler pan or over an open flame, turning until browned on all sides and cooked through. Baste with marinade or additional olive oil. Serve individual skewers on saucers.

Serves 8

MEJILLONES EN SALSA VERDE
(MUSSELS IN GREEN SAUCE)

Excellent with a dry white wine.

1 tablespoon olive oil
1 onion, chopped
3 cloves garlic, chopped
2 tablespoons flour
½ cup dry white wine
1 cup chopped fresh parsley
Salt and pepper to taste
2 dozen mussels

Heat oil in a skillet and sauté onion and garlic in it until onion is soft. Stir in flour and add wine, parsley, and salt and pepper to taste. Simmer for 15 minutes. Add mussels and continue to simmer for 5 minutes or until mussels have opened. Serve 3-5 mussels hot in the sauce on each saucer.

Note: Any of the mussel recipes in this book would make a good addition to this menu. Instead of Mussels and Green Sauce, try the Mussels with Bacon in Chapter 17 or the Mussels with Lemon in Chapter 10 (see index for recipes).

Serves 6

ESTOFADO DE BUEY
(BEEF STEW)

A Spanish brandy would be the ideal partner.

1   pound beef stew meat
3   tablespoons oil
1   onion, sliced
1   clove garlic, chopped
1   tomato peeled and
      chopped
¼   cup dry white wine
1   tablespoon brandy
¼   teaspoon dried thyme
½   teaspoon paprika
1   bay leaf
1   tablespoon flour
      Pinch cinnamon
      Salt to taste
1   cup beef stock or water

Cut meat into bite-size (½-inch) cubes. Heat 2 tablespoons oil in a skillet, sauté meat cubes in it until well browned, and remove. Add 1 tablespoon oil to the skillet, reheat, and sauté onion slices and garlic until onions are soft. Add tomato, white wine, and brandy and continue to cook until liquid is reduced by about a fourth and alcohol evaporates. Add thyme, paprika, bay leaf, flour, cinnamon, and salt to taste; stir until flour is browned. Add meat and stock, mix well, and simmer about 2 hours or until meat is tender. If sauce becomes too dry, add more stock or water. Serve hot.

VARIATION
For a hardy meat-and-potatoes meal, add diced potatoes and peas (or other vegetable) while the meat simmers.

Serves 6

CHAPTER NINE
THE BEST OF TAPAS

There will be times when you'll want to be free from your tapas to greet guests and see that they meet each other, perhaps also meet your guest of honor. You'll want simplicity in your tapas, and some of the more exciting tapas are those that need little preparation. Many of the tapas in this menu can be prepared ahead and reheated, require no watching or last-minute cooking, and taste just as good after sitting for an hour or two on the coffee table (if necessary, in a chafing dish or over ice) as they did when they were just prepared. Cheeses and sausages hold their own very well. Vegetables, on the other hand, often become limp, and the flavors tend to lose their individuality.

The next time you're hosting a party and find yourself short of preparation time, try whipping up a few (or all) of these quick and easy tapas.

MENU

CANAPES DE CABRALES
(Cheese Canapés)

HUEVOS RELLENOS
(Stuffed Eggs)

BUTIFARRA A LA PLANCHA
(Grilled Catalan Sausage)

MEDIANOCHES
(Small Sandwiches)

BARQUITAS DE APIO
(Celery Boats)

CHAMPIÑONES AL AJILLO
(Mushrooms with Garlic)

ALBONDIGAS CON ALMENDRAS
(Meatballs in Almond Sauce)

MIGAS
(Fried Bread)

43

CANAPES DE CABRALES
(CHEESE CANAPES)

Cabrales is a popular cheese from Asturias in northern Spain. To prepare cheese canapés, spread slices of bread with Cabrales or a good Roquefort, cut into desired shapes, and sprinkle with chopped almonds, mushrooms, or other topping; Asturians are partial to piñones (pine nuts). You can also edge each canapé with chopped chives and top with a black olive or a slice of hard-boiled egg. For an extra-creamy spread, mix Cabrales with cream cheese or butter. The addition of Spanish brandy to the spread will provide a more vigorous taste.

HUEVOS RELLENOS
(STUFFED EGGS)

For recipe see Chapter 7, page 33.

BUTIFARRA A LA PLANCHA
(GRILLED CATALAN SAUSAGE)

Of the numerous Spanish sausages that take well to grilling, a particular favorite of tapa-goers is butifarra, a mildly seasoned pork sausage from Catalonia. To prepare grilled butifarra (or any other good link sausage), first puncture the casings to prevent bursting and place on the grill (or in a skillet) over moderate heat; fry until browned on all sides and cooked through. Depending on size, one link should be an adequate tapa serving. A full-bodied red wine would be the perfect partner.

MEDIANOCHES
(SMALL SANDWICHES)

Medianoches (the word means "midnight," but they are eaten at all hours of the night and day) are soft sweet buns, often glazed with egg whites and sprinkled with sugar. They are popular in Spanish tea rooms and cafés accompanied by a cup of late-afternoon tea or hot chocolate. At tapa bars they are sliced and filled with ham, tuna, cheese, and other fillings to form tiny sandwiches.

The easiest way to prepare medianoches is to buy soft dinner rolls at your local bakery, split each in half and stuff with your favorite sandwich ingredients. Serve one sandwich per tapa portion.

BARQUITAS DE APIO
(CELERY BOATS)

Any mixed drink would be an appropriate partner for these cold tapas.

1	bunch celery
1	7-ounce can water-packed tuna, drained
10	medium size green olives, pitted and chopped
2	tablespoons chopped pimientos
2	tablespoons chopped onion
1	tablespoon mayonnaise
1	hard-boiled egg, chopped
	Black olives, pitted

Clean and cut celery into 3- to 4-inch lengths. Mix together tuna, chopped green olives, pimientos, onion, and enough mayonnaise to bind. Fill celery "boats" with the mixture and sprinkle with chopped hard-boiled egg. Place 1 or 2 pitted black olives on each.

Serves 8 or more (3 "boats" each)

CHAMPIÑONES AL AJILLO
(MUSHROOMS WITH GARLIC)

Mushrooms, either wild (setas) or domesticated (champiñones), are a tapa-bar favorite. They are delicious and nutritious with virtually no calories. They are popular sautéed (either whole, caps, quartered, sliced, or chopped) in olive oil or butter (or half-and-half) but perhaps most popular of all cooked with garlic or al ajillo. Whatever the method, and like most other tapa vegetables, be sure to cook mushrooms quickly and a few at a time. Mushrooms are also popular served raw, perhaps accompanied by a favorite sauce or dip. Excellent with dry sherry.

½	pound mushrooms
1	tablespoon olive oil
6	cloves garlic, chopped
	Salt and pepper to taste
2	teaspoons dry sherry
2	tablespoons chopped fresh parsley

Clean and slice mushrooms. Heat oil in a skillet, add sliced mushrooms and chopped garlic, and sprinkle with salt, pepper, and sherry. Sauté until mushrooms are browned, 10–15 minutes. Sprinkle with parsley during the last minute of cooking. Serve hot. This robust tapa favorite becomes a savory first course when served over rice.

Serves 6

ALBONDIGAS CON ALMENDRAS
(MEATBALLS IN ALMOND SAUCE)

A glass of beer or a good red wine would be an appropriate partner.

1 **pound ground beef or mixture of beef and pork**

1 **egg, beaten**

¼ **cup milk**

½ **cup bread crumbs**

1 **small onion, chopped**

2 **tablespoons chopped fresh parsley**

3 **cloves garlic, chopped**

Pinch nutmeg

Salt and pepper to taste

Flour for dusting

1 **tablespoon oil**

1 **slice white or whole wheat bread**

20 **blanched almonds**

4 **peppercorns**

1 **bay leaf**

¼ **teaspoon saffron**

1 **cup beef stock**

Salt to taste

Mix together ground beef, egg, milk, and bread crumbs. Add onion, 1 tablespoon parsley, ⅓ of garlic, nutmeg, and salt and pepper to taste. With your fingers, form beef mixture into small (about ½-inch) balls and dust with flour. Heat oil in a skillet and fry meatballs until browned on all sides. With a slotted spoon, remove and set aside.

In the same oil, fry bread slice, remaining garlic, and almonds until bread is well browned. Remove from the skillet, drain, and crush in a mortar or electric blender with peppercorns, bay leaf, and saffron. Add mixture to the skillet and stir in stock and salt to taste; simmer a few minutes. Add meatballs to the sauce, sprinkle with remaining parsley, and simmer for 15 minutes or until cooked through. Add more stock or water if sauce becomes too thick.

Serves 6 (3–5 meatballs each)

MIGAS
(FRIED BREAD)

Migas are cubes of bread fried crisp. The Spanish use them as croutons in soups (in gazpacho, for example), salads, and casseroles and mix them into tomato, mushroom, and other vegetable dishes, and serve them with eggs (either mixed in or used as garnish). They are also a very popular tapa tradition all by themselves.

To prepare, trim the crusts from as many stale (or fresh) white bread slices as you need and cut the slices into ⅓-inch cubes. Wrap the cubes in wet salted cloth and set aside for several hours or until cubes are soaked through. Heat 3 tablespoons olive oil in a skillet and sauté 3–4 cloves of garlic in it until browned, then discard the cloves. For extra flavor, add bits of ham or bacon to the olive oil. Carefully stir in the bread cubes, making sure they are well coated on all sides. Sprinkle with a little paprika and salt and pepper to taste and fry until bread becomes crisp and golden brown. Serve either warm or at room temperature.

CHAPTER TEN
TAPAS MAGNIFICAS

Perhaps the ideal party setting is an unabashed stand-up buffet where you can offer guests a grand array of tapas and drinks. Don't, however, try for the variety of a typical Madrid tasca. The mere act of replenishing 40 or 50 platters requires dexterity that comes only with years of experience. Rely instead on a good cross section.

There are no hard-and-fast rules for setting a tapa buffet. You can use linen or paper napkins, china or paper plates, silverware or plastic forks, depending on the degree of elegance you want. You will also need appropriate receptacles for your beverages.

In place of the traditional tapa saucers, you can use larger plates that require fewer trips to the table. You should, however, encourage your guests to make at least enough visits so they won't be forced to fill their plates with tapas that don't blend well. Even when using large plates, guests should stick to regular tapa portions and not load up on a favorite dish.

Buffets do involve work, even tapa buffets. But by using tapas it is possible to offer an exciting eating adventure and at the same time take care of a large number of guests in a short time with minimum effort and maximum sociability, which is what Spanish eating is all about.

The first rule of tapa-buffeting is to make it easy for guests to help themselves. If possible, put similar foods together. If you're serving a large crowd, make twin arrangements of tapas, one on each side of the table for two-way traffic, with a good selection of beverages at each end.

A representative buffet of tapas should include some or all of the following.

MENU

TORTILLA ESPAÑOLA	RIÑONES AL JEREZ
(Potato Omelet)	(Kidneys in Sherry)
ALCACHOFAS CON JAMON	ESTOFADO A LA CATALANA
(Artichokes with Ham)	(Catalan Beef Stew)
SOLDADITOS DE PAVIA	ALMEJAS A LA MARINERA
(Codfish Fingers)	(Clams in White Wine)
JAMON SERRANO	LENGUADO CON PIÑONES
(Mountain Ham)	(Sole with Pine Nuts)
PECHUGAS AL JEREZ	MEJILLONES CON LIMON
(Chicken Breasts in Sherry Sauce)	(Mussels with Lemon)
CHAMPIÑONES ADOBADOS	SARDINAS FRITAS
(Marinated Mushrooms)	(Fried Sardines)

TORTILLA ESPAÑOLA
(POTATO OMELET)

Every European country has its own version of the omelet. The madre *of them all—and the one that spawned the French omelet, among others—is the* tortilla española, *a simple combination of eggs, potatoes, and onions. The Spanish tortilla has, of course, nothing in common with the thin cornmeal cakes of Mexico called tortillas, except for the round shape, which the word tortilla describes.*

Although the Spanish omelet contains simple, everyday ingredients, it is not an easy dish to master. The idea is to create an egg-and-potato mixture that is firm, perfectly round, two to three inches thick, golden brown on the outside yet moist and juicy in the middle, with a nutty taste that is robust, solid, and full of flavor. This takes patience and practice.

You'll get the best results if you use a special omelet pan (nonstick if you like), although any frying pan will do. Ideally, your pan should be reserved for omelets and never washed, only wiped clean with a cloth or paper towel. This helps keep the omelets from sticking. Spanish omelet pans are traditionally made of heavy cast iron, 8 to 10 inches in diameter. Recently, tapa cooks have been using long-handled, thick aluminum pans that facilitate flipping and maneuvering ingredients. Still more recently, nonstick pans have come into vogue, as they have in America.

To get the classic nutty taste of the Spanish omelet, you will need a top-grade olive oil as your cooking agent, or at the very least a mixture of one-half vegetable oil and one-half olive oil. Olive oil is also the best possible nonsticking cooking agent. Any drink should go well with this tapa-bar favorite, alcoholic or not.

¼ **cup or more extra-virgin olive oil**

3 **large potatoes, peeled and diced**

1 **large onion, chopped**
Salt to taste

4 **eggs**

Heat about ¼ cup cooking oil in a skillet. Add potatoes and onions, sprinkle lightly with salt, and fry slowly until potatoes are tender but not brown. Remove potato-and-onion mixture with a slotted spoon, drain, and let cool. Beat eggs in a bowl and mix in potatoes and onions. Add a little more olive oil to the skillet, heat, and pour in the mixture. Reduce the heat and cook until the bottom of the omelet begins to brown, shaking occasionally to prevent sticking. Invert a large plate over the skillet and carefully flip the omelet onto the plate. If necessary, add more oil to the skillet. Slide the omelet back into the skillet and continue cooking on the second side until browned. Place on a serving platter and slice like a pie or into squares. Serve hot or, best of all, chilled, one slice per tapa serving.

VARIATIONS

1. You can top with parsley or mushrooms or with a tomato or other sauce, but a properly cooked tortilla española is at its tastiest chilled and unadorned.

2. In place of, or in addition to, potatoes, Spanish tapa cooks also use ham, pureed spinach, eggplant, chicken livers, asparagus, crabmeat, sardines, bits of seafood, peas, whatever.

Serves 8–10

ALCACHOFAS CON JAMON
(ARTICHOKES WITH HAM)

Delicious accompanied by sherry or white wine.

12	fresh artichoke hearts
	Oil
¼	cup chopped ham
1	tablespoon chopped onion
1	tablespoon fresh lemon juice
	Salt to taste
	Lemon wedges

Boil artichoke hearts in a kettle of salted water until barely tender. Remove and drain. Heat oil in a skillet and stir in ham and onion. Add artichoke hearts, cover, and continue to simmer a few minutes or until hearts are heated through. Sprinkle with lemon juice and salt to taste and serve with lemon wedges. Delicious served either hot or cold.

Serves 4 (3 or 4 medium hearts each)

SOLDADITOS DE PAVIA
(CODFISH FINGERS)

Tapas are usually plainly and simply named, often given generic names like fried fish, fish stew, or just plain stew. "Little Soldiers of Pavia" is an exception, named after a 16th-century battle in Pavia, Italy, between the armies of Spain and France. The outnumbered and outgunned Spanish soldiers were not only victorious; they also captured the French king, Francis I. To prevent confusion in the darkness, the Spanish soldiers wore white shirts over their uniforms, with crimson-colored armbands, the colors of their emperor. The deep-fried "Little Soldier" tapas are traditionally served with a tomato sauce, but they are delicious plain with lemon wedges. As a meal, serve with green beans or other vegetable and boiled potatoes. A Spanish brandy would be a suitable companion.

1	pound dried salt cod
	Juice of 1 lemon
1	teaspoon paprika
¼	cup olive oil
	Dash pepper
1	cup flour
½	teaspoon saffron
¼	cup brandy
1½	teaspoons baking powder
	Pinch salt
	Oil for deep-frying

Soak dried cod in cold water 6-8 hours, changing water occasionally. Drain and cut into narrow fingers about 3 inches long and 1 inch wide. Mix lemon juice, paprika, olive oil, and a dash of pepper and sprinkle over cod fingers. Meanwhile, in a bowl mix together flour, saffron, brandy, baking powder, and a pinch of salt. Blend well, adding enough water to form a creamy batter. Cover the bowl and let batter stand in a warm place for an hour or so. Dip each cod finger into the batter and then deep-fry in hot oil at 375°F for 4 minutes, or until crisp and golden brown.

Serves 4-6 (3 or 4 fingers each)

JAMON SERRANO
(MOUNTAIN HAM)

Of Spain's many superb hams, the most popular by far is a raw-cured mountain variety called jamón serrano. A leg of serrano lies poised on nearly every tapa-bar counter in Spain, waiting patiently for a customer to induce one of the bartenders to shave off a saucerful of thin, transparent slivers.

Serrano is made from a special Spanish pig (cerdo ibérico), a close relative of the wild boar, which has been allowed to run free in the forests of southern Spain. Plenty of exercise and a diet of acorns, chestnuts, and other natural foods make the meat lean and tough, yet succulent in flavor. Curing is done naturally without refrigeration in the cool, high-altitude mountain air. In recent years, prepared feeds have become part of the diet, and the pigs themselves are often hybrids of various kinds, but the characteristic flavor and texture of serrano have remained the same.

In America you can sometimes find canned serrano in specialty food stores. Otherwise, the closest you'll come to matching its distinctive flavor is a top-quality Italian prosciutto or perhaps a German Westphalian. Serrano is usually eaten raw but is also popular combined with other foods.

An especially delicious tapa technique is to cut serrano, prosciutto, or other good cured ham into very thin slices and top with thin slices of smoked salmon. Then roll tightly, cut into 1½- to 2-inch-long tubes, and spear with toothpicks. Serrano is also delicious tightly rolled around hunks of tuna, chicken, sardines, pork, or other meat or fish; delicious also wrapped around a favorite meat, fish, cheese, or vegetable spread. Sprinkle each with chopped parsley, top with a black olive, and serve chilled, 4 or 5 tubes per serving. Just about any beverage would go well with serrano, especially a dry wine or cold beer.

PECHUGAS AL JEREZ
(CHICKEN BREASTS IN SHERRY SAUCE)

A dry sherry would be the ideal companion for this tapa.

2	whole chicken breasts
2	tablespoons oil or butter
1	onion, chopped
1	clove garlic, chopped
½	cup dry sherry
¼	cup chicken stock
1	small bay leaf
1	tablespoon chopped fresh parsley
2	tablespoons flour
	Salt to taste

Skin, bone, and cut breasts into strips. Heat oil or butter in a skillet and fry pieces until browned on all sides. Remove, drain, and set aside. In the same skillet, sauté onion and garlic until onion is soft. Add sherry, chicken stock, bay leaf, and parsley. Stir in flour and add salt to taste. Simmer for 10 minutes. Add chicken pieces and continue to simmer for 10 minutes or until pieces are tender, adding more stock if sauce becomes too thick.

Serves 6

CHAMPIÑONES ADOBADOS
(MARINATED MUSHROOMS)

Any drink would be suitable; a white wine or dry sherry would be perfect.

1   pound mushrooms
2   cloves garlic, chopped
⅔   cup white wine
⅓   cup olive oil
5   peppercorns, crushed
1   tablespoon chopped fresh
     parsley

Clean mushrooms and remove the tough ends of the stems. In a bowl, mix together mushrooms and the other ingredients, refrigerate, and marinate overnight. Serve at room temperature and spear with toothpicks.

Serves 6–8

RIÑONES AL JEREZ
(KIDNEYS IN SHERRY)

The taste of dry sherry (both in drinking and cooking) is the perfect complement to kidneys.

1   pound veal kidneys
2   tablespoons olive oil
1   small onion, chopped
1   clove garlic, chopped
1   tablespoon flour
½   cup beef stock
1   small bay leaf
½   cup dry sherry
     Salt and pepper to taste
1   tablespoon chopped fresh
     parsley
     Oil for frying

Clean and wash kidneys, trim away fat and gristle, and drain. Cut kidneys into 1-inch cubes. Heat oil in a skillet and sauté cubes until lightly browned. Remove and set aside. In the same oil, sauté onion and garlic until onion is soft. Return kidneys to the skillet and stir in flour, stock, and bay leaf. Simmer until a thick sauce forms. Add sherry, season with salt and pepper, and simmer 10 minutes or until liquid is reduced. Sprinkle with parsley, simmer a few more minutes, and serve hot.

VARIATIONS
For a slightly different taste for this mainstream tapa, add sliced carrots or mushrooms.

Serves 6–8

ESTOFADO A LA CATALANA
(CATALAN BEEF STEW)

A full-bodied red wine would be an excellent accompaniment.

1	pound beef stew meat
2	tablespoons olive oil
2	onions, chopped
3	cloves garlic, chopped
1	tablespoon flour
1	cup red wine
2	tomatoes, chopped
1	carrot, sliced
1	celery stalk, chopped
1	ounce unsweetened chocolate, grated
¼	teaspoon dried oregano
¼	teaspoon dried basil
¼	teaspoon dried thyme
1	tablespoon chopped fresh parsley
1	bay leaf
1	cup beef stock

Cut meat into bite-size cubes. Heat oil in a skillet, add meat, sauté until well browned, and remove. Add more oil and reheat. Sauté onions and garlic until onions are soft. Stir in flour and add wine, tomatoes, carrot, celery, and chocolate. Season with oregano, basil, and thyme; add parsley and bay leaf and stir in stock. Mix well, cover, and simmer for about 2 hours. Add more stock if sauce becomes too thick. Remove meat and strain sauce through a sieve. Return meat to the sauce and simmer slowly for another 15 minutes.

Serves 6

ALMEJAS A LA MARINERA
(CLAMS IN WHITE WINE)

A dry wine would be an appropriate accompaniment.

3-4	dozen small clams
1	tablespoon oil
1	onion, chopped
2	cloves garlic, chopped
1	tomato, peeled and chopped
1	cup white wine
1	tablespoon flour
2	tablespoons chopped fresh parsley
	Salt and pepper to taste

Soak clams in water for several hours to eliminate sand and grit. Meanwhile, heat oil in a casserole or skillet and sauté onion and garlic in it until onion is soft. Stir in tomato, wine, and flour and simmer for about 5 minutes or until sauce has thickened. Add drained clams and continue to cook uncovered until they have opened; about 10 minutes. Sprinkle with parsley and salt and pepper to taste. Continue to cook, stirring occasionally, 1-2 minutes or until blended. Serve hot.

VARIATIONS
Use the same *a la marinera* or "sailor-style" treatment for mussels and other shellfish.

Serves 4–6 (8 or more small clams each)

LENGUADO CON PIÑONES
(SOLE WITH PINE NUTS)

Spanish sole has one of the mildest, if not the mildest, flavors of all the tapa-bar seafoods. The meat is delicate, yet firm and easy to fillet. Because of its "neutral" flavor, it lends itself to endless cooking possibilities and is able to accept other foods, seasonings, and sauces remarkably well. Sole recipes are interchangeable with most other white fish, especially with hake and flounder. In Spain, a fish known as San Pedro, or John Dory, is a popular substitute for sole, and Spanish cooks often use besugo (sea bream) in this pine-nut tapa. This tapa is excellent with a light white wine.

1	pound boneless fillets of sole
	Flour for dusting
1	tablespoon flour
½	cup dry white wine
1	tablespoon fresh lemon juice
4	tablespoons pine nuts or a combination of pine nuts, almonds, and hazelnuts
1	tablespoon chopped fresh parsley
3	tablespoons olive oil
	Salt to taste

Flake fish with your fingers or cut into large bite-size pieces and dust pieces with flour. Heat oil in a skillet and fry fish pieces until golden. Remove, drain, and transfer to a warm platter. Add 1 tablespoon flour to remaining oil and gradually pour in wine and lemon juice; simmer, continuing to stir, until sauce is smooth. Grind nuts and parsley in a mortar and pestle or an electric blender, adding just enough olive oil to form a smooth paste. Add paste to the sauce and mix well. Add salt to taste. Add fish, cover, and simmer slowly 5 more minutes.

Serves 6

MEJILLONES CON LIMON
(MUSSELS WITH LEMON)

A white wine or a dry sherry would be most suitable.

2	dozen mussels
¼	cup fresh lemon juice
¾	cup olive oil
	Pepper to taste
	Lemon wedges

Clean and wash mussels. With a knife, open each mussel and discard one shell. Mix lemon juice and olive oil and pour over the mussels. Sprinkle well with freshly ground pepper and refrigerate. Serve cold with lemon wedges.

Note: Any of the mussel recipes in this book would be a delicious choice for *tapas magníficas*. Besides this one, consider Mussels with Bacon from Chapter 17 or Mussels in Green Sauce from Chapter 8 (see index for recipes).

Serves 6

SARDINAS FRITAS
(FRIED SARDINES)

Excellent with cold crisp beer.

1 **pound fresh sardines or
   herring
   Flour for dusting
   Salt and pepper to taste
   Oil for deep-frying**

Wash and clean sardines and slit open the bodies, removing intestines. Season flour with salt and pepper. Dust sardines in seasoned flour, shake off excess, and deep-fry in hot oil at 380°F for about 3 minutes. Tapa cooks like to cross the tails of 4 or 5 sardines just before immersing in hot oil. When removed, the tails remain stuck together, to be served in bunches.

Serves 4

CHAPTER ELEVEN
WELL-ROUNDED TAPAS

Usually when you invite a cross section of guests to a party you want to serve a cross section of foods. That's one of the joys of tapas. There's something for everyone: canapés for the traditionalist and squid rings for the sophisticate; fresh fruit salads for Aunt Bess and pigs' ears for that ex-Chicago Bears linebacker who crashes all your parties. There are tapas that require involved cooking methods (Tripe, Madrid Style, for example) and tapas that call for merely slicing up a round of cheese or opening a can of nuts. Here is a representative tapa selection from each recipe group.

MENU

ENSALADA DE JUDIAS VERDES Y CEBOLLAS
(Green Bean and Onion Salad)

TOMATES RELLENOS
(Stuffed Tomatoes)

PAELLA VALENCIANA
(Rice, Valencia Style)

TORTILLA ESPAÑOLA
(Potato Omelet)

CALAMARES FRITOS
(Fried Squid Rings)

ESTOFADO DE LOMO
(Pork Stew)

PERDIZ ESTOFADO
(Stewed Partridge)

OREJAS GUISADAS
(Stewed Pigs' Ears)

ENSALADA DE JUDIAS VERDES Y CEBOLLAS
(GREEN BEAN AND ONION SALAD)

Excellent with white chilled wine, especially a rosé.

1 pound fresh green beans
2 tablespoons vinegar
4 tablespoons olive oil
2 medium onions, sliced thin
1 tablespoon chopped fresh parsley

Wash beans, trim off the ends, and halve lengthwise. Boil beans in salted water for about 5 minutes or until barely tender. Remove, drain, and let cool; set aside the bean stock. Mix together vinegar, oil, onions, parsley, and ¼ cup bean stock. Pour mixture over the beans and refrigerate for 2-3 hours. Serve chilled.

Serves 8

TOMATES RELLENOS
(STUFFED TOMATOES)

It's impossible to conceive of a tapa offering without tomatoes. They are popular in sauces, in salads, stuffed, and combined with all manner of ingredients. They are equally delicious hot or cold, valuable for both flavor and color. Vegetable-stuffed tomatoes are often used in Spain to accompany meat courses. Most appropriate with a cold beer.

6 small tomatoes
Olive oil
Salt and pepper to taste
1 medium potato
1 small carrot
¼ cup peas
3 tablespoons pimientos, chopped
2 tablespoons chopped fresh parsley
¼ cup mayonnaise (preferably homemade; see index for recipe)
1 teaspoon vinegar

Cut the top from each tomato and scoop out the pulp. Turn upside down to drain remaining liquid. Brush all over with olive oil and sprinkle with salt and pepper. Cook potato, carrot, and peas; peel and dice potato and dice the carrot. Mix potato, carrot, and peas with pimientos and parsley. Blend mixture with mayonnaise and vinegar; add salt to taste. Fill tomatoes with the mixture.

VARIATIONS

1. A hardy Tomato Sauce (see index for recipe) will add a bit more flavor to this relatively mild-tasting tapa.

2. Instead of a vegetable filling, you can stuff with the same seafood or meat fillings used for turnovers, tartlets, and croquettes (see index for recipes). Or make up your own filling.

Serves 6

PAELLA VALENCIANA
(RICE, VALENCIA STYLE)

"There is no more royal fare of any kind," wrote Frances Parkinson Keyes, "than a paella." The most famous of all Spanish main dishes, paella is a popular and delicious tapa. The chief difference between the main dish (always serving at least two people at a time) and the tapa (served in scores of miniature portions) is that for a tapa the meats are cut into small pieces. In the traditional meal-size paella, big pieces of chicken and pork are used, including the bones. One drawback of this hardy tapa casserole is that you must prepare it in large amounts.

The traditional version is paella valenciana, *the only one for which there is a recipe. All others, whether complete meals or tapas, are personal variations. Each cook has his or her own way to prepare this dish, with the only two things in common being the special Spanish rice grown in Valencia and saffron. Most will also contain combinations of meat, chicken, seafood, vegetables, and various seasonings. Whatever the combination, when cooked properly with authentic Valencia rice and fresh ingredients, it is excellent. As Somerset Maugham said about paella: "It is never bad and sometimes it is of an excellence that surpasses belief."*

Whether you're following someone else's recipe or concocting your own version, it's important to observe a few simple rules. First, use only short-grain rice, preferably Spanish rice from Valencia. The ideal cooking utensil is a special pan called a paellera (from which this rice casserole gets its name), but any shallow, flat-bottomed pan will do. It should, however, have sloping edges and be about two inches deep. The traditional paellera has a handle on each side. Ideally, the flame should cover the whole bottom of the pan, which ensures even heat and lets you shake the pan to prevent sticking instead of stirring. For the sake of convenience, you can prepare all the ingredients, except the rice, the day before. Be careful not to overcook, which will burst the rice. Popular with either red or white wine.

1	small chicken (about 2½ pounds)
½	pound boneless pork
	Salt and pepper to taste
4	tablespoons olive oil
1	onion, chopped
2	cloves garlic, chopped
2	tomatoes, peeled and chopped
½	cup green peas
½	cup green beans, cut in ½ inch slices
½	tablespoon paprika
2	cups rice
½	teaspoon saffron
5	cups boiling water
½	pound shrimp in their shells
12	small clams, cleaned
12	mussels, cleaned

Cut chicken, skinned and boned, and pork into bite-size pieces and season with salt and pepper. Heat oil in a paella pan and sauté meats 5-10 minutes or until lightly browned on all sides. Add onion, garlic, tomatoes, peas, and beans and cook 5 more minutes, stirring occasionally. Remove pan from the heat, mix in the paprika, and return to the stove. Add rice and brown very lightly. Mix saffron in boiling water, pour into the pan, and cook for 5 minutes. Reduce heat and simmer slowly for another 5 minutes; then bury shrimp, clams, and mussels in the rice and continue to cook uncovered for 10 more minutes. Add a little more hot water if dish becomes dry. Do not stir, but shake the pan occasionally to prevent rice from sticking. After rice and seafood are cooked, allow to stand 5-10 minutes to absorb the liquid and blend the flavors.

Serves 12 or more

TORTILLA ESPAÑOLA
(Potato Omelet)

For recipe see Chapter 10, page 48.

CALAMARES FRITOS
(FRIED SQUID RINGS)

Deep-fried squid is popular in nearly all Mediterranean countries, particularly in Spain and Italy. It's wonderful as a first course and exceptional as a tapa. To the uninitiated, the squid rings are often mistaken for fried onion rings. This tapa standby would be suitable with any drink.

1 **pound small squid**
Flour for dusting
Beaten egg (optional)
Fine bread crumbs (optional)
Oil for deep-frying

Wash squid thoroughly, removing innards and cuttlebone. With scissors, cut across the bodies of the squid to form rings. Dust rings with flour (and then dip in beaten egg and fine bread crumbs, if a heavy coating is desired). Fry in deep hot oil at 380°F for about 2 minutes or until browned. Be careful not to overfry. Serve warm. In Spain, the tentacles as well as the bodies are dusted and fried.

6–8 rings per portion

ESTOFADO DE LOMO
(PORK STEW)

Either a red or white wine would be a suitable partner.

1 **pound pork tenderloin**
3 **tablespoons oil**
1 **onion, chopped**
3 **cloves garlic, chopped**
Flour for dusting
½ **cup dry white wine**
¼ **cup chicken stock**
1 **tablespoon vinegar**
1 **tablespoon flour**
Salt and pepper to taste
Pinch saffron

Cut pork tenderloin into 2-inch cubes. Heat oil in a skillet and sauté onion and garlic in it until onion is soft. Dust pork lightly in flour and fry until browned on both sides. Remove, drain, and set aside. Add wine, stock, and vinegar and stir in 1 tablespoon flour. Add salt and pepper to taste and a pinch of saffron. Return meat to the skillet and simmer for 20 minutes, stirring occasionally, or until a smooth sauce forms and meat is tender.

Serves 6

PERDIZ ESTOFADO
(STEWED PARTRIDGE)

Partridge is one of Spain's most popular game birds, hunted throughout the peninsula. Each province has its favorite method of preparing it. This version comes from New Castile. A dry white wine would stand up well with this tapa.

2   young partridges
     Salt to taste
2   tablespoons olive oil
2   onions, chopped
4   cloves garlic, chopped
1   bay leaf
5   peppercorns
1   carrot, sliced
1   stalk celery, sliced
1   cup dry white wine
¼   cup vinegar
¼   teaspoon dried thyme
¼   teaspoon dried oregano
1   tablespoon chopped fresh
     parsley

Clean the partridges, halve them along the back, and sprinkle with salt. Heat olive oil in a skillet and brown partridge halves on all sides. Add onions, garlic, and bay leaf and sauté until onion is soft. Mix in peppercorns, carrot, and celery; pour in wine and vinegar and add thyme, oregano, and parsley. Cover and simmer for about 40 minutes or until tender. Remove from the skillet and let cool. Cut out the bones and slice meat into large individual tapa-size pieces. Place on a serving dish and strain remaining liquid over the meat. Serve either at room temperature or reheated.

Serves 8 (1 piece each)

OREJAS GUISADAS
(STEWED PIGS' EARS)

Excellent with a full-bodied red wine.

1   pound pigs' (or calves')
     ears
1   onion, chopped
2   cloves garlic, chopped
2   tablespoons chopped fresh
     parsley
1   tablespoon flour
1   tablespoon chopped
     hazelnuts
     Pepper to taste
     Pinch nutmeg

Clean and wash ears and boil in salted water for about 2 hours or until tender. With a mortar and pestle or in an electric blender, mix together onion, garlic, 1 tablespoon parsley, and the flour and blend with enough broth from the kettle to form a smooth, thin sauce. Cut ears into small pieces, place in a skillet, and stir in the sauce. Simmer for 10 minutes or until heated through. Sprinkle with chopped nuts and the remaining parsley and season with freshly ground pepper and a pinch of nutmeg.

VARIATION
For extra flavor, add sliced onion, carrots, leeks, and celery to the kettle when boiling ears and season with garlic cloves and a little basil.

Serves 6

CHAPTER TWELVE
TAPAS AROUND THE YEAR

Both the occasion and the weather can affect the tapas you might plan to serve. No one would think of serving hot casserole tapas during a Fourth of July heat wave. During a blizzard, with guests huddled around the fireplace, a chilled cucumber tapa would be out of place. Here again, you're in luck. There are tapas not only for every occasion but also for all seasons and holidays.

HOT-WEATHER TAPA SUGGESTIONS

For summer serving, you don't have to neglect hot tapas. To prevent overheating the kitchen—and the cook—you can charcoal-broil shish kabobs on the outdoor grill or hibachi. If you do plan to serve both hot and cold tapas, remember that they don't have to be hot meats and cold salads. Offer, instead, a combination of cold meats and fish served with one or two hot vegetable tapas.

Generally speaking, though, this is the time to serve summer's best—ripe fruit, fresh green vegetables, shellfish straight from the sea. Most summertime tapas will be at their best eaten raw or very simply cooked, perhaps with a chilled sauce. They should be light, colorful, and appealing to the eye and palate. Whether you serve them cold or hot, cooked or uncooked, plain, well adorned, or sauced, concentrate on those ingredients that are unique to summer and that will be at their best at this time of year. Center your selections on what are the freshest and most appealing offerings on a given day. Flexibility, freshness, and simplicity are the keynotes of a summer tapa spread.

Ice-cold beer, well-chilled white wine, and, best of all, a frosty pitcher of sangria are perfect summertime accompaniments. Try these cooling-down tapas at your next summertime get-together.

MENU

ENSALADILLA RUSA
(Russian Salad)

LANGOSTA A LA CATALANA
(Lobster in Tomato Sauce)

ENSALADA WALDORF
(Waldorf Salad)

MERLUZA CON MAYONESA
(Cold Hake with Mayonnaise)

COLIFLOR A LA VINAGRETA
(Cauliflower Vinaigrette)

ESTORINO EN ESCABECHE
(Marinated Mackerel)

BROCHETAS DE PEZ ESPADA
(Swordfish Kabobs)

OSTRAS
(Oysters on the Half-Shell)

ENSALADILLA RUSA
(RUSSIAN SALAD)

Russian salad is a popular tapa-bar and first-course salad that, although it varies with locale and the seasons, always includes potatoes, carrots, and peas. You can use canned vegetables, but fresh ones are best. Excellent with a cold, crisp beer.

1	cup peeled and diced cooked potatoes
1	cup diced cooked carrots
½	cup cooked peas
1	cup diced cooked beets
½	cup diced cooked green beans
3	tablespoons olive oil
1	tablespoon vinegar
	Salt and pepper to taste
1	cup mayonnaise for coating
1	hard-boiled egg, sliced
12	stuffed green olives
1	2-ounce jar pimientos

Mix together potatoes, carrots, peas, beets, and green beans. In a bowl, mix oil and vinegar and add mixed vegetables. Add salt and pepper to taste and marinate about 1 hour. Drain and spoon mixed vegetables into a serving dish. Coat (do not toss) with mayonnaise and top with sliced hard-boiled egg, green olives, and pimiento strips. Let stand for 1-2 hours to blend the flavors; serve at room temperature.

Serves 6–8

ENSALADA WALDORF
(WALDORF SALAD)

Waldorf salad is a popular foreign import, probably because it is an ideal application of local seasonal fruits and a perfect summer accompaniment to the crisp white wines of Spain.

½	cup diced apples
1	tablespoon fresh lemon juice
½	cup diced celery
1	cup grapes (white, red, or both), halved and seeded
½	cup diced orange slices
¼	cup seedless raisins
¾	cup mayonnaise
½	cup hazelnuts or chopped walnuts
	Lettuce

Sprinkle diced apples with lemon juice to preserve the color. Combine apples, celery, grapes, oranges, and raisins. Bind with mayonnaise, toss, and sprinkle with nuts. Or you can combine the fruits, shape into a loaf, cover with mayonnaise, and sprinkle with nuts. Chill thoroughly and serve cold on a bed of crisp lettuce.

Serves 6–8

COLIFLOR A LA VINAGRETA
(CAULIFLOWER VINAIGRETTE)

You can cook cauliflower either whole or broken into flowerets. To preserve the flavor, cook only until barely tender or flowerets will become mushy. Raw or lightly cooked flowerets are excellent topped with a homemade mayonnaise, béarnaise, or vinaigrette dressing, perhaps also sprinkled with a little grated cheese or ham. Champagne or a white wine would be the perfect companion.

1	medium head cauliflower
⅓	cup olive oil
2	tablespoons vinegar
1	tablespoon chopped fresh parsley
1	tablespoon chopped onion
	Salt to taste

Wash cauliflower, cut off stem and leaves, and break into flowerets. Boil salted water in a kettle and cook flowerets for about 5 minutes or until barely tender; remove and drain. Mix together olive oil, vinegar, parsley, onion, and salt to taste. Pour over flowerets and serve hot or refrigerate and serve cold.

Serves 6

BROCHETAS DE PEZ ESPADA
(SWORDFISH KABOBS)

Because of its firm flesh and rich flavor, swordfish takes well to grilling. You can, of course, use any firm fish; the hardier the fish, the better. Excellent with a sturdy white wine.

1	pound swordfish steaks
2	tablespoons fresh lemon juice
1	tablespoon vinegar
2	cloves garlic, chopped
1	onion, chopped
1	tablespoon chopped fresh parsley
1	cup olive oil
	Pinch saffron
	Lemon wedges

Cut the swordfish into bite-size cubes and put into a bowl. Mix in lemon juice, vinegar, garlic, onion, parsley, and enough olive oil to cover the swordfish cubes. Add a pinch of saffron. Place in the refrigerator and marinate for several hours. Remove from the marinade and thread the cubes on skewers. Place on a grill or hibachi for 3 or 4 minutes, basting frequently with leftover marinade. You can also pan-fry or broil, being careful not to overcook. Serve 1 skewer on each saucer with lemon wedges.

VARIATION
If you wish, alternate fish cubes with tomato wedges, small onions, strips of peppers, or other vegetables.

Serves 6 (1 skewer, 6–8 pieces fish, each)

LANGOSTA A LA CATALANA
(LOBSTER IN TOMATO SAUCE)

Lobsters are usually served in tapa bars grilled, broiled, or boiled, cut into hunks while still in the shells, and accompanied with lemon wedges or a tomato or other mild sauce. Or the meat can be removed from the shells, as in this Catalan recipe. Live lobsters right out of the seawater tank are the tastiest, but you can also use frozen tails. A dry white wine would be a most suitable partner.

1   **live lobster *or* 1 pound frozen lobster tails, thawed**
2   **tablespoons oil**
1   **small onion, chopped**
2   **cloves garlic, chopped**
2   **tomatoes, peeled and chopped**
    Pinch basil
    Salt and pepper to taste

Carefully put the live lobster into a large kettle of boiling salted water (about 3 quarts of water and 3 tablespoons of salt). Boil for 15 minutes or until cooked. Plunge lobster into cold water and drain. Carefully remove the meat from the shell and cut into pieces. Heat oil in a skillet and sauté onion and garlic in it until onion is soft. Stir in tomatoes. Add a pinch of basil and salt and pepper to taste. Simmer until tomatoes are reduced to a smooth paste; add lobster pieces. Cook only until heated through.

Serves 4

MERLUZA CON MAYONESA
(COLD HAKE WITH MAYONNAISE)

Spanish hake is considered the tastiest member of the cod family. It is Spain's most popular and plentiful fish, highly regarded on both dinner tables and tapa counters. The meat is lean and flakes easily, is less white in color and a bit firmer and more tender than other cods, and has a more delicate flavor. It is the easiest of the cods to bone. No matter how you cook it, it will taste good. Small hake, known as pescadilla, *is served in restaurants whole, usually bent in a circle with its tail between its teeth, as either a first or main course.*

Cold fish, usually served with mayonnaise (or green sauce or other light-tasting dressing) is a traditional tapa standby throughout Spain. Because of its delicate flavor, hake is an excellent choice, but any good fish will do. For best results, the fish should be fresh and the mayonnaise homemade with olive oil (see index for mayonnaise recipe). You can cook the fish in just about any way; grilling, frying, and poaching are the most popular.

To poach, first clean and scale the fish, but you can leave on the head and tail. Place in a kettle of boiling salted water and, when the water returns to the boiling point, cook for about 10 minutes per inch of thickness. (Double this time for frozen fish.) Remove the fish immediately so that it doesn't overcook, and let cool. Cut into strips or squares and refrigerate. Serve chilled, several strips on each saucer, with a homemade mayonnaise. One pound hake serves 6.

ESTORINO EN ESCABECHE
(MARINATED MACKEREL)

Spanish mackerel is a firm, meaty fish with a high oil and fat content. Although more delicately flavored than the mackerel found in other parts of the world, it has, nevertheless, a rather strong and distinctive flavor, but a flavor that deteriorates quickly. Spanish mackerel is excellent grilled, takes well to sauces, and is a first-rate fish for marinating. En escabeche, or "in marinade," is a Spanish food preservation technique that has evolved over the centuries into a delicious way to prepare tapas. You can, of course, use any fish, but the richer mackerel, shark, tuna, and sea bass seem to work best. Excellent with a dry white wine.

1	pound mackerel fillets
	Flour for dusting
	Salt and freshly ground pepper to taste
3	tablespoons oil
2	cloves garlic, chopped
¼	cup wine vinegar
2	tablespoons olive oil
1	onion, sliced
1	bay leaf
6	peppercorns
1	green pepper, sliced
1	small dried chili pepper, broken

Cut mackerel into strips. Roll strips in flour seasoned with salt and pepper. Fry in hot oil until golden on all sides and transfer to a bowl. Add garlic, vinegar, olive oil, onion, bay leaf, peppercorns, green pepper, and chili pepper and stir in enough water for the marinade to cover the fish. Let stand for 24 hours and serve at room temperature.

Serves 6 (4–6 strips each)

OSTRAS
(OYSTERS ON THE HALF-SHELL)

Oysters are usually eaten raw in tapa bars, but they're also fried and sometimes baked; seldom with a sauce. To prepare oysters, first wash and scrub the shells under running water. Then, with a sharp knife, slit open the shells and cut the muscle.

To serve raw oysters on the half-shell, discard the top shells, cut the oysters free from the bottoms, and serve on the bottom shells in the natural juices with lemon wedges. Champagne, a dry white wine, or a light beer would be the ideal partner.

Note: As alternatives, try the other recipes in this book as the oyster tapa in this hot-weather menu: Fried Oysters, Oyster Fritters, or Oysters with Wine, all in Chapter 17.

COLD-WEATHER TAPA SUGGESTIONS

For a blustering winter evening, hot and hearty tapas in larger quantities would be most welcome. Nuts, sausages, and stronger-tasting cheeses are also appropriate.

MENU

ALMENDRAS
(Almonds)

QUESO MANCHEGO
(Manchego Cheese)

BUÑUELITOS DE BACALAO
(Codfish Fritters)

BUTIFARRA A LA PLANCHA
(Grilled Catalan Sausage)

FABADA ASTURIANA
(Asturian Bean Stew)

CALDERETA
(Fish Stew)

ESTOFADO DE TERNERA
(Veal Stew)

ALMENDRAS
ALMONDS

For suggestions on preparing and serving almonds, see Chapter 5, page 20.

QUESO MANCHEGO
MANCHEGO CHEESE

For information on choosing and serving Manchego cheese, see Chapter 5, page 23.

BUÑUELITOS DE BACALAO
(CODFISH FRITTERS)

Excellent accompanied by a cold beer or a full-bodied wine.

½ pound dried salt cod
Buñuelitos Batter (recipe follows)
2 cloves garlic, chopped
2 tablespoons chopped fresh parsley
Oil for deep-frying

Soak dried cod 6-8 hours, changing the water occasionally. Drain and flake into small pieces with your fingers. Stir flaked cod into Buñuelitos Batter and add garlic and parsley. Heat oil in a skillet and drop in fritter mixture, 1 teaspoon at a time. Fry until golden.

Note: For Codfish Fritters in this menu, try substituting any of the ingredients suggested for buñuelitos in Chapter 13.

Serves 6

BUÑUELITOS BATTER

2 cups flour
1 teaspoon baking soda
1 egg, beaten
½ cup water
Salt to taste

Put flour in a bowl and mix in the baking soda, egg, enough water to form a smooth paste, and salt to taste. Use batter as directed in individual buñuelitos recipes.

YIELD: Makes enough batter for 6 Buñuelitos.

BUTIFARRA A LA PLANCHA
(GRILLED CATALAN SAUSAGE)

For suggestions on preparing and serving Spanish sausage, see Chapter 9, page 44.

FABADA ASTURIANA
(ASTURIAN BEAN STEW)

Fabada *was originally an Asturian one-dish stew made of beans (called* fabes*) and lamb. It has evolved into scores of regional variations, including various tapas, and is even sold canned in Spanish supermarkets. To be a true* fabada asturiana, *the beans as well as all the other ingredients must come from Asturias, an improbability except in the home region. Actually, you can substitute any dried white bean and use your own combination of meats. Blood sausage, chorizo, and salt pork have become standard throughout Spain, and pigs' feet and ears are common. Any full-bodied red wine would be a good partner here.*

1½   **pounds dried white beans**
½   **pound blood sausage (morcilla), diced**
½   **pound chorizo or other pork sausage, diced**
½   **pound salt pork, diced**
½   **pound ham or bacon, diced**
½   **teaspoon saffron**
2   **teaspoons paprika**
3   **cloves garlic, crushed**
1   **bay leaf**
   Salt to taste

Soak beans overnight in a large kettle of water. Place kettle on the stove and bring to a boil in the same water used for soaking. After it reaches the boiling point, add blood sausage, chorizo, salt pork, and ham; stir in saffron, paprika, garlic, and bay leaf. Simmer for about 2 hours or until beans are tender. Add a little hot water if the stew becomes dry, but not enough to thin it. Add salt to taste.

Serves 10

CALDERETA
(FISH STEW)

Caldereta *(the word means "small kettle")* *is a fish stew from Asturias, quite flexible as to basic ingredients. Use any combination of fish and shellfish that's available. Fresh, of course, would be the best. Delicious accompanied by dry sherry or white wine.*

12	mussels or large clams
12	small clams
12	small shrimp
2	pounds assorted (at least 3 varieties) white fish
2	tablespoons oil
2	onions, chopped
2	cloves garlic
2	tomatoes, peeled and chopped
1	cup dry sherry or white wine
5	peppercorns, crushed
1	teaspoon paprika
	Salt and pepper to taste
2	tablespoons chopped fresh parsley

Clean mussels and clams, open the shells, remove the meat, and discard shells. Clean and peel shrimp, clean and skin assorted white fish, and cut fish into bite-size cubes. Heat oil in a skillet and sauté onions and garlic in it until onions are soft. Add tomatoes, sherry, peppercorns, and paprika and simmer until liquid is reduced by about a third. Add shellfish and fish pieces and continue to simmer for 10 minutes or until fish is cooked, adding hot water or fish stock if stew becomes too dry. Add salt and pepper to taste and sprinkle with parsley. A heaping saucerful (this is a large recipe with a lot of ingredients) makes a hardy tapa.

VARIATION
Add diced boiled potatoes for a substantial fish-and-potatoes meal.

Serves 10 or more

ESTOFADO DE TERNERA
(VEAL STEW)

Excellent with red wine or sherry.

1   **pound veal**

3   **tablespoons oil**

1   **onion, chopped**

2   **tomatoes, peeled and chopped**

1   **cup dry white wine**

1   **cup veal, chicken, or beef stock**

1   **bay leaf**

¼   **teaspoon dried thyme**

1   **cup chopped mushrooms**

½   **tablespoon flour**

    Salt to taste

8   **blanched almonds, chopped**

2   **cloves garlic, chopped**

¼   **teaspoon saffron**

    Olive oil

1   **tablespoon chopped fresh parsley**

Cut meat into bite-size (½-inch) chunks. Heat 2 tablespoons oil in a skillet, add veal, fry until well browned and remove. Add 1 tablespoon oil to the skillet and sauté onion in it until soft. Add tomatoes and wine and continue to cook until liquid is reduced by a third. Return veal to the skillet and add stock, bay leaf, thyme, mushrooms, flour, and a pinch of salt; cover and simmer gently about 1 hour. With a mortar and pestle or in an electric blender, grind almonds, garlic, saffron, and enough olive oil to form a smooth sauce. Add mixture to the veal, sprinkle with parsley, and simmer another 30 minutes.

Serves 6

A HOLIDAY TAPAS OPEN HOUSE

Holiday patterns are changing. So are Americans and their appetites. Gone are the days when a full-scale family dinner was the only way to celebrate Christmas, New Year's Day, and Thanksgiving. Wedding receptions and anniversary dinners are changing, too. Granted, a Thanksgiving tapa party will never replace a turkey-and-pumpkin-pie dinner back on the farm, but it certainly beats a restaurant or cafeteria meal.

If the holiday season is an inconvenient time for a tapa party, there are scores of Spanish fiesta days, even fiesta weeks, to choose from. Consult your favorite travel book for a list of ever-changing dates. The most important holiday in Spain is not Christmas, but Holy Week. With this in mind we present a typical Lenten tapa party, emphasizing meatless dishes, as is the custom in Spain.

MENU

ARROZ A LA MARINERA
(Seafood Rice)

ACEITUNAS ADOBADAS
(Marinated Olives)

CHAMPIÑONES RELLENOS
(Stuffed Mushrooms)

PATATAS POBRES
(Poor Man's Potatoes)

PIMIENTOS FRITOS
(Fried Peppers)

PISTO
(Vegetable Stew)

RAPE A LA MARINERA
(Anglerfish, Fisherman's Style)

ARROZ A LA MARINERA
(SEAFOOD RICE)

Although not as popular for meals as are some of the other paella dishes, arroz a la marinera *has become a tapa favorite, especially during Lent. A good white wine would be a fine partner for this tapa.*

1	pound flounder, halibut, or other white fish
12	small clams
12	mussels or medium clams
½	pound small shrimp
5	cups water
3	small squid, cleaned
3	tablespoons oil
1	onion, chopped
2	cloves garlic, chopped
½	cup rice
½	teaspoon saffron
3	tablespoons chopped fresh parsley
1	tablespoon chopped canned pimientos
	Lemon wedges

Clean fish and seafood and shell and devein shrimp. Cover the cleaned shrimp, clams, and mussels with 5 cups of water and simmer for 5 minutes or until shells open. Remove and reserve the liquid. Cut out the meat from the shells, discarding shells. Cut white fish into 1-inch cubes and squid into rings and pieces. Heat oil in a paella pan and sauté onion and garlic in it until onion is soft. Add fish cubes and squid rings and continue cooking slowly for 5 minutes or until fish is barely cooked. Add rice, mussels, clams, and shrimp. Mix saffron into the liquid used to cook the shellfish and pour into the pan. Cook uncovered (or bake in a preheated 450°F oven) for 15 minutes or until liquid is absorbed and rice is cooked. Let stand for 10 minutes to blend the seafood flavors. Sprinkle with parsley, top with pimientos, and serve with lemon wedges.

VARIATION
You can use any other combination of seafood and add peas, artichoke hearts, peppers, or other vegetables.

Serves 10

PATATAS POBRES
(POOR MAN'S POTATOES)

Besides being a tasty tapa, this Spanish version of hot potato salad is a popular accompaniment to meat dishes, especially sausage and ham. Also popular with eggs. Ideal with cold beer.

4	medium potatoes
	Salt and pepper to taste
4	tablespoons oil
2	cloves garlic, minced
½	teaspoon paprika
¼	cup vinegar
1	tablespoon chopped fresh parsley

Peel and cut potatoes into thin slices, ⅛ inch thick or thinner, and season with salt and pepper. Heat oil in a large skillet and sauté slices until browned lightly on both sides. Gently mix in garlic and paprika and continue to simmer 10 minutes more or until potatoes are tender. During the last 2 minutes of cooking, pour in vinegar and sprinkle with parsley. Serve hot.

Serves 8

ACEITUNAS ADOBADAS
(MARINATED OLIVES)

Although technically a fruit, olives are usually classed with vegetables. Both the green and black varieties are eaten in tapa bars out of hand just as they come off the tree. They are also popular stuffed with pimientos, lemon peels, almonds, onions, garlic, and anchovies. Most often, they are marinated. You can buy cured olives in specialty food stores, or you can do it yourself. Any drink would be appropriate with this popular tapa; a glass of sherry might taste best.

½   **gallon pitted olives (green or black)**
2-3   **garlic cloves, peeled**
1   **teaspoon dried oregano**
1   **lemon, quartered**
1   **tablespoon wine vinegar**

To marinate, first remove the liquid from a ½-gallon glass jar of pitted olives (the Spanish use large earthenware containers) and fill with water. Add garlic cloves, oregano, quartered lemon, and wine vinegar. Cover the jar and refrigerate for several days. The longer the olives soak, the better the flavor; to speed the curing process, split the olives. Allow 8-10 olives for a generous portion.

VARIATION
Sliced onions, paprika, and thyme are favorite additions, and so are hot peppers.

Serves 15–20

PIMIENTOS FRITOS
(FRIED PEPPERS)

Sweet peppers (pimientos) are a versatile tapa food that come in all sizes and can be eaten in many ways, either raw or cooked. They are excellent in salads and are an important part of several vegetable tapas. Peppers have a special affinity for eggs and are the basis for several Spanish sauces, notably Salsa Romesco (see index for recipe). They are popular in America canned or jarred.

The red pepper (pimiento rojo) and the green pepper (pimiento verde) are produced from the same plant. The pods are green when mature, turning yellow, orange, and finally bright red when fully ripened. Either a good red or white wine would complement this tapa.

16   **small green peppers**
4   **tablespoons oil**
   Salt to taste

Wash and dry small peppers (the smaller they are, the handier they are to eat), leaving the stems on for easy holding. Heat oil in a skillet and fry slowly, turning frequently, until tender and cooked on all sides. Sprinkle with salt and serve hot.

Serves 4 (3–5 small peppers or 1 large pepper each)

RAPE A LA MARINERA
(ANGLERFISH, FISHERMAN'S STYLE)

An impressive tapa as well as a delicious all-in-one meal. Excellent with a white or a rosé wine.

4	tablespoons oil
1	onion, chopped
1	clove garlic, chopped
1½	pounds anglerfish fillets
1	egg, beaten
	Flour for dusting
12	small clams, cleaned
12	small shrimp, cleaned and peeled
¼	cup dry white wine
¼	cup tomato paste
1	hard-boiled egg, chopped

Heat 1 tablespoon of oil in a large skillet and sauté onion and garlic in it until onion is soft. Clean fish and cut into bite-size pieces. Dip pieces in beaten egg and then in flour. Add 3 more tablespoons of oil and fry in hot oil until light brown on all sides. Add clams and peeled shrimp. Mix together white wine and tomato paste and pour into the skillet. Sprinkle with chopped hard-boiled egg and simmer for 15 minutes or until liquid is reduced and clam shells have opened.

Serves 10 or more

CHAMPIÑONES RELLENOS
(STUFFED MUSHROOMS)

A hearty red wine would be a suitable companion.

12	medium-size mushrooms
1½	tablespoons oil
1	small onion, chopped
1	clove garlic, chopped
½	pound ground pork, veal, or other meat
1	tablespoon chopped fresh parsley
1	teaspoon dried basil
¼	cup grated Manchego, Parmesan, or other cheese
1	egg, beaten
1	tablespoon brandy

Wash mushrooms and cut off stems. Heat oil in a skillet and sauté onion and garlic in it until onion is soft. Add mushroom caps and continue to simmer for 2–3 minutes or until glazed. Remove caps and set aside. Finely chop mushroom stems and add to the skillet. Add pork and continue cooking until meat is well browned. Stir in parsley, basil, half the grated cheese, and the beaten egg. Add brandy and mix well. Fill mushroom caps with the mixture. Sprinkle remaining cheese over the caps and bake in a preheated 350°F oven (or in a broiler) about 15 minutes.

Serves 4–6

PISTO
(VEGETABLE STEW)

Pisto *is a hearty vegetable stew found throughout central and northern Spain in scores of regional versions, served as both a meal and a tapa. The word* pisto *is variously translated as "vegetable stew," "vegetable medley," "vegetable hash," even "vegetable mess." Ingredients differ, depending on the season and section of the country. Tomatoes, peppers, zucchini, eggplant, and potatoes are the most popular. You may notice its resemblance to ratatouille. A hearty red wine would be a suitable partner. The basic tapa pisto (if there is one) goes something like this:*

Oil

1 large onion, chopped

2 cloves garlic, chopped

1 medium potato, peeled and diced

2 green peppers, cut into strips

3 large tomatoes, chopped

2 medium zucchini, sliced

1 small eggplant, chopped

Salt and pepper to taste

Heat 1-2 tablespoons oil in a skillet and sauté chopped onion and garlic in it until the onion is soft. Add the diced potato and fry until barely browned. Add green peppers and simmer 5 more minutes, then mix in tomatoes, zucchini, and eggplant. Add salt and pepper to taste. Cover and simmer 30 minutes or until vegetables are tender. Equally delicious cold as a tapa or hot as a meal.

VARIATION

For a meal, add diced ham or bacon and, at the last minute, top with 2 fried eggs or fold in 2 lightly beaten eggs. Serve it piping hot and call it *pisto manchego* (pisto, La Mancha style).

Serves 8

PART THREE
TAPA RECIPES

Part III is an anthology of traditional tapa recipes that have been harvested by the authors from tapa kitchens throughout Spain. Each chapter in Part III covers a specific food category; Salads to Exotics. Besides the more than 200 recipes and recipe variations included here, you will find also, at the end of each chapter, page references to the more than 50 recipes described in Part II: "Tapas Parties."

CHAPTER THIRTEEN
SALAD AND FINGER-FOOD TAPAS (ENSALADAS Y ENTREMESES)

SALADS

Tapa salads are chiefly regional specialities, with a few, like Waldorf Salad, adapted from the salads of other countries. Whatever their origin, all start with fresh ingredients, mostly local seasonal produce. Most are also plainly served, usually accompanied by a vinaigrette, mayonnaise, or other light dressing. Ingredients usually include greens or vegetables, either cooked or raw; fish, shellfish, and meats are also popular.

Salads are a favorite first tapa of the day and a popular first course in the traditional Spanish multicourse meal. During the summer months, they are frequently expanded into light meals, often accompanied by slices of cold meats (*fiambres*), sausage, or seafood.

Whether the salads are tapas, first courses, or light meals, the Spanish seldom toss them—especially green salads. In the typical first-course *ensalada de la casa*, for example, the ingredients (lettuce leaves, tomato slices, olives, rings of onions, etc.) will be arranged in a decorative fashion on a large shallow platter and served undressed with miniature pitchers of olive oil and wine vinegar on the side. Even when a mayonnaise dressing is used (for example, in a potato or Russian salad) it is often spread over the top rather than blended in with the other ingredients.

ENSALADILLA DE PATATAS
(POTATO SALAD)

Just about any drink would go well with potato salad, but perhaps a cold beer would taste best.

3	medium potatoes
1	small onion, chopped
1	small tomato, chopped
¼	cup chopped celery
1	teaspoon vinegar
1	tablespoon chopped fresh parsley
1	teaspoon celery seed
2	teaspoons fresh lemon juice
1	tablespoon olive oil
½	cup mayonnaise
1	hard-boiled egg, sliced
1	2-ounce jar pimientos
	Green olives

Cook potatoes in water; drain and peel. Cut into chunks while still warm. Place in a bowl and add onion, tomato, and celery. Sprinkle with vinegar, parsley, celery seed, lemon juice, and olive oil. Mix well. Shape into a loaf and cover with a thin coating of mayonnaise (preferably homemade) and refrigerate. (You can also mix the mayonnaise throughout, American style.) Top with egg slices, pimiento strips, and green olives.

Serves 6–8

ENSALADA DE BRECOL Y COLIFLOR
(BROCCOLI AND CAULIFLOWER SALAD)

This is a typical ensalada *that can easily pass for a vegetable tapa, and with the addition of thick slices of ham it is transformed into a wonderfully refreshing one-dish summer meal. Any drink would stand up well to this salad, especially a crisp white wine.*

1	medium head cauliflower
1	pound broccoli
1	onion, chopped
1	cup mayonnaise
¼	cup vinegar
8	slices bacon, cooked and crumbled

Wash cauliflower, cut off stem and leaves, and break into flowerets. Wash and trim the tough ends of broccoli stalks. Cut both flowerets and broccoli into small bite-size chunks. Mix all ingredients together, toss, chill, and serve cold.

Serves 8

ENSALADA DE COL
(CABBAGE SALAD)

A beer or red or white wine would be a suitable companion.

1	small head cabbage, chopped
1	bunch celery, chopped
1	onion, chopped
1	green pepper, chopped
1	egg, beaten
½	cup sugar
½	teaspoon saffron or turmeric
½	cup vinegar
2	tablespoons flour
1	teaspoon salt

Mix together chopped cabbage, celery, onion, and green pepper. Mix egg, sugar, saffron, vinegar, flour, and salt to make a thick dressing. Pour over the ingredients and mix well. Refrigerate for several hours and serve chilled. You can make the dressing or even the entire salad the day before.

Serves 8

ENSALADA CATALANA
(CATALAN SALAD)

Ensalada Catalana is a mixed salad found in many wondrous variations throughout Spain. It can be served as a tapa or first course; in larger portions, it is a meal in itself. As a meal, spread over lettuce leaves and surround with sausage or sliced ham. As a tapa, spoon over individual endive leaves. In its classic form, ensalada catalana uses a Catalan sausage called butifarra. Popular with a Spanish brandy.

2	stalks celery, cubed
1	red onion, chopped
2	medium potatoes, boiled and diced
1	green pepper, sliced
⅓	cup diced ham
½	cup butifarra, chorizo, or other pork sausage
1	4-ounce can anchovies, tuna, cod, or other firm-fleshed fish
12	green olives
2	tomatoes, diced
2	hard-boiled eggs, quartered
	Oil and vinegar or mayonnaise and vinegar

Combine all ingredients and toss. For a dressing, use either an oil and vinegar (at least 3 or 4 to 1) or a homemade mayonnaise (see index for recipe) thinned with vinegar (about 4 to 1) and sprinkled over the salad.

Serves 6–8

ENSALADA VALENCIANA
(VALENCIA SALAD)

Accompany with a chilled Spanish champagne or a pitcher of sangria.

2 **oranges, peeled and sliced**
1 **onion, sliced**
1 **small green pepper, sliced**
2 **tablespoons chopped pimientos**
3 **tablespoons olive oil**
1 **tablespoon red wine vinegar**
  Salt and pepper to taste

Cut orange slices into chunks and mix well with onion, green pepper, pimientos, oil, and vinegar. Add salt and pepper to taste and serve cold.

VARIATION
As a salad course, add greens and toss.

Serves 6

ENSALADA DE TOMATES
(TOMATO SALAD)

Tomatoes, either red or green, are a favorite plain-and-simple tapa, served only with a little olive oil and salt. To prepare, cut ripe tomatoes into ¼-inch slices, sprinkle generously with salt and a coating of olive oil, but no vinegar; you can, if you like, add a little lemon juice. Black olives will add a bit more taste, texture, and color. To form a typical mixed salad, add onion rings, chopped garlic, parsley, and hard-boiled egg slices.

Serves 2 per medium-size tomato

ENSALADA DE REMOLACHA
(BEET SALAD)

Beets, both cooked and raw, are much more popular in Spain as salads than as vegetables. Their sweetness is a welcome contrast to the taste of other Spanish salad ingredients, and they stand up well to most tapa drinks. Beets are one of the very few vegetables that are almost as good canned as fresh. A rosé wine would go well with this tapa.

4   fresh medium beets *or* 1 9-ounce can of beets
3   tablespoons olive oil
1   tablespoon red wine vinegar
     Salt to taste
1   onion, chopped
1   tablespoon chopped fresh parsley

Cut off the beet stems just above the bulbs but do not peel. If fresh, boil beets in salted water for about 40 minutes (much less for tiny beets) or until tender. Drain and let cool until you can peel off the skins. Cut slices about ¼ inch thick or leave tiny beets whole. Mix oil and vinegar and drizzle over the beets. Add salt to taste, stir in chopped onion, and sprinkle with parsley. Serve chilled.

Serves 6–7

ENSALADA DE APIO
(CELERY SALAD)

This celery salad is a favorite, simple-to-prepare Catalan tapa. Its secret is freshness and crispness. A light white wine would be an appropriate partner.

12   very tender inner celery stalks
     Olive oil
     Fresh lemon juice
1-2 tablespoons chopped celery leaves
     Salt and pepper to taste

Cut celery into strips about 2 inches long and soak in cold water, 1 hour or more to bring out the crispness. Remove and drain well. Mix olive oil and lemon juice (in a 3-to-1 ratio) and chopped celery leaves. Drizzle over the celery; add salt and pepper to taste.

VARIATION
Braise celery strips with bits of bacon (cook slowly in a covered skillet for about 15 minutes) to prepare a hot celery tapa, called *apios braseados con bacón.*

6 servings (2 stalks each)

ENSALADA PIMIENTOS Y ACEITUNAS
(PEPPER AND OLIVE SALAD)

6   green peppers
1½ tablespoons oil
½   cup chopped green olives
2   tablespoons capers
1   teaspoon wine vinegar
1   teaspoon sugar
½   teaspoon dried oregano
    Salt and pepper to taste

Cut peppers into thin slices. Heat oil in a skillet and sauté pepper slices until soft. Add olives, capers, vinegar, sugar, and oregano and mix well. Add salt and pepper to taste. Simmer for 15 minutes, chill, and serve.

Serves 8

ENSALADA DE POLLO
(CHICKEN SALAD)

2   cups cubed cooked
    chicken
½   cup sliced celery
⅓   cup mayonnaise
⅓   cup chopped almonds or
    whole hazelnuts
1   cup halved green seedless
    grapes
2   tablespoons chopped
    onions
    Salt and pepper to taste
⅛   teaspoon dried thyme
1   hard-boiled egg, sliced
    Pitted black olives

Combine chicken and celery. Mix together mayonnaise, nuts, grapes, and onion. Season with salt, pepper, and thyme. Toss with chicken and celery. Refrigerate 2-3 hours. Top with slices of hard-boiled egg and black olives and serve chilled.

Serves 6-8

ENSALADA DE CALAMARES Y QUESO
(SQUID AND CHEESE SALAD)

2   pounds squid or octopus
½   cup olive oil
2   tablespoons fresh lemon
      juice
½   teaspoon dried oregano
     Salt and pepper to taste
½   pound Manchego or other
      cheese, diced
2   stalks celery, sliced
1   tablespoon chopped fresh
      parsley
1   red pepper, sliced

Clean and wash squid. Remove ink sacs, insides, and heads and peel off the skins. Boil salted water in a kettle and cook squid 2-3 minutes or until barely tender. Remove, drain, and cut bodies into rings and tentacles into pieces. In a bowl, mix together olive oil, lemon juice, and oregano; add salt and pepper to taste. Add squid and refrigerate 2-3 hours. Stir in cheese, celery, and parsley. Taste for salt and top with sliced peppers. Serve chilled.

Serves 8-10

ENSALADA DE BACALAO
(CODFISH SALAD)

1   pound dried salt cod
1   onion, chopped
1   tomato, peeled and
      chopped
½   cup black or green olives
      or a combination
1   tablespoon chopped fresh
      parsley
     Salt and pepper to taste
6   tablespoons olive oil
2   tablespoons vinegar
2   hard-boiled eggs, sliced

Soak cod 6-8 hours, changing the water 2-3 times. Boil salted water in a kettle and cook cod for 15 minutes or until done. Remove, drain, skin, and cut into pieces. Mix together onion, tomato, olives, and parsley. Add cod pieces, salt and pepper to taste, drizzle with oil and vinegar, and toss. Top with egg slices. Serve chilled.

Serves 8

ENSALADA DE GAMBAS Y MEJILLONES
(SHRIMP AND MUSSEL SALAD)

1   pound small shrimp,
     cooked and shelled

6   steamed mussels or
     clams, shelled and diced

1   small onion, chopped

1   small green pepper,
     chopped

1   clove garlic, minced

3   tablespoons olive oil

2   tablespoons vinegar

1   tablespoon chopped fresh
     parsley

    Salt and pepper to taste

    Dash of Tabasco

1   hard-boiled egg, sliced

Combine shrimp, diced mussels, onion, and green pepper. Sprinkle with garlic, olive oil, vinegar, and parsley. Add salt and pepper to taste and a dash of Tabasco and toss. Top with egg slices. Refrigerate 3–4 hours and serve chilled.

Serves 6–8

ADDITIONAL SALADS

FINGER-FOOD TAPAS

Entremeses include the finger-food tapas available in cafés and tapa bars, but they are also served at outdoor and indoor fiestas, in snack bars and cafeterias, and by street vendors to passersby. They include tartlets, croquettes, fritters, miniature sandwiches, and stuffed pastries of various kinds. Because finger-food tapas can be created out of almost any combination of ingredients, they defy categorization under the traditional food headings of meats, fish, and vegetables. When listed on Spanish a la carte menus, they are typically found under the first-course heading *Entremeses y Ensaladas*.

Also invariably listed under this first-course heading are fresh salads, such as those in the first part of this chapter, and the plain-and-simple appetizers, often called *tapas naturales*: marinated olives, steamed mussels, grilled shrimp, sliced sausage. This latter group, the natural tapas, fit conveniently into the traditional food categories and, therefore, will not be presented here but in the appropriate chapters that follow.

TURNOVERS (EMPANADILLAS)

Empanadillas are pastries stuffed with meat or fish and sometimes with vegetables. They are diminutive versions of a large pie or loaf-size Galician specialty called *empanadas*, which, in northern Spain, are cut into large wedges or slices and eaten as complete meals. Snack-size turnovers come with a variety of fillings and in all shapes—usually round, but also oblong, triangular, and square. They are considered by tapa cooks to be the ideal receptacle for leftovers.

The two elements that make up empanadillas are dough and a filling. The latter always includes a moistener, or binding agent, such as mayonnaise, tomato sauce, sherry, or white wine that both enhances flavor and binds together the ingredients, keeping them moist during and after cooking. Traditionally the dough for this tapa is a yeast dough; you may use any unsweetened light yeast dough—bread or pizza dough or a pie crust mixture.

EMPANADILLAS DE ATUN
(TUNA TURNOVERS)

This is a popular filling used both in pie-size empanadas and in finger-size empanadillas. You can, of course, substitute any fish and accompany with any number of ingredients. Mushrooms would be an especially tasty addition. Just about any drink would be suitable, including mixed drinks.

1   **tablespoon oil**
1   **medium onion, chopped**
2   **medium tomatoes, peeled and chopped**
1   **7-ounce can tuna, drained and flaked**
1   **2-ounce jar pimientos, drained and chopped**
2   **tablespoons chopped fresh parsley**
   Salt to taste
1   **hard-boiled egg, chopped**
   Empanadilla Dough (see index for recipe)

Heat oil in a skillet and sauté onion in it until soft. Add tomatoes and continue to fry until a paste begins to form. Add tuna bits, pimientos, and parsley. Mix well and cook briefly. Add salt to taste, remove from the heat, and sprinkle in chopped hard-boiled egg. Spoon filling onto the turnover dough, fold up the sides, and pinch together to seal. Leave in a warm place for 15 minutes. Bake in a preheated 375°F oven for 40 minutes or until golden.

Serves 6 (2–3 small turnovers each)

TARTLETS (TARTALETAS)

Tartaletas are popular party and tapa snacks. They are made from a pie-crust or other dough molded in the form of *barcos*, or small boats (although they can be any shape), and filled with seafood, ham, chicken, or cheeses and covered with sliced olives, chopped parsley, snipped chives, or other toppings.

TARTALETAS DE JAMON Y QUESO
(HAM AND CHEESE TARTLETS)

Accompany these tartlets with a good pilsner.

½ **cup finely chopped cooked ham**

½ **cup grated Manchego, Gruyère, Swiss, or other cheese**

1 **teaspoon good-quality mustard**

1 **tablespoon or more mayonnaise**

Tartlet Shells (see index for recipe)

Garnishes: chopped fresh parsley, paprika, sliced black olives, or chopped green onions

Mix ham, cheese, mustard, and just enough mayonnaise to bind. Fill the shells with the mixture and sprinkle with garnishes of your choice.

Serves 5 (2 small tartlets per serving)

CROQUETAS DE JAMON
(HAM CROQUETTES)

Croquetas *are another excellent way to use leftovers, popular in Spain both as tapas and as predinner appetizers. You can make them ahead, freeze, and fry. They are often served in tapa bars with a béchamel or other sauce (see index for sauce recipes). Excellent with a dry sherry or a crisp beer.*

2   tablespoons oil
3   tablespoons chopped onion
1   tablespoon dry sherry (optional)
2   tablespoons flour
¾   cup chicken stock
1   cup ground ham
¼   cup finely chopped blanched almonds
1   tablespoon chopped fresh parsley
    Salt, pepper, and nutmeg to taste
1   egg, beaten
½   cup bread crumbs
    Oil for deep-frying

Heat oil in a skillet and sauté onion in it until soft. (For added taste, include 1 tablespoon dry sherry.) Stir in flour and slowly pour in stock. Add ham, almonds, and parsley. Mix well and season with a pinch each of salt, pepper, and nutmeg. Spread mixture into a pan and refrigerate until stiff enough to handle. Form the mixture into firm bite-size balls, dip each into beaten egg, and roll in bread crumbs. Place croquettes in a pan and refrigerate for 1 hour or more. Fry in deep oil at 350°F for 3 minutes or until golden. Drain and serve hot.

Serves 4–6 (2–4 croquettes each)

SMALL FRITTERS (BUÑUELITOS)

Buñuelitos are bite-size fritters (or puffs) of fish, meat, and other foods dipped in batter and deep-fried. They are served in tapa bars either warm or hot, often with a sauce. Buñuelitos are easier to make than croquettes, although not as popular. (Meal-size fritters are called buñuelos.)

Besides the buñuelitos in other chapters (as noted below) you can make them with fresh cod or any white fish. Salmon, anchovies, and shrimp are also popular; so are chicken, ham, and sausage. Peas, eggplant, and other vegetables are excellent possibilities, as are chopped hard-boiled eggs. Add grated potatoes for extra firmness. Serve either plain or with a tomato, béchamel, or other sauce (see index for sauce recipes). A good-size fritter would equal a tapa serving.

CHURROS
(DOUGH FRITTERS)

Tapas are seldom eaten for breakfast, with this one exception: churros. *Churros are twisted strips of fried hollow dough sold in tapa bars and cafés and by street vendors. The vendor squirts dough from a large pastry tube (called a* churrera*) into a huge vat of hot oil, creating a long curlicue strip of fried dough. The fried strip is cut into bite-size pieces and served in a scrap of rolled-up newspaper to be eaten out of hand like french fries. Churros are delicious with hot chocolate and popular in tapa bars and cafés with a breakfast café solo. "A splendid invention," as Roger Fry so aptly put it.*

2 cups water
¼ teaspoon fresh lemon juice
¼ teaspoon salt
2 cups flour
   Oil for deep-frying
   Sugar for dusting
      (optional)

Boil water, lemon juice, and salt and immediately add flour. Stir with a wooden spoon until the dough is smooth. Remove from the heat, let cool, and fill a cake decorator or pastry tube with the dough. The opening should be fluted and about ½ inch wide. Heat oil to 350°F in a deep pan and squeeze the dough into the hot oil. Fry 2–3 minutes or until crisp and golden brown. Remove, drain, and cut into 3-inch strips. Serve hot, either plain or dusted with sugar.

Serves 8

FRIED SANDWICHES (EMPAREDADOS)

Emparedados (fried sandwiches) are popular in cafés and tascas and are a snack-bar favorite. Besides the York ham and Manchego cheese combination below, chicken, chorizo, and most other meats and cheeses are also popular.

EMPAREDADOS DE JAMON Y QUESO
(HOT HAM AND CHEESE SANDWICHES)

To prepare a platter of emparedados, remove the crusts of several slices of bread and cut each slice in half or in quarters. Cover half the slices with alternating layers of ham and cheese, then top with remaining bread to form small sandwiches.

Pour milk into a shallow dish and, with toothpicks or a fork, dip each sandwich into the milk only long enough to dampen the bread (this helps prevent the emparedados from breaking up when fried); set aside to dry for 10–15 minutes. Just before serving, dip sandwiches in beaten eggs and pan-fry in hot oil or heat in a broiler until well browned. Drain and serve. A cold beer might be just right with these sandwiches.

> *1–2 miniature sandwiches per serving, depending on size.*

CANAPES

Spanish canapés are simple to prepare, and you can invent as many of your own combinations as your imagination dictates. The base is usually bread, sometimes pastries or crackers, with a meat, fish, cheese, or other covering or spread. Typical coverings include slices of cheese, ham, sausage, smoked salmon, and sardines. Spreads are usually made of meat, fish, or cheese.

To prepare, remove the crust from an unsliced loaf of bread and cut $\frac{1}{3}$-inch (or thinner) slices or use thin presliced bread. Cover slices completely with a covering or filling and cut into small squares, triangles, or other shapes with a sharp serrated knife. Top individually with mayonnaise, sliced olives, chopped almonds, pimiento strips, chopped parsley, bits of tomato, chopped hard-boiled egg yolks, etc.

To save time, slice the bread ahead, wrap tightly, and store at room temperature. You can also prepare fillings and toppings ahead and refrigerate, but be sure to bring to room temperature before spreading. Prepare hot canapés ahead by toasting the bread, spreading with a topping, cutting into shapes, and heating just before serving. Tapa cooks like to grill and deep-fry canapés. Serve 2-3 canapés per portion, depending on size, with just about any beverage accompaniment, alcoholic or not.

CANAPE DE JAMON
(HAM CANAPE)

Another popular canapé is made of pureed ham (or chicken or other meat or fish) blended with either mayonnaise or sherry, seasoned with a little salt and pepper, spread on toast or bread, topped with toasted almonds, and cut into the desired shapes.

To prepare a warm ham canapé, spread a slice of bread with mayonnaise and lay on a piece of ham and then a piece of cheese. Place in a 400° F oven for 4 minutes or until the cheese is melted and sprinkle with minced parsley or sliced olives. Three small ham canapés would make a nice serving.

CANAPE DE ATUN
(TUNA CANAPE)

1   7-ounce can tuna, drained
2   tablespoons chopped hard-
    boiled egg yolks
1   tablespoon minced onion
2   tablespoons minced
    pimientos
    Mayonnaise or Tomato
    Sauce (see index for
    recipes)
4   slices bread
2   hard-boiled eggs, sliced

Mash tuna in a bowl with chopped hard-boiled egg yolks. Add minced onion and pimientos. Blend with enough mayonnaise or Tomato Sauce to bind. Spread on bread, cut into desired shapes, and top each with a slice of hard-boiled egg.

Serves 8

ADDITIONAL FINGER-FOOD TAPAS

CHAPTER FOURTEEN
EGG AND CHEESE TAPAS (HUEVOS Y QUESOS)

EGGS (HUEVOS)

Eggs are a versatile food, and Spanish cooks have devised dozens of ingenious ways to prepare them, many unknown outside the peninsula. Besides tapas, eggs are eaten as a first course, side dish, main course, or light meal, but seldom for breakfast. They are served in tapa bars hard-boiled, stuffed, poached, scrambled, fried, and more; they can be eaten plain and also stand up well to most seasonings and sauces. Their mild flavor and their ability to adapt to all possible cooking methods make them the perfect partner with other tapa foods and drinks.

TORTILLA DE HABAS
(BEAN OMELET)

Spanish broad beans, or habas, are a simple yet tasty omelet filling. The taste would be highlighted by a cold beer.

4   tablespoons extra-virgin olive oil

1   small onion, chopped

1½   cups habas, favas, or lima beans

4   eggs
     Salt to taste

Heat oil in a skillet and sauté onions in it until soft. Add beans, cover, and cook slowly for about 30 minutes or until tender. Remove, drain, and let cool. Beat eggs in a bowl and add beans. Add a little more olive oil to the skillet, heat, and pour in the mixture. Reduce the heat and cook until the bottom of the omelet begins to brown, shaking occasionally to prevent sticking. Invert a large plate over the skillet and carefully flip the omelet onto the plate. If necessary, add more oil to the skillet. Slide the omelet back into the skillet and continue cooking on the second side until browned. Place on a serving platter and slice the omelet like a pie or into squares; serve hot or chilled.

VARIATION
The affinity of habas for ham makes the addition of 2 tablespoons of chopped ham a temptation that tapa cooks can seldom resist.

Serves 8–10

BRILLIANT BEGINNINGS

Clockwise from upper right: Green Bean Salad, Cheese and Ham Rolls, Asparagus with Ham, Garlic Shrimp. Served with red wine.

TAPAS FOR TWO OR THREE
Clockwise from upper right: Stuffed Eggs, Cheese and Potato Balls, Tartaletas, Garlic Chicken, Chicken Liver Pâté. Served with champagne.

BEST OF TAPAS

Clockwise from upper right: Celery Boats, Fried Bread, Cheese Canapés, Small Sandwiches, Meatballs in Almond Sauce, Sausage. Served with beer.

TAPAS MAGNIFICAS
Clockwise from upper right: Chicken Breasts in Sherry Sauce, Marinated Mushrooms, Catalan Beef Stew, Artichokes with Ham, Mussels. Served with sherry.

WELL-ROUNDED TAPAS

Clockwise from upper right: Stuffed Tomatoes, Pork Stew, Green Bean and Onion Salad, Fried Squid Rings. Served with red wine.

HOT-WEATHER TAPAS

*Clockwise from upper right: Cauliflower Vinaigrette, Oysters, Lobster in Tomato Sauce,
Waldorf Salad, Russian Salad. Served with a* **bota** *of wine.*

COLD-WEATHER TAPAS

*Clockwise from upper right: Almonds, Asturian Bean Stew, Sausage and Cheese,
Veal Stew. Served with brandy and espresso.*

HOLIDAY TAPAS (EASTER WEEK)

Clockwise from upper right: Stuffed Mushrooms, Vegetable Stew, Poor Man's Potatoes, Marinated Olives. Served with white wine.

TORTILLA SACROMONTE
(*SACROMONTE* OMELET)

The tortilla al Sacromonte *testifies to the capacity of the Spanish omelet to house the humblest ingredients, yet remain a delectable experience. Created by a monk in the Granada monastery by that name, the Sacromonte is guaranteed to be the center of attention at any tapa table.*

Calves' brains and especially calves' criadillas *(testicles) are the chief ingredients in the authentic tortilla Sacromonte of Granada. If your supermarket is out of testicles, you can substitute, as do many tapa cooks, sweetbreads, kidneys, liver, or even ham and still come away with an acceptable Sacromonte. A good Spanish brandy might stand up best to this hardy omelet.*

1 calf's or sheep's brain
2 calf's testicles, sweetbreads, kidneys, or liver
  Fresh lemon juice
½ cup cooked peas
3 medium potatoes, cooked and diced
4 eggs
  Salt to taste
4 tablespoons extra-virgin olive oil

Wash brain and testicles and cook in salted water with a little lemon juice. Drain, let cool, and chop into small pieces. Add peas and potatoes and sauté 5 minutes. Beat eggs in a bowl, and add brain, testicles, peas, potatoes, and salt to taste. Add olive oil to a skillet, heat, and pour in the egg mixture. Reduce the heat and cook until the bottom of the omelet begins to brown, shaking occasionally to prevent sticking. Invert a large platter over the skillet and carefully flip the omelet onto the plate. If necessary, add more oil to the skillet. Slide the omelet back into the skillet and continue cooking on the second side until browned. Place on a serving platter. Cut into slices and serve hot or chilled.

Serves 8–10

HUEVOS RELLENOS FRITOS
(DEEP-FRIED HARD-BOILED EGGS)

The Spanish have a passion—not to mention an expertise—for deep-frying anything they can lay their hands on, including hard-boiled eggs. Deep-frying gives eggs added flavor, texture, and color, while still maintaining their intrinsic taste, which is the kind of gastronomic objective that tapa cooks continually strive for. Just about any drink would be a proper accompaniment, but perhaps a crisp, cold beer would taste best.

 6   hard-boiled eggs
1½ tablespoons oil or butter
 1   tablespoon chopped onion
 2   tablespoons chopped ham
 2   tablespoons chopped fresh
      parsley
      Salt and pepper to taste
 1   cup White Sauce (see
      index for recipe)
 2   eggs, beaten
 1   cup bread crumbs
      Oil for deep-frying

Peel the hard-boiled eggs, cut in half lengthwise, and carefully remove yolks. Heat oil or butter in a skillet and sauté onion, ham, and parsley in it until onion is soft. Mash egg yolks and mix with ham mixture to form a paste. Season with salt and pepper and fill egg halves with the mixture. Carefully reassemble egg halves to form whole eggs. Dip each egg in White Sauce and refrigerate until sauce hardens on the eggs. Dip coated eggs in beaten eggs, roll in bread crumbs, and deep-fry in hot oil at 350°F for 3 minutes or until golden brown. Drain and serve hot.

VARIATION
You can also stuff with shrimp, anchovies, mushrooms, chicken, or any number of other ingredients.

Serves 6

CROQUETAS DE HUEVOS DUROS
(HARD-BOILED EGG CROQUETTES)

A dry white wine would be an agreeable partner for this tapa.

 6   hard-boiled eggs
 1   tablespoon oil or butter
 1   tablespoon chopped onion
 ¼   cup chopped ham
 ½   cup White Sauce (see
      index for recipe)
      Salt and pepper to taste
 1   cup bread crumbs
      Oil for deep-frying

Peel the hard-boiled eggs and chop into pieces. Heat oil or butter in a skillet and sauté chopped onion and ham in it until onion is soft. Remove from heat and mix with the chopped eggs and enough White Sauce to bind. Add salt and pepper to taste and let cool. Mold into 6 small croquettes, roll in bread crumbs, and deep-fry in hot oil at 350°F, 3-4 minutes. Drain and serve.

Serves 6–8

HUEVOS ESCALFADOS FRITOS
(FRIED POACHED EGGS)

A dry sherry would enhance the flavor of these eggs.

6 eggs
½ teaspoon salt
1 tablespoon vinegar
2 eggs, beaten
1 cup bread crumbs or flour
   Oil for deep-frying
1 tablespoon chopped fresh
   parsley
   Lemon wedges
   Tomato Sauce or other
   sauce (see index for
   recipes)

Poach eggs in boiling water with salt and vinegar. Remove carefully and let cool. If you wish, trim the white with a scissors or a sharp knife to form evenly rounded shapes. Dip poached eggs into the beaten eggs and then into bread crumbs or flour. Deep-fry at 370°F for 3 minutes (or pan-fry on both sides) until golden brown and drain. Sprinkle with parsley and serve with lemon wedges or cover with a tomato, garlic, or other sauce.

Serves 6

HUEVOS REVUELTOS CON TOMATE
(SCRAMBLED EGGS WITH TOMATO)

Scrambled eggs are popular throughout the world, including Spain. Whether a tapa, light meal, or side dish, they take well to numerous seasonings and to many different ingredients, including cheese, peppers, seafood, chicken, and ham. Fried brains are a traditional tapa-bar addition, and tomatoes are perhaps most popular of all. In any case, the technique is basically the same: do not overcook. Always stir the eggs (preferably with a wooden spoon) over low heat and only until the egg mixture is barely set. Scrambled eggs will continue to cook from their own internal heat even after being removed from the stove. A red wine would be a worthy partner.

2 tablespoons oil or butter
3 tablespoons chopped
   onion
3 tomatoes, peeled and
   chopped
6 eggs
   Salt to taste

Heat oil or butter in a skillet and sauté chopped onion and tomatoes in it until onion is tender and tomatoes are reduced to a sauce. Beat eggs and stir into the skillet. Salt to taste and continue stirring over low heat until the eggs have barely reached the creamy stage. Serve hot or cold.

Serves 6

HUEVOS AL NIDO
(EGGS IN A NEST)

Besides being a hardy tapa, eggs in nests are a traditional first course in Spanish homes. Either a cold beer or a hearty red wine would be a proper companion.

2	cups mashed potatoes
1½	tablespoons milk
1½	tablespoons butter
2	tablespoons finely chopped onion
	Salt to taste
6	eggs, separated
2	tablespoons olive oil
	Tomato Sauce or other sauce (optional; see index for recipes)

Mix mashed potatoes, milk, and butter. Add onions and salt to taste. Mix thoroughly. Divide mashed potatoes into 6 thick pancakes; make a hollow in each and drop in 1 egg yolk. Beat egg whites until firm and brush whites on pancakes. Heat oil in a skillet and fry pancakes, continuing to baste with egg whites until cakes are browned and the yolks have set. Remove and drain. Serve with a tomato or other sauce if desired.

VARIATION
You can also use thick slices of bread or soft rolls in place of mashed potatoes. Make a hole in the center of each slice, pour a little milk in each hole, and spread butter thinly over the bread, including the holes. Add egg yolks and proceed as for potato nests.

Serves 6

ADDITIONAL EGG TAPAS
TORTILLA ESPAÑOLA (Potato Omelet); Chapter 10, page 48.
HUEVOS RELLENOS (Stuffed Eggs); Chapter 7, page 33.
HUEVOS DUROS CON QUESO (Hard-boiled Eggs with Cheese); Chapter 6, page 28.

CHEESE TAPAS (QUESOS)

Cheeses, like eggs, are excellent as tapas, either by themselves or as an accompaniment or a background to other ingredients. Just about every tapa bar offers one or more varieties, either cut into thick slices and served by themselves or combined with other foods; usually both. Every region in Spain has its own varieties, and many of them are excellent. Cheeses from northern Spain are made mainly from cow's milk; in central Spain, from sheep's milk; and in arid Andalusia, from the milk of goats. Spanish cheeses come in all sizes, shapes, and colors, ranging from very soft to hard in texture, from bland to very strong in taste.

During multicourse meals, cheeses often substitute for desserts or precede the dessert course and are sometimes served with fruits or honey; they are also a favorite first course. In tapa bars they are frequently the last tapas sampled.

For information on Spanish cheeses, turn to Chapter 5.

BOLAS DE QUESO CALIENTE
(HOT CHEESE BALLS)

A hearty red wine would be a fitting accompaniment.

2	cups grated Manchego, Gruyère, or other cheese
½	cup flour
¼	cup chopped almonds
2	egg whites, beaten
2	tablespoons sherry
1	cup bread crumbs
	Oil for deep-frying

Combine grated cheese, flour, chopped nuts, egg whites, and sherry. Mix well and form into small balls. Roll each ball in bread crumbs and deep-fry in hot oil at 370°F for 3 minutes or until golden brown. Drain, spear with toothpicks, and serve.

Serves 6–8 (5–7 cheese balls each)

ADDITIONAL CHEESE TAPAS
BOLAS DE QUESO Y PATATA (Cheese and Potato Balls); Chapter 7, page 33.
FLAMENQUINES (Cheese and Ham Rolls); Chapter 6, page 28.
QUESO FRITO (Fried Cheese); Chapter 8, page 39.

CHAPTER FIFTEEN
VEGETABLE TAPAS (VERDURAS)

Vegetables hold a prominent place in almost every tapa offering. They are frequently the first tapas consumed during an evening of tasca-crawling and are often used by aficionados to spark the appetite for the heavier items that will follow. They stand up well to all drinks, alcoholic as well as nonalcoholic.

Vegetables go well with Spanish sauces but are also capable of standing on their own, either raw or lightly cooked. At any rate, prepare them as straightforwardly as possible and use sauces only to enhance the natural vegetable flavors. Always try to safeguard original colors, textures, and crispness. Never overcook, which dulls flavors and invariably turns vegetables limp and soggy. Steaming, although not a traditional Spanish cooking method, is an excellent way to prepare vegetable tapas.

Asparagus, artichokes, cauliflower, and Brussels sprouts are tapa favorites. Eggplant, zucchini, and potatoes are popular deep-fried or sautéed in olive oil, often with bits of ham, sausage, mushrooms, shrimp, or other seafood. Carrots, on the other hand, are seldom eaten by themselves, either raw or cooked, but are often chopped and used as a seasoning for other ingredients, especially meats. Where possible, use fresh vegetables, although quick-frozen should be adequate for most recipes. Avoid canned vegetables unless unavailable in any other form.

ARTICHOKES (ALCACHOFAS)

Artichokes are considered a luxury by most Americans; the Spanish think of them as a common ordinary seasonal vegetable. Actually, they're a type of thistle, with the edible parts being the base of the leaves and the heart.

The best way to prepare artichokes is to boil the heads in water, adding a little olive oil and a pinch of salt, but they also take well to microwave cooking. The traditional way to eat artichokes, whether as a tapa or as a first course, is to strip off the inside leaves, dip each into a sauce, and scrape off the soft flesh at the base with your lower teeth. They are equally delicious hot or cold, but always with a sauce—hollandaise, vinaigrette, mayonnaise, or olive oil and salt. For added character, sprinkle with lemon just before serving.

You can buy the hearts canned or frozen, and tiny artichokes are available preserved in olive oil. A saucer of hearts or small whole artichokes makes a delicious tapa, accompanied by a homemade sauce.

ALCACHOFAS RELLENAS
(STUFFED ARTICHOKES)

A Spanish brandy would be an agreeable partner.

10	small artichokes
1	lemon slice
1½	tablespoons oil
2	tablespoons chopped onion
1	clove garlic, chopped
½	pound ground beef, veal, pork, chicken, or other meat
2	tablespoons chopped fresh parsley
1	tablespoon tomato paste
¼	cup white wine or chicken stock
¼	teaspoon ground nutmeg
	Salt and pepper to taste
½	cup bread crumbs

Clean artichokes under running water, remove the tough outer leaves, and cut off the base of each so it will stand flat. Cut off tops and trim the pointed tips of the leaves. Rub with a slice of lemon to keep leaves from turning dark. Cook in salted boiling water about 25 minutes or until tender. Remove and drain. Pull out the inner leaves and spoon out and discard the choke in the center, leaving a small cavity in the middle of each. Heat oil in a skillet and sauté onion and garlic until onion is soft. Add ground meat and cook until browned. Add parsley, tomato paste, and wine. Sprinkle with nutmeg and add salt and pepper to taste. Simmer for 10 minutes or until liquid is reduced. Remove, let cool, and fill artichoke bottoms with the mixture. Sprinkle with bread crumbs. Bake in a preheated 375°F oven for about 15 minutes or until meat is heated through and the crumbs are browned. You can prepare the artichokes ahead, refrigerate, and bake just before serving.

VARIATION

As an alternative stuffing, fill with a shrimp or other seafood mixture and sprinkle with cheese, parsley, or another topping.

Serves 5

ALCACHOFAS FRITAS
(FRIED ARTICHOKES)

Excellent with red wine.

12 small artichokes
1 egg, beaten
  Flour for dusting
  Salt and pepper to taste
  Oil for deep-frying

Clean the artichokes under running water, slice off the tops, and remove the tough outer leaves. Cook in boiling water until tender; do not overcook. Remove, drain, and cut each one into quarters. Dip each quarter in beaten egg and then in flour seasoned with salt and pepper. Deep-fry in hot oil, 370°F, about 4-5 minutes. Drain and serve hot with a sauce or a sprinkling of olive oil.

Serves 8

ASPARAGUS (ESPARRAGOS)

Two kinds of asparagus are eaten in Spanish tapa bars, green and white. The difference is in the cultivation. White asparagus is grown in earth mounds to prevent the greening effect of the sun. It is softer and more tender than the green and has a more delicate flavor. The stalks are thick with almost no scales. If white varieties are unavailable fresh at the market, you can always find them canned.

White asparagus is popular cold with a sauce—hollandaise, béchamel, vinaigrette, or homemade mayonnaise. For added color, texture, and flavor, top with crumbled egg yolks, Manchego cheese, or almonds.

Wild green asparagus is served in tapa bars in the early spring, and a month or two later cultivated varieties appear. As a tapa, green asparagus, like the more popular white varieties, is best when served simply, perhaps merely sautéed in olive oil. Asparagus should be accompanied by a good white wine.

ESPARRAGOS CON QUESO
(ASPARAGUS WITH CHEESE)

A dry sherry would be a worthy companion.

1 pound green or white
  asparagus
2 tablespoons butter
  Salt and pepper to taste
½ cup grated Manchego or
  other cheese

Cut off the ends of asparagus. In a large kettle, boil asparagus in salted water until tender. Remove with a slotted spoon, drain, and place in an earthenware or other casserole. Melt butter in a skillet, season with salt and pepper, and pour over the asparagus. Sprinkle with grated cheese. Cook briefly under a broiler or in a hot oven until lightly browned.

Serves 4-5 (2 stalks per serving)

ESPARRAGOS SALTEADO
(SAUTEED ASPARAGUS)

Choose a pleasant white or rosé for this tapa.

1 **pound green asparagus**
3 **tablespoons oil**
1 **clove garlic, chopped**
   Salt to taste

Cut the hard ends from the asparagus. Heat oil in a skillet and add asparagus and chopped garlic. Simmer for about 15 minutes or until asparagus is tender. Add salt to taste and serve hot.

VARIATION
For added flavor and texture, sprinkle with chopped nuts (almonds, pine nuts, or walnuts) or with grated cheese.

Serves 4–5 (2 stalks per serving)

ESPARRAGOS FRIO
(GREEN ASPARAGUS)

Green asparagus is a favorite cold tapa (espárragos frío). Simply boil the asparagus, let cool, and serve cold, either unadorned or with a homemade mayonnaise or green sauce.

5 to 7 stalks per serving, depending on size

BEANS (HABAS Y JUDIAS)

JUDIAS VERDES CON SALSA DE TOMATE
(GREEN BEANS IN TOMATO SAUCE)

A red wine would be a fitting partner.

1 **pound fresh green beans**
1½ **tablespoons oil**
1 **small onion, chopped**
1 **clove garlic, chopped**
2 **tomatoes, peeled and chopped**
 Salt and pepper to taste
1 **tablespoon chopped fresh parsley**

Cut green beans into 1-inch lengths. Boil salted water in a kettle and drop in cut beans. Cook 5-10 minutes or until barely tender. Remove with a slotted spoon and drain. Heat oil in a skillet and sauté onion and garlic in it until onion is soft. Stir in tomatoes, season with salt and pepper, and simmer until the sauce thickens. Stir in beans, sprinkle with parsley, and continue to simmer until beans are heated through.

Serves 6-8

HABAS CON JAMON
(BROAD BEANS WITH HAM)

Although practically unknown in America, habas *(called in various languages "the meat of the poor") have been a staple in Spain and the rest of Europe since the Stone Age. Habas resemble lima beans but are rounder in shape and have a tougher outer skin. The flavor is more like that of peas than other beans. They are at their tastiest when young and tender and can be eaten in their skins. Otherwise they are tough and should be soaked, and the skins removed. Habas are available in some parts of America under their Italian name, fava beans, or you can substitute a lima or other broad bean.*

Habas are popular as a tapa served plain with perhaps a little chopped parsley; they are also frequently prepared in combination with other foods, including peas and other vegetables. Like most beans, habas have an affinity for ham. An ice cold beer would be a deserving partner.

2 **tablespoons oil**
2 **pounds habas, lima beans, or other broad beans**
¼ **pound serrano or other cured ham or bacon, chopped**
 Salt and pepper to taste
1 **tablespoon chopped fresh parsley**

Heat oil in a skillet, add beans, and cook for about 20 minutes. Add chopped ham and sauté 15 or more minutes or until beans are tender. Season with salt and pepper, sprinkle with parsley, and serve hot.

Serves 8

HABAS A LA CATALANA
(BROAD BEANS, CATALAN STYLE)

This is a well-known Catalan tapa (in large portions, a hardy one-dish meal) that calls for a special Catalan sausage, butifarra. You can substitute any good smoked pork sausage or even hunks of lean bacon. As a meal, serve with whole sausages on the side. Excellent with a crisp, cold beer.

1 tablespoon lard or oil

¼ pound salt pork or sliced bacon, chopped

1 onion, chopped

2 cloves garlic, chopped

½ cup dry white wine or dry sherry

1 tomato, chopped

1 small bay leaf

¼ teaspoon dried thyme

1 tablespoon chopped fresh mint

3 pounds habas, favas, limas, or other broad beans

¼ pound butifarra, chorizo, or other pork sausage, sliced

1 tablespoon chopped fresh parsley

In a large earthenware casserole or skillet, melt lard and add salt pork. Stirring frequently, cook until pieces are crisp and golden. With a slotted spoon, remove pork pieces and drain. Add onion and garlic and simmer until onion is soft. Pour in wine and stir in tomato, bay leaf, thyme, and mint. Add cooked salt pork, beans, and sausage, stirring constantly. Bring to a boil, reduce the heat, cover, and simmer slowly for about 45 minutes or until beans are tender. While cooking, add chicken stock or water if juice becomes too thick. Sprinkle with parsley just before serving.

Serves 8

JUDIAS VERDES CON PIMIENTOS
(GREEN BEANS WITH PEPPERS)

A dry sherry would be an agreeable companion.

1 pound fresh green beans

2 red peppers or 2 4-ounce cans pimientos

2 tablespoons oil

1 clove garlic, chopped

1 tablespoon chopped fresh parsley

½ teaspoon paprika
Salt to taste

1 hard-boiled egg, chopped

Cut green beans into 1-inch lengths. Boil salted water in a kettle and drop in cut beans. Cook 5–10 minutes or until barely tender. Remove with a slotted spoon and drain. Cut red peppers into strips. Heat oil in a skillet and sauté garlic in it until slightly browned; add peppers and continue to cook until tender. Add green beans, sprinkle with parsley and paprika, and simmer 5 more minutes. Salt to taste. Sprinkle chopped hard-boiled egg over the top.

Serves 8

JUDIAS VERDES A LA ROMANA
(BATTER-FRIED GREEN BEANS)

Tasty with a cold beer.

1	**pound fresh green beans**
½	**cup flour**
1	**egg, beaten**
¼	**cup dry white wine or dry sherry**
	Salt to taste
	Oil for deep-frying

Cut off the tips of the green beans. Boil salted water in a kettle and drop in cut beans. Cook 5-10 minutes or until barely tender. Remove and drain. Mix together flour, egg, and wine to form a thick batter; salt to taste. Dip beans in the batter and deep-fry at 370°F (or pan-fry) until golden. Drain and season with more salt.

Serves 6

JUDIAS VERDES CON PIÑONES
(GREEN BEANS WITH PINE NUTS)

A white wine would be an agreeable drink with this tapa.

1	**pound fresh green beans**
2	**tablespoons olive oil**
2	**cloves garlic, chopped**
¼	**cup pine nuts**

Cut beans into 1-inch lengths. Boil salted water in a kettle and drop in cut beans. Cook for 5-10 minutes or until barely tender. Remove and drain. Toss beans with olive oil, garlic, and pine nuts. Serve hot or chilled.

Serves 6–8

BROCCOLI (BRECOL)

BRECOL AL AJO
(BROCCOLI WITH GARLIC)

Broccoli is prepared in tapa bars in much the same way as asparagus, often served with a hollandaise or other sauce or with grated cheese or melted butter. Broccoli is at its best when steamed or boiled very quickly. A red wine might be a fitting accompaniment.

1	**pound broccoli or cauliflower**
3	**cloves garlic, chopped**
¼	**cup olive oil**
2	**tablespoons chopped fresh parsley, grated cheese, or combination**

Separate the head into large individual stalks. Trim off the tough ends of the broccoli stalks to form level bottoms. Stand the broccoli upright in a large saucepan with about 1½ inches of water. Bring water to a boil, cover, and boil about 10 minutes, or until crisp-tender. Remove, drain, and place in a serving dish. Combine garlic and olive oil and pour over the broccoli. Sprinkle with chopped parsley, grated cheese, or both.

Serves 6

BRUSSELS SPROUTS (COLES DE BRUSELAS)

COLES DE BRUSELAS CON QUESO
(BRUSSELS SPROUTS WITH CHEESE)

Brussels sprouts are best when lightly cooked or even raw, perhaps topped with grated cheese or a hollandaise or other sauce, or you can simply season lightly with olive oil. A sprinkling of chopped almonds, hazelnuts, or mushrooms adds extra texture and flavor. Be sure never to overcook, which causes sprouts to become mushy and acquire a strong taste and smell. Test for proper consistency by piercing with a fork. Excellent with cold beer.

1   pound Brussels sprouts
    Salt and pepper to taste
¼   cup olive oil
¼   teaspoon fresh lemon juice
3   tablespoons grated
    Manchego or other
    cheese

Cook Brussels sprouts in boiling salted water about 8-10 minutes or until tender. Remove and drain. Season with salt and pepper. Sprinkle with a mixture of olive oil and lemon juice and then with grated cheese.

Serves 6-8

COLES DE BRUSELAS FRITAS
(FRIED BRUSSELS SPROUTS)

Serve with a cold, crisp beer.

1   pound Brussels sprouts
    Salt to taste
½   cup bread crumbs
1   egg, beaten
    Oil for deep-frying

Cook Brussels sprouts in boiling salted water until tender, 8-10 minutes. Drain, sprinkle lightly with salt, roll in bread crumbs, dip in beaten egg, and roll again in bread crumbs. Deep-fry in hot oil at 370°F, 3-4 minutes or until golden brown. Drain on paper towels and serve.

VARIATION
Use the same treatment for other vegetables: sliced cauliflower, artichokes, zucchini, eggplant.

Serves 6-8

CABBAGE (REPOLLO)

REPOLLO RELLENO
(STUFFED CABBAGE)

Tapa cooks have a knack for stuffing and wrapping one food with another. Cabbage leaves are especially handy wrappers. Ground pork, veal, and beef are typical fillings, but sausages are the easiest to stuff, and, when batter-fried (another favorite Spanish preparation method), they make a truly savory snack. A full-bodied red wine would be a worthy partner.

6 small cabbage leaves
6 chorizo or other cured
    pork sausages
1 egg, beaten
    Flour or bread crumbs for
    dusting
    Salt and pepper to taste
    Oil for deep-frying

Trim cabbage leaves and boil in salted water until tender. Remove and drain. Lay a sausage on each leaf, fold up the ends, and roll the leaf around the sausage. On demand, dip a cabbage roll in beaten egg, roll in flour or bread crumbs seasoned with salt and pepper, and deep-fry in hot oil at 370°F, 3-4 minutes or until golden. Serve hot.

Serves 6

CAULIFLOWER (COLIFLOR)

COLIFLOR FRITA
(FRIED CAULIFLOWER)

Serve with Spanish brandy.

1 medium head cauliflower
    Flour for dusting
1 egg, beaten
½ cup bread crumbs
    Oil for deep-frying

Wash cauliflower, cut off stem and leaves, and divide into flowerets. Dust each floweret in flour, dip in beaten egg, and roll in bread crumbs. Deep-fry in hot oil at 370°F, 3-4 minutes or until golden brown.

Serves 6

CHICKPEAS (GARBANZOS)

GARBANZOS CON JAMON
(CHICKPEAS WITH HAM)

Chickpeas are popular in Spain and also in the other Mediterranean countries, but not in northern Europe or America. "We cannot define it better," wrote the French poet, Théophile Gautier, "than by saying that it is a pea with an only too successful ambition to be a bean." Whether pea or bean, the chickpea has a unique taste with a definite affinity for ham. It is popular in tapa bars refried and roasted. You can usually buy chickpeas in America dried or in cans. Dried chickpeas must be soaked overnight before cooking. Delicious accompanied by a cold beer.

1	pound dried chickpeas
2	tablespoons oil
1	onion, chopped
2	cloves garlic, chopped
¼	cup chopped cooked ham
1	tablespoon chopped fresh parsley

Soak chickpeas overnight. Place in a kettle and cook for 1½-2 hours or until soft. Heat oil in a skillet and sauté onion and garlic in it until onion is soft. Add chopped ham and cooked chickpeas and continue to simmer until heated through. Sprinkle with parsley and serve hot or cold.

Serves 8

GARBANZOS REFRITOS
(REFRIED CHICKPEAS)

Refried chickpeas make an excellent canapé spread. Excellent with a crisp beer or a full-bodied red wine.

1	pound dried chickpeas, cooked
2	cloves garlic, chopped
2	tablespoons chopped onion
¼	cup dry white wine
	Salt and pepper to taste

Puree cooked chickpeas, garlic, and onion in an electric blender or with a mortar and pestle, adding enough white wine to form a smooth paste. Add salt and pepper to taste.

VARIATION
For added flavor, stir in chopped pimientos or ham or sprinkle with grated cheese.

Serves 8

EGGPLANT (BERENJENA)

Eggplant is a tapa favorite that comes in many sizes, shapes, and colors, served either hot or cold, but always cooked. Eggplant is one of the few tapa vegetables never eaten raw. The tender young plants of most varieties have the best flavor and fewest seeds.

BERENJENA FRITA
(FRIED EGGPLANT)

A good dry sherry would be an agreeable partner.

1   **large or 2 small eggplants**
     Salt and pepper to taste
     Flour for dusting
⅓   **cup oil**

Trim off ends of the eggplant and cut into ¼-inch slices. Salt slices and dip in flour seasoned with salt and pepper. Heat oil in a skillet and sauté slices until browned on both sides and tender. Drain and serve warm, either plain or with a hot tomato sauce.

    Another tapa technique is to sprinkle eggplant slices with Manchego or Parmesan cheese, place in a broiler 2-3 minutes, and top with sautéed onion rings or chopped ham or bacon.

Serves 6–8

MUSHROOMS (CHAMPIÑONES)

CHAMPIÑONES FRITOS
(DEEP-FRIED MUSHROOMS)

This beer batter can be used not only for mushrooms, but also for deep-frying eggplant slices, artichoke hearts, broccoli, Brussels sprouts, and cauliflower flowerets. Serve with white wine.

1   **pound mushrooms**
½   **cup flour**
½   **cup beer**
1   **egg, separated**
1   **tablespoon olive oil**
     Salt and pepper to taste
     Oil for deep-frying

Clean the mushrooms and remove the stems. In a bowl, mix together the flour, beer, egg yolk, and olive oil. Season with a pinch of salt and a little freshly ground pepper. Stir the batter in the same direction, mixing thoroughly, and allow to sit 4-5 hours. In a separate bowl, beat the egg white until stiff and fold into the batter. With a fork, dip each mushroom into the batter and deep-fry in hot oil at 370°F, 3-4 minutes.

Serves 4–6

CHAMPIÑONES CON SALSA DE TOMATES
(MUSHROOMS IN TOMATO SAUCE)

Serve with a light red wine.

1   **pound mushrooms**
2   **tablespoons oil**
1   **medium onion, chopped**
2   **cloves garlic, chopped**
2   **medium tomatoes, peeled
      and chopped**
      Salt to taste
      Pinch ground cinnamon
1   **tablespoon chopped fresh
      parsley**

Clean mushrooms and cook in boiling salted water until barely tender. Heat oil in a skillet and sauté onion and garlic in it until onion is soft. Stir in tomatoes and season with salt and a pinch of cinnamon; cook until a smooth sauce forms. Slice mushrooms and add to the sauce, sprinkle with parsley, and simmer 10 minutes more.

VARIATION
Mushrooms are also served in green and other homemade sauces (see index for recipes).

Serves 8

BROCHETA DE CHAMPIÑONES
(MUSHROOMS ON SKEWERS)

A good sherry would be the perfect partner.

1   **pound mushrooms**
3   **cloves garlic, chopped**
⅔   **cup olive oil**
⅓   **cup fresh lemon juice**
2   **tablespoons dry sherry**
¼   **teaspoon dried oregano**
1   **bay leaf**
2   **tablespoons chopped fresh
      parsley**
      Salt and pepper to taste

Clean mushrooms and remove the tough ends of the stems. In a bowl, mix together mushrooms and the other ingredients, refrigerate, and marinate overnight. Thread mushrooms on individual metal or wooden skewers and, on demand, grill quickly in a broiler or over charcoal.

Serves 4–6

CHAMPIÑONES "AU GRATIN"
(MUSHROOMS AU GRATIN)

Excellent with a dry white wine.

¾ pound mushrooms
2 tablespoons grated Manchego or other cheese
1 tablespoon bread crumbs
1 tablespoon chopped fresh parsley
   Salt to taste
   Pinch cayenne pepper
1 tablespoon olive oil
1 cup dry white wine

Clean mushrooms and remove the stems. Chop stems and mix with grated cheese, bread crumbs, and parsley. Place mushrooms, heads down, in a buttered casserole or baking pan and cover with the mixture. Sprinkle with salt, a little cayenne pepper, and olive oil. Carefully pour in white wine. Cook in a preheated 350°F oven for about 15 minutes or until golden brown.

Serves 4-6

CHAMPIÑONES Y ACEITUNAS
(MUSHROOMS AND OLIVES)

A dry sherry would be an especially good companion.

1½ tablespoons oil
1   onion, chopped
2   cloves garlic, chopped
1   pound mushrooms, chopped
½   cup pitted and sliced green olives
½   cup pitted and sliced black olives
½   teaspoon paprika
    Salt to taste
1   tablespoon chopped fresh parsley

Heat oil in a skillet and sauté onion and garlic in it until onion is soft. Stir in mushrooms, green and black olives, and paprika; sauté about 10 minutes or until onions are browned and the flavors well blended. Add salt to taste, sprinkle with parsley, and serve hot.

Serves 6

PEAS (GUISANTES)

Peas blend well with almost any ingredient: sausage (*guisantes con salchichas*), ham (*guisantes soté con jamón*), carrots, beans, and even seafood. *Guisantes a la Catalana* is a simple but tasty mixture of peas, raisins, and pine nuts. Even more simple: *guisantes a la mantequilla*, or buttered peas. Concoct your own combinations.

GUISANTES CON CEBOLLAS
(PEAS WITH ONIONS)

A white wine would be the best accompaniment.

2	tablespoons oil
2	cloves garlic, chopped
½	pound small onions, sliced
1½	pounds peas
¼	cup chopped ham
2	tablespoons white wine
	Salt to taste

Heat oil in a skillet and sauté chopped garlic and sliced onions in it until onions are soft. Add peas, ham, wine, and salt to taste. Simmer for about 10 minutes or until peas are tender. Add water or more wine if necessary.

Serves 8

PEPPERS (PIMIENTOS)

PIMIENTOS ASADOS
(ROASTED PEPPERS)

Besides being a tasty tapa, roasted peppers are also popular as a first course and as a side dish accompanying meat courses. Excellent with either a cold beer or a glass of red wine.

3	large red peppers
2	tablespoons oil
2	tablespoons chopped onion
3	cloves garlic, chopped
	Salt to taste

Wash and dry peppers, place under a broiler or over an open flame and cook, turning frequently, until skins are blistered on all sides. Peel peppers, remove seeds, and cut into thin strips. (If you're using pimientos, you won't need to peel them.) Heat oil in a skillet and sauté onion, garlic, and peppers in it about 5 minutes or until peppers are tender. Season with salt and serve hot.

VARIATION
You can add chopped ham and sprinkle with parsley for added flavor.

Serves 6

POTATOES (PATATAS)

The potato is found in one form or another in every tapa bar in Spain. Its neutral taste offers the ideal accompaniment to other foods, especially as a background for eggs (Spanish omelet, for example) and meats. The potato also is able to stand alone (fried or otherwise cooked), enhanced perhaps with a little olive oil and salt or with garlic, paprika, parsley, or any number of other seasonings.

PATATAS NUEVAS
(FRIED NEW POTATOES)

Patatas nuevas *are a simple, yet delicious, tapa and a popular accompaniment to meat dishes. A crisp, cold beer would be a worthy partner. Another delicious fried potato tapa is* patatas pajas *(shoestring or straw potatoes) deep-fried in sizzling oil.*

1½ **pounds small new potatoes**

2½ **tablespoons oil**

Salt to taste

2 **tablespoons chopped fresh parsley**

Peel and clean potatoes. Heat oil in a skillet and fry new potatoes, turning frequently, about 20 minutes or until cooked through and golden brown on all sides. Add salt to taste and sprinkle with chopped parsley.

Serves 4 (3–5 small potatoes each)

PATATAS CON QUESO
(POTATOES WITH CHEESE)

A dry white wine would be an agreeable partner.

1 **dozen small new potatoes**

Manchego, Gruyére, or other cheese, grated

Flour for dusting

1 **egg, beaten**

1 **cup bread crumbs**

Oil for deep-frying

Boil and then peel new potatoes. Carefully hollow out some of the center of each potato and stuff with grated cheese. Dust each potato in flour, dip in beaten egg, and roll in bread crumbs. Deep-fry in oil at 370°F for 3 minutes or until golden brown.

Serves 4

PATATAS A LA RIOJANA
(POTATOES, RIOJA STYLE)

For a meal, accompany this dish with fried pork sausage. A full-bodied red wine would be just right for this tapa.

2	pounds potatoes
½	pound chorizo, pork loin, or pork sausage
4	tablespoons oil
1	onion, chopped
3	cloves garlic, chopped
½	cup dry white wine
1	teaspoon paprika
1	bay leaf
	Salt to taste

Peel and wash potatoes and cut into thick strips. Cut sausage into cubes. Heat oil in a skillet and sauté onion and garlic in it until onion is soft. Add potato strips and pork cubes and continue cooking until pork and potatoes are lightly browned. Stir in white wine, paprika, and bay leaf. Add salt to taste. Cover and cook slowly for about 20 minutes or until potatoes and sausage are cooked. If necessary, add a little stock or water.

VARIATION
You can top with slices of hard-boiled eggs or sprinkle with chopped parsley or grated cheese.

Serves 6

PATATAS EN SALSA VERDE
(POTATOES IN GREEN SAUCE)

Excellent with a white wine.

4	medium potatoes
3	tablespoons oil
1	onion, chopped
2	cloves garlic, chopped
3	tablespoons chopped fresh parsley
	Hot water or beef or chicken stock
	Salt and pepper to taste

Peel and cut potatoes into ¼-inch rounds. Heat oil in a skillet and sauté onion and garlic in it until onion is soft. Add potato rounds and brown lightly. Stir in parsley and just enough hot water or stock to cover. Add salt and pepper to taste. Continue to cook over low heat, turning once, for about 15 minutes or until potatoes are tender.

Serves 6–8 (5–6 slices each)

PATATAS FRITAS A LA BRAVA
(SPICY FRIED POTATOES)

The amount of garlic and chili you use will determine how much **brava** *you end up with. Aficionados mix a simple combination of olive oil, vinegar, garlic, and chili for the brava sauce. A strong white wine would be a suitable partner.*

4	medium potatoes
6	tablespoons oil
1	small onion, chopped
4	cloves garlic, crushed
2	tablespoons tomato paste
¼	cup dry white wine
1	tablespoon vinegar
1	small dried chili pepper, crushed, or 1 tablespoon paprika

Peel and cut potatoes into ¼-inch rounds. Heat 4 tablespoons of oil in a skillet and sauté potatoes in it until tender and evenly browned on both sides. Meanwhile, heat oil in another skillet and sauté onion and garlic in it until onion is soft. Add tomato paste, wine, vinegar, and crushed pepper or paprika and continue to simmer, stirring well, until a smooth sauce forms. Pour sauce over the fried potatoes.

Serves 6–8 (5–6 rounds each)

TOMATOES (TOMATES)

TOMATES FRITOS
(FRIED TOMATOES)

Either a red or white wine would be an agreeable partner.

6	small red tomatoes
	Salt and pepper to taste
	Flour for dusting
3	tablespoons oil

Cut tomatoes in slices. Season with salt and pepper and dip slices in flour. Heat oil in a skillet and briefly fry tomato slices until lightly browned on both sides.

Serves 6

ZUCCHINI (CALABACIN)

Because of the delicate flavor of zucchini, tapa cooks prepare it simply. Never overwhelm this vegetable with strong seasonings or sauces. The simplest way to prepare zucchini tapas is to boil, slice, and serve with lemon wedges or top with melted cheese. The most popular method is to fry.

CALABACINES FRITOS
(FRIED ZUCCHINI)

A white wine would be an agreeable partner.

6	small zucchini
	Flour for dusting
1	cup bread crumbs
	Oil for deep-frying

Cut zucchini into thick slices. Dust lightly in flour and roll in bread crumbs. (For a thicker coating, dip also in egg batter.) Deep-fry in oil at 370°F (or pan-fry, turning once) for 3 minutes or until golden brown. Drain and serve hot.

Serves 6–8

ADDITIONAL VEGETABLE TAPAS

CHAPTER SIXTEEN
RICE TAPAS (ARROCES)

Spanish cooks can do wondrous things with rice. With the addition of combinations of seafood, chicken, sausage, nuts, and vegetables, any number of inventive tapas can be concocted. Paella is Spain's most famous rice dish, but in and around Valencia all sorts of other rice dishes abound from the most elegant fare to the most economical.

When preparing a rice tapa, be careful not to overcook. Always remove the rice from the heat before it is "done," just as the grains start to get soft. Then add the precooked fish, vegetables, and other ingredients and allow the rice to finish cooking while absorbing the juices from the other foods.

ARROZ CON TALLARINES
(RICE WITH NOODLES)

Rice is one of the staple foods of Valencia. This recipe came by way of North Africa. A good red wine would contrast nicely with this tapa.

½ cup ½-inch-wide egg noodles

2 tablespoons butter

1 cup rice

2 cups chicken stock

1 tablespoon chopped pimientos

Cut noodles into 1- to 1½-inch lengths and drop into a saucepan. Stir in butter and cook about 3 minutes or until noodles are golden in color. Add rice and stir in stock. Bring to a boil, cover tightly, and simmer for 15 minutes. Stir in pimientos, cover again, and simmer slowly for 5 minutes. Fluff with a fork and serve warm.

Serves 8

ARROZ CON HABAS
(RICE WITH BROAD BEANS)

A crisp beer would be a suitable partner.

2 tablespoons olive oil

1 small onion, chopped

1 clove garlic, chopped

1 cup rice

¼ cup blanched almonds (or combination almonds and hazelnuts), chopped

2 cups boiling water

1 cup habas or broad beans, cooked

1 teaspoon salt

12 black olives, pitted

Heat oil in a skillet and sauté onion and garlic in it until onion is soft. Stir in rice and nuts and add boiling water. Cook, stirring constantly, for 5 minutes. Add beans, season with salt, and continue cooking for 5 minutes, stirring occasionally. Cover, remove from the heat, and let stand for 15 minutes or until liquid is absorbed and rice is fluffy. Top with olives.

Serves 6–8

ARROZ CON CHAMPIÑONES
(RICE WITH MUSHROOMS)

A white wine would be an excellent companion.

2   tablespoons olive oil
1   small onion, chopped
1   clove garlic, chopped
1   cup rice
2   cups boiling water
1   green pepper, chopped
1   stalk celery, chopped
¾   cup mushrooms, sliced thin
1   teaspoon salt

Heat oil in a skillet and sauté onion and garlic in it until onion is soft. Stir in rice, add boiling water, and cook, stirring constantly, for 5 minutes. Add pepper, celery, and mushrooms, season with salt, and continue cooking for 5 minutes, stirring occasionally. Cover, remove from the heat, and let stand for 15 minutes or until liquid is absorbed and rice is fluffy.

Serves 6–8

ADDITIONAL RICE TAPAS
PAELLA VALENCIANA (Rice, Valencia Style); Chapter 11, page 57
ARROZ A LA MARINERA (Seafood Rice) Chapter 12, page 71

CHAPTER SEVENTEEN
SEAFOOD TAPAS
(PESCADOS Y MARISCOS)

It's impossible to describe the overwhelming variety of fish and seafood found in the lakes, streams, and offshore waters of Spain. Many varieties harvested along Spain's 2,000-mile coast (the longest coastline in Europe) are unknown elsewhere in the world; some have no translations for their names. Yet thanks to a highly structured and well-organized distribution system, all are available fresh everywhere in Spain. Trucks loaded with *frutas del mar* leave the coast every hour of the day and night (depending on the distance, weather, and day's catch) and speed along designated routes to arrive at each inland market at a precise time. A few tapa bars and restaurants in Madrid have tried to fly in seafood, as is the practice in mid-America, but they found that the airplane was less reliable, more expensive, and saved little if any time over the national trucking system.

Fish and shellfish are tastiest when freshly caught and simply prepared. The traditional tapa accompaniment is two small hunks of crusty bread and a lemon wedge; purists ignore the lemon. Although heavy seasoning is required for some regional tapas, the purpose should be always to enhance, never to alter, the flavor.

Frying is the favorite way to prepare fish; in southern Spain, it's just about the only way. Even when preparing fish casseroles, tapa cooks will often fry first to seal in the juices.

In any case, be careful not to overcook. Fresh fish is delicate and needs very little cooking. You can tell that the fish is done when it begins to lose its transparent look and the meat flakes easily.

Deep-frying is especially popular. To deep-fry fish the traditional tapa way, put the fish (either whole or cut into pieces) in a bowl of flour, toss, and with a sieve shake off the excess flour; then deep-fry in sizzling-hot oil. Besides flour, tapa cooks also use several heavier coatings; the methods are interchangeable, depending on the texture and taste desired. You can, for example, dip the fish in egg batter, either before or after the flour, or both; you can use fine bread crumbs or cornmeal instead of flour, or both; or you can include a béchamel or other sauce in the process.

To achieve the crisp, golden-brown outside and juicy inside that is so important for fish tapas, be sure to immerse the fish completely and deep-fry always in sizzling-hot oil. Quick deep-frying ensures that the fish will be fried, not cooked, and prevents the meat from becoming saturated with oil. Test the temperature with a thermometer or drop in a piece of bread; if the bread turns brown after 60 seconds, the oil is ready. Heat in advance to about 370°F. Large fish may need a bit lower temperature (340–360°F) so that the center cooks properly. Also be sure to deep-fry only a few fish at a time so the hot oil remains at a constant temperature and the coating doesn't rub off.

When pan-frying, turn the fish only once. Because of the high heat needed for proper tapa frying and the relatively low smoking point of olive oil, you may want to substitute, or at least add, a vegetable oil.

Tapa cooks like to prepare individual fish and shellfish tapas on demand in the same miniature earthenware skillets in which they are served. If you plan to follow the Spanish practice, be sure to remove the fish from the stove just before it's done; the heat of the skillet will continue to cook the meat, even as it's being eaten.

When selecting fresh fish in the market, make sure they are indeed fresh. Eyes should be bright, transparent, and bulging; the gills moist and a healthy pink color; the skin shiny; the meat firm. There should be a delicate, almost sweet, deep-sea aroma, never a fishy smell. Shellfish should be bought when still alive to guarantee freshness. Although you usually will not get the same taste, you can, of course, use canned or quick-frozen fish and shellfish.

By using fresh ingredients and simple cooking methods, you'll find that most fish are interchangeable, especially white fish. Halibut can substitute for sole, cod for hake, monkfish for lobster, and so on. Even some of the richer fish are interchangeable: salmon for mackerel and vice versa. Most shellfish, although not the same flavors, will also adapt to different recipes, and shellfish can sometimes double for other seafood—lobster for hake, for instance.

FISH

FRESH ANCHOVIES (BOQUERONES)

In America we usually encounter anchovies in cans, preserved in oil or some other liquid. They are not, however, the same fish as the fresh anchovies of southern Spain. The Spanish anchovy (native to the Mediterranean, averaging about four inches long) is delicious and mild-tasting, lacking the strong flavor of our tinned varieties.

BOQUERONES
(FRESH ANCHOVIES)

Mediterranean anchovies are at their best when fresh and deep-fried. In the beach bars of southern Spain, they are dusted in seasoned flour, deep-fried in fan-shaped bunches pinched together at their tails, usually 4 or 5 at a time (the hot frying causes their tails to stick together), and eaten whole, bones and all, like corn on the cob. A crisp, cold beer would make an ideal accompaniment.

**Fresh anchovies, sardines,
   or herring**
Flour for dusting
Oil for deep-frying
Lemon wedges

Cut off the heads and remove the innards of the anchovies. Dust in flour and shake off the excess. Deep-fry in hot oil at 375°F, 4-5 minutes until golden. Serve hot with lemon wedges, 3 per portion.

BOQUERONES EN ESCABECHE
(PICKLED ANCHOVIES)

A cold beer would be the perfect partner.

12 **small fresh anchovies,
     sardines, or herring**
 2 **cloves garlic, chopped**
 1 **small lemon, quartered**
 1 **bay leaf**
 1 **cup vinegar**
   Salt to taste
   **Oil for deep-frying
     (optional)**
   Lemon wedges

Clean fish, removing insides and heads, but not the tails. Slit the backbone of each and remove spine and bones, leaving the halves attached at the tail. Place in a large casserole. Add garlic, lemon quarters, and bay leaf. Pour in enough vinegar to cover and sprinkle with a little salt. Refrigerate overnight. Remove from the marinade and rinse. Serve either cold in their pickled form (*en escabeche*) or dust lightly and deep-fry briefly in sizzling oil at 375°F until well browned and crisp. Serve with lemon wedges.

Serves 4 (3-4 small anchovies each)

ANGLERFISH (RAPE)

Rape, a member of the shark family, is known throughout the world under various names, including *monkfish*, *frog fish*, and *anglerfish*. It is a delicious fish, prized in Spain, France, and other European countries for its firm, sweet, lobsterlike meat. It has never been as popular in America as it has in Spain, probably because of its appearance—a huge ugly head and a grotesque, dark-gray body tapering back to the tail. When found in American markets, the head, which the Spanish use for soup, is always removed.

Rape is best when baked, broiled, or grilled, cut into strips, and served simply, either with lemon wedges or a mild sauce. It is also popular cubed and batter-fried or cold with homemade mayonnaise.

RAPE AL HORNO
(BAKED ANGLERFISH)

A white wine would be a fitting partner.

1½	pounds anglerfish or other firm white fish
4	tablespoons oil
	Flour for dusting
3	cloves garlic, chopped
1	onion, chopped
1	dozen almonds, chopped
1	tomato, peeled and chopped
2	tablespoons bread crumbs
¼	cup white wine
¼	teaspoon saffron
	Salt and pepper to taste
2	tablespoons chopped fresh parsley

Cut fish into slices about ¾ inch thick. Heat oil in a skillet, dust fish pieces with flour, and fry briefly until pieces are lightly browned. Remove with a slotted spoon, drain, and place pieces in an earthenware or glass casserole. To the same oil, add garlic, onion, almonds, and tomato and sauté until onion is soft. Add bread crumbs and wine and continue simmering until liquid is reduced and a smooth paste forms. Stir in saffron and season with salt and pepper. Pour sauce over the fish slices and bake in a preheated 375°F oven for about 15 minutes. Sprinkle with chopped parsley and serve hot.

Serves 6–8

PESCADO FRITO
(DEEP-FRIED FISH)

Deep-fried fish is a part of just about every tapa offering. The species of fish used depends as much on availability as anything else. Fresh rape is a delicious choice. Try a Spanish brandy with this tapa.

1   **pound anglerfish or other fish**
    Flour for dusting
    Salt and pepper to taste
2   **eggs, beaten**
2   **cups bread crumbs or cornmeal**
    Oil for deep-frying
    Lemon wedges

Cut fish into strips ½ inch thick and 1-2 inches long. Dust strips in flour seasoned with salt and pepper and shake off excess. Dip in egg and roll in bread crumbs or cornmeal. Deep-fry in hot oil at 375°F, 3-4 minutes, or pan-fry on both sides. Remove, drain, and serve hot with lemon wedges.

Serves 6

PESCADO A LA AJO ARRIERO
(FISH STEW, MULE-DRIVER'S STYLE)

You can use any fish or combination of fish in this "mule-driver's" stew. Rape is popular, but the same treatment can be given to cod, hake, and even to shrimp and lobster. Many local versions omit the tomatoes and add more red peppers. Still others braise in white wine instead of frying in olive oil. Popular with a dry white wine.

2   **pounds anglerfish or other seafood**
3   **tablespoons olive oil**
1   **onion, chopped**
5   **cloves garlic, chopped**
2   **tomatoes, peeled and chopped**
2   **red peppers, cut into strips**
2   **tablespoons chopped fresh parsley**
2   **teaspoons paprika**
6   **peppercorns, crushed**
1   **tablespoon vinegar**

Clean fish and cut into pieces. Heat oil in a skillet and sauté fish pieces until barely done. With a slotted spoon, transfer to an earthenware or glass casserole. In the same skillet, sauté onion and garlic until onion is soft. Add tomatoes, red peppers, and parsley and continue to cook until peppers are soft. Stir in paprika, peppercorns, and vinegar and continue to cook until sauce forms. Pour in a little fish stock or hot water if sauce becomes too thick. Pour sauce over fish pieces, reheat, and continue to simmer until well blended. Serve hot.

Serves 8

MERO A LA PIMIENTO VERDE
(ROCK BASS WITH GREEN PEPPERS)

Sea bass in various varieties exists throughout the world. The two species found most often in Spanish tapa bars are mero *(rock bass, sometimes called* sea perch, pollack, *or* grouper) *and* lubina *(sea bass). Both are delicious cooked in the same ways as other white fish, eaten either unadorned or with a sauce; a green sauce is especially tasty with rock and sea bass. Tapa cooks also like to use* besugo *(sea bream) with this green-pepper tapa. A Spanish brandy would be a perfect partner.*

3	tablespoons oil
1	onion, chopped
2	cloves garlic, chopped
3	green peppers, chopped
1	pound rock bass, sea bream, or halibut
	Salt to taste
½	cup Spanish brandy
1	teaspoon fresh lemon juice
	Pinch cayenne pepper
1	tablespoon chopped fresh parsley

Heat oil in a skillet and cook onion and garlic in it until the onion is soft. Add chopped peppers and simmer until peppers are reduced to a pulp. Cut fish into ½-inch-thick slices, season with salt, and simmer in the skillet a few minutes or until brown on both sides. Pour brandy over the slices, light, and let burn until alcohol has burned off. Add lemon juice and cayenne pepper and sprinkle with parsley. Bake in a preheated 400°F oven for 5 minutes or until cooked through.

Serves 6–8

MERO A LA NARANJA
(ROCK BASS WITH ORANGE SAUCE)

A cool sangria would be a perfect complement to this orange-sauce tapa.

1	pound rock bass
2	tablespoons oil
1	tablespoon butter
1	tablespoon flour
1	cup chicken stock
	Salt, pepper, and nutmeg to taste
½	cup orange juice
1	tablespoon fresh lemon juice
	Orange or lemon slices

Cut rock bass into strips ½ inch thick. Heat oil in a skillet and fry fish strips until barely cooked. Transfer to a casserole. In another pan, melt butter, add flour, and stir over low heat for a few minutes. Stir in stock and simmer. Season with salt, pepper, and nutmeg, and slowly add orange and lemon juices. Continue to cook, stirring occasionally, until liquid is reduced and you have a smooth sauce. Pour sauce over the fish and place in a preheated 350°F oven for 5 minutes or until well heated. Serve with orange or lemon slices.

Serves 6

LUBINA EN SALSA AMARILLA
(SEA BASS IN SAFFRON SAUCE)

Accompany with a white wine.

1	pound sea bass, halibut, or other firm white fish
2	tablespoons oil
3	cloves garlic, chopped
15	blanched almonds, chopped
2	tablespoons chopped fresh parsley
1	tablespoon olive oil
1	onion, chopped
½	tablespoon saffron
¼	cup white wine
¼	cup fish stock or water
2	tablespoons flour
	Salt to taste

Cut bass into strips about ½ inch thick and 1½-2 inches long. Heat 2 tablespoons oil in a skillet and fry fish strips until lightly browned. Transfer to a casserole. With a mortar and pestle or in an electric blender, crush garlic, almonds, and parsley, adding enough olive oil to form a smooth paste. Heat 1 tablespoon olive oil in the same skillet used to cook the fish and sauté onion in it until soft. Stir in the garlic mixture. Dissolve saffron in white wine, pour wine and fish stock into the skillet, and stir in flour. Simmer slowly for 5 minutes or until alcohol has evaporated, liquid is reduced, and a smooth sauce forms. Season with salt and pour sauce over fish strips. Bake in a preheated 375°F oven for about 20 minutes or until fish is cooked.

Serves 6

COD (BACALAO)

Codfish (known in several languages as "the beef of the sea") is the world's most important saltwater fish; in the Basque country, it's Spain's most important fish. Basque fishermen were the first to discover cod off the Newfoundland Banks in the 14th century. Although not found in Spanish waters, codfish is, nevertheless, a necessity in tapa bars. One reason for its popularity is that, when salted and dried, cod holds its flavor longer and better than any other fish.

Cod lacks the subtle taste of many other saltwater fish, yet it still has a good, lean flavor. The meat is white, flaky in texture, and never oily; it has comparatively few bones.

You can buy cod in America fresh, frozen, salted, smoked, dried, or canned. Spanish cooks nearly always use dried and salted cod (*bacalao*), but you can substitute fresh or frozen. You can also use any subspecies of cod (haddock, hake, rockfish) or almost any other white fish, including ocean perch.

BACALAO PIL-PIL
(CODFISH "PIL-PIL")

Pil-pil is the classic simmering technique of Basque origin, used for cooking fish and other foods in olive oil and garlic, often with onions or chili peppers. The idea is to simmer slowly in a skillet or earthenware casserole by shaking only, never stirring. This lets the food juices mix naturally with the oil and garlic, producing a smooth, thick *pil-pil* sauce. Most frequently eaten with a glass of white wine, but a cold crisp beer would be excellent.

2　pounds dried cod
⅓　cup olive oil
5　cloves garlic, peeled
1　cup fish stock or water in which the cod was soaked

Soak the cod 6-8 hours, changing the water at least 2-3 times. Remove the scales without breaking the skin; the skin helps give the sauce its rich flavor. Remove the bones, cut into bite-size strips, and dry with a paper towel or cloth. Heat olive oil in a skillet or casserole, add garlic cloves, and simmer slowly until browned; remove the garlic. Put pieces of fish in the skillet and fry, skin side down, shaking and twisting from time to time to prevent sticking. Simmer for about 20 minutes. When the sauce starts to thicken, gradually begin adding stock and continue to cook, shaking the skillet, until juices from the fish and olive oil thicken into a creamy sauce.

For a meal, cut into larger pieces before frying and serve with rice or boiled potatoes.

Serves 8–10

BACALAO A LA VIZCAINA
(CODFISH, BASQUE STYLE)

Excellent with a full-bodied white wine; Basques prefer apple cider.

1 **pound dried cod**
2 **tablespoons oil**
3 **onions, chopped**
6 **red peppers, seeded and chopped**
4 **cloves garlic, chopped**
4 **tomatoes, peeled and chopped**
¼ **cup bread crumbs**
1 **tablespoon chopped fresh parsley**

Soak cod in water 6-8 hours, changing water occasionally. Remove skin and cut into bite-size strips. Heat water in a kettle and cook strips for 10 minutes or until cooked; drain, save the liquid, and place cod pieces in a casserole. Heat oil in a skillet and sauté onions in it until soft. Add peppers, garlic, tomatoes, bread crumbs, and parsley and simmer for 20 minutes to form a sauce. Add cod liquid if sauce becomes too thick. Pour sauce over cod and bake in a preheated 350°F oven, uncovered, for about 15 minutes, or until hot and thoroughly blended. Serve hot.

For a meal, cut pieces into meal-size slices and serve with boiled potatoes.

Serves 8

CONCHAS DE BACALAO
(CODFISH ON SCALLOP SHELLS)

Excellent with white wine, but any drink would be suitable.

1 **pound dried cod**
½ **pound potatoes, peeled, cooked, and diced**
1 **egg yolk**
   Salt to taste
2 **tablespoons chopped fresh parsley**
8 **scallop shells**
¼ **cup bread crumbs**
8 **lemon wedges**

Soak dried cod in water 6-8 hours, changing water occasionally. Remove the skin and cut cod into slices. Heat water in a kettle and boil the cod for about 10 minutes or until cooked. Remove and drain. In an electric mixer, mix cod slices, cooked potatoes, and egg yolk until mixture is well blended and a smooth consistency. Salt to taste and stir in 1 tablespoon parsley. Fill each scallop shell with the mixture. When ready to serve, sprinkle with bread crumbs and place in a broiler for 5 minutes or until well browned; sprinkle with remaining parsley and garnish with lemon wedges.

Serves 8

EEL (CONGRIO)

Eels are a tapa delight, especially tasty cut into small pieces and fried in white wine with onions, garlic, and mushrooms; also popular in Spain in stews and marinated.

The adult conger eel (*congrio*) has a white, oily but firm flesh and a delicate flavor. There are no bones other than the long backbone, which is easy to remove. To prepare eel, you first must skin it. The traditional method is to nail the head to a board (or to the wall) and, with a sharp knife, make a circular cut just below the head, which will detach the skin; then strip off the skin with one long pull. To remove the backbone, slit along both sides of the bone and lift off the meat.

Eels are sold in the States fresh during certain times of the year, especially around Christmas. Smoked eels are available all year long, and you can always find them preserved in cans and jars. In Spain, fresh eels are kept alive until the very minute of cooking.

CONGRIOS FRITOS
(FRIED CONGER EELS)

Especially appropriate with a crisp white wine.

2 conger eels
   Flour for dusting
   Salt and pepper to taste
3 tablespoons oil
1 onion, chopped
   Lemon wedges

Skin and clean eels and cut into 3-inch pieces. Dip pieces in flour seasoned with salt and pepper. Heat oil in a skillet and sauté onion in it until soft. Add eels and continue to sauté until pieces are golden brown. Remove, drain, and spear with toothpicks. Serve hot with lemon wedges.

VARIATION
For added flavor, simmer in $\frac{1}{4}$ cup of white wine and sprinkle in a handful of chopped mushrooms.

Serves 6

ALL I PEBRE
(EELS IN PIQUANT SAUCE)

A favorite Valencian tapa as well as a popular main dish, especially along the Costa Blanca. A cold beer might go best with this piquant tapa.

4	pounds eel
1	tablespoon oil
1	tablespoon paprika
1-2	cups water
3	cloves garlic, chopped
14	blanched almonds
2	tablespoons chopped fresh parsley
¼	teaspoon saffron
1	tablespoon olive oil
	Salt to taste

Clean and skin eels and cut into 1- to 1½-inch pieces. Heat oil in a casserole or skillet, add paprika, and stir in enough hot water to cover eels. Bring to a boil and add pieces of eel. Meanwhile with a mortar and pestle or in an electric blender crush garlic, almonds, parsley, and saffron with enough olive oil to make a smooth paste. Stir mixture into the casserole, add salt to taste, and cook for about 20 minutes or until eels are done. Add more water if sauce thickens. Serve hot.

VARIATION
For an all-in-one meal or a main course, add peas, chopped carrots, or new potatoes (or all three) and serve over rice, as they do in Valencia.

Serves 10

FROGS' LEGS (ANCAS DE RANA)

ANCAS DE RANA PROVENZALE
(SAUTEED FROGS' LEGS)

Perfect with a cool glass of Spanish champagne.

12	pairs frogs' legs
2	cups milk
3	tablespoons oil
1	onion, chopped
2	cloves garlic, chopped
2	tablespoons chopped fresh parsley
	Salt and pepper to taste
	Lemon wedges

Separate the pairs of legs if joined. Soak in milk 20-30 minutes, remove, and drain. Heat oil in a skillet and sauté onion and garlic in it until onion is soft. Add frogs' legs, sprinkle with parsley, and sauté for 5 minutes or until legs are tender. Add salt and pepper to taste. Serve with lemon wedges.

Serves 6-8 (2-4 legs each)

ANCAS DE RANA ADOBADA
(MARINATED FROGS' LEGS)

Perfect with a dry white wine.

12	pairs frogs' legs
1	cup dry white wine
2	cloves garlic, chopped
3	tablespoons fresh lemon juice
6	peppercorns
2	tablespoons chopped fresh parsley
1	bay leaf
½	teaspoon dried thyme
½	teaspoon ground nutmeg
	Flour for dusting
2	eggs, beaten
1	cup bread crumbs
	Oil for deep-frying
	Salt and pepper to taste
	Lemon wedges

Separate the pairs of frogs' legs if joined. In a bowl, mix together wine, garlic, lemon juice, peppercorns, parsley, bay leaf, thyme, and nutmeg. Place legs in the bowl and refrigerate for 3-4 hours. Remove legs and drain. Dust in flour, shake off excess, dip in beaten egg, and roll in bread crumbs. Deep-fry at 375°F, 2-3 minutes or until golden brown. Remove and drain. Add salt and pepper to taste and serve with lemon wedges.

Serves 6-8

HAKE (MERLUZA)

MERLUZA EN SALSA VERDE
(HAKE IN GREEN SAUCE)

This green-sauce tapa is of Basque origin (often called a la Vasca or "Basque style") and is based on a popular main dish that usually includes small clams. Try a dry white wine with this tapa.

2	pounds hake
3	tablespoons oil
3	cloves garlic, chopped
2	tablespoons chopped fresh parsley
1	cup fish stock or asparagus liquid
¼	teaspoon fresh lemon juice
1	cup cooked peas
1	dozen cooked asparagus tips
2	hard-boiled eggs, chopped

Cut hake into strips about 2 inches long. Heat oil in an earthenware casserole or skillet, add garlic and parsley, and simmer until garlic begins to brown. Add fish slices to the casserole and pour in fish stock and lemon juice. Cook until tender, shaking occasionally. During the last 5 minutes, add peas and asparagus tips; sprinkle with chopped hard-boiled eggs just before serving. Serve hot.

Serves 8

MERLUZA ROMESCO
(HAKE IN ROMESCO SAUCE)

Salsa Romesco, *which hails from Tarragona, calls for a special local hot pepper, but you can substitute chili powder, cayenne, or paprika; each gives a slightly different bite to the dish. Salmonete (red mullet) is also popular with salsa romesco. A full-bodied red wine would be a worthy partner.*

1½ **pounds hake or other white fish**
¼ **cup olive oil**
2 **tablespoons fresh lemon juice**
1 **tablespoon oil**
1 **small onion, chopped**
2 **tomatoes, peeled and chopped**
3 **cloves garlic, chopped**
2 **dozen almonds, chopped**
2 **teaspoons wine vinegar or fresh lemon juice**
1 **teaspoon paprika, chili powder, or cayenne pepper**
   Salt to taste
2 **tablespoons chopped fresh parsley**

Cut hake into strips about 1 inch thick and 2-3 inches long. Marinate in olive oil and lemon juice for 2-3 hours. Heat oil in a skillet and fry onion in it until soft. Remove onion and put into a mortar or electric mixer and mash together with tomatoes, garlic, and almonds to form a puree. Add mixture to the skillet along with vinegar, paprika, and a little salt. Mix well and simmer over a low flame, stirring continually, for a few minutes. Remove fish strips from marinade, drain, place on a hot grill or fry in a skillet, and cook until tender. Do not overcook. Pour sauce over grilled fish sticks and sprinkle with parsley.

Serves 6–8 (2–4 sticks each)

MACKEREL (ESTORINO)

ESTORINO CON CEBOLLA
(MACKEREL WITH ONIONS)

1½ **pounds onions**
2 **tablespoons oil**
1½ **pounds mackerel**
   Flour for dusting
   Salt and pepper to taste
   Oil for deep-frying

Slice onions into thin rings. Heat oil in a skillet and sauté onions in it until soft. Clean mackerel and cut into strips. Dust strips in flour seasoned with salt and pepper and deep-fry in hot oil at 375°F, 3-4 minutes (or pan-fry, turning once). Place on a serving dish and top with sautéed onions; serve hot.

Serves 8

SARDINES (SARDINAS)

Fresh Spanish sardines are of the same family as herring and are similar to Spanish anchovies, but larger, about 6 inches long. Tapa cooks prepare them in many of the same ways as anchovies—deep-fried, marinated, broiled—but grilling is considered best. As in America, sardines also appear in Spain in cans, preserved in oil. Fresh or canned, they make excellent tapas.

The simplest way to present canned sardines is right out of the can in their oil with lemon wedges and hunks of bread. Another tapa technique is to grill canned sardines and sprinkle with chopped parsley. Or place sardines on a baking sheet, sprinkle with Manchego, Swiss, or Gruyère cheese, and broil. Excellent with chilled white wine or ice-cold beer.

SARDINAS REBOZADAS
(BATTER-FRIED SARDINES)

1 **pound fresh sardines or herring**
Flour for dusting
Salt and pepper to taste
1 **egg, beaten**
2 **cups bread crumbs or cornmeal**
Oil for deep-frying
2 **tablespoons chopped fresh parsley**
Tomato Sauce (optional; see index for recipe)

Wash and clean the sardines, removing head, tail, spine, and intestines of each. Dip first in flour seasoned with salt and pepper, then in beaten egg, next in bread crumbs or cornmeal. Deep-fry in hot oil at 375°F for about 3 minutes, drain, and sprinkle with parsley. Popular served in a thick tomato sauce.

Serves 4–6 (3–4 sardines each)

SARDINAS A LA CATALANA
(SARDINES, CATALAN STYLE)

Excellent with a cold beer, dry white wine, or mixed drinks.

1 **pound fresh sardines or herring**
6 **cloves garlic, chopped**
2 **tablespoons chopped fresh parsley**
1 **cup olive oil**
¼ **cup fresh lemon juice**
Flour for dusting
Salt and pepper to taste
1 **egg, beaten**
2 **cups bread crumbs**
Lemon wedges

Wash and clean sardines and split open the bodies, removing the insides, head, tail, spine, and bones of each, leaving the two halves attached to the tail. Crush garlic and 1 tablespoon of parsley with a mortar and pestle or electric blender, slowly adding olive oil, drop by drop, until a thick, heavy paste forms. Add lemon juice and stir in the remaining olive oil until the mixture thickens to a smooth, creamy consistency. Add salt to taste. Open each sardine and spread some of the mixture on the inside. Close each to its original form, dust with flour seasoned with salt and pepper, dip in beaten egg, and roll in bread crumbs. Heat oil in a skillet and fry on both sides. Sprinkle with remaining parsley and serve with lemon wedges.

Serves 6 (2-3 sardines each)

SARDINAS A LA GRANADA
(SARDINES, GRANADA STYLE)

Excellent with a cold white wine.

1 **pound fresh sardines or herring**
2 **tablespoons oil**
1 **tablespoon fresh lemon juice**
¼ **cup white wine**
2 **cloves garlic, chopped**
1 **tablespoon chopped fresh parsley**

Wash and clean sardines and remove intestines. Heat oil in a skillet or casserole. Place fish in the skillet and pour in lemon juice and white wine, add chopped garlic, and sprinkle with parsley. Cover and cook for about 10 minutes or until sardines are done. Serve hot.

Serves 6

SHARK (CAZON)

CAZON EN ESCABECHE
(MARINATED SHARK)

Cazón, or dogfish, is a member of the shark family. Shark meat is solid, with a hardy flavor, making it a favorite fish for marinating en escabeche. A good red wine would be a suitable accompaniment.

1 **pound shark, sea bass, or other solid-fleshed fish**
2 **cloves garlic, chopped**
1 **onion, sliced**
2 **teaspoons paprika**
1 **teaspoon dried oregano**
1 **teaspoon ground cumin**
1 **green pepper, sliced**
¼ **cup fresh lemon juice**
Olive oil
Flour for dusting
Salt and pepper to taste
Oil for deep-frying

Cut shark meat into cubes or strips about 2 inches thick and put into a bowl. Mix in garlic, onion, paprika, oregano, cumin, green pepper, lemon juice, and enough olive oil to cover. Refrigerate and let stand overnight. Drain fish cubes, dust with flour seasoned with salt and pepper, and pan-fry or deep-fry in hot oil at 375°F, 2-3 minutes or until golden on all sides. Spear cubes with toothpicks and serve hot.

Serves 6

SOLE (LENGUADO)

LENGUADO AL CHAMPAÑA
(SOLE IN CHAMPAGNE)

Champagne would be the ideal companion, but any drink would go well with this tapa.

1 **pound sole, flounder, other white fish, shrimp, or other shellfish**
1½ **cups champagne**
1 **teaspoon fresh lemon juice**
¼ **teaspoon cayenne pepper**
½ **cup cream**
1 **teaspoon paprika**
Salt to taste

Flake sole into large pieces. Place pieces in a skillet and add champagne, lemon juice, and cayenne pepper. Simmer until sole is golden. With a slotted spoon, carefully remove fish from the skillet and transfer to a platter. Continue to simmer until liquid is reduced by about half and then add cream and paprika. Simmer slowly (do not boil), stirring until sauce is thick and smooth. Add salt to taste and pour sauce over the fish.

Serves 6

POPIETAS DE LENGUADO
(LITTLE TUBES OF SOLE)

Any drink would be appropriate, including mixed drinks.

1   **pound sole or other white fish**

1   **7-ounce can oil-packed tuna, drained**

¼   **cup diced green olives**

1   **2-ounce jar pimientos, diced**

   Flour for dusting

2   **eggs, beaten**

2   **cups bread crumbs**

¼   **cup diced black olives**

2   **tablespoons chopped fresh parsley**

⅓   **cup oil for frying**

Clean and scale sole, leaving head and tail intact. Poach by dropping fish into a kettle of boiling salted water. When water returns to boiling point, boil for about 10 minutes or until cooked. Remove and let cool. Cut into thin fillets. Mix together tuna, green olives, and pimientos. Spoon some of the mixture onto each fish fillet, roll into a tube, and fasten with a toothpick. Dust with flour, dip in beaten eggs, and roll in bread crumbs. Fry in hot oil at 375°F, 2-3 minutes or until browned and heated through. Drain and let cool. With a sharp knife, carefully cut into slices about ½ inch thick. Sprinkle with chopped black olives and parsley.

Serves 8 (2-3 slices each)

SWORDFISH (PEZ ESPADA)

Although found in every ocean in the world, the swordfish (*pez espada*) breeds and spawns only in the Mediterranean. It has a firm, meatlike flesh, rich in flavor and rather oily. Swordfish retains its firmness when cooked but tends to dry out if not continually basted, and it will lose its richness if overcooked. Its hardy flavor makes swordfish a favorite in tapa bars throughout the peninsula.

On Spanish restaurant menus, swordfish is popular broiled or fried as steaks; in tapa bars, it is usually grilled, often on skewers. In any case, it should be served simply, perhaps merely with parsley and lemon wedges. Tapa cooks are careful not to mask the rich but delicate flavor by overcooking or by drenching in heavy sauces. Most swordfish is marketed frozen in America, but occasionally it's available fresh as steaks or fillets.

TUNA (ATUN)

Spanish tuna (*atún*) is a superb tapa, table, and game fish. "The king of *all* fish" and "the ruler of the Valhalla of fishermen," according to one sportsman, Ernest Hemingway.

The meat of the Spanish, or Mediterranean, tuna is firm and compact and a bit heavy, likened more often to veal than to other saltwater fish. Tapa cooks will sometimes even substitute tuna in their veal recipes.

Tuna is best known in America in cans, but you can also find it in fillets, in steaks, and smoked. Although the taste is not the same, you can use canned tuna in most recipes that call for fresh, as the Spanish often do; also you may interchange tuna with mackerel, which is the Spanish tuna's closest living relative. As a tapa, Spanish tuna is excellent grilled in olive oil or white wine with a little chopped onion and garlic.

ATUN CON TOMATE
(TUNA WITH TOMATO SAUCE)

A dry white wine would be a suitable accompaniment.

2	pounds fresh tuna
	Salt and pepper to taste
	Flour for dusting
4	tablespoons oil
½	cup dry white wine
1	onion, chopped
2	cloves garlic, chopped
4	tomatoes, peeled and chopped
2	tablespoons chopped fresh parsley

With a fork, flake tuna into hunks (about 2-inch squares), season with salt and pepper, and dust in flour. Heat oil in a skillet and fry tuna hunks in it until light brown on all sides. Remove, arrange in the bottom of a casserole or baking dish, and pour in white wine.

In the same oil used for browning tuna (adding more oil, if necessary), sauté onion and garlic until onion is soft. Mix in tomatoes and simmer until liquid is reduced by about a fourth and a sauce forms. Season with salt and pepper. Pour sauce over tuna hunks, sprinkle with parsley, and bake in a preheated 350°F oven, 10-15 minutes. Serve hot.

Serves 8

ATUN A LA SEVILLANA
(MARINATED TUNA, SEVILLE STYLE)

Any drink would be suitable; a dry sherry would be perfect.

1	pound fresh tuna or mackerel
2	cloves garlic, chopped
1	onion, sliced
2	tablespoons olive oil
¼	cup vinegar
6	peppercorns
¼	teaspoon dried thyme
2	tablespoons chopped fresh parsley
2	tablespoons oil
¾	cup green olives, pitted
	Salt to taste

With a fork, flake tuna into hunks and place in a bowl. Stir in garlic, onion, olive oil, vinegar, peppercorns, thyme, and 1 tablespoon chopped parsley. Let stand for 3-4 hours, remove tuna flakes, and drain. Heat oil in a skillet and sauté tuna for 5 minutes or until barely browned. Add green olives and a little of the marinade and simmer for 15 minutes or until tuna is cooked. Add salt to taste and sprinkle with remaining parsley. Serve hot.

Serves 6

MARMITAKO
(TUNA CASSEROLE)

Marmitako hails from the Basque country, where it is served as a savory tapa and in larger portions as a hearty one-dish meal.

2	tablespoons oil
1	onion, chopped
2	cloves garlic, chopped
2	tomatoes, peeled and chopped
½	tablespoon paprika
	Pinch cayenne pepper
	Salt to taste
1	pound potatoes, peeled and diced
1	pound fresh tuna, mackerel, halibut, or canned tuna

Heat oil in a casserole or skillet and sauté onion and garlic in it until onion is soft. Add chopped tomatoes and, stirring occasionally, cook until liquid is reduced and a smooth sauce forms. Sprinkle with paprika, a pinch of cayenne pepper, and salt to taste. Add diced potatoes, cover, and cook about 15 minutes or until potatoes are barely cooked through. Cut tuna into cubes and add to the casserole. Cover and cook 10-15 minutes or until tender.

Serves 6-8

SEAFOOD

CLAMS (ALMEJAS)

Clams (*almejas*) exist all along the Spanish coast in many species and all sizes. They are usually eaten raw, but are also added to paella dishes, stews, and casseroles.

Like all shellfish, clams must be cleaned well before eating. Either wash in running water or soak them for several hours, preferably both. If you're preparing a sauce to accompany your clams, be sure to strain the liquid and add to the ingredients. You can buy clams fresh, canned, or frozen; fresh is, of course, best. Most tapa recipes for clams, oysters, and mussels are interchangeable. Tapa cooks especially like to steam clams.

ALMEJAS RELLENOS
(STUFFED CLAMS)

A crisp, cold beer would be an ideal companion.

1 dozen large clams
2 tablespoons oil
1 small onion, chopped
2 cloves garlic, chopped
3 tablespoons bread crumbs
2 tablespoons minced ham
1 tablespoon fresh lemon juice
2 tablespoons chopped fresh parsley
Tabasco sauce
Salt and pepper to taste
Lemon wedges

Wash and clean clams in running water. Open clams with a knife and discard half the shells. Cut out meat and chop into small pieces. Heat oil in a skillet and sauté onion and garlic in it until onion is soft. Stir in bread crumbs, ham, lemon juice, and parsley. Mix with clam meat and place mixture on the open clam shells. Add to each a dash of Tabasco and salt and pepper to taste. Bake in a preheated 350°F oven or grill about 10 minutes or until browned. Serve with lemon wedges.

Serves 4 (3–4 clams each)

ALMEJAS CON CERDO
(CLAMS WITH PORK)

A white wine would be an agreeable companion.

4 dozen small clams
½ cup dry white wine
2 teaspoons fresh lemon juice
2 cloves garlic, chopped
½ pound boneless pork
2 tablespoons oil
1 tablespoon chopped fresh parsley

Wash clams in water to eliminate sand and grit. Place clams in a large saucepan with about ¼ inch of white wine, lemon juice, and garlic. Cover and steam over high heat for about 5 minutes or until the shells open. Discard any clams that remain closed or are cracked. Cut pork into bite-size pieces. Heat a little oil in a skillet and sauté pork in it until cooked. Add clams and juice to the skillet and simmer until liquid is reduced and the pork and clam flavors are well blended. Sprinkle with parsley and serve hot.

Serves 6

ALMEJAS AL VAPOR
(STEAMED CLAMS)

A dry sherry would be a fitting partner.

18 large clams **Lemon wedges**	To steam, thoroughly scrub the shells and place in a saucepan with about ½ inch of salted water. Cover the pan and steam over high heat about 5 minutes or until the shells open. Discard any clams that remain closed or are cracked. Serve in their juices on the half- or whole-shell and accompany with lemon wedges.

Serves 4–6 (3–4 large clams each) |

SEA CRABS (CANGREJOS)

Crabs, like most other seafood, are often served in Spain in their shells, which help retain the fresh sea flavor of the meat. In the Basque country, small whole sea crabs (or pieces of larger ones) are boiled and served as tapas. To eat, simply twist off the legs and suck the meat from the shell and legs.

To cook, drop live crabs into well-salted boiling water and cook for about 20 minutes. Then quickly plunge the crabs into cold water to stop the cooking. Drain and cut into serving pieces (or serve small ones whole), accompanied by lemon wedges. Excellent with a glass of dry sherry.

TXANGURRO
(STUFFED CRAB)

Txangurro (a Basque word also spelled shangurro *or* changurro*) is a Bay of Biscay favorite, wonderful as a meal and exceptional as a tapa along with a dry white wine. Use either crab or scallop shells for stuffing.*

6-8 small live crabs **1 tablespoon oil** **1 onion, chopped** **1 clove garlic, chopped** **2 tomatoes, peeled and chopped** **2 tablespoons chopped fresh parsley** **½ cup dry white wine** **½ cup Spanish brandy** **Pinch cayenne pepper** **Salt and pepper to taste** **¼ cup bread crumbs** **2 tablespoons butter**	Boil crabs in salted water for about 15 minutes. Drain and let cool. Remove the meat from bodies and legs. Wash and clean shells and set aside. Heat oil in a skillet and sauté onion and garlic in it until onion is soft. Add tomatoes, 1 tablespoon parsley, wine, brandy, a pinch of cayenne pepper, and salt and pepper to taste. Cook for 10 minutes or until liquid is reduced and a smooth sauce forms. If sauce becomes too thick, add liquid from cooking the crabs. Mix in the crabmeat and blend well. Stuff the cleaned crab shells (or fill scallop shells) with the mixture. Sprinkle with remaining parsley and the bread crumbs and dot with butter. Bake in a preheated 400°F oven for 10 minutes or until golden. Serve hot.

Serves 4 |

MUSSELS (MEJILLONES)

The mussel is an oblong, black shellfish, about the size of a large oyster. It is delicious and nutritious, neglected by many Americans but *the* shellfish for serious tapa eaters, much more popular than oysters or clams. Spain is, in fact, the world's largest commercial mussel producer, with a quarter of a million mussels grown annually in floating offshore nurseries.

Test mussels as you would any other shellfish. Gently squeeze open the shell; if it closes, the mussel is alive; if it stays open, toss it. Also discard any mussels with cracked or open shells. To clean, soak in cold water for a few hours and then rinse well under running water to get rid of the sand and grit and scrape each shell with a stiff brush or knife and cut off the hairy growth ("beard").

Mussels are eaten in tapa bars deep-fried, baked, stuffed, smoked, grilled, skewered, and occasionally raw. Fried or grilled mussels are often served cold with mayonnaise and are excellent accompanied by a cold crisp beer.

Another popular cooking method is to steam briefly in salted water. To steam mussels, place several in a saucepan in a half inch of salted water. Then cover and steam over high heat for about 5 minutes or until the shells open. For a more distinctive flavor, use a good dry white wine in place of water. Strain the liquid and serve mussels in their shells (or on half-shells) either with lemon wedges or a sauce made from the liquid.

MEJILLONES AL BACON
(MUSSELS WITH BACON)

Delicious with cold beer.

2   **dozen mussels**
12   **strips smoked bacon**
1   **egg, beaten**
1   **cup bread crumbs**
    Oil for deep-frying
    Lemon wedges

Clean and wash mussels. With a knife, open each shell and carefully cut out the meat. Wrap each mussel with a half-slice of bacon and fasten with a toothpick. When ready to serve, dip each in egg, then in bread crumbs, and deep-fry in hot oil at 375°F, 2-3 minutes. Serve hot with lemon wedges.

Serves 6 (about 4 mussels each)

OCTOPUS (PULPO)

Octopus is a highly regarded tapa delicacy, especially in Spain's northern provinces. The meat is chewy, with a taste sometimes compared to that of lobster. Unlike squid and cuttlefish, it is the tentacles of the octopus, not the body, that provide the best eating, although both body and tentacles are used. Octopus is popular in casseroles and salads; also found in tapa bars fried, boiled, or baked, and cut into small pieces and served in a simple mixture of olive oil, parsley, and lemon. Delicious accompanied by a white wine.

PULPO A LA GALLEGA
(OCTOPUS GALICIAN STYLE)

Excellent with a white wine.

2   pounds octopus
½   cup oil
1   small onion, chopped
2   cloves garlic, chopped
2   tablespoons chopped fresh parsley
1   teaspoon paprika
   Salt to taste
4   medium potatoes, peeled and diced
   Pimientos for topping

Clean, skin, and wash the octopus, removing internal organs and suction cups. If octopus is difficult to skin and clean, boil it in a kettle of salted water for an hour or until tender; skin and suckers should then come off easily. Cut tentacles and body into 1-inch squares. Heat 4 tablespoons of oil in a skillet and sauté onion and garlic in it until onion is soft. Add octopus, 1 tablespoon parsley, and paprika. Add salt to taste. Cook for about 1 hour or until octopus is tender and browned on all sides.

Meanwhile, heat 4 more tablespoons of oil in another skillet and fry diced potatoes until cooked and well browned. Remove, drain, and add potatoes to the octopus. Cook 5 more minutes. Top with pimientos and the remaining parsley.

Serves 8–10

PULPO CON CEBOLLAS
(OCTOPUS WITH ONIONS)

Any drink should go well here, but a brandy or a dry white wine might taste best.

2   large onions, sliced
4   tablespoons oil
2   pounds octopus
1   cup brandy
1   teaspoon ground cinnamon
1   tablespoon chopped pimientos
   Salt to taste
2   tablespoons chopped fresh parsley

Heat oil in a skillet, add sliced onions and simmer until soft. Clean, skin, and wash octopus, removing internal organs and suction cups. Cut tentacles and body into 1½- to 2-inch pieces. Add octopus to the skillet and cook for an hour or until tender and browned on all sides. Add brandy, cinnamon, and pimientos and simmer until alcohol evaporates, about 20 minutes. Add salt to taste and sprinkle with parsley just before serving.

Serves 8–10

OSTRAS FRITAS
(FRIED OYSTERS)

A cold beer might be best with this recipe.

1	**dozen oysters**
	Juice of 2 lemons
	Cornmeal for coating
3	**tablespoons oil**
	Salt and pepper to taste
1	**tablespoon chopped fresh parsley**
	Lemon wedges

Open the oysters with a knife and clean and wash both oysters and shells in cold water. Remove the meat from the shells. Dip first in lemon juice and then in cornmeal. Using a slotted spoon or fork, fry in hot oil for 2-3 minutes or until brown on all sides. Drain and return each oyster to one of the shells. Add salt and pepper to taste and sprinkle with parsley. Serve with lemon wedges.

Serves 4 (about 3 oysters each)

BUÑUELITOS DE OSTRAS
(OYSTER FRITTERS)

Excellent with a crisp, light beer.

1	**dozen oysters**
2½	**cups flour**
1	**teaspoon baking powder**
1	**clove garlic, chopped**
2	**onions, chopped**
1	**cup beer**
	Oil for deep-frying
	Salt and pepper to taste
2	**tablespoons chopped fresh parsley**

Open and clean oysters in cold water, cut out the meat, and discard both shells. Mix flour, baking powder, garlic, and onions together. Slowly stir enough beer into the mixture to make smooth batter. Dip each oyster in the beer batter and deep-fry at 375°F, 2-3 minutes or until well browned. Drain, add salt and pepper to taste, and sprinkle with parsley.

Serves 6 (about 2 large fritters each)

OSTRAS CON VINO
(OYSTERS WITH WINE)

A pleasant experience with a dry white wine.

1 **dozen oysters**
2 **tablespoons oil**
1 **small onion, chopped**
5 **strips bacon, fried and crumbled**
1 **chorizo or other cured sausage, diced**
1 **cup dry white wine**
1 **tablespoon chopped fresh parsley**
   Oil for frying

Open and clean oysters in cold water and discard the top shells. Place in a casserole and bake in a preheated 450°F oven for about 5 minutes. Heat oil in a skillet and sauté onion in it until soft. Mix crumbled bacon and diced sausage in the skillet and drizzle on top of the oysters. Pour white wine over the oysters and sprinkle with parsley. Bake a few more minutes, until heated through. Serve hot.

Serves 4-6

SCALLOPS (VIEIRAS)

Scallop shells (often called *conchas de peregrino* or "pilgrim shells") have been for centuries a religious symbol associated with the pilgrimage to the shrine at Santiago de Compostela in northwestern Spain. In Galician tapa bars, they are considered the perfect seafood receptacle and fun to eat out of.

Scallops are served whole in Spain; in this country, only the muscle is eaten. Small scallops are served in tapa bars raw with lemon wedges; larger ones are fried or otherwise cooked, often accompanied by a béarnaise or other sauce.

VIEIRAS FRITAS
(FRIED SCALLOPS)

A manzanilla sherry would make a most agreeable partner.

1 **dozen scallops**
   Flour for dusting
3 **tablespoons oil**
1 **onion, chopped**
2 **cloves garlic, chopped**
   Salt and pepper to taste
2 **tablespoons chopped fresh parsley**

Pry open the shells, cut out scallops, and wash and clean in cold water. Drain and dust lightly with flour. Heat oil in a skillet and sauté onion and garlic in it until onion is soft. Add scallops and sauté until lightly browned. Add salt and pepper to taste and sprinkle with parsley. Either serve in their shells or spear with toothpicks and serve on saucers.

Serves 4 (about 3 each)

VIEIRAS AL HORNO
(BAKED SCALLOPS)

Accompany with a cool medium-dry white wine.

1	**dozen scallops**
1	**onion, chopped**
2	**cloves garlic, chopped**
3	**tablespoons bread crumbs**
1	**tablespoon fresh lemon juice**
2	**tablespoons chopped fresh parsley**
¼	**cup white wine**
	Tabasco, butter, or paprika
	Salt and pepper to taste
	Lemon wedges

Pry open each scallop, cut out the meat, wash and clean in cold water, and set aside one shell from each scallop. Chop meat into pieces and mix together with onion, garlic, bread crumbs, lemon juice, and parsley; stir in white wine. Fill scallop shells with the mixture. As a topping, give each either a dash of Tabasco, a dab of butter, or a sprinkle of paprika, and season with salt and freshly ground pepper. Bake in a preheated 350°F oven or grill about 15 minutes or until browned. Serve with lemon wedges.

Serves 4-6 (3 medium-size shells)

VIEIRAS REBOZADAS
(BATTER-FRIED SCALLOPS)

Excellent with a cold beer.

1	**dozen scallops**
	Salt and pepper to taste
1	**cup bread crumbs**
1	**egg, beaten**
	Oil for deep-frying
	Lemon wedges

Pry open the scallops with a sharp knife, carefully cut out the meat, and clean. Add salt and pepper to bread crumbs. Roll each scallop in the crumbs and dip it in beaten egg. Deep-fry in hot oil at 375°F, 3-4 minutes or until golden. Serve hot on toothpicks with lemon wedges.

Serves 4

GAMBAS REBOZADAS
(BATTER-FRIED SHRIMP)

Just about any drink would be a worthy accompaniment for this popular tapa.

1 **pound medium-large shrimp**
1 **cup flour**
1 **teaspoon baking soda**
½ **teaspoon salt**
1 **clove garlic, chopped**
2 **eggs, beaten**
¾ **cup milk**
   Oil for deep-frying

Wash, peel, and devein shrimp. In a bowl, mix together flour, baking soda, and salt. Add garlic and beat in eggs and milk until smooth. Dip shrimp into the batter and deep-fry at 375°F, 3-4 minutes or until golden. Remove with a slotted spoon, drain, spear with toothpicks, and serve hot.

Serves 4 (4-6 each)

GAMBAS VINAGRETA
(SHRIMP VINAIGRETTE)

A dry sherry would be an agreeable companion.

1 **pound medium-large shrimp**
1 **small onion, chopped**
1 **tablespoon chopped green pepper**
2 **hard-boiled egg yolks, chopped**
½ **cup vinegar**
2 **tablespoons olive oil**
1 **tablespoon chopped fresh parsley**
¼ **teaspoon saffron**
   Salt and pepper to taste
   Dash Tabasco

Cook shrimp 3-4 minutes, never more, in boiling salted water and then wash, peel, and devein. Combine all ingredients and marinate shrimp, 4-6 hours. Spear with toothpicks and serve cold.

Serves 4

GAMBAS AL JEREZ
(SHRIMP IN SHERRY SAUCE)

A dry sherry or a light white wine would be a suitable companion.

1	pound medium-large shrimp, peeled and cleaned
½	cup dry sherry
2	cloves garlic, chopped
1	tablespoon chopped fresh parsley
¼	cup olive oil
½	teaspoon salt

Combine all ingredients and marinate shrimp for 4-6 hours. Cook shrimp mixture briefly in a skillet, on a hibachi, or in a broiler for about 4 minutes or until pink, spear each with a toothpick, and serve hot.

Serves 4

GAMBAS A LA PLANCHA
(GRILLED SHRIMP)

A la plancha, or "grilled on a hot plate," is the simplest and probably the most popular no-risk way to fix shrimp tapas. A cold beer would make an agreeable accompaniment.

18	jumbo shrimp
	Salt and pepper to taste
	Lemon juice
	Olive oil
	Lemon wedges or Garlic Sauce (see index for recipe)

Wash jumbo shrimp in their shells and place on a grill. Sprinkle with salt and freshly ground pepper and brush with a mixture of lemon juice and olive oil. Cook for 3-5 minutes on each side (turning once), or until the shells become orange. Serve hot in their shells with lemon wedges or Garlic Sauce.

Serves 4-6 (3-5 shrimp each)

SNAILS (CARACOLES)

Snails are a tapa treat, a specialty of the Basque country, where they are eaten fresh, usually in a tomato or other sauce. Snails are available in America canned, sometimes frozen, but not often fresh.

CARACOLES
(SNAILS IN TOMATO SAUCE)

Excellent with a glass of white wine.

4	dozen canned or frozen snails in their shells
2	tablespoons oil
1	onion, chopped
2	cloves garlic, chopped
2	tomatoes, peeled and chopped
1	cup bread crumbs or 2 tablespoons flour
1	cup white wine
	Salt to taste
2	tablespoons chopped fresh parsley

Remove snails from cans and rinse under running water. If you're using fresh snails, soak first in several changes of warm water until water is clear and then boil in salted water for about 30 minutes. Remove from shells, discard membranes, and rinse well in cold water or dry white wine. Heat oil in a skillet and sauté onion in it until soft. Add garlic, tomatoes, bread crumbs or flour, and wine. Sauté until alcohol evaporates. Pass through a sieve to make a puree. Return sauce to the skillet and add salt to taste. Add snails, bring to a boil, and simmer for 30 minutes, stirring occasionally. Add water if sauce becomes too thick. Sprinkle with parsley and serve hot.

Serves 6

CARACOLES CON JAMON
(SNAILS WITH HAM)

A red wine would be a suitable partner.

4	dozen canned or frozen shelled snails
4	tablespoons oil
1	onion, chopped
2	cloves garlic, chopped
½	cup chopped cooked ham
2	tablespoons chopped green peppers
	Salt to taste
2	tablespoons chopped fresh parsley

Remove snails from cans and rinse under running water. Heat oil in a skillet and sauté onion and garlic in it until onion is soft. Add ham, peppers, snails, and salt to taste. Continue to simmer slowly for 30 minutes, stirring occasionally, or until snails are cooked. Sprinkle with parsley during the last few minutes of cooking.

Serves 6-8

CARACOLES A LA SANTANDERINA
(SNAILS, SANTANDER STYLE)

A hardy red wine would stand up best to this spicy tapa.

4 dozen canned or frozen snails in their shells
2 tablespoons oil
1 onion, chopped
4 cloves garlic, chopped
¼ pound ham, diced
¼ pound chorizo or other cured sausage, diced
2 tomatoes, peeled and chopped
5 peppercorns, crushed
1 small hot chili pepper, seeded and chopped
½ cup fish stock
1 cup dry white wine
1 tablespoon flour
½ teaspoon dried thyme
1 tablespoon paprika
   Salt to taste
2 tablespoons chopped fresh parsley

Remove snails from the cans and rinse well under running water. Heat oil in a skillet and sauté onion and garlic in it until onion is soft. Add diced ham and sausage and brown for 5 minutes. Stir in tomatoes, peppercorns, chili pepper, stock, and wine. Sprinkle in flour to make a sauce. Add snails, sprinkle in thyme and paprika, and simmer for 45 minutes, stirring occasionally. If necessary, add more stock to maintain a smooth sauce. Season with salt and sprinkle with parsley. Serve hot.

Serves 8–10

SQUID (CALAMARES)

Squid is a tapa delicacy; in the States it is used mainly as bait, but this is beginning to change. Squid is on the verge of becoming the "in" seafood appetizer in continental-type restaurants throughout America.

Squid is a mollusk (like mussels, clams, and oysters) but without an external shell. The meat is white with a firm chewy texture and a sweet delicate flavor, often likened to abalone.

CALAMARES RELLENOS
(STUFFED SQUID)

A medium-dry white wine would be an appropriate partner.

12	small squid
½	pound ham, minced
6	stuffed olives, chopped
2	tomatoes, peeled and chopped
1	tablespoon chopped fresh parsley
	Salt to taste
3	tablespoons oil
1	onion, chopped
2	cloves garlic, chopped
	Flour for dusting
	Oil for frying

Clean and wash squid, discarding ink sacs, heads, and insides, and peel off skins. Remove tentacles and chop fine. Mix chopped tentacles, ham, olives, tomatoes, and parsley. Add salt to taste. Stuff squid with the mixture and close the openings with toothpicks. Heat oil in a skillet and sauté onion and garlic until onion is soft. Dust squid with flour and fry with onion and garlic for about 30 minutes or until golden on all sides.

VARIATION

If you want a sauce with your squid, remove the squid to a warming oven. Then add to the skillet ½ cup dry white wine and 2 peeled and finely chopped tomatoes. Continue cooking until the liquid is reduced and you have a smooth sauce. Spoon sauce over the stuffed squid.

Serves 4–6 (1–3 squid each)

CALAMARES AL JEREZ
(SQUID IN SHERRY)

A dry sherry or a good white table wine would be an appropriate partner.

2 **pounds squid**
2 **tablespoons oil**
2 **onions, chopped**
4 **cloves garlic, chopped**
20 **blanched almonds, chopped**
¼ **teaspoon saffron**
2 **tablespoons olive oil**
1 **cup dry sherry**
2 **tablespoons chopped fresh parsley**
Oil for frying

Clean and wash squid, removing ink sacs, heads, and insides, and peel off skins. Cut the bodies into rings and tentacles into pieces. Heat oil in a skillet and fry onions and garlic in it until onions are soft. With a mortar and pestle or in an electric blender, grind blanched almonds and saffron, adding enough olive oil to form a smooth paste. Add almond paste and sherry to the skillet and mix well. Add squid, cover, and simmer slowly for about 1 hour or until squid is tender. Add hot water if sauce becomes too thick. Sprinkle with parsley just before serving.

Serves 8

ADDITIONAL FISH AND SEAFOOD TAPAS

CHAPTER EIGHTEEN
PORK, BEEF, AND SAUSAGE TAPAS (CARNES)

According to a popular Spanish saying, in the north of Spain they stew, in the central region they roast, and in the south they fry. Tapa cooks, regardless of their province of origin, do all three, but with the emphasis on frying. Pan-frying is popular because it is convenient, especially in the cramped quarters of the typical tapa-bar kitchen. More important, pan-frying takes advantage of the concentrated meat juices from which creative tapa cooks can evoke any number of savory sauces.

Meats are eaten young and fresh. Aging has never been common. Beef (*carne de vaca*) is tough and not very tasty, used mainly for tapas that call for long marinating, slow cooking, or both. Veal (*ternera*) is excellent and prepared in many imaginative ways, including as the basis of several stews. Suckling lamb and pig are also popular, especially in Castille. Like other meats, lambs are seldom allowed to mature, and Spanish hams are at their tastiest from pigs slaughtered when only a few months old.

Marinades are popular both to enhance flavor and to tenderize tougher cuts. The basis for nearly all Spanish marinades is wine: a dry white or full-bodied red, a hearty brandy, or a crisp dry sherry. When marinating, be sure to allow enough time for the juices to penetrate the meat—overnight for larger pieces and even longer for tougher cuts. Three to four hours should suffice for cubes of meat. To let the juices penetrate, slit larger pieces in several places.

Meat stews served in individual earthenware casseroles (*cazuelitas*) are popular in tapa bars. These hearty, stick-to-the-ribs snacks take well to clever seasoning and are especially delicious when served piping hot in their own sealed-in-flavor containers. You can make most stews the day before and reheat individual portions with no loss of flavor; reheating, in fact, often enhances flavor.

BEEF (CARNE DE VACA)

HAMBURGUESA A LA TARTARA
(TARTARE)

A Spanish brandy would be an especially good companion.

1   pound lean beef steak, freshly and finely ground

¼ pound serrano ham, freshly ground

1   raw egg yolk

1   clove garlic, minced

¼ cup finely chopped onion

2   tablespoons chopped fresh parsley

Salt and pepper to taste

Spanish bread

Lemon wedges, parsley sprigs, Tabasco, or Worcestershire sauce

Garlic Sauce or Tomato Sauce (optional; see index for recipes)

Mix together beef, ham, egg yolk, garlic, onion, parsley, and salt and pepper to taste. Shape into a mound. Serve on slices of thick Spanish, French, or Italian bread with lemon wedges, sprigs of parsley, or with a bottle of Tabasco or Worcestershire sauce on the side. Many Spaniards are partial to a pungent garlic sauce; others prefer a milder tomato sauce.

Serves 8 (3–4 slices bread with Tartare each)

ROLLO DE CARNE
(MEAT ROLL)

A good red wine might be a suitable partner.

½ pound ground beef

¼ pound ground pork

¼ pound cooked ham, chopped fine

⅓ cup bread crumbs

1 egg, beaten

2 cloves garlic, chopped

1 small onion, chopped

2 tablespoons fresh chopped parsley

Salt and pepper to taste

Pinch ground nutmeg

3-4 hard-boiled eggs, peeled

3 tablespoons oil

3 strips bacon

Tomato Sauce (optional; see index for recipe)

Mix together beef, pork, ham, bread crumbs, and beaten egg. Add garlic, onion, and parsley. Season with salt, pepper, and a pinch of nutmeg. Carefully roll the meat mixture, forming a long thick tube, around 3-4 hard-boiled eggs laid end to end, covering the eggs completely. Heat oil in a large skillet and sauté meat roll in it until browned. Remove from the skillet, place bacon strips around meat to keep the meat moist, and place in a preheated 350°F oven for 45 minutes or until cooked through. Remove from the oven, remove bacon strips, let cool, and cut into slices. Serve either unadorned or with Tomato Sauce.

Serves 6-8 (1 thick or 2 medium slices each)

VEAL (TERNERA)

HAMBURGUESAS
(HAMBURGERS)

Hamburgers are popular in Spain both in sandwiches and miniaturized as tapas. Usually, however, they are not made of ground beef but of a combination of meats. One of the most popular combinations, especially for tapas, is half veal and half pork, often also including leftover minced chicken, ham, bacon, or all three. The result is more like a meatball or meat loaf mixture than the typical American hamburger. A cold beer would be the perfect accompaniment.

½	**pound ground veal or beef**
½	**pound ground pork**
2	**eggs, beaten**
1	**clove garlic, minced**
1	**tablespoon bread crumbs**
	Salt and pepper to taste
	Flour for dusting
3	**tablespoons oil**
	Tomato Sauce or other sauce (optional; see index for recipes)

Mix together veal, pork, half the egg mixture, the garlic, and the bread crumbs; sprinkle with salt and pepper. Divide meat mixture into 10-12 small balls and flatten into patties. Sprinkle patties with flour, dip in remaining egg and again in flour, and fry in oil in a skillet until browned and cooked through. Serve either unadorned or with Tomato Sauce or other sauce.

Serves 6 (1–2 patties each)

TERNERA CON GUISANTES
(VEAL STEW WITH PEAS)

Excellent with a medium-dry white wine.

1   pound veal
     Salt and pepper to taste
3   tablespoons oil
1   small onion, chopped
     Flour for dusting
1   cup green peas
½   cup dry white wine
2   tablespoons brandy
¼   cup meat stock or water
¼   teaspoon dried thyme
     Pinch saffron
1   tablespoon chopped fresh
        parsley

Cut veal into 1-inch cubes and season with salt and pepper. Heat oil in a skillet and sauté onion in it until soft. Dust veal cubes with flour and fry until browned on all sides. Add peas, wine, brandy, and enough stock to cover. Stir in thyme, saffron, and parsley. Simmer for 20 minutes or until liquid is reduced and meat cooked. Add more stock if sauce becomes too thick.

Serves 6

ROLLO DE TERNERA
(VEAL ROLL)

Any drink would be suitable; perhaps a cold beer would taste best.

1 pound veal

¼ pound cooked ham, sliced thin

¼ pound chorizo or other cured pork sausage, sliced thin lengthwise

2 hard-boiled eggs, peeled and quartered

1 2-ounce jar pimientos

2 cloves garlic, chopped

1 small onion, chopped

2 tablespoons chopped celery

2 tablespoons chopped fresh parsley

2 eggs, beaten

1 cup bread crumbs

Salt and pepper to taste

4 tablespoons oil

Tomato Sauce or other sauce (optional; see index for recipes)

Cut veal into 1 or more very thin slices. Trim and discard fat and gristle. Cover each veal slice with layers of ham and sausage, quartered eggs, and pimiento strips. Sprinkle with garlic, onion, celery, and 1 tablespoon parsley. Roll veal slices into cylinders and skewer the ends to secure the filling. Dip veal rolls in beaten egg and roll in bread crumbs seasoned with salt, pepper, and the remaining parsley. Heat oil in a skillet and sauté veal rolls in it until browned on all sides and cooked through. Remove, drain, let cool, and carve into slices. Serve either plain or with Tomato Sauce or other sauce.

Serves 6 (2–4 slices each)

LAMB (CORDERO)

CORDERO A LA CHILINDRON
(LAMB WITH PEPPERS)

A full-bodied red wine would be an excellent accompaniment to this popular tapa, which in larger portions becomes the centerpiece for a delicious multicourse meal.

2 **pounds boneless lamb**
   Salt and pepper to taste
3 **tablespoons oil**
1 **onion, chopped**
2 **cloves garlic, chopped**
¼ **cup diced ham**
4 **green peppers, cut into strips**
2 **tablespoons chopped fresh parsley**
½ **cup red wine**
3 **tomatoes, chopped**
5 **peppercorns, crushed**
1 **bay leaf**

Cut lamb into 1½- to 2-inch cubes and season with salt and pepper. Heat oil in a skillet and sauté cubes in it until browned. Add onion, garlic, ham, and green peppers and continue to cook for 10 minutes. Stir in parsley, red wine, tomatoes, peppercorns, and bay leaf; simmer for 1 hour or until meat is tender.

Serves 10

CALDERETA EXTREMEÑA
(LAMB, EXTREMADURA STYLE)

A hearty red wine makes an especially compatible partner.

1½	pounds boneless lamb
	Salt and pepper to taste
3	tablespoons oil
4	cloves garlic, peeled
1	lamb's liver
1	small onion, chopped
1	bay leaf
¼	teaspoon dried thyme
2	teaspoons paprika
1	tablespoon flour
1	cup white wine
½	cup beef stock
5	peppercorns
1	small red bell pepper
1	tablespoon chopped fresh parsley

Cut lamb into 1½- to 2-inch cubes and season with salt and pepper. Heat oil in a skillet and sauté garlic cloves in it until brown. Remove garlic and set aside. In the same oil, brown lamb cubes and whole lamb's liver. Remove liver and set aside. Add onion and sauté until soft. Stir in bay leaf, thyme, paprika, flour, white wine, and stock. Cover and simmer for 30 minutes. Meanwhile, with a mortar and pestle or in an electric blender, crush browned garlic, peppercorns, red pepper, and browned lamb's liver with just enough liquid from the stew to form a smooth sauce. Add sauce to the stew and continue to cook slowly for 1 hour or until meat is tender. Sprinkle with parsley.

Serves 8

COCHIFRITO
(LAMB FRICASSEE)

A chilled rosé might embrace the flavor of this tapa.

1½	pounds boneless lamb
	Salt and pepper to taste
3	tablespoons oil
1	onion, chopped
3	cloves garlic, chopped
¼	cup fresh lemon juice
1	teaspoon paprika
1	tablespoon chopped fresh parsley
½	cup chicken stock or water

Cut lamb into 1½- to 2-inch cubes and season with salt and pepper. Heat oil in a skillet and sauté lamb in it until browned on all sides. Add onion and garlic and sauté until onion is soft. Add lemon juice, paprika, parsley, and enough stock to cover. Continue to cook slowly for 1 hour or until meat is tender, adding more stock if necessary.

Serves 8

PORK (CERDO)

LOMO ADOBADO
(MARINATED PORK LOIN)

In tapa bars throughout Spain, marinated pork, sliced thin, has become almost as popular as sliced ham. As usual, marinades vary with locale. This one is typical. A hearty red wine would be a suitable partner.

3   cloves garlic, chopped
1   teaspoon paprika
¼   teaspoon dried oregano
6   peppercorns
¼   cup olive oil
    Salt to taste
1   pound boneless pork loin
      roast
2   tablespoons oil

With a mortar and pestle, crush garlic, paprika, oregano, and peppercorns. Dissolve mixture in olive oil and sprinkle with salt. Coat the meat on all sides and refrigerate overnight, preferably longer. Remove from the refrigerator, drain, and cut into thin slices. Heat oil in a skillet and sauté pork until cooked through, basting occasionally with remaining marinade.

Serves 6

FILETITOS DE CERDO
(GRILLED PORK FILLETS)

A dry sherry might be the best partner.

1   pound pork tenderloin
4   cloves garlic, chopped
3   tablespoons fresh lemon
      juice
2   tablespoons chopped fresh
      parsley
    Salt to taste
3   tablespoons oil
1   onion, chopped

Slice pork tenderloin paper-thin and cut into 2-inch squares. Combine garlic, lemon juice, and parsley in a bowl. Add pork and season with salt. Marinate in the refrigerator 2-3 hours. Heat oil in a skillet, sauté onion in it until soft, add pork squares, and simmer until well browned on both sides and cooked through.

Serves 6

CERDO CON ALMEJAS
(PORK WITH CLAMS)

A dry white wine would be the perfect companion.

3-4 dozen small clams
½ cup dry white wine
2 teaspoons fresh lemon juice
1 pound boneless pork loin
3 tablespoons oil
1 onion, chopped
2 cloves garlic, chopped
2 tomatoes, peeled and chopped
1 tablespoon chopped fresh parsley

Wash clams in cold water to eliminate sand and grit. Place clams in a large saucepan with about ¼ inch of white wine and lemon juice. Cover and steam over high heat for about 5 minutes or until the shells open. Remove the clams from the saucepan, set aside, and discard any clams that remain closed or are cracked. Cut pork into bite-size cubes. Heat oil in a skillet and sauté pork in it until browned and cooked through. Remove and set aside. In the same skillet, sauté onion and garlic until onion is soft. Add tomatoes and continue to simmer until a sauce begins to form. Add clams (still in their shells) and pork cubes to the skillet and simmer until pork and clam flavors are well blended, adding a little of the wine/clam juices from the saucepan if sauce becomes too thick. Sprinkle with parsley and serve hot.

VARIATION
For extra flavor, marinate pork as in the recipe for Marinated Pork Loin before browning.

Serves 8

CHULETAS EMPANADAS
(BREADED PORK CUTLETS)

Any drink would stand up well to this tapa, including mixed drinks.

1   **pound pork tenderloin**
2   **tablespoons fresh lemon juice**
1   **egg, beaten**
½   **cup bread crumbs**
Salt and pepper to taste
2   **tablespoons chopped fresh parsley**
3   **tablespoons oil**

Cut pork tenderloin into 2-inch squares. Sprinkle with lemon juice, dip in beaten egg, and roll in bread crumbs seasoned with salt, pepper, and parsley. Heat oil in a skillet and fry pork squares in it on both sides until well browned and cooked through.

VARIATION
For *Chuletas Asadas* (roasted pork cutlets), skip the beaten egg and, instead of frying, place pork squares in a broiler and cook on both sides until browned and cooked through.

Serves 6

JAMON DE YORK A LA PLANCHA
(GRILLED BOILED HAM)

Jamón de York, or Yorkshire ham, is a boiled ham comparable to American and English boiled hams. One of the simplest and tastiest ways to prepare boiled ham as a tapa is to fry ½-inch-thick slices over a large hot plate (a la plancha) or in a skillet in either olive oil or butter (sherry and Madeira wine are also popular cooking agents). Serve plain or with finely chopped mushrooms or truffles.

Sliced boiled ham is also perfect for enclosing any number of tapa fillings. To prepare a tapa called Canutillos de Jamón, roll thin slices into tubes or cone shapes and stuff with your favorite meat, cheese, or vegetable filling. Serve either chilled or a la plancha, 2–3 tubes per portion, depending on size.

For an even simpler tapa, called Jamón al Pepinillos, roll slices of ham around dill pickles and secure with toothpicks. Just about any drink stands up well to ham, but perhaps a crisp, cold beer would taste the best.

ROLLITOS DE JAMON CON DATILES
(HAM ROLLS WITH DATES)

Sherry, mixed drinks, or a vermouth would be most appropriate companions.
    Slit open pitted dates and insert a blanched almond (or 2 hazelnuts) into each date. Roll a small strip of boiled ham 1½–2 turns around each date and fasten with toothpicks. Instead of ham, you can serve dates con bacón *by rolling small bacon slices around each nut-filled date and either broiling or pan-frying until bacon is crisp on all sides.*

4–5 small ham rolls per serving

JAMON FRITO
(FRIED HAM)

A cold beer would go well with this tapa.

1   **pound cooked ham**
1   **egg, beaten**
½   **cup bread crumbs**
     Oil for deep-frying

Cut ham into 1-inch chunks. Dip chunks in beaten egg, roll in bread crumbs, and deep-fry in hot oil at 350°F, 2–3 minutes or until golden. Serve hot.

VARIATION
For a slightly different taste, first dip chunks in White Sauce (see index for recipe), refrigerate to set the sauce, and then dip in beaten egg and bread crumbs. Deep-fry.

Serves 6

MAGRAS CON TOMATES
(HAM IN TOMATO SAUCE)

Try a white wine with this tapa.

1   **pound cooked ham or**
     cooked pork
2   **tablespoons oil**
1   **small onion, chopped**
4   **large tomatoes, peeled and**
     chopped fine
     Salt to taste
     Oil for frying

Cut ham or pork into bite-size chunks. Heat oil in a skillet and sauté onion in it until soft. Add the chopped tomatoes and continue to cook, stirring frequently, until reduced to a sauce. Add ham and continue to simmer until heated through. Add salt to taste and serve hot.

Serves 6

CHORIZO
(SAUSAGE)

Chorizo is Spain's most popular sausage, produced in endless regional variations. It is a tasty, highly seasoned (but never hot!) link sausage, a careful blend of meats and spices (always including pork, peppers, and garlic) that has been cured in wood smoke.

Chorizos are made in other European countries, in the Americas, and in Mexico (a fiery hot sausage), but they are not the same. Spanish chorizos come closest in taste to Italian pepperoni. Spanish chorizo combines well with other tapa ingredients and is an important addition to many stews. You can sometimes find chorizo in imported food shops, occasionally fresh but most often canned.

In tapa bars, chorizo is usually sliced and served raw or grilled, sometimes on bits of toast. Small whole chorizos are also popular grilled, often accompanied by a handful of wild mushrooms (setas). The sausages of Spain, including the chorizos, seem to stand up best to Spain's full-bodied red wines.

MORCILLAS FRITAS
(FRIED BLOOD SAUSAGES)

Blood sausage, or black pudding, is prepared throughout Europe. Spanish morcilla is made from pig's blood, pork, garlic, and spices. Rice is a popular filling in many parts of the country, and hard-boiled eggs are sometimes included. Asturias and Aragon have some of the best varieties.

Cook morcilla as you would any other sausage. The classic method is to slice and fry in a little olive oil, sprinkle with chopped parsley, and serve hot. The addition of broad beans or bits of bacon enhances the flavor. Excellent with any hearty wine.

LIVER (HIGADO)

HIGADO A LA PLANCHA
(FRIED LIVER)

A crisp, ice-cold beer would be the perfect accompaniment.

1	**pound calf's liver**
	Salt and pepper to taste
1	**egg, beaten**
½	**cup bread crumbs**
3	**tablespoons oil**
1	**tablespoon chopped fresh parsley**
	Lemon wedges

Cut liver into 2-inch strips and sprinkle with salt and pepper. Dip strips in beaten egg and roll in bread crumbs. Heat oil in a skillet and fry until cooked through and golden brown on both sides. Drain, sprinkle with parsley, and serve hot with lemon wedges.

VARIATION
You can also grill strips without a coating and simply sprinkle with parsley, olive oil, and a little crushed garlic.

Serves 6 (5–7 strips each)

HIGADO CON PIMIENTOS
(LIVER WITH PEPPERS)

Either a cold beer or a hearty red wine seems to stand up best to liver tapas.

1 pound calf's liver
1 tablespoon fresh lemon juice
3 tablespoons oil
1 onion, chopped
1 clove garlic, chopped
2 red or green peppers or 1 of each, diced
¼ cup red wine
¼ cup diced mushrooms
1 tablespoon chopped fresh parsley
   Salt and pepper to taste

Cut liver into cubes and sprinkle with lemon juice. Heat oil in a skillet and sauté onion and garlic in it until onion is soft; add peppers and continue to simmer until soft. Pour in wine, add liver, and cook slowly for 10 minutes or until meat is done. Add mushrooms, parsley, and salt and pepper to taste and cook another 15 minutes.

Serves 6

HIGADO CON CHAMPIÑONES
(LIVER WITH MUSHROOMS)

Beer seems to be the best companion for liver tapas.

1 pound calf's liver
1 tablespoon fresh lemon juice
   Flour for dusting
   Salt and pepper to taste
3 tablespoons oil
½ cup sliced mushrooms
¼ cup white wine

Cut liver into 2-inch strips and sprinkle with lemon juice. Dust pieces with flour seasoned with salt and pepper. Heat oil in a skillet and fry liver in it until cooked through and golden on all sides; remove and drain. In the same oil, sauté sliced mushrooms until golden, pour in wine, add liver, and simmer for 15 minutes.

Serves 6

RIÑONES A LA ASTURIANA
(KIDNEYS, ASTURIAN STYLE)

A good Spanish brandy would be a compatible partner.

1	pound veal kidneys
3	tablespoons oil
1	small onion, chopped
1	clove garlic, chopped
4	tablespoons cooked and crumbled bacon
1	cup cider or dry sherry
2	tablespoons brandy
1	tablespoon flour
1	tablespoon chopped fresh parsley

Clean and wash kidneys and trim away fat and gristle. Drain and cut into 1-inch cubes. Heat oil in a skillet and sauté cubes in it until lightly browned. Remove and set aside. In the same oil, sauté onion, garlic, and bacon until onion is soft and bacon is crisp. Return kidneys to the skillet and pour in cider and brandy; stir in flour. Mix well and continue cooking until the sauce thickens. Sprinkle with parsley and serve hot. Serve over rice as a meal.

Serves 6–8

BROCHETA DE RIÑONES
(KIDNEYS ON SKEWERS)

Excellent with a dry wine, beer, or sherry.

1	pound veal kidneys
3	tablespoons fresh lemon juice or wine vinegar
12	mushroom caps
½	pound bacon, ham, or both, cubed
2	eggs, beaten
½	cup bread crumbs
	Salt and pepper to taste
2	tablespoons chopped fresh parsley
3	tablespoons oil

Soak kidneys in water to cover and lemon juice or wine vinegar for about ½ hour. Trim away fat and gristle and cut into 1-inch cubes. Rinse in hot water and drain. Thread 4–5 kidney cubes on individual thin metal or wooden skewers, alternating with mushroom caps, bacon, and ham cubes. Coat kidneys, mushrooms, and meat cubes with egg and roll in bread crumbs seasoned with salt, pepper, and parsley. Heat oil in a skillet and, on request, fry individual brochettes (or broil in the oven or grill on a hibachi) until browned on all sides and liver is cooked.

Serves 6–8

LENGUA ESTOFADA
(TONGUE STEW)

A full-bodied red or white wine or a medium-dry sherry would be a worthy companion.

1 **pound beef tongue**

2 **tablespoons oil**

1 **onion, chopped**

2 **cloves garlic, chopped**

2 **tomatoes, chopped**

1 **green or red pepper, chopped**

1 **carrot, chopped**

¼ **teaspoon dried thyme**

1 **tablespoon chopped fresh parsley**

1 **cup white wine**

1 **cup beef stock or water**

Salt and pepper to taste

Boil tongue in salted water for 45 minutes or until tender. Remove and, when cool, peel off skins. Cut into fine slices. Heat oil in a skillet and sauté onion and garlic in it until onion is soft. Stir in tongue slices, tomatoes, green or red pepper, carrot, thyme, parsley, white wine, and enough stock or water to cover. Season with salt and pepper and simmer for 30 minutes or until well blended and the liquid is reduced.

Serves 6–8

ADDITIONAL PORK, BEEF, AND SAUSAGE TAPAS

CHAPTER NINETEEN
POULTRY AND GAME TAPAS (AVES Y CAZA)

The forests, mountains, valleys, brushlands, marshes, and high plains of Spain are natural breeding grounds for wild game of every sort. And since Spain is on the direct migratory path between northern Europe and Africa, it's only natural that game plays an important part in tapa cookery—which is, after all, a wild kind of cuisine.

Spanish seasonings (garlic, oregano, bay leaves, saffron) are well suited to poultry and game. Pine nuts, chorizo, olives, and other typical tapa ingredients blend perfectly, and the hearty red and white wines of Spain make ideal partners.

CHICKEN (POLLO)

Birds and other animals in Spain, whether domesticated or not, live close to nature; there has never been a clear distinction between domesticated and wild animals. Up until the last few years, for example, chickens were never confined to cages or subjected to prepackaged diets. Even today, many are raised organically, allowed to run wild to scratch for bugs, worms, and grit. Spanish chickens (*pollos*) have, therefore, less fat and more texture and flavor than our battery-raised birds. Yet because they are one of the very few animals in Spain not harvested when young, they are heavier and bigger than our chickens, weighing up to 4 or 5 pounds each. Stewing hens (*gallinas*) weigh around 8 pounds.

Chicken is a versatile tapa food that goes well with Spanish sauces and can complement any number of ingredients, including most vegetables. During an evening of tapa-sampling, you can insert a chicken tapa just about anywhere among the meats, seafood, and vegetables, and it will never seem out of place. Chicken will interchange with other meats in most tapa recipes, especially with rabbit, duck, and other game and poultry, but even with fish.

PECHUGA DE POLLO FRITO
(DEEP-FRIED CHICKEN BREAST)

A dry white wine or a light red wine might go nicely with this chicken tapa.

2   whole chicken breasts
    Flour for dusting
    Salt and pepper to taste
2   eggs, beaten
1   cup bread crumbs
    Oil for deep-frying
    Almond Sauce or other
        sauce (see index for
        recipes)

Skin, bone, and cut chicken breasts into bite-size strips. Dust strips with flour seasoned with salt and pepper, remove excess flour, dip in beaten eggs, and roll in bread crumbs. Deep-fry at 375°F or pan-fry on all sides until golden brown. Drain and serve speared on toothpicks or in Almond Sauce or other sauce.

Serves 6

POLLO EN SAMFAINA
(CHICKEN AND VEGETABLE STEW)

Pollo en Samfaina *(the word* samfaina *means "symphony") is a Catalan specialty (also known as* Pollo a la Catalana*) made of chicken and assorted vegetables in season, usually including eggplant, peppers, and tomatoes. It is popular throughout Spain as a main course and in Catalonia as a tapa. A white wine would be a suitable partner.*

1   small chicken
    Salt to taste
4   tablespoons oil or,
        traditionally, lard
1   cup diced cured ham
1   onion, chopped
1   clove garlic, chopped
1   small zucchini, cubed
1   small eggplant, peeled and
        cubed
2   green or red peppers or 1
        of each, cut into strips
3   tomatoes, peeled and
        chopped
1   small bay leaf
    Pinch dried thyme
¼   cup white wine
¼   cup chicken stock
    Salt and pepper to taste

Skin, bone, and cut chicken into pieces about 2 inches long. Season with salt. Heat oil in a skillet and sauté chicken pieces in it until browned. Add ham, onion, and garlic and continue to sauté until onion is soft. Add zucchini, eggplant, and peppers and simmer 5 more minutes. Add tomatoes, bay leaf, and thyme and stir in wine and stock. Add salt and pepper to taste. Continue to simmer about 1 hour or until liquid is reduced, a good sauce forms, and the flavors have blended.

Serves 8

PECHUGAS CON NARANJAS
(CHICKEN BREASTS WITH ORANGES)

Sangria would be a refreshing accompaniment to this chicken tapa.

2 whole chicken breasts
Salt and pepper to taste
3 tablespoons oil or butter
2 large oranges, peeled and chopped, or 1 cup orange juice
1 tablespoon chopped fresh mint
⅛ teaspoon ground cloves
Pinch ground nutmeg

Skin, bone, and cut breasts into bite-size strips. Sprinkle with salt and pepper. Heat oil or butter in a skillet and fry chicken in it until golden on all sides. Remove meat and set aside. In the same skillet, simmer orange pieces (or juice), stirring constantly, until pieces are reduced to a pulp. Add mint, cloves, and nutmeg. Return meat to the skillet and cook gently for about 15 minutes or until tender. Season again with salt to taste. Serve in the sauce or, for a milder orange flavor, remove chicken pieces with a slotted spoon, strain orange sauce through a sieve, pour over the meat, and reheat.

Serves 6

POLLO CHILINDRON
(CHICKEN WITH RED PEPPERS)

This centuries-old chilindrón *(the word means "cooked with red peppers") hails from the ancient kingdom of Aragon. Either a light red or a white wine would be appropriate.*

1 chicken (3½ pounds) or lamb (3½ pounds)
4 tablespoons oil
½ cup chopped serrano or other cured ham
1 onion, chopped
1 clove garlic, chopped
3 red or green peppers, cut into strips
3 tomatoes, peeled and chopped
Salt and pepper to taste
Extra pepper or pimiento strips for garnish

Cut chicken into large individual tapa-size pieces (or into larger serving pieces for a meal). Heat oil in a skillet and fry chicken pieces in it until browned on all sides. Add chopped ham, onion, garlic, and peppers and continue to fry, stirring frequently, until peppers and onion are soft, about 10 minutes. Add tomatoes, salt, and pepper to taste, and simmer until chicken is tender and liquid reduced. Chilindrón sauce should appear almost dry, never thin or runny. Top each piece with an extra strip of pepper or pimiento.

Serves 8

POLLO EN PEPITORIA
(CHICKEN FRICASSEE)

This hearty chicken fricassee, or stew, is one of the great dishes of Spain. Convenient to serve as a tapa, it has many regional variations, usually including eggs, almonds, sherry (or white wine), garlic, saffron, and often ham, among other ingredients. Excellent with a light red wine or a dry sherry.

1	chicken (3½ pounds)
	Salt and pepper to taste
	Flour for dusting
4	tablespoons oil
½	cup chopped ham
1	onion, chopped
2	cloves garlic, chopped
½	cup dry sherry
1	cup chicken stock
1	bay leaf
2	tablespoons chopped fresh parsley
20	blanched almonds, chopped
¼	teaspoon saffron
2	hard-boiled egg yolks
2	tablespoons chicken stock
	Salt and pepper to taste

Cut chicken into bite-size pieces and season with salt and pepper. Dip pieces in flour and remove excess. Heat oil in a skillet and brown pieces in it on all sides. Add ham, onion, and garlic and simmer until onion is soft. Stir in sherry and enough stock to cover, then add bay leaf and parsley. With a mortar and pestle, crush almonds, saffron, and egg yolks and add enough stock to form a paste. Stir mixture gradually into the skillet and add salt and pepper to taste. Continue cooking for 10 minutes or until chicken is tender. Add more stock if sauce thickens.

Serves 8

JAMONCITO DE POLLO
(STUFFED CHICKEN LEGS)

A cold beer would be a congenial partner.

6 small chicken legs
1½ tablespoons oil
1 clove garlic, chopped
⅓ cup chopped mushrooms
1 tablespoon fresh lemon juice
1 tablespoon chopped fresh parsley
Salt and pepper to taste
Flour for dusting
2 eggs, beaten
1 cup bread crumbs
Oil for deep-frying

Slit sides of chicken legs and carefully remove leg bones. Heat oil in a skillet and sauté garlic in it until browned. Add mushrooms to the skillet, sauté gently until well browned, and transfer to a bowl. Sprinkle with lemon juice and parsley, season with salt and pepper, mix well, and let cool. Stuff legs with the mixture. Dust legs with flour, dip in beaten eggs, roll in bread crumbs, and deep-fry at 375°F or pan-fry on all sides until chicken legs are cooked and golden brown.

Serves 6

HIGADILLOS
(CHICKEN LIVERS)

A white wine would go well with this tapa.

3 tablespoons oil
2 onions, chopped
1 pound chicken livers, trimmed
Salt and pepper to taste
1 cup white wine

Heat oil in a skillet and sauté onions in it until soft. Add chicken livers and salt and pepper to taste, and simmer until livers are browned. Pour in the wine and simmer for 20 minutes or until liquid is reduced and livers are cooked.

VARIATION
Sliced chicken livers also make delicious kabobs, popular in tapa bars, strung on skewers alternating with mushrooms, small onions, or sweetbreads and grilled on a flat plate, a la plancha.

Serves 6

ALAS DE POLLO
(CHICKEN WINGS)

6   chicken wings
2   cloves garlic, chopped
⅓   cup olive oil
1   tablespoon fresh lemon
    juice
1   teaspoon dried thyme
1   bay leaf, crumbled
    Pinch dried rosemary
    Salt and pepper to taste
    Tomato Sauce or other
    sauce (optional; see
    index for recipes)

Clean wings and, if you like, cut off the wing tips. Mix together in a bowl garlic, olive oil, lemon juice, thyme, bay leaf, and rosemary. Add chicken wings and salt and pepper to taste; marinate for 2-3 hours. Remove, drain, and place wings in a casserole. Broil for about 10 minutes on each side or until well browned and cooked through. Tapa cooks usually add a tomato or other homemade sauce to the dish during the last 3-4 minutes of cooking. Serve hot.

Serves 6

DUCK (PATO)

PATO CON ACEITUNAS
(DUCK WITH OLIVES)

Wild duck with olives (also known as Pato a la Sevillana *or "Pato Seville style") is a popular Andalusian main dish that is often miniaturized into hearty tapas. Olives contrast with the duck to provide a stunning flavor combination. Excellent with a light red wine or dry sherry.*

1   duck (4-5 pounds)
6   tablespoons oil
1   onion, sliced
2   cloves garlic, chopped
1   red bell pepper, chopped
1   tablespoon chopped fresh
    parsley
2   tomatoes, chopped
1   cup dry sherry
1   cup chicken stock
    Salt and pepper to taste
    Pinch dried rosemary
1   cup chopped pimiento-
    stuffed green olives or
    pitted green or black
    olives

Clean the duck and cut into individual tapa-size pieces (or into 6 large pieces for a meal). Heat 4 tablespoons of oil in a skillet and fry sliced onion and duck in it until meat is browned on all sides. Transfer to a casserole and pour off excess fat. In a small skillet, heat 2 tablespoons of oil and sauté garlic, red pepper, parsley, and tomatoes until tomatoes are soft. Pour over the meat and stir in sherry and enough stock to barely cover the meat. Add salt and pepper to taste and rosemary. Cover and simmer for about 30 minutes or until meat is tender. Just before removing from the heat, sprinkle with chopped olives.

Serves 8

PARTRIDGE (PERDIZ)

PERDIZ CON CHOCOLATE
(PARTRIDGE WITH CHOCOLATE)

Chocolate is one of those seasonings that tapa cooks use to give a distinctive yet subtle taste to their meats. Chocolate is especially effective with partridge, rabbit, and other game. An exciting tapa treat when accompanied by a fine red wine.

2 young partridges
   Salt to taste
4 tablespoons olive oil
1 onion, chopped
2 cloves garlic, chopped
½ cup red wine
½ cup chicken stock
¼ cup wine vinegar
1 bay leaf
1 tablespoon flour
   Partridge giblets and hearts
1 ounce unsweetened chocolate, grated

Clean partridge, cut in halves along the back, and sprinkle with salt. Heat olive oil in a large skillet or deep casserole and brown partridge in it on all sides. Add onion and garlic and continue cooking until onion is soft. Add wine, stock, vinegar, and bay leaf and slowly stir in flour to form a smooth sauce. Cover and continue to cook for 30 minutes or until tender, adding more stock if necessary. Remove from the heat and let cool. Transfer the meat to a platter, reserving the sauce in a skillet. Cut out the bones and cut meat into large individual serving pieces. Chop giblets and hearts of partridges and add to the sauce; stir in the chocolate. Return partridge pieces to the skillet, cover, and simmer for 10 minutes or until cooked through and well blended.

Serves 8

QUAIL (CODORNIZ)

CODORNICES EN ESCABECHE
(MARINATED QUAIL)

A white wine would be a compatible beverage.

4	**large quail or 2 young partridges**
	Salt to taste
5	**tablespoons oil**
2	**cloves garlic, crushed**
1	**onion, sliced**
1	**bay leaf**
1	**teaspoon dried thyme**
1	**teaspoon dried oregano**
½	**teaspoon paprika**
½	**cup dry white wine**
½	**cup wine vinegar**
½	**cup chicken stock or water**
8	**peppercorns, crushed**
	Salt to taste

Clean quail and sprinkle with a little salt. Heat oil in a skillet and brown on all sides. When well browned, transfer to a casserole. In the same skillet, sauté garlic, onion, bay leaf, thyme, and oregano for 5 minutes. Stir in paprika and pour the sauce over the quail. Add wine, vinegar, stock, and crushed peppercorns and sprinkle with more salt. Cover and simmer for about 30 minutes or until meat is tender, adding more stock if necessary and basting from time to time. Remove from heat, let cool, and remove quail. Bone quail and cut the meat into bite-size pieces. (Tapa cooks like to serve tiny quail and other small birds whole, bones and all, one bird per tapa serving.) Place meat in an earthenware dish and strain sauce over the meat; marinate for several hours. Serve at room temperature or reheat and serve warm.

Serves 8

PICHONES AL VINO TINTO
(PIGEONS IN RED WINE)

Young and tender wild pigeons are a delicacy in Spain. You can use chicken, quail, dove, rabbit, or almost any other bird or game for this full-flavored red wine, brandy, and chorizo recipe. A hearty red wine would be the perfect partner.

2   pigeons or doves or 1 chicken

Salt to taste

4   tablespoons oil

Flour for dusting

1   onion, chopped

2   cloves garlic, chopped

3   tablespoons chopped chorizo or other smoked sausage

1   small carrot, chopped

2   tablespoons Spanish brandy

1   cup red wine

1   bay leaf

¼   teaspoon dried thyme

1   tablespoon chopped fresh parsley

1   tablespoon flour

Clean and cut pigeons into individual serving pieces, leaving bones in the legs, wings, and wherever else it is convenient. Sprinkle pieces with salt. Heat oil in a skillet. Dust pieces with flour, remove excess, and fry in a skillet until browned on all sides. Add onion, garlic, sausage, and carrot; sauté until onion is soft. Add brandy, light it, and allow the alcohol to burn off. Add red wine and bay leaf and sprinkle in thyme, parsley, and about 1 tablespoon flour to form a sauce. Cover and simmer for 30 minutes or until liquid is reduced; add more wine if sauce becomes too thick.

Serves 8

LIEBRE AL VINO BLANCO
(HARE IN WHITE WINE)

Since ancient times, rabbits have run wild throughout the peninsula and still do. The name Spain *comes from the Phoenician word that meant "island of rabbits." A dry white wine would be the best partner for this tapa.*

1	hare or rabbit
4	tablespoons oil
1	onion, chopped
2	cloves garlic, chopped
	Flour for dusting
1	cup white wine
1	bay leaf
¼	teaspoon dried thyme
1	tablespoon chopped fresh parsley
	Salt to taste

Skin, bone, and cut hare into individual serving pieces. Heat oil in a skillet and sauté onion and garlic in it until onion is soft. Dust hare with flour and brown on all sides. Pour in wine and add bay leaf, thyme, parsley, and salt to taste. Simmer slowly for 1 hour or until liquid is reduced and pieces are tender. Add more wine or warm water if sauce becomes too thick.

Serves 6–8

LIEBRE ESTOFADA CON HABAS
(STEWED HARE WITH BEANS)

Accompany with a light red wine.

½	pound habas (broad beans)
1	hare
	Flour for dusting
4	tablespoons oil
2	onions, chopped
4	cloves garlic, chopped
½	cup diced salt pork or bacon
3	tomatoes, peeled and chopped
¼	teaspoon dried thyme
¼	teaspoon dried tarragon
1	bay leaf
1	cup dry white wine
¼	cup wine vinegar
2	tablespoons chopped fresh parsley

Soak beans in cold water overnight. Shell and cook beans in kettle in boiling salted water for about 10 minutes or until tender. Clean hare, remove bones, and cut meat into individual serving pieces. Dust pieces with flour. Heat oil in a skillet and brown pieces in it on all sides. Remove and set aside. In the same skillet, sauté onions, garlic, and salt pork for 5 minutes. Stir in tomatoes, thyme, tarragon, bay leaf, white wine, and vinegar. Return meat to the skillet, cover, and simmer for 1 hour or until tender. Add beans and continue to simmer a few minutes or until well blended and beans and meat are cooked through. Sprinkle with parsley.

Serves 8

CONEJO CON SALSA DE ALMENDRAS
(RABBIT IN ALMOND SAUCE)

Delicious accompanied by a light red wine.

1	rabbit
4	tablespoons oil
1	onion, chopped
3	cloves garlic, chopped
	Flour for dusting
20	blanched almonds or almonds and pine nuts, chopped
1	tablespoon olive oil
8	peppercorns
1	bay leaf
¼	teaspoon dried thyme
2	cloves
1	tablespoon chopped fresh parsley
¼	teaspoon ground cinnamon
1	cup white wine

Skin, clean, bone, and cut rabbit into large individual serving pieces. Heat oil in a skillet, add onion and garlic, and sauté until onion is soft. Dust rabbit pieces with flour and brown on all sides. With a mortar and pestle, crush almonds and add olive oil to form a smooth paste. Add to the skillet the almond paste, peppercorns, bay leaf, thyme, cloves, parsley, and cinnamon and stir in wine. Simmer slowly for one hour or until meat is tender, adding hot water if sauce becomes too thick. Remove meat, place in a warm casserole, and strain sauce over the meat.

Serves 6–8

ADDITIONAL POULTRY AND GAME TAPAS
POLLO AL AJILLO (Garlic Chicken); Chapter 7, page 35
PECHUGAS AL JEREZ (Chicken Breasts in Sherry Sauce); Chapter 10, page 50
PASTELILLO DE HIGADILLOS (Chicken Liver Pâté); Chapter 7, page 34
PERDIZ ESTOFADO (Stewed Partridge); Chapter 11, page 59

CHAPTER TWENTY
SAUCES FOR TAPAS (SALSAS)

According to a popular Spanish saying, "There's no sauce like a good appetite." Sauces have never reached the stature in Spain that they enjoy in France and in many other countries. At least they haven't if we mean sauces extracted from bottles and poured over foods. Sauces *are* important, however, if we mean the kinds extracted from the foods themselves—those that we in America call "gravy" or "juices." Even when a sauce is prepared separately, Spanish cooks will usually incorporate it into the tapa through simmering or marinating.

Of the Spanish sauces prepared apart, tomato is the most popular and most versatile. Sherry, almond, and especially garlic are also favorites, as are some of the seafood sauces from the provinces. Mayonnaise, which originated in Mahón in the Balearic Islands, is the *número uno* "topping."

Besides the sauces described in this chapter, there are others, mainly of French origin, that are frequently used in tapa cookery. Béarnaise (*salsa bearnesa*), for example, is popular with some of the richer tapas, including the richer fish dishes; hollandaise (*salsa holandesa*) is a favorite with vegetables, eggs, and fish tapas, especially with poached fish; and vinaigrette is used on salads and with some of the more delicate vegetable tapas.

A sauce, to be a proper tapa sauce, must have a purpose—namely, it must help create a distinguished dish out of simple ingredients. It should add texture, color, and flavor, and it should help stimulate the appetite.

Like the ingredients they enhance, Spanish sauces are flavorful, with plenty of body, yet they should never overpower or mask the taste of food. Tapa cooks, especially in the northern provinces, like their sauces on the heavy side, sometimes even dry, never thin or watery. A sauce should be thick enough to spoon over the ingredients as a coating without running off, yet thin enough to be sopped up with hunks of bread.

You may want to use a thickening agent to create the proper consistency. Flour is used throughout Spain, but bread crumbs, which give added texture and act as a better absorbent, are also popular. Spanish cooks often toast bread crumbs and even flour before stirring into a dish, which gives tapas a slightly nutty flavor.

Although most tapa cooks concentrate on a few standard sauces, each sauce will have numerous variations. With mayonnaise, for example, you can create several quick and easy combinations by adding chopped parsley or grated cheese or sprinkling with saffron or paprika. Or you can stir in cooked egg yolks or sliced olives, thin with lemon juice or vinegar, or thicken by whipping.

You'll have the tastiest results if you make your own sauces out of fresh ingredients, even for the standards like mayonnaise. But to save time, you will also want to experiment with some of the bottled, packaged, and frozen varieties available in stores.

SALSA DE TOMATE
(TOMATO SAUCE)

Tomato Sauce, sometimes called "red sauce" (Salsa Colorada or Salsa Roja) is popular with fish and shellfish tapas and with cold meats and vegetables. In its classic form, Salsa de Tomate is simply a mixture of fresh tomatoes and chopped onions. Over the decades, Spanish cooks have added their own personal touches: wine, egg yolks, chili peppers, garlic, almonds, or whatever strikes their taste buds and will best enhance the dish at hand. Some cooks even substitute red peppers for tomatoes in their Salsa de Tomate.

1 tablespoon olive oil
1 onion, chopped
1 clove garlic, chopped
4 tomatoes (about 1 pound), peeled and chopped
1 tablespoon chopped fresh parsley
½ teaspoon dried basil
Salt to taste
Pinch dried thyme

Heat oil in a skillet and sauté onion and garlic in it until onion is soft. Add tomatoes, parsley, basil, salt, and thyme. Simmer until sauce has thickened. Puree in electric blender or strain through a sieve and return to the skillet to simmer for 15–20 minutes or until sauce is desired consistency. Delicious either hot or cold.

Yield: 1½ cups sauce

SALSA VERDE
(GREEN SAUCE)

Green sauce is most popular with fish tapas, especially when broiled or baked.

1 cup chopped fresh parsley
¼ cup olive oil
1 tablespoon wine vinegar or lemon juice
1 tablespoon dry sherry
Salt to taste

Grind chopped parsley with a mortar and pestle, gradually adding olive oil until you have a smooth paste. Slowly blend in vinegar; add sherry and salt to taste. If you're using an electric blender, you can mix all ingredients at once.

VARIATIONS
1. For a bit more pungent taste, include a clove of finely minced garlic.
2. Regional versions of Green Sauce feature green peppers, peas, and green asparagus in place of, or in addition to, parsley.

Yield: one-half cup sauce

SALSA MAYONESA
(MAYONNAISE)

You can, of course, use bottled mayonnaise. The chief difference is that bottled mayonnaise, besides lacking fresh ingredients and containing preservatives, is made with bland vegetable oils; the classic Salsa Mayonesa *must have olive oil. If you use bottled mayonnaise, you can beat in a couple of tablespoons of olive oil, which gives more of a homemade taste and creates a bit heavier sauce. You should store all homemade mayonnaise combinations in the refrigerator, but before preparing, make sure all ingredients and even the mixing bowl are at room temperature.*

2	egg yolks
2	teaspoons vinegar or fresh lemon juice
1	teaspoon good mustard (optional)
¼	teaspoon salt
1	cup olive oil

Mix egg yolks with 1 teaspoon vinegar or lemon juice, the mustard, and the salt. Slowly, drop by drop, add olive oil while stirring constantly with a wooden spoon or whisk, always in the same direction; you can also use an electric mixer. As the mixture thickens, add the remaining vinegar, stirring all the while, until the sauce has a good, thick consistency. If too thick, thin with warm water.

VARIATION
Besides (or in addition to) mustard, you can season mayonnaise with any number of other ingredients, including freshly ground white pepper, tarragon, cayenne pepper, tomato sauce, saffron, and chopped parsley.

Yield: 1 cup sauce

SALSA AMARILLA
(YELLOW SAUCE)

Serve chilled with cold meats and with chicken tapas.

6	hard-boiled eggs
1	tablespoon Malaga wine or sweet sherry
1	tablespoon brandy
2	tablespoons olive oil
	Salt and pepper to taste
½	cup beef or chicken stock
1	tablespoon wine vinegar
½	teaspoon dry mustard

Separate cooked egg whites from yolks and pass the whites through a sieve. Mash yolks and thoroughly mix with the wine and brandy. Add olive oil, drop by drop, until creamy. Season with salt and pepper and stir in stock, vinegar, and dry mustard. Beat in egg whites.

Yield: 2 cups sauce

SALSA BECHAMEL
(WHITE SAUCE)

Béchamel *is a French import that has been popular in Spain as a white sauce (Salsa Blanca)* *for centuries. Its popularity lies mainly in its ability to blend quickly with any number of* *foods; merely add it to chopped meats, fish, poultry, or vegetables. It is especially* *appropriate over poached fish. Béchamel should not, however, be used to camouflage* *overcooked tapas or to conceal a lack of freshness. Like most tapa sauces, it is simple to* *make—basically flour, butter, milk, and perhaps a little chopped onion.*

1   **tablespoon finely chopped onion**
2   **tablespoons butter**
2   **tablespoons flour**
1   **cup milk, light cream and milk, or light stock and milk**
¼   **teaspoon grated nutmeg**
   Salt and freshly ground white pepper to taste

In a skillet, sauté onion in melted butter. Mix in flour and continue to cook over a low flame, stirring continually, until well blended and smooth. Slowly stir in milk; add nutmeg and salt and pepper to taste. Simmer over low heat, stirring occasionally, for 8-10 minutes or until a thick, smooth sauce forms.

VARIATIONS

1. For a richer sauce, remove from the heat, add 1-2 egg yolks, and reheat but do not boil.
2. Tapa cooks like to sprinkle in a little lemon juice just before serving.

Yield: 1 cup sauce

SALSA DE PATATAS
(POTATO SAUCE)

Potato Sauce is a simple-to-prepare fish sauce from Andalusia also used with meat.

2   **tablespoons oil**
½   **pound potatoes, peeled and finely chopped**
1   **red bell pepper, chopped**
2   **medium tomatoes, peeled and chopped**
1   **clove garlic, chopped**
1   **bay leaf**
½   **cup water**
   Salt to taste

Heat oil in a skillet and sauté potatoes, peppers, and tomatoes in it for about 5 minutes. Add garlic, bay leaf, water, and salt to taste. Continue cooking, stirring continually, until potatoes are soft, adding more water if necessary. Pass through a sieve or mix in an electric blender. Reheat and serve hot.

Yield: 2½ cups sauce

SALSA AL JEREZ
(SHERRY SAUCE)

This Andalusian specialty suits most meats, especially game and poultry; it is a classic kidney sauce.

2	**tablespoons oil**
2	**onions, chopped**
2	**tablespoons flour**
½	**cup dry sherry**
½	**cup chicken stock, beef stock, or water**
2	**cloves garlic, chopped**
1	**bay leaf**
4	**peppercorns, crushed**
	Salt to taste

Heat oil in a skillet and sauté onions in it until tender. Stir in flour, sherry, and stock. Continue stirring until sauce begins to thicken. Add garlic, bay leaf, peppercorns, and salt to taste and continue to simmer for 30–40 minutes, adding more stock or sherry if sauce becomes too thick. Pass through a sieve, reheat, and serve hot.

Yield: 1⅓ cups sauce

ALL-I-OLI
(GARLIC SAUCE)

All-i-Oli *(Latin for "garlic-and-oil") is a classic Catalan sauce, dating back to the 11th century. It most often accompanies the blander-tasting tapas—for example, dishes featuring lamb, eggs, potatoes, and poached fish.*

4	**garlic cloves, chopped**
1	**cup olive oil**
2	**egg yolks, beaten**
2	**tablespoons fresh lemon juice or wine vinegar**
	Salt to taste

Peel and crush garlic with a mortar and pestle or in a garlic press. Slowly add about 1 teaspoon olive oil, drop by drop, until a heavy, thick paste forms. Gradually blend in egg yolks, stirring constantly. Add lemon juice and slowly stir in remaining olive oil and continue to mix until sauce thickens to a creamy consistency, or use an electric blender. Add salt to taste.

VARIATION
The traditional Catalan version (still in favor today along Spain's Costa Brava) contains no egg yolks and is simply a combination of raw garlic and olive oil. If you're a purist and a good sport, try the classic version. Other variations add crushed almonds, thyme, or soft cheese.

Yield: 1 cup sauce

SALSA ROMESCO
(ROMESCO SAUCE)

Romesco *is a hot-sauce specialty from the ancient city of Tarragona in Catalonia, used primarily with fish. Its peppery taste is also popular with vegetables and the blander-tasting tapas—lamb, for example. One of the very few "hot" items of Spain, Romesco is made from a small hot pepper native to Catalonia. You can substitute any local hot chili pepper or cayenne pepper.*

2   **small dried hot chili peppers**

2   **tomatoes, peeled and chopped**

3   **cloves garlic, chopped**

2   **dozen hazelnuts, pine nuts, almonds, or a combination, shelled and toasted**

1   **cup olive oil**

½   **cup wine vinegar**
    Salt to taste

Grind dried chilies, tomatoes, garlic, and nuts together with a mortar and pestle or in an electric blender. Gradually mix in olive oil and vinegar until sauce has thickened. Add salt to taste.

Yield: 2¼ cups sauce

SALSA DE ALMENDRAS
(ALMOND SAUCE)

This is a classic meatball salsa.

2   **tablespoons olive oil**

1   **slice bread**

20   **blanched almonds**

2   **cloves garlic**

5   **peppercorns**

½   **teaspoon saffron**

1   **bay leaf**

1   **cup stock (or water)**
    Salt to taste

Heat oil in a skillet and fry bread, almonds, and garlic until bread is browned on both sides. Remove all ingredients and crush in a mortar with peppercorns, saffron, and bay leaf. Return to the skillet, stir in meat stock, salt to taste, and simmer about 10 minutes. Add the meat, fish, or other tapa ingredients to the sauce and cook for another 10 minutes.

Yield: 1 cup sauce

CHAPTER TWENTY-ONE
EXOTIC TAPAS

One of the culinary stumbling blocks in the acceptance of Spanish cuisine, including Spanish tapas, has been the array of unconventional ingredients found in much of Spain's regional cooking—at least unconventional when compared with other European cuisines. Granted, most tapas are created out of ordinary, everyday foods—fried potatoes, scrambled eggs, chicken legs, bell peppers, sausage, fish fillets, chickpeas. And, of course, many other delicious tapas are based on such gourmet treats as snails, pheasant, squid, artichokes, and lobster. But some of the tastiest tapas use ingredients that, although ordinary and everyday to Juan Español, are new to John Doe. Baby eels, lamb's testicles, sea barnacles, and sweetbreads ("Andalusians," quipped Somerset Maugham, "have a passion for other animals' insides") can be frightening fare for even the most worldly gourmet—that is, until prepared *a la española*.

The French writer, George Sand, a cosmopolitan if ever there was one, related how she and Frédéric Chopin spent a winter on the Spanish island of Majorca sampling regional specialities. "One day," Sand wrote, "we bought a large *calamar*, or cuttlefish, for the sake of examining it. I have never seen a more repulsive creature. Its body is as large as a turkey-cock's, its eyes as big as oranges, and its limp, hideous tentacles, when uncurled, were four or five feet long. The fishermen assured us that it was a great delicacy." And it was. After preparation by their Majorcan cook, Chopin and Sand devoured their repulsive creature "with a great smacking of lips."

CALAMARES EN SU TINTA
(SQUID IN THEIR OWN INK)

There are dozens of tapa recipes using squid; the two most popular call for deep-frying "in rings" and serving en su tinta, "in their own ink." Squid is also considered by creative tapa cooks to be perfect for stuffing.

Squid is available in American markets fresh, canned, and frozen. The flavor seems to deteriorate only slightly with quick freezing. To clean squid, first remove the interior shell, head, insides (including the cuttlebone), and ink sac. Separate the sac if you plan to use it for sauce. Cut off the tentacles, peel the skin from the body, and wash well under running water.

This dish is excellent with a full-bodied white or red wine.

1	**pound baby squid**
2	**tablespoons oil**
1	**clove garlic, chopped**
1	**onion, chopped**
1	**tomato, peeled and chopped**
1	**tablespoon chopped fresh parsley**
½	**cup red wine**
1	**tablespoon flour**
	Salt to taste

Clean and wash baby squid, discard insides and cuttlebones, peel off the skins, and carefully remove ink sacs to use later. (If you can't find baby squid in the market, use larger squid and cut the bodies into rings and tentacles into pieces.) Heat oil in a skillet and sauté garlic and onion in it until onion is soft. Add squid and cook a few minutes or until golden on all sides. Add tomato, parsley, and red wine; sprinkle in flour and add salt to taste.

Meanwhile, with a wooden spoon, mash sacs through a strainer, extracting the black ink. Add ink to the squid, mix well, and cook over low heat for 15-20 minutes or until well blended and the squid is tender. If sauce becomes too thick, add a bit more wine.

For a meal, serve over rice or with boiled potatoes.

Serves 6–8

JIBIA CON GUISANTES
(CUTTLEFISH WITH PEAS)

The cuttlefish is an eight-armed sea creature, a large version of the squid, and is prepared in much the same way as squid. Recipes for squid and cuttlefish (and often for octopus) are interchangeable. Cuttlefish is popular combined with other seafood and is found in numerous rice dishes. It is more difficult to clean than squid and is therefore usually sold in American markets cleaned and ready for cooking. Any fine dry wine would be a nice accompaniment.

2	pounds cuttlefish
3	tablespoons oil
1	onion, chopped
1	bay leaf
1	cup bread crumbs
2	cloves garlic
16	blanched almonds, chopped
1	teaspoon saffron
6	peppercorns
2	tablespoons olive oil
1	cup white wine
2	cups green peas

Clean and wash cuttlefish and cut into pieces. Heat oil in a skillet and fry onion in it until soft. Add bay leaf and cuttlefish pieces to the skillet. Meanwhile, crush bread crumbs, garlic, chopped almonds, saffron, and peppercorns with a mortar and pestle or in an electric blender, adding enough olive oil to form a smooth paste. Add the mixture and the wine to the cuttlefish and cook for 30 minutes or until cuttlefish is tender. Add peas, cover, and simmer for 15 minutes. Add fish stock or hot water if sauce becomes too thick.

Serves 8–10

ESPINAS DE BOQUERONES
(ANCHOVY BONES)

Backbones of anchovies, small sardines, herring, or similar fish
1 **cup milk**
Flour for dusting
Oil for deep-frying

Soak backbones in milk 20-30 minutes. Remove, drain, dust with flour, and deep-fry in hot oil at 375°F for about 6 minutes or until crisp and golden.

4 or 5 large backbones per tapa serving

CHANQUETES
(WHITEBAIT)

Chanquetes, *the Spanish version of whitebait, are tiny thin fish, almost transparent, an inch or so long, caught at night along the coastal waters of the Mediterranean by fishermen using huge lights. Theoretically, at least, Mediterranean chanquetes are a species all their own, a member of the family of gobies. Actually, they are fast becoming an endangered species; today chanquetes are usually a mixture of small fry of a number of fish, including herring, sprats, sardines, anchovies, and even immature forms of larger fish like sole and sea bass, all of which easily pass for chanquetes. No matter. When batter-fried and eaten whole like popcorn, they are an Andalusian tapa favorite and a gourmet treat—"fried sea spray," as the Andalusians sometimes call them. Either a red or white wine is the most popular whitebait accompaniment.*

Chanquetes or immature forms of anchovies, sardines, etc.
Flour for dusting
Oil for deep-frying
Lemon wedges

Drain chanquetes thoroughly and dust lightly with flour. Shake off excess flour in a sieve. Deep-fry in sizzling oil at 375°F for 1 minute or until golden crisp. Serve piping hot with lemon wedges.

ANGULAS
(FRIED BABY EELS)

Baby eels—called angulas *by the Spanish (the name comes from the Basque seacoast town of Aguinaga) and "tiny bean sprouts" by Ernest Hemingway—are traditionally cooked with garlic and olive oil in individual earthenware dishes. They are often the tapa "specialty of the day"; also very popular in restaurants as one of a series of courses. Angulas go well with either a good red or white wine.*

½ **cup olive oil**
4 **cloves garlic**
1 **pound live angulas**

Heat olive oil in a large skillet and brown garlic cloves in it. Add live baby eels and cook very briefly, perhaps 30 seconds or less, or until done, stirring with a wooden spoon. Serve immediately! Traditionally eaten with small wooden forks.

Serves 6

PERCEBES
(GOOSE BARNACLES)

Barnacles are finger-shaped sea animals, 3–4 inches long, that grow in clusters on rocks in the offshore waters of northwestern Spain. Chances are you won't find these tapa delights in your local market, even in cans, and that's unfortunate. If you do, be sure to prepare them simply, preferably raw, sprinkled with a little olive oil and chopped garlic. Or you can poach and serve with lemon wedges. Any drink would be an appropriate accompaniment, but a cold, crisp beer might taste best.

2–3 fingers per serving

MANITAS DE CORDERO A LA RIOJANA
(LAMBS' FEET, RIOJA STYLE)

An ice-cold beer would be the ideal partner.

6   lambs' feet
1   onion, sliced
3   cloves garlic
1   carrot, sliced
1   stalk celery, sliced
1   tablespoon chopped fresh parsley
2   tablespoons vinegar
    Salt and pepper to taste
2   tablespoons oil
1   onion, chopped
2   cloves garlic, chopped
3   tomatoes, peeled and chopped
1   red bell pepper, cut into strips
    Salt and paprika to taste

Clean lambs' feet, place in bottle with water to cover, boil for 10 minutes, and discard water. Put enough fresh water into the kettle to cover the feet and add sliced onion, whole garlic cloves, carrot, celery, parsley, and vinegar and sprinkle with salt and pepper. Bring to a boil and simmer for 2 hours or until tender. Remove, drain, and set aside. Heat oil in a skillet and sauté chopped onion, chopped garlic, and chopped tomatoes in it until a sauce forms. Add pepper strips and lambs' feet, sprinkle with salt and paprika, and simmer for 10 minutes or until peppers are soft and feet are cooked through.

Serves 6

CRIADILLAS EMPANADAS
(DEEP-FRIED LAMBS' TESTICLES)

Serve with red or white wine.

½   **pound lambs', veal, or beef testicles**
3   **tablespoons fresh lemon juice**
1   **egg, beaten**
½   **cup bread crumbs**
    Salt and pepper to taste
    Oil for deep-frying

Clean testicles in cold water and remove the skins. Cut into bite-size pieces and sprinkle generously with lemon juice. When ready to serve, dip pieces in beaten egg and in bread crumbs seasoned with salt and pepper. Deep-fry in hot oil at 375°F for about 3 minutes or until golden brown, drain, and serve hot.

Serves 4–6 (6–8 each)

MANOS DE CERDO A LA CATALANA
(PIGS' FEET, CATALAN STYLE)

Excellent with beer or a dry red wine.

4   **pigs' feet**
2   **cloves garlic, chopped**
1   **onion, sliced**
1   **carrot, sliced**
1   **stalk celery, sliced**
2   **tablespoons chopped fresh parsley**
    Salt and pepper to taste
1   **egg, beaten**
½   **cup bread crumbs**
    Oil for deep-frying

Wash feet in cold water, boil for 10 minutes, and throw out the water. Put enough fresh water into the kettle to cover the feet and add garlic, onion, carrot, celery, parsley, and salt and pepper to taste. Bring to a boil and simmer for 2 hours or until tender. Remove feet, drain, and carefully remove the bones, keeping the feet whole. Slice the meat into bite-size hunks. Dip each in the beaten egg, roll in bread crumbs, and deep-fry in hot oil at 375°F, 3-4 minutes or until brown.

Serves 4

MOLLEJAS FRITAS
(FRIED SWEETBREADS)

Sweetbreads are the thymus glands from the neck and heart of a calf; sometimes from a lamb, kid, or other young animal; occasionally from the pancreas ("stomach sweetbreads") of young animals. They are a luxury food in Spain, France, and most other European countries. When sold in American butcher shops, sweetbreads are usually already washed, soaked, and dressed.

Sweetbreads are soft in texture with a delicate, somewhat bland taste. To take advantage of their delicate flavor, you should fry or otherwise cook simply. Tapa cooks like to use sweetbreads in combination with stronger foods, often threaded on skewers with pork, lamb, or other meats; batter-frying is also popular. A full-bodied red wine would be a proper accompaniment.

1 **pound veal sweetbreads**
2 **teaspoons fresh lemon juice or vinegar**
1 **tablespoon chopped fresh parsley**
1 **onion, sliced**
   Salt and pepper to taste
1 **egg, beaten**
   Flour or bread crumbs for dusting
   Oil for deep-frying

To clean sweetbreads, first rinse thoroughly in cold running water. Boil in salted water with lemon juice or vinegar, parsley, and sliced onion for 5 minutes. Drain, rinse in cold water, and remove skin, membranes, and fat. Dry and slice into bite-size pieces. Add salt and pepper to taste, dip in beaten egg, roll in flour or bread crumbs, and deep-fry at 375°F or pan-fry 2–3 minutes or until golden.

Serves 6 (8–10 pieces each)

MOLLEJAS CON JAMON
(SWEETBREADS WITH HAM)

A cold glass of beer would be an appropriate partner.

1 **pound veal sweetbreads**
2 **teaspoons fresh lemon juice**
2 **tablespoons oil**
⅓ **cup chopped serrano or other cured ham**
1 **onion, chopped**
1 **carrot, chopped**
½ **cup stock**
   Salt and pepper to taste

Rinse sweetbreads thoroughly in cold running water. Place in boiling salted water with a little lemon juice for 5 minutes. Remove, drain, rinse in cold water, and remove the skin, membranes, and fat. Dry and slice into bite-size pieces. Heat oil in a skillet and add sweetbreads, ham, onion, and carrot. Sauté until sweetbreads are browned, stirring occasionally. Add stock, continue stirring, and simmer for 15 minutes. Add more stock if sweetbreads become dry. Add salt and pepper to taste.

Serves 6

SESOS A LA ROMANA
(DEEP-FRIED BRAINS)

Brain is quite tender, with a soft, creamy texture and a rather bland taste. Calves' brains are considered the best eating, but those of sheep, pigs, and beef are also popular. Fried or deep-fried brains are a tapa delight. Tapa cooks also like to use calves' brains as a background for other foods, often with a béchamel or other sauce. A dry sherry would taste good with this tapa.

1 calf's brain
2 tablespoons vinegar
  Flour for dusting
  Salt and pepper to taste
1 tablespoon chopped fresh parsley
1 egg, beaten
½ cup bread crumbs
  Oil for deep-frying

Clean the brains and wash in cold water, removing any skin and veins. Boil in salted water containing 2 tablespoons vinegar for 30 minutes. Remove, drain, and cut into bite-size pieces. Dust pieces with flour seasoned with salt, pepper, and parsley; dip in beaten egg and then in bread crumbs. Deep-fry in hot oil at 375°F for 3 minutes, drain, and serve hot.

Serves 6

CAP I POTA
(CALF'S HEAD AND TAIL)

Originally, this Catalan specialty was made with a calf's head and tail; today, usually only the head is used. At its best when prepared at least a day in advance. Excellent with a crisp beer or a dry red wine.

1 calf's head, cleaned and washed
2 onions, chopped
¼ cup olive oil
  Juice of 1 lemon
1 tablespoon chopped fresh parsley
  Salt and pepper to taste
¼ cup chopped black olives

Remove the meat from the head and cut into small pieces, including bits of fat and gelatin. Spread pieces on the bottom of an earthenware or glass casserole and sprinkle with chopped onions. Mix together olive oil, lemon juice, and parsley, season with salt and pepper, and pour over the meat. Refrigerate for 24 hours. Sprinkle with chopped olives and serve at room temperature.

Serves 6

CALLOS A LA MADRILEÑA
(TRIPE, MADRID STYLE)

Tripe is the stomach of cattle (especially veal), sheep, and other ruminating animals. Stomach linings of pigs and other nonruminants are sometimes used, as are organs other than the stomach. Because tripe has virtually no flavor of its own, it is most often combined with other foods that can benefit from its unique texture.

The cleaning and preparation is long and involved. Fortunately, tripe is sold in America already cleaned, washed, and usually partially cooked. It's one of the few tapa meats that cannot be overcooked, so you may want to allow for extra cooking to make sure it is tender. Tapas containing tripe gain flavor when prepared a day or more ahead and then reheated.

Madrid-style is the best known of the tripe recipes and one of the great dishes of Spain, either as a first course or as an all-in-one meal; in Madrid, it's a flavorful tapa. Prepare it the day before. Traditionally eaten with a hearty red wine as a partner.

1	pound tripe
1	pig's foot, split lengthwise
1	carrot, sliced
1	onion, sliced
3	cloves garlic
1	bay leaf
8	peppercorns, crushed
¼	teaspoon dried thyme
1	tomato, chopped
½	cup sherry
½	cup white wine
1	cup beef stock
2	tablespoons oil
¼	cup diced serrano or other cured ham
¼	pound chorizo or other smoked pork sausage, sliced
1	teaspoon paprika
	Salt and pepper to taste

Boil cleaned and washed tripe for about 15 minutes. Remove, drain, and cut into bite-size pieces. In a kettle, combine tripe, split pig's foot, carrot, onion, garlic, bay leaf, peppercorns, thyme, tomato, sherry, white wine, and stock. Bring to a boil and simmer for 4 hours. Remove from the heat and let cool, preferably overnight for added flavor. Remove bay leaf and pig's foot; bone pig's foot, cut up the meat, and return to the kettle; discard the bone. Heat oil in a skillet and sauté ham and sausage in it. Sprinkle with paprika and cook until browned. Add ham and sausage to the kettle and simmer for 60 minutes or until liquid is further reduced and ingredients are tender and blended. Add more stock if necessary.

Serves 8–10

ADDITIONAL EXOTIC TAPAS
OREJAS GUISADAS (Stewed Pigs' Ears); Chapter 11, page 59

APPENDIX
TAPAS TALK
A GLOSSARY OF SPANISH TERMS

Aceite—Olive oil
Aceitunas—Olives
Adobado—Marinated; pickled
Agua mineral—Mineral water
Ahumado—smoked
Ajo—Garlic
Ajo arriero, al—Mule-driver's style; with garlic
Al, a la, a lo—In the style of; with
Albahaca—Basil
Albóndigas—Meatballs
Alcachofas—Artichokes
All-i-Oli—A popular garlic and olive oil sauce
All i pebre—A piquant sauce
Almejas—Clams
Almendras—Almonds
Amáraco—Oregano
Amontillado—A medium-dry sherry
Ancas de rana—Frog's legs
Anchoa—Anchovy
Andaluza, a la—Andalusian style
Anguillas—Eels
Angulas—Baby eels
Apio—Celery
Aragonesa—Style of Aragon
Arroz—Rice
Asado—Roasted
Asar—To barbecue
Asturiana, a la—Asturian style
Atún—Tuna
Aves—Poultry
Azafrán—Saffron

Bacalao—Dried salt codfish
Bebidas—Drinks
Berenjena—Eggplant
Bilbaína, a la—Bilbao style
Bocadilla—Sandwich
Bodega—Wine cellar; wine producer
Boquerones—Anchovies
Bota—Leather wine bag
Brasa, a la—Charcoal-broiled
Brécol—Broccoli

Brocheta—Skewered
Buey—Beef
Buñuelito—Small fritter
Butifarra—Catalan pork sausage

Caballa—Mackerel
Café—Espresso coffee
Café con leche—Espresso coffee with milk
Café solo—Black espresso coffee
Calabacines—Zucchini
Calamares—Squid
Caldereta—Fish stew
Caliente—Hot
Callos—Tripe
Cangrejos—Crabs
Cantina—Bar; wine cellar
Caracoles—Snails
Carta—Menu
Casa, de la—Of the house
Catalana, a la—Catalonian style
Caza—Game
Cazón—Shark
Cazuela—Earthenware casserole dish
Cazuelita—Individual tapa casserole dish
Cebolla—Onion
Cerveza—Beer
Champaña—Champagne
Champiñones—Mushrooms
Chanquetes—Whitebait
Chilindrón—Tomato sauce
Chorizo—A Spanish pork sausage
Chuletas—Chops
Churros—Fried doughnuts
Cocido—Boiled; cooked
Cocido al vapor—Steamed
Codornices—Quail
Coles de Bruselas—Brussels sprouts
Coliflor—Cauliflower
Coñac—Brandy
Concha—Seafood shell; individual tapa serving dish
Condimentos—Seasoning
Conejo—Rabbit

Congrios—Eels
Copa—Glass of wine
Copita—Small glass of wine or sherry
Cordero—Lamb
Criadillas—Lamb or veal testicles
Cuenta—Bill or check

Día, del—Of the day
Dos salsas—With two sauces

Elección, a—Of your choice
Empanadilla—Small fried turnover
Empanado—Breaded
Emparedado—Sandwich
Entremeses—Appetizers
Entremeses variados—Assorted appetizers
Escabeche—Marinated; pickled
Española—Spanish style
Espárragos—Asparagus
Especialidad de la casa—Specialty of the house
Especialidades locales—Local specialties
Estofado—Stew
Estorino—Mackerel

Fabada—Asturian bean stew
Fiambres—Cold cuts
Fino—A dry sherry
Fresco—Fresh
Frío—Cold; chilled
Frito—Fried
Frutas del mar—Seafood

Gallega, a la—Galician style
Gambas—Shrimp
Garbanzos—Chickpeas
Gazpacho—A popular cold soup
Ginebra—Gin
Granada, a la—Granada style
Guisantes—Peas
Gusto, al—Of your choice

Habas—Broad beans
Hervido—Poached
Hígado—Liver
Horchata—A popular soft drink
Horno, al—Baked
Huevos—Eggs

Jamón—Ham
Jamón serrano—A popular cured "mountain ham"
Jardinera—With fresh vegetables
Jerez—Sherry
Jibia—Cuttlefish
Judías—Beans

Langosta—Lobster
Legumbres—Vegetables
Lengua—Tongue
Lenguado—Sole

Liebre—Hare
Limón, al—With lemon
Lomo—Loin of pork
Lonchas, en—Sliced
Lubina—Sea bass

Madrileña, a la—Madrid style
Manzanilla—A very dry sherry
Manos de cerdo—Pigs' feet
Marinar—To marinate
Marinera, a la—Sailor style
Mariscos—Seafood
Mayonesa—Mayonnaise
Medianoches—Small sandwich buns
Mejillones—Mussels
Merienda—Late-afternoon snack
Merluza—Hake
Mero—Rock bass
Mesón, de la—Of the restaurant
Migas—Fried bread
Mollejas—Sweetbreads
Morcillas—Blood sausages

Natural, al—Plain; natural; unadorned
Navarra, a la—Navarrese style

Oloroso—A semisweet sherry
Ostras—Oysters

Paella—A classic rice dish; pan for cooking rice
País, del—From the area
Palillo—Toothpick
Palitos de queso—Cheese sticks
Pan—Bread
Parrilla, a la—Grilled
Pastelería—Pastry shop
Pastora, a la—Shepherd's style
Patatas—Potatoes
Pato—Duck
Pechuga—Chicken breast
Percebes—Goose barnacles
Perdiz—Partridge
Perejil—Parsley
Pescadillas—Small hake
Pescado—Fish
Pez espada—Swordfish
Picadillo—Chopped
Picante—Spicy; well seasoned
Pichón—Pigeon
Pierna—Leg
Pil-pil—Simmered, Basque style
Pimentón—Paprika
Pimientos—Bell peppers
Pimienta—Black pepper
Pinchitos—Tapa-size kabobs
Piñones—Pine nuts
Pisto—Vegetable stew
Plancha, a la—Grilled on a flat plate
Plato, de—Plate or assortment of

Pollo—Chicken
Pulpo—Octopus

Queso—Cheese
Queso Manchego—Spain's best-known cheese
Quesos extranjeros—Foreign cheeses
Quisquillas—Small shrimp

Rabo de buey—Oxtail
Ración—A large individual ration of tapas
Ranas—Frog legs
Rape—Anglerfish
Rebozada—Batter-fried
Relleno—Stuffed
Riñones—Kidneys
Riojana, a la—Riojan style
Romana, a la—Deep-fried
Romesco—A Catalan hot pepper sauce
Ron—Rum

Sal—Salt
Salazón, en—Cured
Salchichas—Sausages
Salsa—Sauce
Salteado—Sautéed
¡Salud!—Cheers!
Samfaina—A Catalan sauce
Sangría—A popular wine and fruit drink
Santanderina, a la—Santander style
Sardinas—Sardines
Secado—Dried

Sepia—Cuttlefish
Servilleta—Napkin
Sesos—Brains
Setas—Wild mushrooms
Sevillana, a la—Sevillian style
Sidra—Hard cider
Sofrito—A thick tomato sauce
Solera—Sherry blending system; flavored with sherry
Surtidos—Assortment

Taberna—Tavern
Tartaleta—A pastry filled with meat or fish
Tasca—Tapa bar
Ternera—Veal
Tertulia—A small group of close friends
Tiempo, del—In season
Tomillo—Thyme
Tortilla—Omelet

Vaca—Beef
Variados—Assorted
Vasca, a la—Basque style
Venta—Informal country restaurant
Verduras—Vegetables
Vermout—Vermouth
Vieiras—Scallops
Vino—Wine
Vino corriente—Open or carafe wine
Vino de espumoso—Sparkling wine
Vino de mesa—Table wine
Vizcaína, a la—Biscayan style

INDEX